President Dwight D. Eisenhower addressing a press conference. (UPI PHOTO)

Adlai E. Stevenson, former Governor of the State of Illinois, Democratic nominee for President in 1952 and 1956, and United States ambassador to the United Nations from 1961 until his death in London in 1965. (UPI PHOTO)

Michelangelo's "Pieta" in the Vatican Pavilion at the New York World's Fair in 1964 and 1965. The 3000-pound white Carrara marble sculpture depicting Mary mourning the dead Christ was insured for $10,000,000 for the move from the Vatican to New York. While at the Fair it was encased behind bulletproof glass with an armed guard on constant duty.
(UPI PHOTO)

A PICTORIAL HISTORY of THE SPACE AGE GENERATION

The last four Presidents, whose terms in office span the period of the atomic energy and space years, shown at the funeral of former Speaker of the House, Sam Rayburn. From left to right are John F. Kennedy, Lyndon B. Johnson, Dwight D. Eisenhower, and Harry S Truman. (UPI PHOTO)

The Trials

TWO DYNA

WITH SPECIAL ARTICLES

The Changing World of Sport by Harold Rosenthal

Show Business in the Space Age by Robert Landry

and Triumphs of

MIC DECADES

by David C. Whitney

Edited by Thomas C. Jones
Assisted by Harriet B. Helmer

Published by

J. G. Ferguson Publishing Company / Chicago

BOUND IN HANDCRAFTED MISSION LEATHER
BY BROWN AND BIGELOW, ST. PAUL, MINNESOTA
A DIVISION OF STANDARD PACKAGING CORPORATION

*Lithographed in the United States of America
by Photopress, Inc., Broadview, Illinois*

*Library of Congress Catalog Card No. 68–
17666*

1 2 3 4 5 6 7 8 9 10

Preface

The idea for this volume originated during a discussion with my son, Douglas, upon reaching his twenty-first year. The subject of our conversation involved a narration of political events that occurred during his early childhood, following the end of World War II. This was before the Cold War, before television, before the rise of nationalism, before the Korean War, before sputnik, before accelerated education, before Vietnam, before hippies' demonstrations, before LSD manifestations and all the other evidences of civilian rebellion against conditions of the times.

From our talks it occurred to me that Douglas and his generation have grown up in a period of the most cataclysmic social and scientific changes of any generation in history. Yet, there has been no single publication tying together, objectively, the political, social and cultural developments that were part of their path to maturity. His generation is the product of this crucible of change. Perhaps there should be some publication that gives these young people quick access to the story of their years of growth.

I dedicate this book specifically to Douglas, and his generation, which is an exciting, challenging and engaging group. We of the preceding generation, scarred by the depression, and disillusioned by World War II and its aftermath, hope that *they* may find more solutions to national and world problems than we have been able to evolve.

A review of the events of the last quarter of a century brings to light many happenings, important at the time but quickly forgotten. The war crimes trials after World War II, for example, are a dim memory to many. To the generation just becoming twenty-one they are part of a maze of words vaguely recalled from some history text. In some of the discussions of the moral and patriotic aspects of the Vietnam War there have been attempts to draw analogies between the moral positions of the contestants in World War II and the present conflict. The fact that criminals in Germany confessed to the killing of millions of Jews, by gas or otherwise, seems to place World War II in a class by itself in terms of moral values. The McCarthy period has an aura of unreality about it. The Korean War was one of the bloodiest in our history—certainly comparable to Valley Forge in terms of physical hardship and discomfort—and yet it is remembered very sketchily today by all except those who were there.

The fact that sixty-three separate new nations have come into existence during the last twenty years has caused adjustments in international considerations and changes in attitude toward the rights of small nations. The Marshall Plan, which helped rebuild Europe and saved parts of the world from joining the communist countries, seems to have little significance today, but the results are impressive. The civil rights movement, while not directly related to the rise of new nations, certainly has been influenced by international encouragement and criticism. Although the problems of segregation go back many years, the wise and fair solutions to related questions must come from this new generation.

The impact of electronics on all phases of our daily lives is so great that it would take an entire volume to point out the changes that have occurred in the last quarter century. Business in this age would simply not function without the gadgetry that was unknown before World War II. The bookkeeping alone would be impossible to handle. How did business ever get along before the copying machine was developed? One of the least realized yet most important applications of electronics is in the entertainment industry. Many people immediately think of television, stereophonic recording, and wide-screen theatres as the electronic applications of the industry. Yet the product itself is probably most affected by it. The big sound and the many techniques for changing, adding to, and blending sounds have given performers an advantage that previously never existed. Thus an unknown individual or group can go from obscurity to hit status literally overnight.

Sputnik injected a whole new approach to education. Still, it took nearly ten years for the federal government to implement much needed new schools and tools for teaching. When government aid programs were finally passed in a size to be effective, very few citizens related them to sputnik. Our space program was greatly stimulated by the Russian space achievements. Now the race to be the first to land astronauts or cosmonauts on the moon appears to be very close.

These few references to some of the occurrences covered in this volume point up the ease with which events become blurred and blended into one total mass, with the passing of time. Perhaps this is a good thing, but it is also worth while to review, now and then, the course that brought us to our present niche in this confused world. From junior high school students to veterans of World War II, there seems to be something of interest here for everybody. We hope it is informative and entertaining.

A work of this nature can only reach completion through teamwork. I should like to mention a few of those who have been most helpful in producing this volume.

First and foremost, David Whitney has created a manuscript that is a pleasure to read, even though it covers much purely factual material. Robert Landry has prepared an absorbing article with accompanying photographs, telling about developments, in *Show Business in the Space Age*. Harold Rosenthal, in *The Changing World of Sport*, has covered the last twenty-five years of sports in a manner that should be exciting and informative to all followers of the sports pages.

We appreciate the patient and understanding help from the Creative Department of Brown & Bigelow. In the highly important photo research, essential to a work such as this, we are indebted to the United Press International for their generous cooperation—particularly to John Fletcher and Ralph Murthey in New York, and Henry Schaefer in Chicago.

In the indispensable work of final page layout, the achievement of Al Josephson and the entire Photopress organization, we believe, speaks for itself. My assistant, Harriet Helmer, gave unstintingly of her time and effort. We are also indebted to Richard Whittemore and Barbara Crawford for their various contributions toward the completed project. To the A-1 Composition Company and The Poole Clarinda Company, we are grateful for excellent performance and fine service. And finally, we thank our binder, A. C. Engdahl and Company, Incorporated.

THOMAS C. JONES

Contents

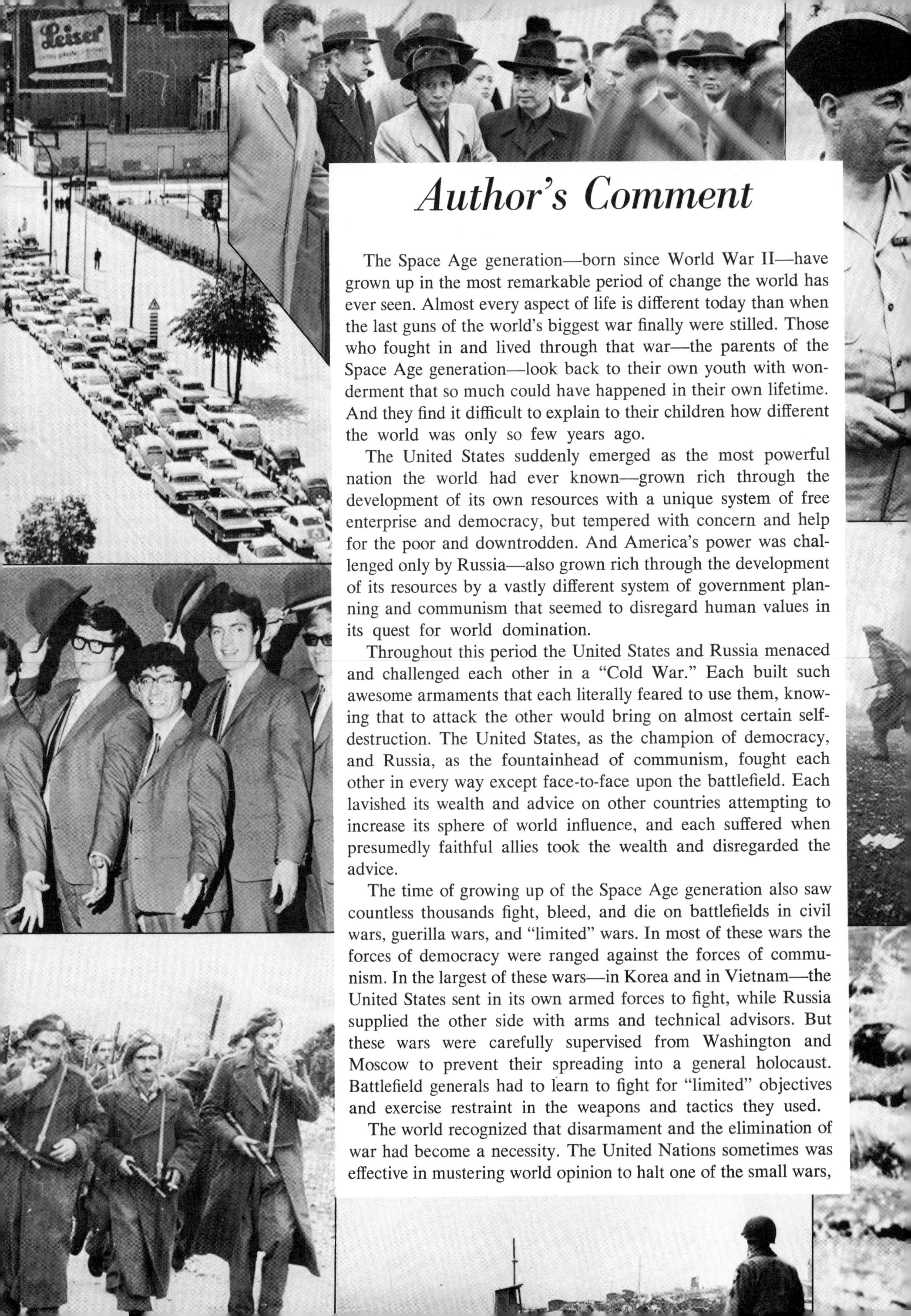

Author's Comment

The Space Age generation—born since World War II—have grown up in the most remarkable period of change the world has ever seen. Almost every aspect of life is different today than when the last guns of the world's biggest war finally were stilled. Those who fought in and lived through that war—the parents of the Space Age generation—look back to their own youth with wonderment that so much could have happened in their own lifetime. And they find it difficult to explain to their children how different the world was only so few years ago.

The United States suddenly emerged as the most powerful nation the world had ever known—grown rich through the development of its own resources with a unique system of free enterprise and democracy, but tempered with concern and help for the poor and downtrodden. And America's power was challenged only by Russia—also grown rich through the development of its resources by a vastly different system of government planning and communism that seemed to disregard human values in its quest for world domination.

Throughout this period the United States and Russia menaced and challenged each other in a "Cold War." Each built such awesome armaments that each literally feared to use them, knowing that to attack the other would bring on almost certain self-destruction. The United States, as the champion of democracy, and Russia, as the fountainhead of communism, fought each other in every way except face-to-face upon the battlefield. Each lavished its wealth and advice on other countries attempting to increase its sphere of world influence, and each suffered when presumedly faithful allies took the wealth and disregarded the advice.

The time of growing up of the Space Age generation also saw countless thousands fight, bleed, and die on battlefields in civil wars, guerilla wars, and "limited" wars. In most of these wars the forces of democracy were ranged against the forces of communism. In the largest of these wars—in Korea and in Vietnam—the United States sent in its own armed forces to fight, while Russia supplied the other side with arms and technical advisors. But these wars were carefully supervised from Washington and Moscow to prevent their spreading into a general holocaust. Battlefield generals had to learn to fight for "limited" objectives and exercise restraint in the weapons and tactics they used.

The world recognized that disarmament and the elimination of war had become a necessity. The United Nations sometimes was effective in mustering world opinion to halt one of the small wars,

especially if the objectives of the war were not of much concern to either Russia or the United States. But the UN had little effect in stopping any war in which either the United States or Russia had a stake. The diplomats continued to search for ways that disarmament could be achieved without leaving any advantage to the United States over Russia or of Russia over the United States.

Although the threat of atomic destruction hung above everyone's head, the world came to live with the thought. There were those who believed that everyone should build a bomb or fallout shelter in his own backyard. But for the most part people adopted a fatalistic attitude that there was little any individual could do about preparation against a cataclysmic future.

Instead of worrying about the atomic bomb, most people turned their attentions to trying to make the world a better place in which to live for themselves and their families. And the world enjoyed the greatest prosperity it had ever known. Almost everywhere people lived better than they ever had before. Countries whose cities had lain in rubble at the end of World War II—friend and foe alike—rebuilt themselves and prospered. Hunger and starvation persisted in many countries, but even there the people had more to eat than before and the world was making determined efforts to help them to a better share.

This period saw the greatest burgeoning of human rights the world had ever known. The United Nations drew up a Universal Declaration of Human Rights that set forth the rights that every man should expect from his own government. Although millions of people in various countries continued to be deprived of these rights, they were on the world's conscience, and millions of others gained their rights for the first time. The break-up of the British, French, Belgian, and Dutch colonial empires brought independence to scores of new countries that began to exercise the rights of self-government. And in the United States individual rights received greater protection under the law than ever before, particularly as Negroes made greater gains in achieving equal rights than at any time since the Civil War.

The world seemed to grow smaller with revolutionary changes in communication and transportation. Television suddenly made it possible for millions of people to see as well as hear events that previously could be viewed by no more than a few persons. World leaders became familiar guests in living rooms around the world. And with a flick of the switch anyone could have his choice of culture or entertainment. Jet airliners made it easy to travel anywhere in the world in just a few hours time. The numbers of

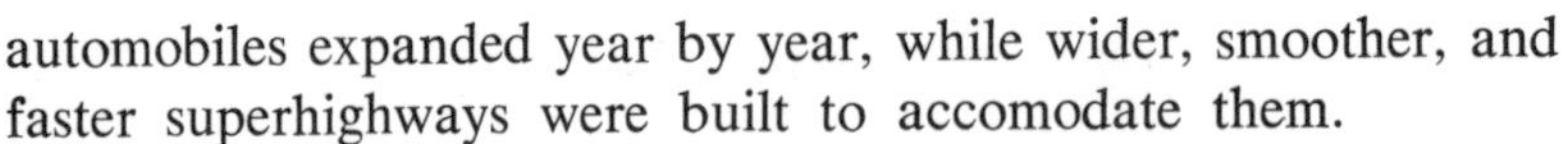

automobiles expanded year by year, while wider, smoother, and faster superhighways were built to accomodate them.

Using the technology of rocket engines developed in Germany in World War II, the United States and Russia launched a race that gave the Space Age generation its name. They sent rockets higher and higher above the earth's surface until they were set free from the earth's gravity. Astronauts and cosmonauts rode spacecraft in orbit around the earth. Plans were pushed forward to explore the moon and the planets—ideas that at the beginning of this period were reserved for comic strips and science fantasy magazines. The space race also had practical side benefits as communications satellites made it possible to broadcast live TV from one continent to another, while weather satellites provided improved information for weather forecasting.

An explosion of scientific and technical knowledge brought change after change. The development of electronic computers freed office workers from the drudgery of record keeping and improved business management. Automation equipment made possible the construction of factories that no longer needed workers to tend the machines. Anthropologists and archaeologists discovered that man had lived on earth much longer than had been known previously. Astronomers using new radio telescopes discovered that the universe was larger than they had thought and that there were new kinds of phenomena in the distant heavens. And doctors and medical researchers found new ways to prolong man's life while eliminating one dread disease after another.

As science and technology eased the burden of man's day-to-day work, families found themselves with more leisure time. Cultural activities, such as concerts, plays, and painting exhibitions, drew bigger and bigger audiences. New sports, such as boating and skiing, gained popularity. More and more people traveled farther and farther on vacation holidays. And education boomed as more and more persons required better knowledge to keep up with their changing world.

Both in pictures and words this book endeavors to portray the kaleidoscope of events that have shaped the world of the Space Age generation. By seeing as well as reading about this time of change, it is possible to view the events less as discrete happenings than as part of a broader pattern of history in the making.

David C. Whitney
Chappaqua, N. Y.

Subject Index

MAJOR EVENTS in the HISTORY of THE SPACE AGE GENERATION

1945

Jan. 9 U.S. troops begin landing on Luzon Island, Philippines.

17 Russian forces capture Warsaw, Poland, from Germans.

Feb. 2 Conference of Big Three leaders opens in Yalta, Russia, to plan final stages of World War II.

3 U.S. troops enter Manila, capital of the Philippines.

13 Russians capture Budapest, Hungary, from the Germans.

19 U.S. Marines start landng on Japanese-held Iwo Jima.

25 U.S. B-29's make first mass fire-bomb raid on Tokyo.

Mar. 3 Finland declares war on Germany.

7 U.S. troops capture Cologne, Germany, and seize a bridge over the Rhine River at Remagen.

22-31 Allied troops cross the Rhine into Germany at many points.

Apr. 1 U.S. troops begin invasion of Japanese-held Okinawa.

7 Russian forces fight their way into Vienna, Austria.

11 Japanese begin attacking U.S. warships off Okinawa with kamikaze suicide pilots.

12 U.S. President Franklin D. Roosevelt dies; succeeded by Harry S Truman.

18 U.S. troops enter Czechoslovakia.

23 Russians begin storming Berlin, capital of Germany.

25 American and Russian armies meet at Torgau, south of Berlin.

28 Italian partisans capture and kill Italian dictator Benito Mussolini.

30 German dictator Adolf Hitler kills himself in Berlin.

May 7 German high command signs unconditional surrender at General Eisenhower's headquarters in Rheims, France.

9 All fighting ends at 12:01 a.m. in the European phase of World War II.

June 26 United Nations charter signed in San Francisco.

July 16 First atomic bomb successfully tested in New Mexico.

17 Big Three begin conference in Potsdam, Germany.

25 British election overthrows Conservative party; Prime Minister Winston Churchill succeeded by Labour party leader Clement Attlee.

26 Potsdam Declaration calls on Japan to surrender unconditionally or face "prompt and utter destruction."

30 Japan rejects Potsdam ultimatum.

Aug. 6 U.S. drops atomic bomb on Hiroshima, Japan.

8 Russia declares war on Japan.

9 U.S. drops atomic bomb on Nagasaki, Japan.

12 Russian troops enter North Korea.

14 President Truman announces Japanese have accepted unconditional surrender.

17 Indonesia declares its independence from the Netherlands.

Sep. 2 Japanese sign unconditional surrender aboard U.S. battleship Missouri in Tokyo Bay, ending World War II.

2 Communist leader Ho Chi Minh proclaims independence of North Vietnam.

6 President Truman outlines his "Fair Deal" domestic program in message to Congress.

8 U.S. troops occupy South Korea, taking over from Japanese.

Nov. 29 Yugoslavia becomes a communist nation, abolishing its monarchy.

1946

Jan. 5 Mongolia becomes an independent communist republic.

10 First session of United Nations General Assembly meets in London.

11 Communists take over government of Albania.

20 Charles de Gaulle resigns as president of France.

31 Marshal Tito becomes head of communist government of Yugoslavia.

Feb. 24 Juan Peron begins nine-year rule as dictator of Argentina.

Mar. 5 Winston Churchill warns in speech at Fulton, Mo., that a communist "iron curtain has descended" across Europe.

22 Great Britain grants independence to Arab country of Jordan, then called Transjordan.

June 2 Italy votes to abolish monarchy and establish republic, sending King Humbert II into exile.

July 4 United States grants independence to the Philippines.

Sep. 1 Election in Greece returns George II to throne, communists begin civil war.

8 Bulgarians overthrow boy king Simeon II, establish a communist government.

17 First commercial television sets go on sale in the United States.

30 Nuremberg war crimes trial sentences 11 top Nazi leaders to death and 11 others to prison.

Oct. 11 Roman Catholic Archbishop Aloysius Stepinac of Yugoslavia sentenced to prison on charges of helping Nazis in World War II.

Mohandas K. Gandhi. Often called Mahatma Gandhi (Mahatma meaning "great soul"), this great Indian leader gained freedom for his country before his assassination January 30, 1948. (UPI PHOTO)

Nov. 19 Elections give communists control of government of Romania; U.S. denounces elections as unfair and undemocratic.

Dec. 31 U.S. Atomic Energy Commission assumes civilian control of the atomic energy program.

1947

Jan. 1 British Labour party government begins socializing the coal and communications industries in Great Britain.

19 Communists take over government of Poland.

Feb. 10 World War II peace treaties signed with Germany's former allies Italy, Bulgaria, Romania, Hungary, and Finland; they become effective Sep. 15, 1947.

Mar. 12 President Truman proposes "Truman Doctrine" of American aid to help Greece and other nations fight communism.

Apr. 1 King George II of Greece dies; succeeded by his brother Paul I.

2 United Nations places former Japanese-controlled Pacific islands under U.S. trusteeship.

May 15 U.S. Congress approves $400 million for "Truman Doctrine" military aid to Greece and Turkey.

June 5 U.S. Secretary of State George Marshall proposes "Marshall Plan" U.S. financial aid to help Western Europe recover from the war and prevent further communist takeovers of government—in next four years U.S. sends about $12 billion to Europe under the plan.

20-23 Congress overrides President Truman's veto to pass Taft-Hartley labor law.

Aug. 15 Great Britain grants independence to Hindu India and Moslem Pakistan as dominions in the British Commonwealth. Both later become republics, India in 1950 and Pakistan in 1956.

31 Communists take over government of Hungary.

Oct. 14 U.S. Air Force Capt. C. E. Yeager makes first flight faster than speed of sound in X-1 rocket plane.

Dec. 30 Communists force King Michael of Romania to abdicate.

1948

Jan. 1 British Labour government socializes railroads and other land transportation in Great Britain.

4 Great Britain grants independence to Burma.

Prince Souvanna Phouma, Laotian neutralist leader, spoke with newsmen in front of the ornate royal palace at Luang Prabang, Laos, after his meeting with Laotian King Savang Vatthana June 4, 1962. (UPI PHOTO)

30 Hindu leader Mohandas K. Gandhi assassinated in India.

Feb. 4 Ceylon becomes an independent dominion in the British Commonwealth.

25 Communists seize the government of Czechoslovakia.

Apr. 30 Charter for Organization of American States signed at Bogota, Colombia.

May 15 Israel declares independence as British troops withdraw from Palestine mandate.

June 24 Russians begin land blockade of West Berlin.

28 U.S. begins airlift of supplies into West Berlin, carrying over 2 million tons of food and fuel by plane in next year.

28 Moscow-controlled international communism denounces Marshal Tito of Yugoslavia for his independence.

Aug. 15 South Korea becomes an independent republic.

Sep. 9 North Korea proclaimed an independent communist republic.

Nov. 2 President Truman elected to second term in surprise victory over Republican candidate Thomas Dewey.

15 Canadian Prime Minister W. L. Mackenzie King retires; succeeded by Louis St. Laurent.

Dec. 10 United Nations General Assembly adopts Universal Declaration of Human Rights.

23 Former Japanese Premier Hideki Tojo and 6 others hanged in Tokyo for war crimes.

1949

Jan. 1 Cease-fire in fighting over Kashmir between India and Pakistan.

20 President Truman takes office for second term—the first presidential inaugural ever televised.

Feb. 8 Roman Catholic Joseph Cardinal Mindszenty of Hungary sentenced to life imprisonment on charges of treason.

Apr. 4 U.S. signs first peacetime military alliance in its history—the North Atlantic Treaty Organizations (NATO)—with Canada and Western European nations.

18 Ireland declares itself an independent republic outside the British Commonwealth.

May 12 Communists end blockade of West Berlin in face of continuing U.S. airlift of supplies.

July 1 South Vietnam granted independence by France.

19 Laos becomes an independent monarchy in the French Union.

Aug. 29 Russia explodes its first atomic bomb.

Oct. 16 Greek government brings 3-year civil war to end with defeat of communists.

21 Federal court sentences 11 U.S. communist leaders to prison for advocating overthrow of U.S. government.

Dec. 7 Marshal Chiang Kai-shek and Chinese Nationalist army flees to Formosa as communists under Mao Tse-tung complete conquest of mainland China after 3-year civil war.

28 Indonesia, formerly the Dutch East Indies, wins independence from the Netherlands.

The imposing "Gateway to Freedom" in Panmunjom, Korea, through which Communist prisoners of war passed on their way to the Communist version of freedom in operation "Big Switch" in August 1953. (UPI PHOTO)

General Douglas MacArthur, the deposed United Nations supreme commander, smiled and waved at the officials who greeted him as he arrived at Idlewild International Airport in New York April 19, 1951, for the nation's largest welcome to a conquering hero. On the left is Mayor Vincent Impellitteri, and on the right, New York's official greeter, Grover Whalen. (UPI PHOTO)

1950

Jan. 25 **Former U.S. State Department official Alger Hiss sentenced to 5 years in prison for perjury in denying he aided communist spy ring.**

June 25 **North Korean communist troops invade South Korea.**

27 **UN Security Council, with Russia absent, calls on member states to help South Korea repel attack.**

27 **President Truman orders U.S. air force and navy to aid South Korea.**

30 **President Truman orders U.S. army into South Korea.**

July 9 **Gen. Douglas MacArthur named Supreme Commander of UN forces in the Far East.**

Aug. 3 **U.S. and South Korean troops finally halt North Korean troops at Pusan in southeast corner of Korea.**

27 **President Truman orders army to take over railroads to prevent nationwide rail strike.**

Sep. 15 **UN troops turn tide of Korean War with amphibious landing at Inchon behind North Korean lines.**

26 **UN forces recapture Seoul, capital of South Korea.**

Oct. 7 **MacArthur's UN troops cross 38th parallel into North Korea.**

19 **UN troops capture Pyongyang, capital of North Korea.**

25 **Chinese troops enter Korean War on side of North Korea.**

Nov. 1 **Two Puerto Ricans attempt to assassinate President Truman.**

21 **MacArthur's forces reach the border of China, the Yalu River.**

26 **Overwhelming attack by Chinese army sends UN troops into retreat in Korea.**

Dec. 11 **U.S. Supreme Court rules that no one can be forced to testify against himself under the 5th Amendment.**

18 **President Truman appoints Gen. Dwight D. Eisenhower as Supreme Commander of NATO forces in Europe.**

24 **U.S. fleet rescues over 200 thousand trapped UN troops from North Korea.**

1951

Jan. 4 **Communists recapture Seoul, capital of South Korea.**

The space age generation has been marked by trials and triumphs in political, social, scientific and economic phases of life, but it is exciting, challenging and promising for a better future for the world of mankind.

(NASA)

On a gray day in July 1948, the funeral cortege of General John J. Pershing, Commander of the A.E.F. in World War I, crossed the Potomac en route to Arlington National Cemetery. (UPI PHOTO)

Dean Acheson signing the North Atlantic Treaty Alliance, April 4, 1949. (UPI PHOTO)

Feb. 27 Amendment 22 to U.S. Constitution ratified, limiting length of presidential service to two terms.

Mar. 15 UN troops recapture Seoul from the communists.

Apr. 8 MacArthur's UN troops again cross into North Korea.

11 President Truman removes Gen. MacArthur from his command, on charges of insubordination for urging Korean War be extended to attacks on China.

May 18 UN General Assembly votes to have all member nations stop arms shipments to communist China.

July 10 Truce talks begin between UN and communists, but fighting goes on as discussions continue for next 15 months.

16 King Leopold III of Belgium abdicates in favor of his son Baudoin I.

Sep. 1 U.S. signs mutual defense treaty with Australia and New Zealand.

4 First coast-to-coast TV broadcast, as President Truman opens Japanese peace treaty conference in San Francisco.

Oct. 19 U.S. formally ends World War II state of war with Germany.

26 British Conservative party wins general election, returning Winston Churchill to power as prime minister.

Dec. 20 Atomic energy used for first time to generate electricity at Arco, Idaho.

24 Former Italian colony of Libya becomes independent kingdom.

1952

Feb. 6 King George VI of Great Britain dies; succeeded by his daughter Queen Elizabeth II.

Apr. 8 President Truman orders government seizure of steel mills to prevent nationwide steel strike.

28 Japan again becomes independent nation as Japanese peace treaty goes into effect.

May 2 First international jet airline service begun by British, between England and South Africa.

July 23 Military junta takes over government of Egypt, forcing King Farouk to abdicate in favor of his baby son Fuad II.

25 Puerto Rico granted self-government as a commonwealth of the United States.

Oct. 3 Great Britain successfully tests first atomic bomb in the south Pacific.

Members of the 17th Regiment, 7th Infantry Division, literally planted the American flag on the solidly frozen Yalu River, when they reached the Korean-Manchurian border in November 1950. (UPI PHOTO)

Vietnam's Foreign Minister Nguyen Quog Dinh (left) and French Foreign Minister Georges Bidault (right) on the steps of the French Foreign Minister's villa at Geneva after a meeting with representatives of the United States and Great Britain May 3, 1954. (UPI PHOTO)

8 UN breaks off Korean War truce talks and the fighting continues.
Nov. 1 U.S. successfully tests first hydrogen bomb at Eniwetok in the Marshall Islands.
4 Gen. Eisenhower wins U.S. presidential election with landslide victory over Democratic candidate Adlai Stevenson.

1953
Mar. 5 Russian dictator Joseph Stalin dies.
Apr. 26 Korean War truce talks resume.
May 29 Sir Edmund Hillary and a guide become first men to climb 29,000-foot Mount Everest, the world's highest mountain.
June 17 Uprising in East Berlin against communists put down by Soviet Russian troops.
18 Egypt abolishes monarchy and becomes a republic.
19 Julius and Ethel Rosenberg executed for giving U.S. atomic bomb secrets to Russia.
July 27 Korean War armistice ends fighting.
Aug. 12 Russia successfully tests its first hydrogen bomb.
Oct. 31 First hour-long color TV show broadcast in U.S.
Nov. 9 Cambodia declares its independence from France.

1954
Jan. 21 U.S. launches first atomic powered submarine, U.S.S. Nautilus.
May 7 French fortress Dien Bien Phu surrenders after 55-day siege by communists in Indochina War.
17 U.S. Supreme Court rules that racial segregation in public schools is unconstitutional.
Aug. 11 Seven-year French-Indochina War ends with armistice signed at Geneva, Switzerland; Vietnam divided into communist North Vietnam and free South Vietnam.
Sep. 8 U.S. signs Southeast Asia Treaty Organization (SEATO), a military alliance for defense of Southeast Asia.
Oct. 5 Italy and Yugoslavia divide the free territory of Trieste.
Nov. 14 Gen. Gamal Abdel Nasser assumes control of Egyptian government as president.

1955
April Polio vaccine developed by Dr. Jonas Salk announced as effective preventative of the dread disease.
5 80-year-old British Prime Minister Winston Churchill resigns, succeeded by Anthony Eden.
May 5 U.S., Great Britain, and France recognize independence of West Germany.
14 Russia and seven communist satellite nations sign Warsaw Pact military alliance.
15 Austrian peace treaty signed in Vienna.
July 18-23 President Eisenhower and Russian dictator Nikita Khrushchev meet in summit conference in Geneva.
27 Austrian peace treaty becomes effective.
Sep. 19 Dictator Juan Perón of Argentina overthrown by military junta.
Dec. 5 A.F.L. and C.I.O. labor unions merge.

1956
Jan. 1 Sudan declares its independence from Great Britain and Egypt.
Feb. 14 Russian dictator Khrushchev denounces former dictator Stalin and calls for "peaceful coexistence" between communist and non-communist countries.
Mar. 2 France grants Morocco its independence.
Apr. 13 Tunisia becomes independent of France.
June 28 Uprising against communists in Poznan, Poland.
July 26 Egypt takes over Suez Canal from private British and French ownership.
Oct. 17 First full-scale atomic energy station to produce electric power begins operation at Calder Hall, England.
23 Hungarian people revolt against communist rulers, appeal by radio for outside help.

29-31 Israel, Great Britain, and France attack Egypt in retaliation for seizure of Suez Canal.

Nov. 4 Russian troops and tanks crush Hungarian revolt.

6 President Eisenhower elected to second term over Democratic candidate Adlai Stevenson.

7 UN obtains a cease-fire in fighting in Egypt.

1957

Jan. 9 British Prime Minister Anthony Eden resigns and is succeeded by Harold Macmillan.

16-18 First jet non-stop flight around the world by three U.S. Air Force B-52's.

Mar. 6 Great Britain grants independence to Ghana, former Gold Coast colony.

7 Congress approves "Eisenhower Doctrine" of U.S. military aid to any Middle Eastern country trying to preserve its independence.

25 European Common Market treaty signed by France, West Germany, Italy, Belgium, Netherlands, and Luxembourg.

May 15 Great Britain successfully tests its first hydrogen bomb.

June 21 John Diefenbaker becomes prime minister of Canada after his Conservative party wins general election.

July 29 International Atomic Energy Agency comes into being.

Aug. 26 Russia announces successful test of an international ballistics missile.

Oct. 4 Russia successfully launches first man-made space satellite, Sputnik I.

1958

Jan. 31 U.S. launches its first space satellite, Explorer I.

June 1 Charles de Gaulle returns to power in France as premier.

July 15 U.S. sends troops to Lebanon under "Eisenhower Doctrine" to prevent communists from taking over government.

Aug.-Sep. Chinese communists shell islands off shore of Nationalist Chinese Formosa.

Oct. 2 Former French colony of Guinea becomes independent.

4 British begin first regular transatlantic jet passenger flights.

Dec. 10 First regular domestic jet airliner service begun in U.S. by National Airlines between New York City and Miami.

The mammoth airliner which brought Soviet Premier Khrushchev to the United States provided a dramatic background for the welcoming ceremonies for the Russian leader as he, President Eisenhower, and others assembled on the speakers' stand at Andrews Air Force Base, Maryland, September 15, 1959. (UPI PHOTO)

1959

Jan. 3 Alaska enters Union as 49th state.

8 Charles de Gaulle takes office as first president of the fifth republic of France.

8 Rebel leader Fidel Castro enters Havana, Cuba, after dictator Fulgencio Batista flees from country.

Mar. 19 Communist China takes Tibet; Dalai Lama flees to India.

July 1 First successful atomic-powered rocket engine tested in New Mexico.

21 First atomic-powered merchant ship, the Savannah, christened at Camden, N.J.

Aug. 21 Hawaii joins the Union as the 50th state.

Sep. 15-28 Russian dictator Khrushchev visits the United States.

Oct. 27 Russia releases first photographs of hidden side of moon taken by spacecraft Lunik III.

Dec. 1 Antarctica Treaty signed by U.S., Russia, and 10 other nations guaranteeing continent's political and military neutrality.

1960

Jan. 1 Former French colony of Cameroon becomes independent.

19 U.S. and Japan sign a mutual defense treaty.

Feb. 13 France successfully tests its first atomic bomb in Algeria.

Apr. 27 Former German colony of Togo becomes independent.

May 1 Russia shoots down U.S. U-2 spy plane over Russia.

3 European Free Trade Association formed by Great Britain and 6 other Western European countries.

16 Russian dictator Khrushchev angrily breaks off summit conference with President Eisenhower in Paris because of the U-2 incident.

June 26 France grants independence to Malagasy, formerly the island of Madagascar.

30 Congo (Léopoldville) wins independence from Belgium.

July 1 Somalia becomes independent republic, made up of former British and Italian colonies.

Aug. 1 France grants independence to former colony Dahomey.

3 Former French colony of Niger becomes independent.

5 Former French colony of Upper Volta becomes independent.

7 Former French colony of Ivory Coast becomes independent.

11 Former French colony of Chad becomes independent.

13 Former French colony of Ubangi-Shari becomes the independent Central African Republic.

15 Congo (Brazzaville) wins independence from France.

Austrian President Adolf Schaerf (center) was host at a State Dinner in Vienna June 3, 1961. With him here, before the dinner, are (left to right) United States President John F. Kennedy, Mrs. Nina Khrushchev, Soviet Premier Nikita S. Khrushchev, and Mrs. Jacqueline Kennedy. (UPI PHOTO)

16 Great Britain grants independence to island of Cyprus.
17 Former French colony of Gabon becomes independent.
20 Former French colony of Senegal becomes independent.
27 Great Britain grants Sierra Leone its independence.
May 5 U.S. Astronaut Alan B. Shepard Jr. becomes first American rocketed into space in 15-minute flight.
30 Assassination of Dominican Republic dictator Rafael Trujillo who had ruled for 31 years.
31 South Africa withdraws from British Commonwealth to become independent republic.
June 3-4 President Kennedy and Russian dictator Khrushchev confer in Vienna, Austria.
19 Great Britain grants independence to Kuwait.
23 Antarctica Treaty becomes effective.
25 Olympic Games open in Rome, Italy.
Sep. 22 Former French colony Mali becomes independent.
Oct. 1 Great Britain grants independence to Nigeria.
Nov. 1 Benelux Economic Union formed to end customs taxes among Belgium, Netherlands, and Luxembourg.
8 John F. Kennedy wins U.S. presidential election over Republican candidate Richard Nixon.
28 Former French colony of Mauritania becomes independent.
Dec. 18-19 India invades and takes over Portuguese colonies in India.

1961

Jan. 3 U.S. breaks off diplomatic relations with Cuba.
20 President John F. Kennedy inaugurated.
Mar. 1 Peace Corps created by President Kennedy for American volunteers to help underdeveloped countries.
Apr. 3 Amendment 23 to Constitution ratified enabling residents of Washington, D.C., to vote for President.
12 Russian Maj. Yuri Gagarin becomes first man to orbit earth in spacecraft Vostok I.
17-20 Cuba defeats invasion attempt aided by U.S. government at Bay of Pigs.
Aug. 13 Communists begin building wall to seal off East Berlin from West Berlin.

Guns boomed salutes and mobs shouted "Viva!" as Fidel Castro triumphantly arrived at Havana, Cuba, January 8, 1959.

(UPI PHOTO)

Sep. 1 Russia resumes testing of atomic weapons in atmosphere.
13 UN troops begin fighting in Congo (Léopoldville) to put down civil war.
15 U.S. resumes underground testing of atomic weapons.
18 UN Secretary General Dag Hammarskjöld killed in plane crash in Congo; succeeded by U Thant of Burma.
27 UN admits its 100th member nation, Sierra Leone, having started in 1946 with 51 nations.
Oct. 19 Chinese communist Premier Chou En-lai denounces Russia, challenging its control over world communism.
30 Russian dictator Khrushchev orders Stalin's body removed from tomb in Moscow's Red Square as part of campaign of "de-Stalinization" of communism.
Dec. 2 Cuban dictator Fidel Castro reveals publicly that he is a communist.
9 Great Britain grants independence to Tanganyika.

1962

Jan. 1 Western Samoa, formerly administered by New Zealand, becomes independent.
Feb. 4 U.S. begins using helicopters in Vietnam to aid South Vietnam in civil war with communists.
20 U.S. Astronaut John H. Glenn Jr. becomes first American to orbit earth in spacecraft Friendship 7.
Mar. 19 Cease-fire ends seven-year French-Algerian War.
Apr. 25 U.S. resumes testing of atomic weapons in atmosphere.
May 17 U.S. troops arrive in Thailand to prevent communist invasion.

The United Nations Security Council held a second-day session regarding the Cuban missile crisis on October 24, 1962. Discussing the United States' demand for a United Nations commission to supervise the withdrawal of Soviet missiles from Cuban soil are (left to right) Valerian Zorin of Russia, Mario Garcia-Inchaustegui of Cuba, and Adlai Stevenson of the United States. (UPI PHOTO)

31 Israel executes Adolf Eichman for crimes against Jews in World War II.

June 27 President Kennedy pledges to defend Formosa from any attack by Communist China.

July 1 Rwanda, and Burundi, former Belgian, mandates, become independent countries.

3 Algeria wins independence from France after long and bloody fighting.

23 Agreement signed at Geneva guaranteeing independence of Laos.

Aug. 6 Great Britain grants independence to Jamaica.

31 Great Britain grants independence to Trinidad and Tobago.

Oct. 9 Great Britain grants independence to Uganda.

20 Chinese communist troops invade India.

22 President Kennedy announces Russia has placed missiles in Cuba; demands their removal; places a naval blockade around Cuba.

28 Russian dictator Khrushchev agrees to withdraw missiles from Cuba.

Nov. 11 U.S. announces Russian missiles have been removed from Cuba.

20 U.S. ends naval blockade of Cuba after Castro agrees to remove Russian jet bombers from the island.

20 Cease-fire ends China-India War.

1963

Jan. 14 De Gaulle vetoes admittance of Great Britain to European Common Market.

22 France and Germany sign mutual defense and friendship treaty.

Apr. 22 Liberal Lester B. Pearson becomes prime minister of Canada, replacing Conservative John Diefenbaker.

May 1 Netherlands gives up Western New Guinea to Indonesia.

10-11 Canadian Prime Minister Pearson and President Kennedy meet in Hyannis Port, Mass.; agree U.S. will provide atomic warheads for Canadian defense missiles.

June 3 Pope John XXIII dies; later succeeded by Paul VI.

17 U.S. Supreme Court rules Bible reading and recitation of Lord's Prayer in schools is unconstitutional.

20 U.S. and Russia set up direct telephone communication between White House and Kremlin to prevent start of an accidental war.

23-26 President Kennedy visits West Germany and West Berlin to emphasize U.S. commitment to oppose communism.

July 5-20 Russian and Chinese leaders meet in Moscow, but are unable to settle their disagreements.

29 France announces it will not sign an atomic test ban treaty.

Aug. 5 U.S., Great Britain, and Russia agree to ban testing of atomic bombs in the atmosphere. Treaty goes into effect Oct. 10, 1963.

Sep. 16 Federation of Malaysia formed, joining Malaya, Singapore, Sarawak, and North Borneo.

Oct. 15 German Chancellor Konrad Adenauer retires after 14 years as leader of Germany, succeeded by Ludwig Erhard.

18 Conservative Prime Minister Harold Macmillan of Great Britain resigns because of ill health, succeeded by Sir Alec Douglas-Home.

Nov. 19 Cambodia ends diplomatic relations with U.S. and strengthens ties with Communist China.

22 President Kennedy assassinated in Dallas, Texas; succeeded by Lyndon B. Johnson.

Dec. 10 Great Britain grants Zanzibar independence.

12 Great Britain grants Kenya independence.

1964

Jan. 23 Amendment 24 to U.S. Constitution ratified, outlawing poll tax requirements in federal elections.

27 France establishes diplomatic relations with Communist China.

Feb. 17 U.S. Supreme Court rules that Congressional districts must have nearly equal populations to insure that each man's vote is of equal value.

Mar. 6 King Paul I of Greece dies; succeeded by his son Constantine I.

14 UN sends troops to Cyprus to end civil war between Greek and Turkish groups.

Apr. 26 Tanganyika and Zanzibar unite and later change the name of the new country to Tanzania.

May 27 U.S. Supreme Court extends one-man one-vote rule to require both houses of state legislatures to be reapportioned so that districts have nearly equal populations.

19 Telephone cable service opened between Japan and Hawaii.

30 UN troops leave Congo (Léopoldville) after 4-year effort to put down civil war.

July 6 Malawi, former British colony of Nyasaland, wins independence.

Aug. 5 U.S. planes make first bombing raid on North Vietnam in the Vietnam War.

Sep. 21 Great Britain grants independence to island of Malta.

Oct. 10 Olympic Games open in Tokyo—first ever held in Asia.

15 Leonid I. Brezhnev and Aleksei N. Kosygin oust Nikita Khrushchev from leadership of Communist Russia.

16 China successfully tests first atomic bomb.

16 Labour party leader Harold Wilson becomes prime minister of Great Britain after his party wins general election.

24 Zambia, former British colony of Northern Rhodesia, becomes independent republic.

Nov. 3 Lyndon Johnson elected to a second term as President in landslide victory over Republican candidate Barry Goldwater.

9 Liberal Democrat Eisaku Sato becomes premier of Japan, is brother of Nobusuke Kishi who was premier from 1957 to 1960.

President Paul E. Magloire of Haiti (left) and President Rafael Trujillo of the Dominican Republic (right) February 24, 1951. (UPI PHOTO)

24-27 Belgian and U.S. forces make an air rescue of 1,700 whites from Congo (Léopoldville) after rebels massacred 96.

1965

Feb. 18 Former British west African colony of Gambia wins independence.

Apr. 28 U.S. marines land in Dominican Republic, first of a buildup of 20,000 U.S. troops to prevent communists from taking over the Latin American country.

May 2 First regular intercontinental TV broadcasts begin between Europe and America using Early Bird satellite.

July 26 Maldive Islands declare their independence from Great Britain.

28 President Johnson announces number of U.S. troops fighting in Vietnam will be substantially increased.

Aug. 5 War breaks out between India and Pakistan over Kashmir.

9 Singapore withdraws from Malaysia to become independent republic.

Sep. 9 French President De Gaulle announces France will secede from NATO military alliance in 1969.

Oct. 1-8 Indonesian generals prevent communists from taking over government, slay thousands of suspected communists.

4 Paul VI becomes first Pope to visit United States.

Nov. 11 Rhodesia declares independence from Great Britain.

Dec. 15 U.S. astronauts achieve first successful rendezvous in space with spacecraft Gemini 6 and Gemini 7.

1966

Jan. 1 European Economic Community integrates coal and steel, economic, and atomic energy organizations.

10 India and Pakistan agree to cease-fire in their war over Kashmir.

Mar. 12 Military junta takes over government of Indonesia, reducing leftist President Sukarno to a figurehead.

May 26 Guyana, formerly British Guiana, becomes independent.

June 1 Indonesia and Malaysia agree to cease-fire in their 3-year-old undeclared war.

29 U.S. makes first bombing attack on Hanoi, capital of North Vietnam.

July 1 U.S. Medicare program goes into effect providing federal aid for hospital care for citizens over 65.

1 France withdraws its troops from NATO, asks removal of all NATO military forces from French soil.

20 Officials ousted from China's government as Mao-Tse-tung's "cultural revolution" begins purging his "enemies" from Chinese communist party.

Sep. 30 Botswana, former British protectorate of Bechuanaland, becomes independent.

Oct. 4 Lesotho, former British protectorate of Basutoland, wins independence.

19 President Johnson flies to Southeast Asia to confer with leaders of countries aiding U.S. in the Vietnam War; returns to U.S. Nov. 2.

Nov. 30 Barbados granted independence by Great Britain.

31 Former Nazi Kurt Kiesinger becomes chancellor of West Germany.

1967

Jan. 27 U.S., Great Britain, Russia and 76 other nations sign Space Treaty to protect world from use of space for military purposes.

Feb. 10 Amendment 25 to Constitution ratified providing changes in presidential succession.

15 North Vietnam President Ho Chi Minh rejects proposal by President Johnson to hold talks for a truce in the Vietnam War.

Mar. 16 U.S. Senate approves first bi-lateral treaty with Russia since the beginning of the Cold War, providing for resumption of consular service between the two nations.

May 30 Eastern region of Nigeria declares itself the independent republic of Biafra, precipitating a civil war.

June 5-10 Israel defeats Egypt, Syria, and Jordan in a six-day war, doubling the size of its territory.

17 China explodes its first hydrogen bomb.

23 and 25 President Johnson and Russia's Premier Kosygin meet in Glassboro, N.J., to discuss world problems, particularly trying to reach agreement on a settlement of Middle Eastern problems.

Aug. 24 Russia and the U.S. agree to text of a draft treaty for the control of nuclear weapons.

Oct. 18 Venus 4 makes a soft landing on the planet Venus after a 4-month journey from Soviet Russia.

AN END and A BEGINNING

V-E Day was a time to celebrate in Paris, on the Champs Elysées, with the "Arc de Triomphe" in the background—but V-E Day was a time to contemplate on Okinawa, where fighting men of the Army's 77th Infantry Division listened to the news of Germany's surrender on May 8, 1945 a few yards behind the front line. The war was not yet over for them. (UPI PHOTOS)

General Dwight D. Eisenhower holding pens used to sign surrender documents at Rheims, France, May 7, 1945. On his right is his chief of staff, Lt. Gen. W. B. Smith, and on his left is Air Marshall Sir Arthur Tedder.
(UPI PHOTO)

The year 1945 opened in the midst of the most widespread war the world had ever known and it ended in peace that seemed to hold hope for a better world. The Space Age generation was being born this year as London was bombarded by German V-2 missiles—the fore-runners of giant rockets that within a few years would lift man into space and send him soaring to the moon, the planets, and eventually the stars. The Atomic Age as well was launched this year with great mushroom clouds that marked the obliteration of Japanese cities while heralding a new source of power that in time could help man overcome the scourges of poverty, starvation, and want. And this year also saw the nations of the world solemnly pledge themselves to work together to keep the peace in a new experiment called the United Nations.

V-E—Victory in Europe

In the early months of 1945 the dreams of empire of the dictators Adolf Hitler and Benito Mussolini were collapsing. German armies fought a losing war on all fronts. In the East, Russian troops captured Warsaw in January and Budapest in February. In the West, American, British, French, and Canadian troops swarmed across the Rhine River into Germany in March.

During April the Allies closed in on Germany's heartland. The Russians fought their way into Berlin. The British swept north to the Baltic Sea. And American troops captured Nuremberg and Munich. Then on April 25, U.S. and Russian troops joined up at Torgau, south of Berlin, splitting Germany in two pieces. Three days later, on the 28th, the big-jawed dictator of Fascist Italy, Benito Mussolini, was captured by Italian partisans while trying to sneak out of the country he had promised to turn into a new Roman Empire. He was promptly shot and strung up by his heels as an object of scorn. Hiding in an underground fortress in Berlin, the Nazi dictator of Germany, Adolf Hitler, swore he would not allow himself to be captured and punished for starting the war and for the deaths he had inflicted on millions of Jews. On the last day of April, Hitler put a pistol to his head and killed himself. A faithful servant burned his body.

A week later, at 2:41 a.m. on May 7, the German high command surrendered unconditionally in a red brick schoolhouse at Reims, France, that was the headquarters of the Allied Supreme

Commander, Dwight D. Eisenhower. The German Colonel-General Alfred Jodl, who signed the surrender, later was hanged as a war criminal. The capitulation called for fighting to cease at 12:01 a.m. on May 9.

V-E Day brought exuberant celebrations in the Allied countries. As British Prime Minister Winston Churchill said, "Weary and worn, impoverished but undaunted and now triumphant, we had a moment that was sublime."

But there were many dead to mourn. About eleven million soldiers, sailors, and airmen had died in the European phase of World War II. Uncounted millions of civilians had died. And about six million Jews had been exterminated in German concentration camps.

The German Surrender

—signed May 7, 1945

We, the undersigned, acting by authority of the German High Command, hereby surrender unconditionally to the Supreme Commander, Allied Expeditionary Force, and simultaneously to the Soviet High Command, all forces on land, sea, and in the air who are at this date under German control.

V-J—Victory over Japan

The war went on in the Pacific. American troops had begun landing on Luzon Island in the Philippines in January, 1945, and had fought their way into Manila within a few weeks. In February the U.S. Marines waded ashore on the island of Iwo Jima. More than 5,000 were killed before they wrested the tiny rocky piece of land from the Japanese in a month of fighting.

The war moved closer and closer to the Japanese homeland. Carrier aircraft of the U.S. fleet attacked Japan itself in mid-March. Then on the first of April troops of the U.S. Tenth Army began swarming ashore on Okinawa—the last stepping stone before the invasion of Japan. In desperation the Japanese launched a violent attack against the American fleet with hundreds of kamikaze pilots who killed themselves by crashing their explosive-laden planes into U.S. warships. On the ground the fighting on Okinawa raged as the bloodiest and most furious of the Pacific war with nearly 200,000 Americans,

General Douglas MacArthur broadcasting to the Philippines on October 29, 1944 that he had landed on Leyte Island and had returned to liberate the Philippines. (UPI PHOTO)

The official flag raising on the fortress island of Corregidor, upon General Douglas MacArthur's return in March 1945 for the first time since 1942. He can be seen, in the center, saluting. In the background are 503rd airborne troops. (UPI PHOTO)

On September 2, 1945 General Yoshijiro Umeza signed the surrender agreement on behalf of Japanese Imperial General Headquarters aboard the U.S. battleship Missouri in Tokyo Bay, as General MacArthur looked on. (UPI PHOTO)

Japanese, and Okinawans killed before the island was subdued in July.

The world waited with bated breath for the next step—the invasion of Japan—that was expected to cost millions of lives. In mid-July the Big Three—the leaders of the United States, Great Britain, and Russia were assembling at Potsdam, Germany, to agree on strategy for the final defeat of Japan and to resolve questions concerning the occupation of Germany. Just before the conference began, a coded message of great portent was delivered to President Truman. It said: "'Babies satisfactorily born." These words signalled the successful conclusion of the best-kept secret of the war, the development and testing of the super-powerful atomic bomb. The Big Three issued the Potsdam Declaration on July 26 calling for the "unconditional surrender" of Japan's armed forces and warning that if the ultimatum was not heeded Japan faced "prompt and utter destruction."

When the Japanese government refused to yield, President Truman ordered the atomic bomb to be used. The first A-bomb was dropped on Hiroshima on August 6, destroying the city and killing an estimated 70,000 persons. Russia declared war on Japan on August 8, and the next day the second A-bomb was dropped on Nagasaki, killing an estimated 36,000 persons. Six days later, on Tuesday, August 14, President Truman announced that the Japanese had accepted "unconditional surrender." But World War II did not officially end until more than two weeks later, when on September 2, Japanese generals officially signed the surrender aboard the U.S. battleship *Missouri* in Tokyo Bay.

With V-J America went wild from coast-to-coast. Bells rang. Parades formed spontaneously. And total strangers hugged and kissed each other in the streets. While on troop transports and on military bases, American servicemen poised for the final assault on Japan breathed sighs of relief and congratulated themselves on their luck at still being alive. Everyone was ready for peace and wondered what it would bring.

The Japanese Surrender

—signed September 2, 1945

We hereby proclaim the unconditional surrender to the Allied Powers of the Japanese Imperial General Headquarters and of all Japanese armed forces and all armed forces under Japanese control wherever situated.

We hereby command all Japanese forces wherever situated and the Japanese people to cease hostilities forthwith, to preserve and save from damage all ships, aircraft, and military and civil property and to comply with all requirements which may be imposed by the Supreme Commander for the Allied Powers or by agencies of the Japanese Government at his direction. . . .

The authority of the Emperor and the Japanese Government to rule the state shall be subject to the Supreme Commander for the Allied Powers, who will take such steps as he deems proper to effectuate these terms of surrender.

Looking to a Peaceful World

Even before the United States had been drawn into World War II plans had begun to be made for the peace that would follow the ending of the war. In August, 1941, four months before the Japanese attack on Pearl Harbor, President Franklin D. Roosevelt and Prime Minister Churchill met in Newfoundland and signed the Atlantic Charter. This document expressed the ideals sought by the two Western democracies. In its most telling phrase it called for a world in which "all the men in all lands may live out their lives in freedom from fear and want."

Two years later when Churchill and Roosevelt met at Tehran, Iran, with Marshal Joseph Stalin of Russia for the first time, the Big Three issued a communique that reaffirmed the Atlantic Charter with the words:

> "We look with confidence to the day when all peoples of the world may live free lives, untouched by tyranny, and according to their varying desires and their own consciences."

The Atlantic Charter

—August 12, 1941

The President of the United States of America and the Prime Minister, Mr. Churchill, representing His Majesty's Government in the United Kingdom, being met together, deem it right to make known certain common principles in the national policies of their respective countries on which they base their hopes for a better future for the world.

First. Their countries seek no aggrandizement, territorial or other.

Second. They desire to see no territorial changes that do not accord with the freely expressed wishes of the peoples concerned.

Third. They respect the right of all peoples to choose the form of government under which they will live; and they wish to see sovereign rights and self-government restored to those who have been forcibly deprived of them.

Fourth. They will endeavor, with due respect for their existing obligations, to further the enjoyment by all States, great or small, victor or vanquished, of access, on equal terms, to the trade and to the raw materials of the world which are needed for their economic prosperity.

Fifth. They desire to bring about the fullest collaboration between all nations in the economic field, with the object of securing for all improved labor standards, economic advancement, and social security.

Sixth. After the final destruction of the Nazi tyranny they hope to see established a peace which will afford to all nations the means of dwelling in safety within their own boundaries, and which will afford assurance that all the men in all the lands may live out their lives in freedom from fear and want.

Seventh. Such a peace should enable all men to traverse the high seas and oceans without hindrance.

Eighth. They believe that all the nations of the world, for realistic as well as spiritual reasons, must come to the abandonment of the use of force. Since no future peace can be maintained if land, sea, or air armaments continue to be employed by nations which threaten, or may threaten, aggression outside of their frontiers, they believe, pending the establishment of a wider and permanent system of general security, that the disarmament of such nations is essential. They will likewise aid and encourage all other practicable measures which will lighten for peace-loving peoples the crushing burden of armaments.

Concrete steps were taken to begin planning a world peace-keeping organization at a conference of representatives of the U.S., Great Britain, Russia, and China that was held in Washington, D.C., from August to September, 1944. The Dumbarton Oaks conference, as it came to be called because of the name of the estate where it was held, drew up the outline for what was to become the United Nations.

In February, 1945, Roosevelt, Churchill, and Stalin met again, this time at Yalta in Russia. At this conference the Big Three agreed that the nations of the world should assemble in San Francisco in April to prepare a charter for the world organization.

Delegates of many nations gathered in San Francisco in April. While they worked on the charter, the war in Europe came to an end. Jan Christian Smuts, the prime minister of South Africa and a longtime champion of world government, was largely responsible for the writing of the preamble to the United Nations charter which poetically expressed mankind's hopes for a better world. Finally, the charter was signed on June 26, 1945, by the delegates of fifty countries—later Poland also was allowed to join its signature as an original charter member.

By the time the UN charter was officially ratified by the governments of the member nations, World War II had come to an end in the Pacific. The first organizational meeting of the UN General Assembly convened in London in January, 1946. At this meeting the delegates voted to accept an invitation to make its permanent headquarters in the United States.

In the years that lay ahead the United Nations sometimes succeeded in preventing wars and

One of the many wartime summit conferences Churchill held with Allied leaders was the February 1945 meeting at Yalta, U.S.S.R. In the front row are (left to right) Britain's Prime Minister Winston Churchill, United States President Franklin D. Roosevelt, and Soviet Premier Joseph Stalin. (UPI PHOTO)

Members of the United Nations Conference Executive Committee met at the San Francisco War Memorial Opera House May 8, 1945. Around table from left to right are: Mastafa Adl, Iran; Jan Masaryk, Czechoslovakia; W. L. Mackenzie King, Canada; Herbert Evatt, Australia; Sir Alexander Cadogan, Great Britain; V. K. Wellington Koo, China; Edward R. Stettinius, Jr., United States Secretary of State; Alger Hiss, Secretary General of the Conference; Vyacheslav M. Molotov, Russia; Georges Bidault, France; Ezequil Padilla, Mexico; Ivan Subasic, Yugoslavia; Eelco N. Van Kleffens, Netherlands. (UPI PHOTO)

quickly stopping those that did start. But the UN also was to have many failures, largely because its most powerful body, the Security Council, could only take effective action that was agreed to by the United States, Great Britain, Russia, France, and China. Any one of these five powers had the right to veto, or block, any action that it opposed. And Russia in particular came to exercise its veto power with great regularity in almost every instance where the world organization's views conflicted with its own self-interest.

But the United Nations became most useful as a forum where most of the world's nations could express themselves and help mold world public opinion, sometimes forcing the great powers to modify their views. Various agencies of the UN worked to solve problems of health, communication, weather information, and other matters.

In the long view perhaps the UN's greatest contribution came in the setting forth of goals and ideals for all mankind in the Universal Declaration of Human Rights adopted by the General Assembly in 1948. In this document, the world organization spelled out "the equal and inalienable rights of all members of the human family." Forever more oppressed peoples would have this document to point to as a goal for the way life should be.

On V-E Day, May 8, 1945, the speech given by U.S. Secretary of State Edward R. Stettinius at the conference in San Francisco was broadcast over the world, reminding the United Nations that although hostilities had ceased in Europe, there was still an all-important job to be done in the Pacific. Pictured with Stettinius are (left to right) British Foreign Minister Anthony Eden; Georges Bideault, Chairman of the French delegation; and V. K. Wellington Koo, of the Chinese delegation. (UPI PHOTO)

Preamble to the Charter of the United Nations

—signed June 26, 1945

WE THE PEOPLES OF THE UNITED NATIONS DETERMINED to save succeeding generations from the scourge of war, which twice in our lifetime has brought untold sorrow to mankind, and

to reaffirm faith in fundamental human rights, in the dignity and worth of the human person, in the equal rights of men and women and of nations large and small, and

to establish conditions under which justice and respect for the obligations arising from treaties and other sources of international law can be maintained, and

to promote social progress and better standards of life in larger freedom,

AND FOR THESE ENDS to practice tolerance and live together in peace with one another as good neighbors, and

to unite our strength to maintain international peace and security, and to ensure, by the acceptance of principles and the institution of methods, that armed force shall not be used, save in the common interest, and

to employ international machinery for the promotion of the economic and social advancement of all peoples,

HAVE RESOLVED TO COMBINE OUR EFFORTS TO ACCOMPLISH THESE AIMS.

Accordingly, our respective Governments, through representatives assembled in the city of San Francisco, who have exhibited their full powers found to be in good and due form, have agreed to the present Charter of the United Nations and do hereby establish an international organization to be known as the United Nations.

Universal Declaration of Human Rights

—Adopted by the UN General Assembly, December 10, 1948

PREAMBLE

WHEREAS recognition of the inherent dignity and of the equal and inalienable rights of all members of the human family is the foundation of freedom, justice and peace in the world,

WHEREAS disregard and contempt for human rights have resulted in barbarous acts which have outraged the conscience of mankind, and the advent of a world in which human beings shall enjoy freedom of speech and belief and freedom from fear and want has been proclaimed as the highest aspiration of the common people,

WHEREAS it is essential, if man is not to be compelled to have recourse, as a last resort, to rebellion against tyranny and oppression, that human rights should be protected by the rule of law,

WHEREAS it is essential to promote the development of friendly relations between nations,

WHEREAS the peoples of the United Nations have in the Charter reaffirmed their faith in fundamental human rights, in the dignity and worth of the human person and in the equal rights of men and women and have determined to promote social progress and better standards of life in larger freedom,

WHEREAS Member States have pledged themselves to achieve, in co-operation with the United Nations, the promotion of universal respect for and observance of human rights and fundamental freedoms,

WHEREAS a common understanding of these rights and freedoms is of the greatest importance for the full realization of this pledge,

NOW, THEREFORE,

The General Assembly

Proclaims this Universal Declaration of Human Rights as a common standard of achievement for all peoples and all nations, to the end that every individual and every organ of society, keeping this Declaration constantly in mind, shall strive by teaching and education to promote respect for these rights and freedoms and by progressive measures, national and international, to secure their universal and effective recognition and observance, both among the peoples of Member States themselves and among the peoples of territories under their jurisdiction.

Article 1.

All human beings are born free and equal in dignity and rights. They are endowed with reason and conscience and should act towards one another in a spirit of brotherhood.

Article 2.

Everyone is entitled to all the rights and freedoms set forth in this Declaration without distinction of any kind, such as race, color, sex, language, religion, political or other opinion, national or social origin, property, birth or other status.

Furthermore, no distinction shall be made on the basis of the political, jurisdictional or international status of the country or territory to which a person belongs, whether it be independent, trust, non-self-governing or under any other limitation of sovereignty.

Article 3.

Everyone has the right to life, liberty and security of person.

Article 4.

No one shall be held in slavery or servitude; slavery and the slave trade shall be prohibited in all their forms.

Article 5.

No one shall be subjected to torture or to cruel, inhuman or degrading treatment or punishment.

Article 6.

Everyone has the right to recognition everywhere as a person before the law.

Article 7.

All are equal before the law and are entitled without any discrimination to equal protection of the law. All are entitled to equal protection against any discrimination in violation of this Declaration and against any incitement to such discrimination.

Article 8.

Everyone has the right to an effective remedy by the competent national tribunals for acts violating the fundamental rights granted him by the constitution or by law.

Article 9.

No one shall be subjected to arbitrary arrest, detention, or exile.

Article 10.

Everyone is entitled in full equality to a fair and public hearing by an independent and impartial tribunal, in the determination of his rights and obligations and of any criminal charge against him.

Article 11.

1. Everyone charged with a penal offense has the right to be presumed innocent until proved guilty according to law in a public trial at which he has had all the guarantees necessary for his defense.

2. No one shall be held guilty of any penal offense on account of any act or omission which did not constitute a penal offense, under national or international law, at the time when it was committed. Nor shall a heavier penalty be imposed than the one that was applicable at the time the penal offense was committed.

Article 12.

No one shall be subjected to arbitrary interference with his privacy, family, home or correspondence nor to attacks upon his honor and reputation.

Everyone has the right to the protection of the law against such interference or attacks.

Article 13.

1. Everyone has the right to freedom of movement and residence within the borders of each state.

2. Everyone has the right to leave any country, including his own, and to return to his country.

Article 14.

1. Everyone has the right to seek and to enjoy in other countries asylum from persecution.

2. This right may not be invoked in the case of prosecutions genuinely arising from non-

President Harry S. Truman addressing the United Nations San Francisco Conference in May 1945. (UPI PHOTO)

Openly admiring the 39-story edifice to peace, President Harry Truman and Governor Thomas Dewey sat side by side on the speakers' platform at the dedication of the United Nations Secretariat Building in New York October 24, 1949. (N.Y. DAILY MIRROR PHOTO FROM INTERNATIONAL)

political crimes or from acts contrary to the purposes and principles of the United Nations.

Article 15.

1. Everyone has the right to a nationality.

2. No one shall be arbitrarily deprived of his nationality nor denied the right to change his nationality.

Article 16.

1. Men and women of full age, without any limitation due to race, nationality or religion, have the right to marry and to found a family. They are entitled to equal rights as to marriage, during marriage and at its dissolution.

2. Marriage shall be entered into only with the free and full consent of the intending spouses.

3. The family is the natural and fundamental group unit of society and is entitled to protection by society and the state.

Article 17.

1. Everyone has the right to own property alone as well as in association with others.

2. No one shall be arbitrarily deprived of his property.

Article 18.

Everyone has the right to freedom of thought, conscience and religion; this right includes freedom to change his religion or belief, and freedom, either alone or in community with others and in public or private, to manifest his religion or belief in teaching, practice, worship and observance.

Article 19.

Everyone has the right to freedom of opinion and expression; this right includes freedom to hold opinions without interference and to seek, receive and impart information and ideas through any media and regardless of frontiers.

Article 20.

1. Everyone has the right to freedom of peaceful assembly and association.

2. No one may be compelled to belong to an association.

Article 21.

1. Everyone has the right to take part in the government of his country, directly or through freely chosen representatives.

2. Everyone has the right of equal access to public service in his country.

3. The will of the people shall be the basis of the authority of government; this will shall be expressed in periodic and genuine elections which shall be by universal and equal suffrage and shall be held by secret vote or by equivalent free voting procedures.

Article 22.

Everyone, as a member of society, has the right to social security and is entitled to realization, through national effort and international cooperation and in accordance with the organization and resources of each state, of the economic, social and cultural rights indispensable for his dignity and the free development of his personality.

Article 23.

1. Everyone has the right to work, to free choice of employment, to just and favorable conditions of work and to protection against unemployment.

2. Everyone, without any discrimination, has the right to equal pay for equal work.

3. Everyone who works has the right to just and favorable remuneration ensuring for himself and his family an existence worthy of human dignity, and supplemented, if necessary, by other means of social protection.

4. Everyone has the right to form and to join trade unions for the protection of his interests.

Article 24.

Everyone has the right to rest and leisure, including reasonable limitation of working hours and periodic holidays with pay.

Article 25.

1. Everyone has the right to a standard of living adequate for the health and well-being of himself and of his family, including food, clothing, housing and medical care and necessary social services, and the right to security in the event of unemployment, sickness, disability, widowhood, old age or lack of livelihood in circumstances beyond his control.

2. Motherhood and childhood are entitled to special care and assistance. All children, whether born in or out of wedlock, shall enjoy the same social protection.

Article 26.

1. Everyone has the right to education. Education shall be free, at least in the elementary and fundamental stages. Elementary education shall be compulsory. Technical and professional education shall be made generally available and higher education shall be equally accessible to all on the basis of merit.

2. Education shall be directed to the full development of the human personality and to the strengthening of respect for human rights and fundamental freedoms. It shall promote understanding, tolerance and friendship among all nations, racial or religious groups, and shall further the activities of the United Nations for the maintenance of peace.

3. Parents have a prior right to choose the kind of education that shall be given to their children.

Article 27.

1. Everyone has the right freely to participate in the cultural life of the community, to enjoy the arts and to share in scientific advancement and its benefits.

2. Everyone has the right to the protection of the moral and material interests resulting from any scientific, literary, or artistic production of which he is the author.

Article 28.

Everyone is entitled to a social and international order in which the rights and freedoms set forth in this Declaration can be fully realized.

Article 29.

1. Everyone has duties to the community, in which alone the free and full development of his personality is possible.

2. In the exercise of his rights and freedoms, everyone shall be subject only to such limitations as are determined by law solely for the purpose of securing due recognition and respect for the rights and freedoms of others and of meeting the just requirements of morality, public order and the general welfare in a democratic society.

3. These rights and freedoms may in no case be exercised contrary to the purposes and principles of the United Nations.

Article 30.

Nothing in this Declaration may be interpreted as implying for any state, group or person any right to engage in any activity or to perform any act aimed at the destruction of any of the rights and freedoms set forth herein.

CHANGING LEADERSHIP

Throughout the world the Space Age generation saw new leaders rise to power supplanting the famous names and faces who had led their peoples through the Great Depression and through World War II. Franklin D. Roosevelt, Adolf Hitler, Benito Mussolini, and Hideki Tojo all had become names for the history books by the time the war was over.

In the childhood of the Space Age generation such names as Harry Truman, Winston Churchill, Clement Attlee, Joseph Stalin, Nikita Khrushchev, Konrad Adenauer, and Jawaharlal Nehru held the spotlight. But by the time the Space Age generation had come to voting age these names, too, had passed into history to be replaced by Lyndon Johnson, Harold Wilson, Aleksei Kosygin, Leonid Breshnev, Kurt Kiesinger, and Indira Gandhi.

A few men clung to power, however, throughout most of this period. Charles de Gaulle, who led the Free French to victory in World War II, remained the strongest leader in France for two decades after the war. Such dictators as Franco of Spain, Salazar of Portugal, Tito of Yugoslavia, Ho Chi Minh of North Vietnam, and Mao Tse-tung of China continued to hold the reins of governments they had seized. And on the island of Formosa aging Chiang Kai-shek, who had led

The "Big Three" in the palace garden at Potsdam, Germany, in August 1945 just before the final conference meeting. Seated, from left to right, are: Prime Minister Clement Attlee of Great Britain; President Harry Truman of the United States; and Marshal Joseph Stalin of Russia. Standing, from left to right, are: Admiral William Leahy, chief of staff to President Truman; Hon. Ernest Bevins, Britain's Foreign Minister; U.S. Secretary of State, James F. Byrnes; and Russia's Foreign Minister, V. M. Molotov. (UPI PHOTO)

Soldiers, Sailors, and Marines gathered in the park across from the White House to listen to news reports on Japan's surrender from a radio broadcasting car stationed at the curb August 12, 1945. (UPI PHOTO)

China in World War II, remained hopeful that someday the Chinese would throw off communism and welcome him back.

In the United States—

As the Space Age generation grew up, the United States for the first time was generally recognized as the most powerful nation in the world. Therefore, the American President now held the most powerful office in the world. During this period the United States experienced four changes of leadership in the White House. Three of the new Presidents—Truman, Kennedy, and Johnson—were Democrats. One—Eisenhower—was a Republican. These four Presidents represented widely varying personalities and backgrounds. They included the oldest President the country ever had—Eisenhower, who left the office at the age of 70; and the youngest ever elected to the office—Kennedy, who at 43 was the first President born in the twentieth century and most nearly represented the youthful vigor of the new generation.

Harry S. Truman

In 1945 the United States government had been led for more than a dozen years by Democratic President Franklin Delano Roosevelt. Many young people could not remember back to a time when anyone else but F.D.R. had been President. He had come to the office when the country was deep in the Great Depression with millions of workers unable to find jobs. In his inaugural address in 1933 he had told the people that "the only thing we have to fear is fear itself," and almost at once conditions began to get better.

The scene at Times Square in New York on V-E Day, May 8, 1945. (UPI PHOTO)

He became the champion of the "common man" and pushed through laws that for the first time safeguarded Americans from unemployment and old age, and guaranteed workers the right to bargain with their employers for higher wages and better working conditions. Then Roosevelt boldly opposed the Fascist dictators of Germany, Italy, and Japan who were pushing the world down the path to World War II. And when America was attacked he guided the building of the mightiest military force in history that by 1945 was winning victories for the Allies on all fronts.

All of which explains why almost every American felt a deep sense of personal shock and grief when Roosevelt died unexpectedly on April 12, 1945. And perhaps the most shocked was Harry S Truman, Roosevelt's Vice-President, who found himself precipitously propelled into world leadership.

A Missouri farm boy who had been a professional politician most of his adult life, the new President told newspaper reporters, "Boy, if you ever pray, pray for me now. I don't know whether you fellows ever had a load of hay fall on you, but when they told me yesterday what had happened, I felt like the moon, the stars, and all the planets had fallen on me."

The country and the world anxiously waited to see what kind of President this 60-year-old Missourian would be. His pre-presidential record was not particularly impressive. After graduating from high school at 17, Truman had worked at odd jobs for a few years, then ran his grandmother's farm until he was 33. World War I ended his career as a farmer. He went to France as a National Guard artilleryman and rose to the rank of captain. Returning from the war, Truman and a war buddy opened a men's clothing store in Kansas City, but this business went broke in 1922. After that Truman turned to politics. With the aid of the Pendergast political machine of Kansas City, he won several elections to county offices, and then was elected to the U.S. Senate in 1934, and re-elected in 1940. As a Senator, he made a name for himself as chairman of a war investigating committee that saved the country an estimated $15 billion in military contracts. In 1944 Roosevelt chose Truman as his running mate in his fourth-term campaign against Thomas E. Dewey. After helping win the election, Truman had served less than three months as Vice-President when Roosevelt died.

President Truman quickly demonstrated that he was capable of making important decisions. Within minutes after taking office he gave the go-ahead for the organizational meeting of the United Nations in San Francisco. He had been President less than a month when Germany surrendered and he was able to make the announcement of V-E Day on his own 61st birthday—May 8. In June he flew to San Francisco to take part in ceremonies establishing the new United Nations. In July he traveled to Potsdam, Germany, to confer with the heads of the British and Russian governments, and was amazed to find that his own 5-feet 10-inches stature made him taller than either the renowned Churchill or Stalin. On his way back from Europe he okayed the dropping of A-bombs on Japan to hasten the end of the war. Less than five months after Truman became President, he was able to proclaim V-J Day and the end of World War II.

But somehow "Harry," as almost everyone called him, didn't get much credit for his big decisions. Many people felt he was just carrying out policy that already had been set by Roosevelt. They thought he looked more like a small-town clothing store owner than a President. And when he surrounded himself with old friends from Missouri, many feared the country might be in for another Harding administration with government-by-crony. On the other hand he was generally admired for his straightforward talk that sometimes included swear words seldom before used in public by a President. Everyone liked his wife Bess and his daughter Margaret, who was becoming a concert singer. But some people thought it wasn't very dignified to have a President who would sit down to play the "Missouri Waltz" on a piano while movie star Lauren Bacall reclined atop it.

Harry Truman, however, was more concerned with being a good President than with what people said about him. He soon demonstrated his ability to be President in his own right. He replaced most of Roosevelt's cabinet with men of his own choosing and when such New Deal stalwarts as Harold Ickes and Henry Wallace disagreed with his policies he removed them, too.

In fact, the only member of Roosevelt's cabinet to be retained was Secretary of the Navy James V. Forrestal, whom Truman appointed in 1947 as the nation's first Secretary of Defense.

When it became apparent that Russia was determined to rule the world, taking over one country after another by communist subversion, Truman exercised world leadership to halt the spread of communism. With his "Truman Doctrine" he sent aid to Greece and Turkey, saving those countries from falling to Russian influence. Then with the "Marshall Plan" he provided billions of dollars of aid to Western Europe to rebuild its economy and save it from the ruin that Russia's leaders predicted was in store for all capitalist nations.

In the 1948 presidential campaign, few people gave Truman much of a chance to win. He was opposed by a strong Republican candidate, Gov. Thomas E. Dewey of New York. In addition two minor parties fought him: the States' Rights party, made up of Southern Democrats who believed Truman was too liberal in proposing to extend greater civil rights to Negroes, and the Progressive party, whose candidate, former Vice-President Henry Wallace, believed Truman's foreign policy was too harsh toward Russia. Truman took his campaign to the people, making a "whistle stop" campaign by train back and forth across the United States. He blasted the Republican-controlled Congress as "do-nothing" and he pointed out that Dewey rhymed with "hooey." He drew big crowds and the people shouted for him to "Give 'em Hell." But the public opinion polls and the news commentators said he couldn't win. And he didn't, until after dawn on the day after the election when Ohio's vote finally swung the balance into the Democratic column. By that time the staunchly Republican Chicago *Tribune* had produced a headline, "DEWEY DEFEATS TRUMAN," that Harry Truman would chortle over and treasure to the end of his days.

In Truman's inaugural address as he started his second term, he proposed a bold new step in American foreign policy—a plan that he called only "Point Four"—that the United States should share its scientific and technical know-how to help the world's underdeveloped nations. This plan that became a cornerstone of American foreign policy in the years ahead was to win the United

President Harry Truman the morning after his surprise victory in 1948 showing the early edition of the Chicago Tribune, which had conceded victory to Dewey before the final count of the votes indicated the Truman victory.
(UPI PHOTO)

Harry Truman took the oath of office as President of the United States on the death of President Franklin D. Roosevelt, April 12, 1945, eighty-three days after becoming Vice President (UPI PHOTO)

States many new friends among the have-not nations.

The most important decision of Truman's second term came in June, 1950, when communist North Korean troops invaded South Korea. To show the world that the United States had drawn a line and would allow no further communist aggression, Truman ordered U.S. troops to go to the aid of the South Koreans. The war dragged on through the rest of Truman's administration—a war that was no more popular with Americans than the later Vietnam War of the 1960's—but a war that most Americans agreed was necessary.

After his retirement to Independence, Missouri, at the end of his second term in 1953, Truman had the satisfaction of seeing that the foreign policies he had established continued to be carried out by his successors.

from Harry S. Truman's Inaugural Address

—January 20, 1949

. . . Today marks the beginning not only of a new administration, but of a period that will be eventful, perhaps decisive, for us and for the world.

It may be our lot to experience, and in large measure to bring about, a major turning point in the long history of the human race. The first half of this century has been marked by unprecedented and brutal attacks on the rights of man, and by the two most frightful wars in history. The supreme need of our time is for men to learn to live together in peace and harmony. . . .

The American people stand firm in the faith which has inspired this Nation from the beginning. We believe that all men have a right to equal justice under law and equal opportunity to share in the common good. We believe that all men have the right to freedom of thought and expression. We believe that all men are created equal because they are created in the image of God.

From this faith we will not be moved.

The American people desire, and are determined to work for, a world in which all nations and all peoples are free to govern themselves as they see fit and to achieve a decent and satisfying life. Above all else, our people desire, and are determined to work for, peace on earth—a just and lasting peace—based on genuine agreement freely arrived at by equals.

In the pursuit of these aims, the United States and other like-minded nations find themselves directly opposed by a regime with contrary aims and a totally different concept of life.

That regime adheres to a false philosophy which purports to offer freedom, security, and a greater opportunity to mankind. Misled by this philosophy, many peoples have sacrificed their liberties only to learn to their sorrow that deceit and mockery, poverty and tyranny, are their reward.

That false philosophy is communism.

Communism is based on the belief that man is so weak and inadequate that he is unable to govern himself, and therefore requires the rule of strong masters.

Democracy is based on the conviction that man has the moral and intellectual capacity, as well as the inalienable right, to govern himself with reason and justice.

Communism subjects the individual to arrest without lawful cause, punishment without trial, and forced labor as the chattel of the state. It decrees what information he shall receive, what art he shall produce, what leaders he shall follow, and what thoughts he shall think.

Democracy maintains that government is established for the benefit of the individual, and is charged with the responsibility of protecting the rights of the individual and his freedom in the exercise of his abilities.

Communism maintains that social wrongs can be corrected only by violence.

Democracy has proved that social justice can be achieved through peaceful change.

Communism holds that the world is so deeply divided into opposing classes that war is inevitable.

Democracy holds that free nations can settle differences justly and maintain lasting peace. . . .

Since the end of hostilities, the United States has invested its substance and its energy in a great constructive effort to restore peace, stability, and freedom to the world. . . .

In the coming years, our program for peace and freedom will emphasize four major courses of action.

First. We will continue to give unfaltering support to the United Nations and related agencies, and we will continue to search for ways to strengthen their authority and increase their effectiveness. We believe that the United Nations will be strengthened by the new nations which are being formed in lands now advancing toward self-government under democratic principles.

Second. We will continue our programs for world economic recovery.

This means, first of all, that we must keep our full weight behind the European recovery program . . .

Third. We will strengthen freedom-loving nations against the dangers of aggression.

We are now working out with a number of countries a joint agreement designed to strengthen the security of the North Atlantic area. . . .

Fourth. We must embark on a bold new program for making the benefits of our scientific advances and industrial progress available for the improvement and growth of underdeveloped areas. . . .

On the basis of these four major courses of action we hope to help create the conditions that will lead eventually to personal freedom and happiness for all mankind . . .

President Truman spoke at the ceremonies marking the laying of the cornerstone for the United Nations Secretariat Building, October 24, 1949. Seated behind him are (left to right) Wallace K. Harrison, Director of Planning; Brazilian Ambassador M. C. de Freitas Valle; Dr. Tingfu F. Tsiang of China; M. Chauvel of France; Pakistan's Mohammed Zafrulla Khan, and Governor Thomas E. Dewey. (UPI PHOTO)

In September 1959 President Eisenhower entertained Premier Nikita Khrushchev during his visit to the United States. They are informally conversing here, with Mrs. Eisenhower at left. (UPI PHOTO)

Dwight D. Eisenhower

Winning generals have never had much difficulty being elected President of the United States. "We like Ike" was enough of a slogan to carry Dwight D. Eisenhower into the White House as Harry Truman's successor. Almost everyone liked this genial, smiling Kansan whose generalship had led the Allies to victory in Europe in World War II. He retained his personal popularity throughout the eight years he served as President, but was unable to transfer the people's affection to his Republican party. As a consequence, the Democrats controlled Congress through all but the first two years of his administration.

Although he was born in Texas, Eisenhower grew up in the small town of Abilene, Kansas. Admitted to West Point when he was twenty, he became a career officer in the army. In the 1930's, while serving as assistant to General Douglas MacArthur in the Philippines, he learned to fly, and thus later was to become the first President ever to hold a pilot's license. When the United States was plunged into World War II by the Japanese attack on Pearl Harbor, Eisenhower was a brigadier general. Although he was among the most junior of all the generals in the army, Chief of Staff Gen. George Marshall picked him to plan American strategy for invading France and then put him in command of U.S. forces in Europe. In 1943 he was placed in command of all Allied forces in Europe, directed the D-Day invasion of France, and then supervised the final winning of the war in Europe. After the war he served for three years as Chief of Staff of the U.S. Army under President Truman, retired from active duty for two years to serve as president of Columbia University, and then was appointed by Truman as supreme commander of NATO forces in Europe, holding that post from 1950 to 1952.

As early as 1945, at the Potsdam Conference, President Truman offered to help Eisenhower become President in 1948. But at that time Ike said he was not interested. In the following years he repeatedly rebuffed efforts by the leaders of both the Democratic and the Republican parties

A prophetic photograph taken in 1932 during the Bonus Army march on Washington, showing General Douglas MacArthur, then chief of staff of the United States Army, with his fellow officers, including his second in command, Colonel Dwight D. Eisenhower (to right in picture). (UPI PHOTO)

to get him to run, for he had not disclosed which party he favored. Then early in 1952 Eisenhower announced that he was a Republican, and that party's national convention offered him the nomination for President on its first ballot. In the 1952 presidential election Eisenhower won a landslide victory over the Democratic candidate, Gov. Adlai E. Stevenson of Illinois. And in the 1956 presidential election he again defeated Stevenson with an even larger majority.

During the 1952 presidential campaign, Eisenhower pledged himself to fly to Korea, if elected, in an effort to bring the war there to a close. While President-elect and before assuming office, he did fly to Korea, but his efforts had no appreciable effect, for the war dragged on for another six months after he assumed office.

Regarding himself as a middle-of-the-roader, Eisenhower made no sweeping changes in either foreign or domestic policy during his administration. He approved the expansion of social welfare legislation begun under his Democratic predecessors, and he continued to implement Truman's policies of the containment of communism. He made many sincere efforts to reach an understanding with Russia that could end the "Cold War," but his efforts were frustrated as the Russian leaders seemed determined to press on with their efforts to make the entire world communist.

During Eisenhower's administration the Space Age began as Russia successfully launched its satellite Sputnik I into orbit in October, 1957, and the United States launched its satellite Explorer I three months later.

Eisenhower's easy smile and warm disposition made even those who disagreed with his policies like him. He and his wife Mamie enjoyed entertaining at the White House, and he sometimes cooked steaks outdoors for special guests. His favorite sport was golf, which provided him relax-

At President Eisenhower's Gettysburg farm in September 1956, the President shows the first lady's "Ike Dress" to Vice President and Mrs. Richard Nixon. (UPI PHOTO)

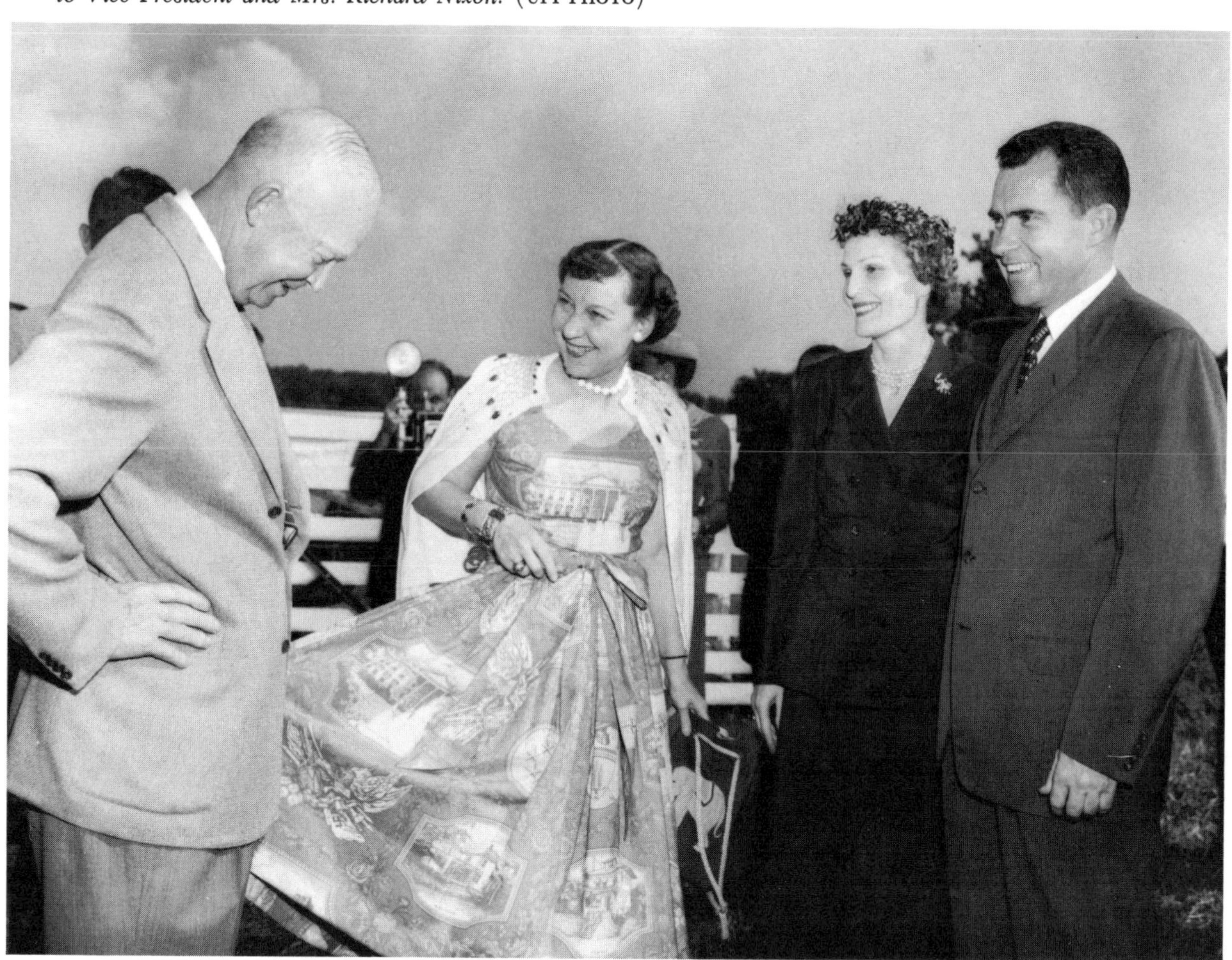

ation on the fairways. When he completed his second term in 1961, he and his wife retired to a farm he had bought near Gettysburg, Pennsylvania.

from Dwight D. Eisenhower's First Inaugural Address
—January 20, 1953

The world and we have passed the midway point of a century of continuing challenge. We sense with all our faculties that forces of good and evil are massed and armed and opposed as rarely before in history. . . .

Since this century's beginning, a time of tempest has seemed to come upon the continents of the earth. Masses of Asia have awakened to strike off shackles of the past. Great nations of Europe have fought their bloodiest wars. Thrones have toppled and their vast empires have disappeared. New nations have been born.

For our own country, it has been a time of recurring trial. We have grown in power and in responsibility. We have passed through the anxieties of depression and of war to a summit unmatched in man's history. Seeking to secure peace in the world, we have had to fight through the forests of the Argonne, to the shores of Iwo Jima, and to the cold mountains of Korea.

In the swift rush of great events, we find ourselves groping to know the full sense and meaning of these times in which we live. In our quest of understanding, we beseech God's guidance. We summon all our knowledge of the past and we scan all signs of the future. We bring all our wit and all our will to meet the question:

How far have we come in man's long pilgrimage from darkness toward light? Are we nearing the light—a day of freedom and of peace for all mankind? Or are the shadows of another night closing in upon us? . . .

We must be ready to dare all for our country. For history does not long entrust the care of freedom to the weak or the timid. . . .

General Dwight D. Eisenhower shook hands with a young admirer on September 28, 1952, as he and Mrs. Eisenhower left their residence to attend services at St. Paul's Chapel, Columbia University, New York. (NEW YORK MIRROR PHOTO FROM INTERNATIONAL)

from Dwight D. Eisenhower's Second Inaugural Address
—January 21, 1957

. . . We live in a land of plenty, but rarely has this earth known such peril as today.

In our Nation work and wealth abound. Our population grows. Commerce crowds our rivers and rails, our skies, harbors, and highways. Our soil is fertile, our agriculture productive. The air rings with the song of our industry—rolling mills and blast furnaces, dynamos, dams, and assembly lines—the chorus of America the bountiful.

This is our home—yet this is not the whole of our world. For our world is where our full destiny lies—with men, of all people, and all nations, who are or would be free. And for them—and so for us—this is no time of ease or of rest.

In too much of the earth there is want, discord, danger. New forces and new nations stir and strive across the earth, with power to bring, by their fate, great good or great evil to the free world's future. From the deserts of North Africa to the islands of the South Pacific one-third of all mankind has entered upon a historic struggle for a new freedom; freedom from grinding poverty. Across all continents, nearly a billion people seek, sometimes almost in desperation, for the skills and knowledge and assistance by which they may satisfy from their own resources, the material wants common to all mankind.

No nation, however old or great, escapes this tempest of change and turmoil. Some, impoverished by the recent World War, seek to restore their means of livelihood. In the heart of Europe, Germany still stands tragically divided. So is the whole Continent divided. And so, too, is all the world.

The divisive force is international communism and the power that it controls.

The designs of that power, dark in purpose, are clear in practice. It strives to seal forever the fate of those it has enslaved. It strives to break the ties that unite the free. And it strives to capture—to exploit for its own greater power—all forces of change in the world, especially the needs of the hungry and the hopes of the oppressed. . . .

So we voice our hope and our belief that we can help to heal this divided world. Thus may the nations cease to live in trembling before the menace of force. Thus may the weight of fear and the weight of arms be taken from the burdened shoulders of mankind.

This, nothing less, is the labor to which we are called and our strength is dedicated.

And so the prayer of our people carries far beyond our own frontiers, to the wide world of our duty and our destiny.

May the light of freedom, coming to all darkened lands, flame brightly—until at last the darkness is no more.

May the turbulence of our age yield to a true time of peace, when men and nations shall share a life that honors the dignity of each, the brotherhood of all.

John F. Kennedy

More than any other President of the period, John F. Kennedy represented the vigor and promise of the Space Age. He expressed the ideals of the twentieth century in words and phrases that captured the imagination of youth. But he was struck down by an assassin's bullets midway through his first term as President, leaving it to his successor to carry out his program.

The son of a wealthy father, Kennedy was born in 1917 in Brookline, Massachusetts—thus becoming the first President born in the twentieth century. After graduating from Harvard University, he published a best-selling book, "Why England Slept," concerned with the steps that had led to World War II. He enlisted in the U.S. Navy three months before the Japanese attack on Pearl Harbor.

During the war Kennedy became commander of a torpedo boat in the South Pacific, PT 109. When the boat was sunk by a Japanese destroyer, he heroically helped rescue his crew, damaging his own health by his exertions. Discharged from the Navy for health reasons a few months before the end of the war, Kennedy became a newspaper reporter for a short time, and then entered politics.

He served six years as a Democratic Congressman from Boston, winning election in 1946, 1948, and 1950. Then in 1952 he was elected Senator from Massachusetts and re-elected in 1958. While a Senator he wrote another best-selling book, "Profiles in Courage," that won him the 1957 Pulitzer prize for biography. In his first effort at national politics in 1956, Kennedy was defeated in an attempt to win the Democratic nomination for Vice-President as the running mate of Adlai Stevenson. Four years later he was chosen as the Democratic candidate for President, defeating Sen. Lyndon B. Johnson of Texas for the nomination, then asking Johnson to be his running mate as Vice-Presidential nominee.

In the 1960 presidential campaign Kennedy was regarded as the underdog. He was not as well known as the Republican nominee, Vice-President Richard M. Nixon, who had the active backing of the popular President Eisenhower. And politicians also expected him to be handicapped in the campaign because he was a Roman Catholic, none of whom had ever before been elected President.

But Kennedy made himself known to the American people by thorough use of the twentieth century's new communications medium, television. He challenged Nixon to a series of four face-to-face TV debates, so for the first time millions

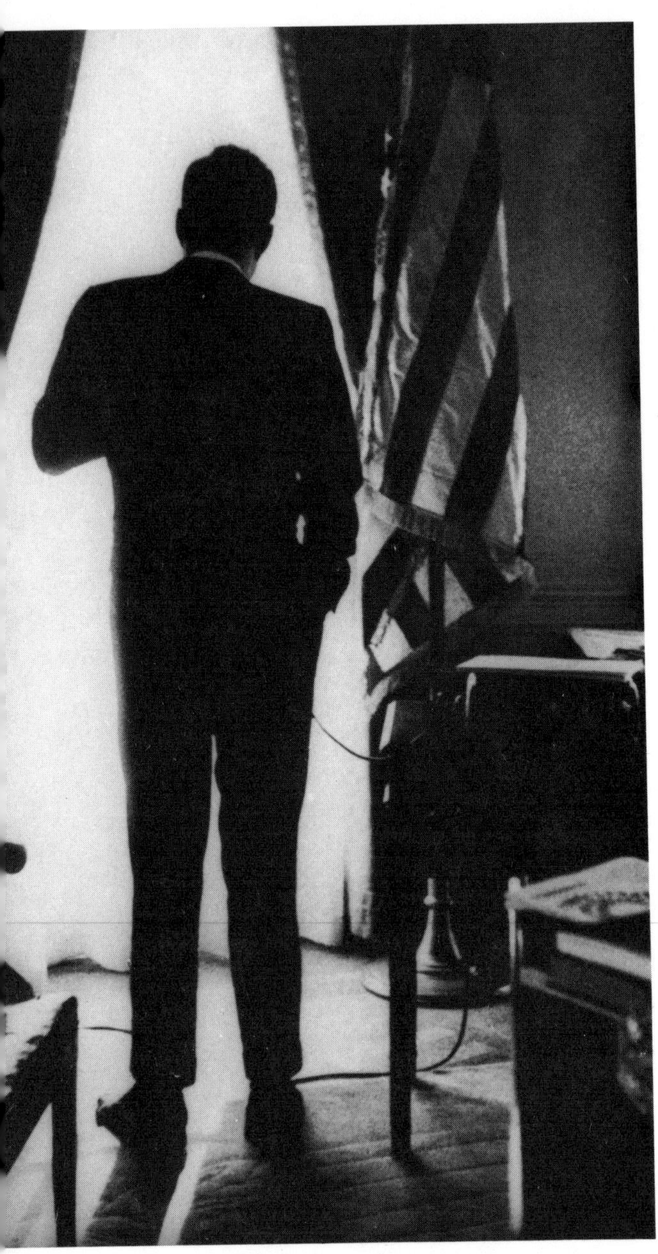

A thoughtful President Kennedy is seen in two moods which depict the lonely, burdensome office of the Chief Executive. (UPI PHOTO FROM CBS NEWS)

of American families were able to see and compare the two major presidential candidates in debate with each other. That Kennedy won these debates with his personality and ability to think on his feet was confirmed when he defeated Nixon in the November election.

As the youngest man ever elected President, the 43-year-old Kennedy inspired the youth of the nation in his inaugural address in 1961, particularly with his phrase: ". . . ask not what your country can do for you; ask what you can do for your country. . . ."

Kennedy's greatest successes as President came in the field of foreign policy. Two months after assuming office, he inaugurated his Peace Corps program in which American volunteers, especially college students, were sent to the world's underdeveloped nations to help educate their peoples in the ways of modern science and technology. The greatest crisis of his administration came in October, 1962, when his firmness in the face of a possible World War III forced Russia to withdraw atomic missiles that had been secretly installed in communist Cuba. His administration then brought some relaxing of tension in the "Cold War" by signing a treaty with Russia in 1963 calling for an end to the testing of atomic weapons in the earth's atmosphere.

In the field of domestic policy, Kennedy advocated a liberal program called the "New Frontier," which called for further extensions of social welfare and civil rights. But a coalition of Republicans and conservative Democrats in Congress blocked most of the laws he proposed.

Kennedy's popularity with youth was matched only by that of his beautiful young wife Jacqueline. She went with him on many of his speaking tours both in the United States and abroad, and he often half-jokingly said that more people turned out to see her than to greet him. As First Lady, she devoted much time and effort as a patron of the arts, endeavoring to interest the American people in cultural activities.

from John F. Kennedy's Inaugural Address

—January 20, 1961

. . . Let the word go forth from this time and place, to friend and foe alike, that the torch has been passed to a new generation of Americans—born in this century, tempered by war, disciplined by a hard and bitter peace, proud of our ancient heritage—and unwilling to witness or permit the slow undoing of those human rights to which this Nation has always been committed, and to which we are committed today at home and around the world.

Let every nation know, whether it wishes us well or ill, that we shall pay any price, bear any burden, meet any hardship, support any friend, oppose any foe, in order to assure the survival and the success of liberty.

Soviet Premier Nikita Khrushchev and Mrs. John F. Kennedy smiling at each other at the reception given by President Adolf Schaerf of Austria at Schoenbrunn Palace in Vienna in 1961. (UPI PHOTO)

This much we pledge—and more.

To those old allies whose cultural and spiritual origins we share, we pledge the loyalty of faithful friends. United, there is little we cannot do in a host of cooperative ventures. Divided, there is little we can do—for we dare not meet a powerful challenge at odds and split asunder.

To those new States whom we welcome to the ranks of the free, we pledge our words that one form of colonial control shall not have passed away merely to be replaced by a far greater iron tyranny. We shall not always expect to find them supporting our view. But we shall always hope to find them strongly supporting their own freedom—and to remember that, in the past, those who foolishly sought power by riding the back of the tiger ended up inside.

To those peoples in the huts and villages across the globe struggling to break the bonds of mass misery, we pledge our best efforts to help them help themselves, for whatever period is required—not because the Communists may be doing it, not because we seek their votes, but because it is right. If a free society cannot help the many who are poor, it cannot save the few who are rich.

To our sister republics south of our border, we offer a special pledge—to convert our good words into good deeds, in a new alliance for progress, to assist free men and free governments in casting off the chains of poverty. But this peaceful revolution of hope cannot become the prey of hostile powers. Let all our neighbors know that we shall join with them to oppose aggression or subversion anywhere in the Americas. And let every other power know that this hemisphere intends to remain the master of its own house.

To that world assembly of sovereign states, the United Nations, our last best hope in an age where the instruments of war have far outpaced the instruments of peace, we renew our pledge of support—to prevent it from becoming merely a forum for invective—to strengthen its

In his office on October 31, 1962 President Kennedy (right) discussed the Army's general readiness and its Cuban crisis activities with (left to right) Lt. Gen. Theodore W. Parker, Lt. Gen. Hamilton H. Howze, and Gen. Earle Wheeler, Army Chief of Staff. (UPI PHOTO)

shield of the new and the weak—and to enlarge the area in which its writ may run.

Finally, to those nations who would make themselves our adversary, we offer not a pledge but a request: that both sides begin anew the quest for peace, before the dark powers of destruction unleashed by science engulf all humanity in planned or accidental self-destruction. . . .

So let us begin anew—remembering on both sides that civility is not a sign of weakness, and sincerity is always subject to proof. *Let us never negotiate out of fear. But let us never fear to negotiate.*

Let both sides explore what problems unite us instead of laboring those problems which divide us.

Let both sides, for the first time, formulate serious and precise proposals for the inspection and control of arms—and bring the absolute power to destroy other nations under the absolute control of all nations.

Let both sides seek to invoke the wonders of science instead of its terrors. Together let us explore the stars, conquer the deserts, eradicate disease, tap the ocean depths, and encourage the arts and commerce.

Let both sides unite to heed in all corners of the earth the command of Isaiah—to "undo the heavy burdens and to let the oppressed go free."

And if a beachhead of cooperation may push back the jungle of suspicion, let both sides join in creating a new endeavor, not a new balance of power, but a new world of law, where the strong are just and the weak secure and the peace preserved.

All this will not be finished in the first 100 days. Nor will it be finished in the first 1,000 days, nor in the life of this administration, nor even perhaps in our lifetime on this planet. But let us begin.

In your hands, my fellow citizens, more than in mine, will rest the final success or failure of our course. Since this country was founded, each generation of Americans has been summoned to give testimony to its national loyalty. The graves of young Americans who answered the call to service are found around the globe.

Now the trumpet summons us again—not as a call to bear arms, though arms we need; not as a call to battle, though embattled we are; but a call to bear the burden of a long twilight struggle, year in, and year out, "rejoicing in hope, patient in tribulation"—a struggle against the common enemies of man: tyranny, poverty, disease, and war itself.

Can we forge against these enemies a grand and global alliance, North and South, East and West, that can assure a more fruitful life for all mankind? Will you join in that historic effort?

In the long history of the world, only a few generations have been granted the role of defending freedom in its hour of maximum danger. I do not shrink from this responsibility—I welcome it. I do not believe that any of us would exchange places with any other people or any other generation. The energy, the faith, the devotion which we bring to this endeavor will light our country and all who serve it—and the glow from that fire can truly light the world.

And so, my fellow Americans, ask not what your country can do for you: Ask what you can do for your country.

My fellow citizens of the world: Ask not what America will do for you, but what together we can do for the freedom of man. . . .

On November 22, 1963, Kennedy and his wife were in Dallas, Texas, on a speaking tour in which he hoped to improve his relationship with Texas Democrats. As Kennedy's open automobile drove slowly along the crowd-lined streets, rifle shots rang out. Kennedy was struck in the neck and head and died almost instantly. One of the bullets also wounded Texas Gov. John B. Connally, who later recovered. Mrs. Kennedy, riding beside the President, was unhurt, but was drenched with her husband's blood as he lay dying in her lap. A few hours later, Lee Harvey Oswald, a former U.S. marine who had once given up his American citizenship to live in Russia, was arrested as the assassin after he had killed a policeman while trying to escape. Oswald denied his guilt, but before he could be brought to trial he in turn was slain by a nightclub owner named Jack Ruby, who said he was avenging Kennedy's death. This last shooting took place as millions of persons were watching on television while Oswald was being transferred from one jail to another. Months later a commission headed by Chief Justice Earl Warren ruled that Oswald had acted alone in the assassination, but this did not stop public speculation that the slaying was part of a conspiracy.

The shocked nation watched in grief on television the sad aftermath of events. They saw Mrs. Kennedy, still wearing her bloodstained dress, accompany her husband's coffin as it was returned to Washington. They saw the new President, Lyndon B. Johnson, pledge to carry forward Kennedy's program. And they watched the solemn funeral ceremonies and the burial of Kennedy's body at Arlington National Cemetery.

On the first anniversary of the assassination of President Kennedy, November 22, 1964, Senator-elect Robert F. Kennedy is shown here placing a flower near the eternal flame on his brother's grave. (UPI PHOTO)

Lyndon B. Johnson

As shocked and bewildered by the assassination of President Kennedy as everyone else, Lyndon B. Johnson was sworn in as the nation's chief executive aboard the plane that carried Kennedy's body back to Washington. Upon arriving at the nation's capital he pledged the nation that he would "do my best." After Kennedy's funeral, Johnson called on Congress to carry forward the fallen President's program with the words, "Let us continue."

The new President was a 6-foot 3-inch Texan who had spent 33 of his 55 years in public service. He had worked his way through Southwest Texas State Teachers College as a youth, taught school briefly, then became secretary to a Texas Congressman in the early days of President Roosevelt's New Deal administration. Starting in 1936 he was elected to six terms as a U.S. Representative from Texas, and then in 1948 was elected to the U.S. Senate, remaining there for a dozen years. During Eisenhower's administration, Johnson was majority leader of the Senate, and as such was regarded as the most powerful man in Washington next to the President. At the Democratic national convention in 1960, he was disappointed not to be chosen as the party's presidential nominee, but when asked by John Kennedy to run for Vice-President he accepted. As Vice-President he continued to take an active role in the government sitting in regularly at Cabinet meetings, chairing important commissions and committees, and traveling throughout the world as the President's representative.

In his address to Congress immediately after Kennedy's death, Johnson challenged Congress to pass all the legislation that Kennedy had asked for to prove that he "did not live—or die—in vain." In the remaining fourteen months that would have completed Kennedy's first term, Congress passed almost every measure he had asked for, including a new stronger civil rights act.

In the 1964 presidential campaign, Johnson won the Democratic nomination by acclamation to oppose Republican candidate Sen. Barry Goldwater of Arizona. Johnson chose as his Vice-Presidential runningmate Sen. Hubert Humphrey of Minnesota. Goldwater represented the conservative wing of the Republican party, and many liberals within his own party refused to support him. Johnson called for a further expansion of the social welfare programs of Roosevelt, Truman, and Kennedy, calling his proposals the "Great Society." In the election in November Johnson won the presidency in his own right by one of the greatest majorities of popular votes in history —61 percent.

With a huge Democratic majority in both houses of Congress, Johnson had little difficulty in getting any legislation that he wanted. Congress passed a Medicare act providing federal assistance for medical care for citizens over 65. It approved an expansion of federal aid to education from primary school to college. And it passed new civil rights legislation to help insure Negroes the right to vote.

But Johnson was less successful in winning popular support for his foreign policy program. In April, 1965, he used U.S. troops to intervene in a civil war in the Dominican Republic, explaining that it was necessary to prevent communists from taking over the government. He was criticized as having acted too hastily and on too little evidence that the communist threat was real, but his critics were on weak ground because they had no counter evidence.

On the other side of the world in Vietnam, Johnson had even greater problems that overshadowed his whole second term. The United States had begun sending military supplies and advisers to Vietnam in 1950 under President Truman to aid the French and South Vietnamese in a war against communist guerrillas. U.S. military aid had been expanded under Presidents Eisenhower and Kennedy. But when it became apparent that the communist forces were being supported by North Vietnam, China, and Russia, Johnson decided to order U.S. military forces directly into action. In an effort to end the war he sent more than 400,000 American troops into the ground fighting and used the navy and air force to bomb North Vietnam. But, as in the case of the Korean War of the 1950's, many Americans were unsympathetic with a war so far from home, and Johnson reaped the brunt of their unhappiness.

In the Congressional elections of 1966 the Democratic party retained control of both houses of Congress, but with reduced majorities. As a

President Kennedy with Vice President Lyndon Johnson, February 7, 1961, just after telling his Congressional leaders that he would send ten special messages to Congress in the following few weeks, including one on medical care for the aged. (UPI PHOTO)

consequence, Johnson faced greater difficulties in the latter half of his second term in winning Congressional approval for his legislative program.

For relaxation President Johnson liked best to go to his ranch in Texas. His wife, best known by her nickname Lady Bird, was credited by her husband with having built the family fortune through her good business sense and careful management of a radio and television station in Austin, Texas. As First Lady, Mrs. Johnson became a leader in the Keep America Beautiful movement to improve the appearance of public highways and recreation areas, and to protect the nation's natural beauties.

Lyndon B. Johnson's Inaugural Address

—January 20, 1965

On this occasion, the oath I have taken before you—and before God—is not mine alone, but ours together. We are one nation and one people. Our fate as a nation, and our future as a people rest not upon one citizen, but upon all citizens.

That is the majesty and the meaning of this moment.

The Inaugural parade January 21, 1965, with President Lyndon B. Johnson in a limousine surrounded by Secret Servicemen and news photographers following a motorcycle police escort down historic Pennsylvania Avenue in Washington, D.C. (UPI PHOTO)

For every generation, there is a destiny. For some, history decides. For this generation, the choice must be our own.

Even now, a rocket moves toward Mars. It reminds us that the world will not be the same for our children, or even for ourselves in a short span of years.

The next man to stand here will look out on a scene that is different from our own, because ours is a time of change—rapid and fantastic change—baring the secrets of nature—multiplying the nations—placing in uncertain hands new weapons for mastery and destruction—shaking old values and uprooting old ways.

Our destiny in the midst of change will rest on the unchanged character of our people—and on their faith.

They came here—the exile and the stranger, brave but frightened—to find a place where a man could be his own man. They made a covenant with this land. Conceived in justice, written in liberty, bound in union, it was meant one day to inspire the hopes of all mankind, and it binds us still. If we keep its terms we shall flourish.

First, justice was the promise that all who made the journey would share in the fruits of the land.

In a land of greath wealth, families must not live in .hopeless poverty.

In a land rich in harvest, children just must not go hungry.

In a land of healing miracles, neighbors must not suffer and die untended.

In a great land of learning and scholars, young people must be taught to read and write.

For more than 30 years that I have served this nation, I have believed that this injustice to our people—this waste of our resources—was our real enemy. For 30 years or more, with the resources I have had, I have vigilantly fought against it. I have learned and I know that it will not surrender easily.

But change has given us new weapons. Before this generation of Americans is finished, this enemy will not only retreat—it will be conquered.

Justice requires us to remember: When any citizen denies his fellow, saying, "His color is not mine or his beliefs are strange and different," in that moment he betrays America, though his forebears created this nation.

Liberty was the second article of our covenant. It was self-government. It was our Bill of Rights. But it was more. America would be a place where each man could be proud to be himself, stretching his talents, rejoicing in his work, important in the life of his neighbors and his nation.

This has become more difficult in a world where change and growth seem to tower beyond the control, and even the judgment, of men. We must work to provide the knowledge and the surroundings which can enlarge the possibilities of every citizen.

The American covenant called on us to help show the way for the liberation of man, and that is today our goal. Thus, if as a nation there is much outside our control, as a people no stranger is outside our hope.

Change has brought new meaning to that old mission. We can never again stand aside prideful in isolation. Terrific dangers and troubles that we once called "foreign" now constantly live among us.

If American lives must end and American treasure be spilled in countries that we barely know, then that is the price that change has demanded of conviction, and of our enduring covenant.

Think of our world as it looks from that rocket that is heading toward Mars. It is like a child's globe, hanging in space, the continents stuck to its side like colored maps. We are all fellow passengers on a dot of earth. And each of us, in the span of time, has really only a moment among our companions.

How incredible it is that in this fragile existence we should hate and destroy one

An intimate view of President John F. Kennedy and Vice President Lyndon B. Johnson. (UPI PHOTO)

Civil-rights marchers guarded by nearly 1000 policemen during a demonstration against racial discrimination in housing in Chicago, August 13, 1966. (UPI PHOTO)

another. There are possibilities enough for all who will abandon mastery over others to pursue mastery over nature. There is world enough for all to seek their happiness in their own way.

And our nation's course is abundantly clear. We aspire to nothing that belongs to others. We seek no dominion over our fellow man, but man's dominion over tyranny and misery.

But more is required. Men want to be part of a common enterprise—a cause greater than themselves. And each of us must find a way to advance the purpose of the nation, thus find new purpose for ourselves. Without this, we will simply become a nation of strangers.

The third article is union. To those who were small and few against the wilderness, the success of liberty demanded the strength of the union. Two centuries of change have made this true again.

No longer need capitalist and worker, farmer and clerk, city and countryside struggle to divide our bounty. By working shoulder to shoulder together, we can increase the bounty of all.

We have discovered that every child who learns, and every man who finds work, and every sick body that is made whole—like a candle added to an altar—brightens the hope of all the faithful.

So let us reject any among us who seek to reopen old wounds and rekindle old hatreds. They stand in the way of a seeking nation.

Let us now join reason to faith and action to experience, to transform our unity of interest into a unity of purpose. For the hour and the day and the time are here to achieve progress without strife, to achieve change without hatred; not without difference of opinion, but without the deep and abiding divisions which scar the union for generations.

Under this covenant of justice, liberty and union, we have become a nation: prosperous, great and mighty. And we have kept our freedom.

But we have no promise from God that our greatness will endure. We have been allowed by Him to seek greatness with the sweat of our hands and the strength of our spirit.

I do not believe that the "Great Society" is the ordered, changeless and sterile battalion of the ants.

It is the excitement of becoming—always becoming, trying, probing, falling, resting, and trying again—but always trying and always gaining.

In each generation—with toil and tears—we have had to earn our heritage again.

If we fail now, then we will have forgotten in abundance what we learned in hardship: that democracy rests on faith, that freedom asks more than it gives, and the judgment of God is harshest on those who are most favored.

If we succeed, it will not be because of what we have, but it will be because of what we are; not because of what we own, but rather be-

Unveiling Leonardo da Vinci's "Mona Lisa" on its historic showing at the National Gallery of Art, Washington, D. C., January 8, 1963, President John F. Kennedy thanked France for permitting the world's most famous work of art to be shown in the United States. (UPI PHOTO)

President John F. Kennedy during a period of relaxation, with Mrs. Jacqueline Kennedy in the background. (UPI PHOTO)

Scenes at Arlington National Cemetery during the funeral of President John F. Kennedy, November 25, 1963.
(UPI PHOTO)

LEFT: *A view of President John F. Kennedy and his wife, Mrs. Jacqueline Kennedy, aboard the yacht Marlin.* (UPI PHOTO)

At the ceremony dedicating the John F. Kennedy Memorial, May 14, 1965, at Runnymede, England, the site of the signing of the Magna Carta, former Prime Minister Harold Macmillan addressed the gathering. Seated in front row, from left to right, are Mrs. Jacqueline Kennedy, Queen Elizabeth and Prince Philip. In second row, from left to right, are Mrs. Edward Kennedy, Senator Edward Kennedy, Senator Robert Kennedy and Caroline Kennedy. (UPI PHOTO)

The Fathers of the Second Vatican Council gathered in St. Peter's Basilica, Vatican City, Rome. The Council was convoked by Pope John XXIII "to procure the good of the Christian people and to be an invitation to the separated communities to join in the search for unity." The Council opened on October 11, 1962. When Pope John died it continued under Pope Paul VI and closed on December 8, 1965. (UPI PHOTO)

A view of some of the Fathers who attended the opening of the final session of the Second Vatican Council on September 14, 1965. An average of 2200 Fathers attended each of the four sessions of the Council, and sixteen official pronouncements aimed at updating the Roman Catholic Church were adopted.

cause of what we believe.

For we are a nation of believers. Underneath the clamor of building and the rush of our day's pursuits, we are believers in justice and liberty and union, and in our own union. We believe that every man must some day be free. And we believe in ourselves.

And that is the mistake that our enemies have always made. In my lifetime—in depression and in war—they have awaited our defeat. Each time, from the secret places of the American heart, came forth the faith that they could not see or that they could not even imagine. And it brought us victory, and it will again.

For this is what America is all about. It is the uncrossed desert and the unclimbed ridge. It is the star that is not reached and the harvest that is sleeping in the unplowed ground.

Is our world gone? We say farewell. Is a new world coming? We welcome it—and we will bend it to the hopes of man.

And to these trusted public servants, and to my family, and those close friends of mine who have followed me down a long, winding road, and to all the people of this union and the world, I will repeat today what I said on that sorrowful day in November last year (1963):

I will lead, and I will do the best I can. But you—you must look within your own hearts, to the old promises and to the old dream. They will lead you best of all.

For myself, I ask only in the words of an ancient leader: "Give me now wisdom and knowledge that I may go out and come in before this people: for who can judge this, thy people, that is so great?"

This unusual photograph of President Johnson embracing Vice President Hubert Humphrey and Mrs. Johnson greeting Mrs. Humphrey on the Humphreys' return from a Far East tour won top prize in the UPI news picture contest for February 1966. (UPI PHOTO)

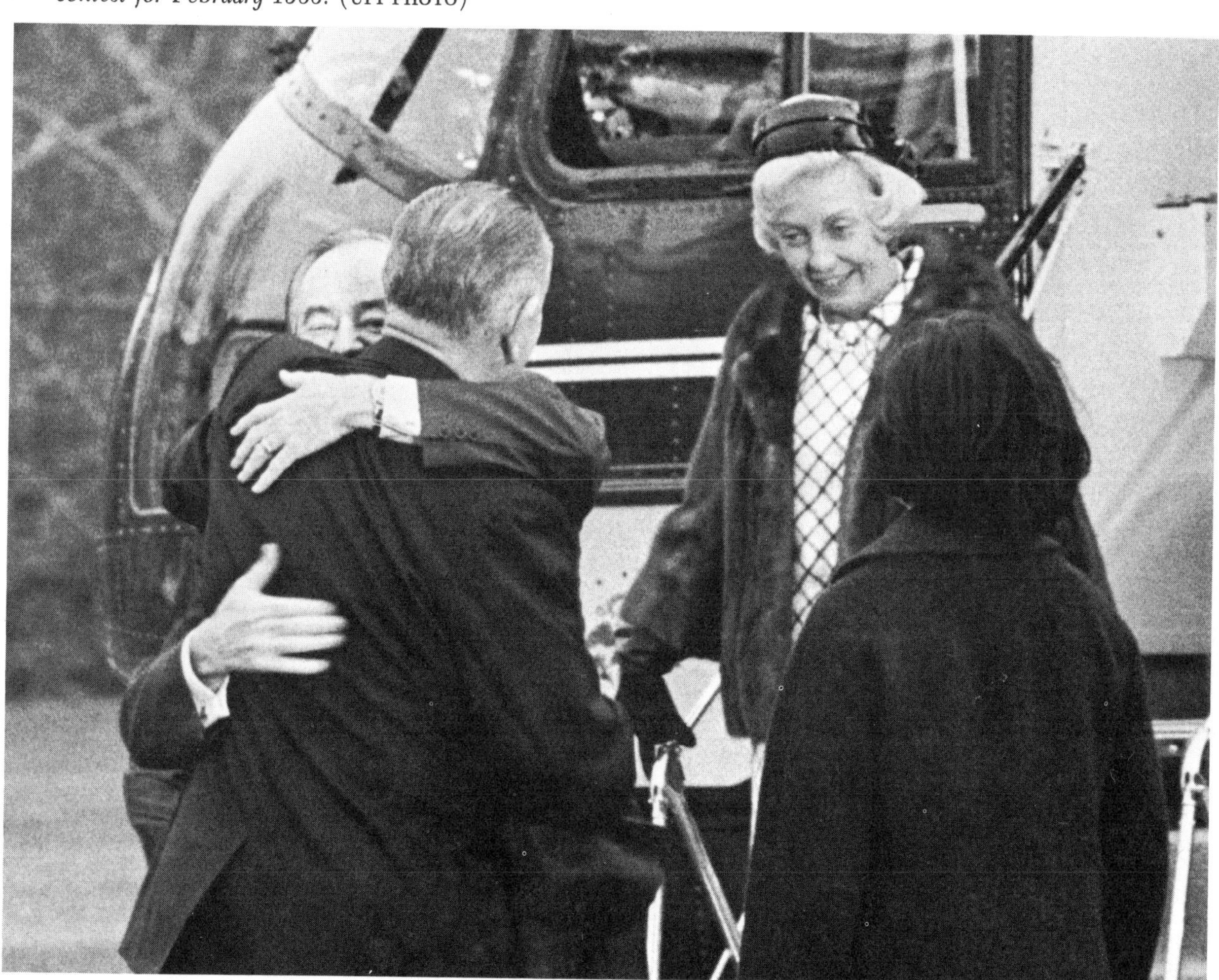

In Great Britain

In the two decades since World War II, Great Britain, like the United States, experienced changes of direction both in its leaders and in public support of its two major political parties. Throughout the first part of the period the titular ruler was King George VI. Upon his death in the early 1950's, he was succeeded by his daughter Elizabeth II. However, the real leadership of the country was in the hands of the six men who in turn held the office of prime minister. Four of these prime ministers were leaders of the Conservative party—Winston Churchill, Sir Anthony Eden, Harold Macmillan, and Sir Alec Douglas-Home. Two were members of the Labour party—Clement R. Attlee and Harold Wilson.

King George VI

George VI ruled during the darkest days of Britain when it looked as though the island might be invaded and conquered by Hitler. But George VI exhibited unwavering confidence, helping buoy the spirits of his people.

He had never expected to be king, and had been as shocked as the rest of his countrymen in 1936 when his popular elder brother, Edward VIII, abdicated in order to marry an American divorcee. Known as the Duke of York before ascending the throne at the age of 40, George had always been overshadowed by the more flamboyant Edward.

But in his own quiet way George VI was perhaps best fitted to be the first British monarch to rule the Space Age generation, because he was the first British king to be able to fly an airplane. He had obtained his wings at the end of World War I as an officer in the Royal Naval Air Service.

Although respected and admired by his subjects, George VI never exerted powerful personal leadership. He left the running of World War II to the elected government, and after the war he passively gave up his title of "emperor of India" when that country was granted self-government in 1948.

Queen Elizabeth II

George's subjects mourned his death in 1952, but they also looked forward hopefully to the ascension of his attractive eldest daughter as

From the balcony of Buckingham Palace in London, England's royal family acknowledged the cheers of the throngs on V-E Day. From left to right are Princess Elizabeth, Queen Elizabeth, King George, and Princess Margaret Rose. (UPI PHOTO)

At the Tomb of the Unknown Soldier in Paris, Prime Minister Winston Churchill, wearing the uniform of the Royal Air Force, and General Charles de Gaulle, head of the French Provisional Government, saluted during Armistice Day services November 11, 1944. (UPI PHOTO)

perhaps a signal of rejuvenation of British glory such as the country had experienced under queens Elizabeth I and Victoria.

The formal coronation ceremonies for the 27-year-old Queen Elizabeth II took place on June 2, 1953—after more than a year of mourning for her father. The glittering pageantry of the coronation procession and the crowning in Westminster Abbey lifted British spirits and reminded the country and the world of the country's powerful past. The new queen and her escort, Prince Philip, in the following years made many trips to the far-flung parts of the British Commonwealth, rallying loyalty to British influence. But royal leadership had become more symbolic than real, and the fate of Britain rested more in the hands of the country's two main political forces, the Conservative and the Labour parties.

Winston Churchill

The most powerful British leader during the growing-up of the Space Age generation was Conservative Prime Minister Wiston Churchill. He had ruled Great Britain during most of World War II, inspiring the British people to sacrifices and great deeds. In June, 1940, a month after Churchill took office, Hitler's forces had crushed France and forced Britain to pull its troops off the European continent. But in that dark hour, the 65-year-old prime minister rallied his people with these stirring words:

"We shall go on to the end, we shall fight in France, we shall fight on the seas and the oceans, we shall fight with growing confidence and growing strength in the air, we shall defend our island, whatever the cost may be, we shall fight on the beaches, we shall fight on the landing grounds, we shall fight in the fields and in the streets, we shall fight in the hills; we shall never surrender, and even if, which I do not for a moment believe, this island or a large part of it were subjugated and starving, then our Empire beyond the seas, armed and guarded by the British Fleet, would carry on the struggle until, in God's good time, the new world, with all its power and might, steps forth to the rescue and the liberation of the old."

President Franklin D. Roosevelt and Prime Minister Winston Churchill conferring with each other in the palace at Yalta in February 1945. (UPI PHOTO)

British Prime Minister Harold Wilson chatting with Rear Admiral Sir Michael Pollock after arrival at Gibraltar aboard the British warship HMS Tiger to meet with Rhodesian Premier Ian Smith in December 1966. (UPI CABLEPHOTO)

Churchill was a descendant of the Duke of Marlborough, a famous British general of the early 1700's. A brilliant writer as well as a politician, Churchill published many books, including multi-volume histories of both World War I and World War II. He had served as a representative in the British parliament since 1903, switching back and forth between the Conservative and Liberal parties and holding cabinet posts under prime ministers of both parties. As wartime prime minister in World War II, Churchill ruled Britain with the powers of a dictator, willingly given to him by the people because they knew he would relinquish them once the war was done.

Almost as soon as the war ended in Europe in 1945, the British called a general election to elect a new parliament to hammer out the country's post-war policies. Churchill could not imagine that, after leading his country to victory, the voters would turn him out of office. He attacked the opposing Labour party as socialists who would change Britain into a totalitarian state, and he failed to emphasize a positive program for the Conservatives to rebuild war-torn Britain. He was shocked at the results of the election in July, 1945, in which, in his own words, he was "dismissed by the British electorate from all further conduct of their affairs."

Clement R. Attlee

The man who succeeded Churchill was as vastly different from his predecessor as night from day. Where Churchill was forceful and aggressive, Attlee was quiet and unassuming. Although a lawyer by training, he spent most of his early life as a social worker in the slums of London, and as a college lecturer in social science.

Attlee entered politics in the 1920's, first as mayor of a London suburb and then as a Labour member of parliament for the slum district of Limehouse. He served in cabinet posts under Labour Prime Minister Ramsay MacDonald from 1929 to 1932. Then in 1935 he became leader of the Labour party. During World War II, he was deputy prime minister in Churchill's four-man coalition War Cabinet.

When the Labour party victory swept Attlee into power as prime minister in 1945, he was 62 years old. In the six years he led the British government, Attlee quietly but determinedly helped restructure the British economy along socialist lines. In 1948 he described the philosophy of his party and himself:

"Our task is to work out a system of a new and challenging kind which combines individual freedom with a planned economy; democracy with social justice. The task which faces not only ourselves but all the Western democracies requires a government inspired by a new conception of society with a dynamic policy in accord with the needs of a new situation. It could not be accomplished by any of the old parties, nor by a totalitarian party, whether Fascist or Communist."

Conservative Prime Ministers Return to Power

Having quickly recovered from his 1945 defeat, Winston Churchill became a vigorous opponent of Attlee as leader of the opposition Conservative party. Churchill hammered at the Labour party government as following a program of "strength through misery." He deplored their socialization of industry at home and their weakness in foreign affairs abroad. Finally, in the British election of October, 1951, he was rewarded as the Conservatives were returned to power with a majority in the House of Commons and at the age of 76 again became prime minister.

During his nearly four-year administration as a peacetime prime minister from 1951 to 1955, Churchill surprised both his friends and his foes by the relative calm and lack of radical change of his government. In April, 1953, he was knighted by Queen Elizabeth, and six months later was awarded the Nobel Prize for literature.

In April, 1955, the 80-year-old Churchill resigned for reasons of age and sickness, turning the prime ministership over to 57-year-old Sir Anthony Eden, who had served in cabinet positions in Conservative governments since he was 27. Eden had won his greatest fame as Britain's foreign minister in both of Churchill's administrations. Eden's government lost face when he sent British troops to aid France and Israel in an invasion of Egypt and then was forced to withdraw them in the face of American and Russian opposition. In January, 1957, Eden resigned, giving ill health as an excuse.

Harold Macmillan, the 52-year-old Conservative leader who succeeded Eden as prime minister, was a wealthy book publisher who had been a member of parliament since 1924. During World War II he had served as Britain's official representative at Eisenhower's headquarters. He held various cabinet posts under Churchill and Eden, being at various times in charge of foreign affairs, defense, and the treasury.

During Macmillan's six years as prime minister, he traveled widely to all parts of the world, restoring good relations with the United States, and endeavoring to ease international tensions with Russia. His Conservative party won a substantial majority in a general election in 1959. In 1963 Macmillan's government was shaken when France refused to allow Britain to join the European Common Market, and later the same year a sex scandal in the private life of one of his cabinet ministers, John Profumo, also hurt the Conservative party. Macmillan resigned in October, 1963, citing his poor health.

Macmillan's successor as prime minister was his foreign secretary, the Earl of Home, who in order to sit in the House of Commons gave up his title and adopted the name Sir Alec Douglas-Home. The new prime minister had first been elected to parliament in 1931, when he was then known as Lord Dunglass. He inherited his father's title and fortune in 1951, and in 1957 became the Conservative leader of the House of Lords. Douglas-Home was 60 when he was appointed prime minister. He was unable to restore public confidence in the Conservative party, and just short of a year after he had assumed office the Labour party won a general election and ended his administration.

Harold Wilson

After thirteen years of Conservative party government, the Labour party returned to power in October, 1964, with 48-year-old Harold Wilson as prime minister—the youngest in 70 years and the first to be born in the twentieth century. A civil servant in various government ministries during World War II, he entered politics in 1945 with election to parliament in the Labour party victory. He became a member of Prime Minister's Attlee's cabinet at the age of 31. During the 1950's and 1960's, while the Conservatives controlled the government, Wilson continused to be re-elected to parliament and slowly climbed to leadership of the Labour party. As prime minister, Wilson pressed forward stringent plans to aid the British economy and attempt to eliminate the deficit balance in British exports over imports.

In Western Europe

Many leaders rose and fell in the various countries of Western Europe, but the two towering figures of the times were Charles de Gaulle of France and Konrad Adenauer of Germany. They rebuilt their countries as the two strongest democracies on the continent. And for the first time in more than a hundred years the leaders of France and Germany worked together in a spirit of cooperation rather than in the spirit of military rivalry that previously had led to the two World Wars.

Charles de Gaulle of France

The 6-foot 4-inch Charles de Gaulle was 53 years old when he triumphantly entered Paris on August 25, 1944, with the Allied liberation forces. De Gaulle, a career soldier, had been a colonel in charge of a tank regiment when World War II began. Then as German forces crashed into France in May, 1940, he had been promoted to brigadier general and made undersecretary of defense in the tottering French government. When France surrendered to the Nazis in June, 1940, de Gaulle escaped to London and won Winston Churchill's support as head of a Free French government in exile. He took command of French forces in France's African colonies, and helped rally French resistance movements during the war.

Upon his return to France in 1944 de Gaulle became president of the provisional government. He ruled with the powers of a dictator, but made it clearly understood that he intended to restore the country's democratic institutions. As soon as French prisoners had been repatriated after the German surrender, de Gaulle called an election in October, 1945, for the election of a constituent assembly and for an expression of opinion as to whether the country should be governed under its old constitution of the Third Republic. The voters called for a new constitution and elected a majority of delegates who were communists, socialists, and other leftists.

In a speech to the constituent assembly in November, 1945, de Gaulle called upon the delegates to rebuild France and make it an important "Third Force" between East and West. He said: "Placed where it is, in Europe, Africa, and Asia, and oriented traditionally toward West and East, France can be and wants to be a link and not, at any price, a pawn."

When it seemed that the communists aided by the socialists were winning control of the constituent assembly, de Gaulle abruptly decided to resign as president on Jan. 20, 1946. He believed

From a reviewing stand on the Champs Elysées in Paris (left to right) Prime Minister Winston Churchill, General Charles de Gaulle, and British Foreign Secretary Anthony Eden watched the parade of Allied troops on Armistice Day, November 11, 1944. (UPI PHOTO)

that the people would demand that he return to power, and, like Winston Churchill in Britain, he was shocked when they did not immediately call him back to office. Instead the country adopted a new constitution for a Fourth Republic, that was not much different in structure than the old Third Republic, and a socialist, Vincent Auriol, was elected president in 1947. A coalition of leftist parties, excluding the communists, controlled the French parliament.

De Gaulle helped form a political movement called the Rally of the French People in 1947. For a time it appeared that this organization was similar to the pre-war fascist groups that brought Hitler and Mussolini to power. But in 1953 de Gaulle dropped out of the RPF, as it was called, and said he was retiring to private life.

Throughout the late 1940's and early 1950's, the French government was headed by one premier after another, each unable to retain the support of parliament for more than a few months because no single party had a majority. Auriol was succeeded as president in 1954 by René Coty, but under the constitution of the Fourth Republic the president was a mere figurehead.

In the spring of 1958 a revolt by French generals in Algeria brought a crisis in the French government. And on June 1, the parliament voted to ask 67-year-old de Gaulle to become premier with the powers of a dictator in order to restore order. De Gaulle accepted, and immediately set about preparing a new constitution for a Fifth Republic in which the president would have strong powers, comparable to that of the President of the United States. In November, 1958, voters approved the new Constitution, and the following month elected de Gaulle as president. He was inaugurated on Jan. 8, 1959.

De Gaulle dedicated himself to increasing France's stature on the world scene in line with his belief, "France cannot be France without greatness." In his efforts to restore France's prestige, de Gaulle sometimes appeared to be obstructing the best interests of his Allies. For example he prevented Britain from joining the European Common Market in 1958. He did not allow France to sign the nuclear test-ban treaty in 1963, because he wanted his country to be free "to equip herself with an atomic force of her own." And in 1965 he announced that France

General and Mme. Charles de Gaulle, November, 1941. (UPI PHOT

was withdrawing from the North Atlantic Treaty Organization, the mutual defense organization that linked the Western European nations with the United States, because he felt that further French participation "hands our fate over to foreign authority."

De Gaulle was 75 years old in 1965, and many persons did not expect him to run for president again in the national election that year. However, he announced his candidacy, warning that if he were not re-elected the French people could expect political chaos "more disastrous than it experienced in the past." In the election in early December, de Gaulle won only 45 per cent of the vote, and so was forced into a run-off with the second place candidate of the socialist party, Francois Mitterrand. In the second vote later in December, de Gaulle won by a 55 per cent majority. In his second term he continued to press his policies for a greater French voice in world affairs.

Konrad Adenauer of Germany

Much older than most of the other national leaders of the era, 6-foot 2-inch Konrad Adenauer was already 72 when he was elected president of the constitutional convention in 1948 that outlined the post-war government for West Germany. For the next 15 years as chancellor, or head of the West German parliament, this aus-

On his arrival in Bonn, Germany, July 13, 1956, Indian Prime Minister Jawaharlal Nehru was greeted by West German Chancellor Konrad Adenauer. (UPI PHOTO)

tere, leathery old man vigorously led his country in establishing it as one of the most important nations of the free world. By the time he retired in 1963, he was 87 years old. Germans affectionately called him "Der Alte," which meant "the Old One."

In the period between the World Wars, Adenauer had been mayor of Cologne from 1917 to 1933. Under Hitler he was imprisoned twice by the Nazis on charges of plotting against the German dictator.

After World War II, the Roman Catholic Adenauer helped organize the middle-of-the-road Christian Democratic party, which became the largest political force in the country. He led his party to national election victories in 1949, 1953, 1957, and 1961, despite constant speculation throughout the time that he would soon retire because of his age. Under the parliamentary form of government, Adenauer, as chancellor, overshadowed the presidents of the republic—Theodor Heuss, who served from 1949 to 1959, and his successor Heinrich Lübke.

Adenauer cooperated wholeheartedly with the West, bringing Germany into active partnership with its former enemies in the North Atlantic Treaty Organization. The culmination of his career came in 1963, shortly before his retirement, when he and France's President de Gaulle signed a treaty of friendship. Adenauer called this treaty a "pillar of peace," and said, "This treaty ends a conflict that has stretched over 400 years. It is that fact which gives the treaty its place in history. . . . German-French friendship is the guarantee of peace in Europe."

Upon retirement Adenauer spoke sadly of the fact that he had been unable to obtain the reunification of West and East Germany as a single nation. "I am convinced it will come," he said, "because unity cannot be denied to a people like the Germans when they want to create it in peace."

Ludwig Erhard, who had been Adenauer's minister of economics and had helped guide the country's remarkable post-war economic recovery, succeeded Adenauer as chancellor and as leader of the Christian Democrats. The 66-year-old Erhard led his party to a clear-cut election victory in 1965, but he lost the voter's confidence the following year. In 1966 Erhard was succeeded as leader of his party and as chancellor by Kurt Kiesinger, a former Nazi party member, who formed a coalition government with the Social Democrats.

In Russia

Like other leading nations of the world, Russia underwent several major changes of leadership. Because so much secrecy surrounded the communist government of Russia, the world was never sure exactly why and how these changes in leadership took place, or what

President Harry Truman and Marshal Joseph Stalin at the time of the Potsdam Conference in August 1945. (UPI PHOTO)

they meant toward the long-range future of international relations.

Joseph Stalin

At the end of World War II Russia was ruled by the ruthless dictator Joseph Stalin, whose last name meant "Man of Steel." The son of a shoemaker, he had taken part in the Bolshevik revolution of 1917, and became secretary-general of the Communist party in 1922. Upon the death of the Russian dictator Lenin in 1924, Stalin became ruler at the age of 44. Stalin saw to it that anyone who opposed him in the Russian government or the Communist party was purged from power, tried, and executed. When Russian farmers opposed his plans to take their land away from them to form collective farms, he had millions of them slain and deported to prison camps in Siberia.

The world learned to mistrust Stalin's words and deeds, because he would observe a treaty with another country only so long as it served his plans for domination of the world by the communists. In August, 1939, Stalin concluded a 10-year nonaggression pact with Hitler that freed the German dictator to make his attack on Poland the following month, starting World War II. At the same time Stalin's troops took the eastern third of Poland, attacked Finland, and captured the Baltic countries of Estonia, Latvia, and Lithuania. On June 22, 1941, Hitler turned on Stalin, sending his German armies driving into Russia. For a time it appeared that Hitler would defeat Russia, but the United States rushed military supplies to Stalin's forces, realizing that if Russia fell Hitler could easily mount his threatened invasion of Great Britain. Altogether the United States gave Russia 11 billion dollars of Lend-Lease aid during the war, but Stalin gave little credit to the Allies and at the end of the war told the Russian people that they alone were responsible for defeating Hitler. Because Roosevelt and Churchill felt it was important to keep Russia in the war, they made many concessions to Stalin at the various meetings of the Big Three that resulted in Russia being in a commanding position in Eastern Europe and in Asia at the end of the war.

Although Stalin was friendly to Roosevelt and Churchill as long as he needed their help, and although he promised that after the war the countries Russia had liberated would be given their freedom, he had no intention of keeping his word. Stalin was dedicated to the idea that communism should rule the world, and as soon as

Russian Foreign Minister Andrei Vishinsky signed the historic Sino-Soviet 30-year treaty in Moscow in February 1950, as Stalin and Mao-Tse-Tung (standing together behind him) and others looked on. At right, with his hand at his chest, is Georgi Malenkov. (UPI PHOTO)

On the left, Leonid Brezhnev, who became President of the Presidium of the Supreme Soviet upon the occasion of the retirement of Kliment Voroshilov (front right) May 7, 1960, with Premier Nikita Khrushchev (center).
(UPI PHOTO)

World War II was finished he began trying to take over as many countries as possible for communism. The leaders of the United States and Great Britain could hardly believe that anyone could be so treacherous as Stalin. As the dictator of Russia and the leader of communism, Stalin single-handedly was responsible for the Cold War that split the world into East and West opposing camps.

The world was startled when Moscow announced on March 5, 1953, that the 73-year-old Stalin had died four days after having had a stroke. There were unverified rumors that Stalin had been killed. Three months after Stalin's death Lavrenti Beria, who had been the head of the dead dictator's feared secret police, was arrested on charges of being a foreign agent, was tried in secret, and was executed in December. Because of Moscow's secrecy no one knew whether Beria did or did not have something to do with Stalin's death.

Georgi M. Malenkov

Stalin's successor as premier of Russia was Georgi M. Malenkov, the 51-year-old secretary of the communist party. Malenkov had been close to Stalin all his life, having become the dictator's private secretary at the age of 23. But for reasons that the world did not learn, Malenkov lost out in the struggle for power that followed Stalin's death. He lasted as premier less than two years, then was demoted to become minister of electricity. In 1957 he was demoted again to become manager of an electric power station in the remote state of Kazakhstan.

Nikita S. Khrushchev

Less than two weeks after Stalin's death in 1953, 58-year-old Nikita S. Khrushchev became secretary, or head, of the communist party in Russia. A former miner and plumber, Khrushchev had joined the communist party in 1918, and then slowly worked his way up through the party ranks until he was named to the central governing body in 1939. He was largely responsible for the removal of Malenkov as premier in 1955 and the naming of Nikolai Bulganin to succeed Malenkov. In a secret speech to the communist party congress in 1956, Khrushchev denounced the former dictator Stalin as a tyrant, and the next year he managed to have most of Stalin's supporters in the government, including former premier Malenkov, removed from their high positions and sent into obscurity. In 1958 Khrushchev took over the premiership from Bulganin, and for the next six years ruled as dictator.

During Khrushchev's rule he made many speeches calling for "peaceful coexistence" with the West. But his actions spoke louder than words as he continued Russia's policies of aggression, bringing the world close to another widespread war at several times.

Leonid I. Brezhnev and Aleksei N. Kosygin

Moscow suddenly announced without warning on October 15, 1964, that the 70-year-old Khrushchev had resigned because of his age and ill health. The world assumed that he had lost out in a power struggle with younger Russian leaders, but no details were made public. He was succeeded as premier by Aleksei N. Kosygin and as first secretary of the communist party by Leonid I. Brezhnev. For the next several years Kosygin and Brezhnev seemed to rule as equals with neither having more power than the other.

Brezhnev was 57 when he became head of the communist party. He had grown up under communism, receiving training as an engineer. As one of Khrushchev's loyal supporters for many years, he had risen in power with his leader. In 1960 Khrushchev installed Brezhnev in the figurehead role of president of the Soviet Union, a post that he held until a few months before Khrushchev's overthrow.

Kosygin was 60 when he became premier. After receiving an education in economics and administration, he had advanced rapidly in the communist party. At the age of 34 he held a position equivalent to mayor of the city of Leningrad, and at 42 he became the youngest member of the communist party's central governing body, the politburo. Under Khrushchev, Kosygin ranked second to the premier in the Russian government and specialized in economic planning.

Communist leaders viewing the military parade from the top of the Lenin Mausoleum in Moscow, November 7, 1961, on the 44th anniversary of Russia's birth as a Communist state, are (left to right) Blas Roca, Cuban delegate to the Soviet Communist Party Congress; Ho Chi Minh, president of North Vietnam; Soviet Premier Nikita Khrushchev; Janos Kadar, Hungarian Communist Party boss; Soviet President Leonid Brezhnev; Soviet Deputy Premier Frel Koslov; Presidium member Mikhail Suslov; First Deputy Premier Anastas Mikoyan. (UPI RADIOTELEPHOTO)

In Canada

During the growing up of the Space Age generation in Canada, there were four major changes in national leadership. Three of the Canadian prime ministers in this period were Liberals, and one was a Conservative.

William Lyon Mackenzie King

Just as President Roosevelt had served more years in the White House than any other American chief executive, Liberal Prime Minister W. L. Mackenzie King headed the Canadian government longer than any of his predecessors—21 years in all. At the age of 34, King became Canada's first Minister of Labour in 1909, because of his background as a labor lawyer. In 1921, when he was 46, King became the first Liberal prime minister of Canada in twenty years.

King served as prime minister from 1921 to 1930, except for a few months in 1926 when the Conservative party briefly won power. The Liberals were turned out of office in 1930, largely because of the Great Depression, but King was restored to power as prime minister in 1935 and continued to hold the office until 1948. During his administration King spearheaded the drive that won complete self-government for Canada within the British Commonwealth of Nations. Under his guidance Canada also adopted its first national social welfare legislation with an old age pension law in 1927. With his leadership Canada made important contributions in men and supplies to the winning of World War II. Because of his advanced age, the 73-year-old King retired as prime minister in 1948 and died two years later.

Louis S. St. Laurent

As leader of the Liberal party, Louis S. St. Laurent helped his party win national election victories in 1949 and 1953. Born in Quebec, near the Canadian border with Vermont, St. Laurent was a French-Canadian. He had become one of Canada's most outstanding lawyers before entering the government as minister of justice in 1941. He was 66 when he succeeded to the office of prime minister upon the resignation of W. L. Mackenzie King.

Canadian Prime Minister Mackenzie King in New York in June 1941. (UPI PHOTO)

As prime minister, St. Laurent played a leading role in the formation of the North Atlantic Treaty Organization that welded North America to Western Europe in a military alliance. He also spearheaded the sending of aid to Britain and Western Europe to help the war-torn Allies recover from World War II.

The Liberal party was defeated in national elections in June, 1957, and the next year the 76-year-old St. Laurent retired from parliament and as party leader.

John G. Diefenbaker

The first Conservative prime minister of Canada in 22 years, John G. Diefenbaker came to the office in 1957 at the age of 61. A well-known criminal and civil rights lawyer, he ran for office unsuccessfully many times before winning a seat in parliament in 1940 when he was 45. In the election of 1957, Diefenbaker's Conservative party emphasized Canadian nationalism and urged the voters that it was time for a change from the long rule of the Liberal party. The Conservatives won by a slim majority and Diefenbaker became prime minister.

In order to strengthen his party's majority, Diefenbaker called a new national election in

Canadian Prime Minister Lester Pearson (left) with President John F. Kennedy on the patio of the Kennedy summer home at Hyannis Port, Massachusetts. (UPI PHOTO)

1958. This time his party won by the largest parliamentary majority in Canadian history, capturing 78 per cent of the seats in the House of Commons. The Conservative government proceeded to expand Canada's social welfare legislation with increased old age pensions and a national health plan.

Economic conditions deteriorated in Canada in the early 1960's, with a rapid rise in unemployment. As a result, in the national election of 1962, the Conservative party lost many of its seats. Diefenbaker retained power as prime minister only because he received the support of the Social Credit party which held 30 parliamentary seats.

In 1963 Diefenbaker accused the United States of interference in Canadian affairs because of its insistence that Canada arm its defensive missiles with atomic warheads that would be controlled by the United States. Diefenbaker's government failed on a no-confidence motion passed by parliament in February. And the Conservatives fell from power after losing a national election held in April.

Lester B. Pearson

Liberal Prime Minister Lester B. Pearson celebrated his 66th birthday the day after assuming the nation's most important office in April, 1963. While still in his teens, "Mike" Pearson, as he was nicknamed, fought in World War I as an infantryman and then as a pilot. After the war, he was graduated from Oxford University in England, where he was an outstanding athlete and played on the British Olympic hockey team.

After teaching history for several years at the University of Toronto, he became an official in Canada's department of external affairs, or state department, holding various important posts, including ambassador to the United States at the end of World War II. In 1948, he won election to Canada's House of Commons as a Liberal in order to accept Prime Minister King's appointment as secretary of external affairs, or foreign minister. He continued in that office through the administration of Prime Minister St. Laurent. His success in ending the fighting between Britain, France, Israel, and Egypt in the Suez Canal crisis of 1956 brought him the Nobel Peace Prize in 1957—the first Canadian to win this honor.

After St. Laurent's retirement in 1958, Pearson became leader of the Liberal party. Although his party suffered defeats in national elections in 1958 and 1962, he finally led the Liberals to victory in 1963. A month after becoming prime minister, Pearson met with U.S. President John F. Kennedy to give assurance of Canadian friendship and pledge acceptance of atomic warheads to be used on Canadian defensive missiles—the issue that had won the national election for the Liberals.

Under Pearson's administration Canada's economy steadily improved, but he had many difficulties obtaining passage of legislation because, although the Liberals held more seats in parliament than any other party, they did not have a majority, and were therefore dependent on the support of minority parties. In an effort to strengthen his party's position, Pearson called a national election in November, 1965. The Liberals won, but with two seats short of an absolute majority in parliament, so Pearson again was forced to rely on minority party support to remain in power.

In Latin America

Throughout the postwar decades many of the countries of Latin America continued to have unstable governments. Short-lived revolutions and palace coups d'état frequently brought changes in leadership. Most of Latin America's leaders were too busy with local affairs or in office too short a time to make much impact on the world. However, two Latin American dictators in particular were watched carefully by the world for fear that their ambitions might bring aggression to other countries—Juan Perón of Argentina and Fidel Castro of Cuba.

Juan Perón of Argentina

An admirer of Adolf Hitler and Benito Mussolini, Juan Perón was the leader of a group of young army officers who seized control of the government of Argentina in June, 1943. For several years he ran the government as war minister, and then, as head of a Labor party that he had created, he won election as president of the country in 1946. During the 1946 election campaign the United States state department exposed Perón's wartime negotiations with Nazi Germany and his efforts to turn neighboring countries to fascism, but this did not have the hoped for effect of defeating Perón.

Perón attracted much support from the Argentine working classes and made use of general strikes by the workers to demonstrate his power over the labor movement. At the same time he restricted most civil rights and eliminated political opposition. His government took over ownership of most large industries, and when newspapers criticized him he seized them.

Argentine President Juan D. Perón (in center, wearing overcoat). Lt. Col. Raul Dario Carenzo (left), and Army Minister General Franklin Lucero (right) inspected the garrison of Campo de Mayo in Buenos Aires after the revolution was quelled in Argentina on September 28, 1951. (UPI PHOTO)

From the reviewing stand at the Lenin Mausoleum in Moscow's Red Square (left to right in center) Cuban Premier Fidel Castro, Soviet Premier Nikita Khrushchev, and Soviet Defense Minister Rodion Malinovsky viewed the May Day parade on May 1, 1963. (UPI RADIOTELEPHOTO)

After revising the country's constitution so that he could remain as president, Perón was re-elected in 1951 in an election that his opponents claimed was rigged. In 1955 he fell into a dispute with the Roman Catholic Church in an effort to separate church and state, and in September, 1955, army leaders overthrew him and sent him into exile. However, Perón retained his popularity with labor unions in Argentina, and ten years after his exile his supporters, called Peronists, still staged strikes from time to time demanding that he be permitted to return from Spain.

Fidel Castro of Cuba

An even more menacing dictator arose on the island of Cuba. The son of a well-to-do sugar planter, Fidel Castro was a professional revolutionary from the time he was a college student. In 1947, three years before he obtained a law degree from the University of Havana, he took part in an unsuccessful movement to overthrow the dictator of the Dominican Republic, Rafael L. Trujillo. On July 26, 1953, he led an attack on an army installation in Santiago de Cuba as part of a revolutionary plan to overthrow the Cuban dictator Fulgencio Batista. Castro and his younger brother Rául were captured and sentenced to prison. After being released in an amnesty in 1954, Castro went to Mexico where he organized a small revolutionary army called the "26th of July" movement.

Castro made an armed landing in Cuba late in 1956. Most of his supporters were killed, but he escaped into the Sierra Maestra mountains, where he set up a guerrilla headquarters. He soon gathered considerable support from the Cuban people with his promise to overthrow Batista's dictatorship and restore civil rights and freedom. Within a little over two years Castro grew so strong that early in 1959 Batista fled from Cuba, and the 32-year-old Castro marched into Havana to take over the government.

The Cuban people soon learned that they had substituted only one dictator for another. Castro made no pretense of restoring constitutional government or civil liberties, and instead inaugurated a secret police state. He stamped out all opposition with executions, imprisonment, and exile. He took over industry and plantations from their private owners, confiscating American-owned property.

Late in 1961 he announced to the world that he had always been a communist and that he was turning Cuba into the first communist nation of the Western Hemisphere. With arms imported from Russia and other communist countries he began building Cuba into the strongest military power in the Americas next to the United States, and made plans to spread communist power to other Latin American countries. When American intelligence discovered in 1962 that Castro was arming himself with Russian missiles and bombers capable of attacking the United States with atomic warheads, the United States blockaded Cuba with its Navy and a world war threatened to break out until Russia agreed to withdraw the missiles and bombers from Cuba. In the mid-1960's Castro continued to portray the United States as Cuba's greatest enemy and proceeded to send subversives to other Latin American countries to help promote communism.

In Asia

The end of the Japanese colonial empire and the decline of British, French, and Dutch colonialism gave independence to one Asian nation after another under the guidance of newly important national leaders. As the East and West contested for influence over the continent's nearly two billion people, most leaders of Asian countries were forced to take one side or the other, although some tried to remain neutral. Three prominent Asian leaders of the period represent the three main courses of action that were followed: Chiang Kai-shek of Nationalist China sided closely with the United States; Jawaharlal Nehru of India attempted to follow a middle course; and Mao Tse-tung of Red China rose to power with the aid of Russia.

Chiang Kai-shek of Nationalist China

The graduate of military schools in China and Japan, Chiang Kai-shek was only 24 when he helped Sun Yat-sen overthrow the Manchu empress of China in 1912 and establish the Chinese Republic. In the early 1920's he furthered his military education by attending an academy in the Soviet Union. After Sun's death in 1925, Chiang took command of the Nationalist Chinese army and began trying to weld China into a unified nation by conquering the war lords and bandits who ruled the country's provinces. He broke off ties with Communist Russia, and then in 1928 became the president and undisputed ruler of China at the age of 40.

After Japan invaded and conquered China's northern province of Manchuria in the early 1930's, Chiang reached an understanding with his Chinese communist opponents who agreed to cooperate under his leadership in an effort to stem the Japanese. In 1937 Japan launched new attacks on China, and from then until 1945 Chiang was kept busy directing the Chinese war effort and endeavoring to prevent Japan from taking over all of China. As head of the largest Allied army in Asia he took part in discussions with President Roosevelt and Winston Churchill on military strategy for the region. But Chiang's task was made difficult because Japan cut off his access to military supplies from the United States and Great Britain.

After Japan's defeat in 1945, Chiang turned his attention to trying to root out and defeat Chinese communist armies that were being supported by Russia. The United States attempted to get Chiang to invite communist leaders into his government and resume the coalition that had been effected during the war years. When Chiang refused, the United States withdrew from his support. Chiang fought a losing civil war with the communists, and in 1949 fled to Formosa.

Chiang set up his Nationalist China government on Formosa, where the United States continued to recognize him as China's legitimate ruler even though the Chinese communists controlled the entire China mainland. By the time Chiang reached the age of 80 in 1967 there seemed little likelihood that he would achieve his goal of taking his Nationalist armies back into China to recapture the country.

Mao Tse-tung of Communist China

Only six years younger than Chiang Kai-shek, Mao Tse-tung also fought for Sun Yat-sen's revolution in 1911-1912. As leader of the communist party in Hunan province, Mao cooperated with Chiang in the early 1920's in an effort to unify China. But after Chiang broke with the communists, Mao helped organize Chinese communist armies and in 1931 became head of a Russian-supported "Soviet Republic of China." During World War II, Mao again aided Chiang in the fight with Japan. But after the war he resumed his plans for communist domination of China. In

When China opened it new National Assembly at Nanking on November 15, 1946, Generalissimo Chiang Kai-shek formally handed over to the people of China the powers vested in the government. The event coincided with the birthday of Dr. Sun Yat-sen, whose tomb Chiang Kai-shek (center) is shown visiting (UPI PHOTO)

A display of rocket launchers at a military parade celebrating Nation Day at Tien An Men Square, Peking, China, October 1, 1953. (UPI PHOTO)

the ensuing civil war he directed the military and political strategy that brought Chiang's defeat.

A poet and prolific writer, Mao published many books that provide the basic philosophy for the Chinese communists. Many of his writings can be interpreted in various ways, but the central theme is that communism, and particularly Chinese communism, should rule the world. In the 1960's Mao openly broke with the Russian communists because he felt they were not continuing to be aggressive enough in trying to force communism onto non-communist nations. In the late 1960's Mao stirred up an unusual revolutionary movement in China in which militant young Red Guards terrorized and purged leaders of the Chinese communist party who had indicated disagreement with some of Mao's policies.

Jawaharlal Nehru of India

The first prime minister of India when it gained its independence from Great Britain in 1947, Jawaharlal Nehru guided his nation for 17 years until his death in 1964. Unlike many of the new nationalist leaders of Asia, Nehru believed strongly in democracy and led his people as the head of a constitutional government. As a youth he was educated in England, graduating from Cambridge University and then being admitted to the bar as a lawyer in London. After returning to India and practicing law for a number of years, he became a disciple of Mohandas K. Gandhi and a leader in the Congress party that was seeking independence for India. From the 1920's through the early 1940's Nehru was arrested and imprisoned many times for demonstrating against the British authorities. He spent most of World War II in a British prison for demanding India's independence as the price of India's cooperation in the war effort.

When the British Labour government finally gave in to demands that India be given self-rule in 1946, the 56-year-old Nehru was appointed head of a temporary government. The following year,

On a tour of Asian capitals, Premier Chou En-lai of China (left) was welcomed by Prime Minister Jawaharlal Nehru of India on his arrival in New Delhi, November 28, 1956. (UPI PHOTO)

when complete independence had been achieved, Nehru's Congress party was elected as the major political party in the country's parliament and he became prime minister. Nehru believed in socialism and guided India's development along the lines of state ownership of industry. At the same time he preserved free elections and civil rights.

As the Cold War developed between the East and West, Nehru tried to remain friends with both sides through a policy that he called nonalignment. He refused to join in military alliances intended to prevent communist aggression and repeatedly expressed his friendship for Communist Russia and Communist China. This policy was generally judged a failure when the Red Chinese attacked and invaded India in a brief war in 1962. Possibly as a result of his great disappointment in the turn of world events, Nehru's health began to fail and he died less than two years later at the age of 74.

In Africa

At the end of World War II there were only four independent countries in Africa—Egypt, Ethiopia, Liberia, and South Africa. But in the years since then more than thirty African countries have won independence from Belgian, British, French, and Italian colonial rule. The leaders of most of these new countries have been far too busy with internal affairs to play a large role on the world scene. The most prominent leader to rise to power in the period was Gamal Abdel Nasser of Egypt, or the United Arab Republic as he renamed the country.

Gamal Abdel Nasser

One of the few world leaders of the period to have been born in the twentieth century, Gamal

Abdel Nasser was 34 when he helped lead a military junta that seized control of the government of Egypt in 1952. A career military officer, Nasser at first remained in the background of the new government as it forced the abdication of King Farouk and then established Egypt as a republic in 1953. Then Nasser came forward to publicly take power in 1954, first as prime minister and then as president.

Nasser forcibly set forth to make himself the leader of the Arab countries of Africa and Asia. He abolished political parties and restricted civil liberties in order to perpetuate his dictatorship. His government took over most industries, many of which had been owned by foreign investors, and he instituted land reforms to break up large estates into small farms.

Like Nehru, Nasser attempted to follow a middle course in foreign affairs, accepting aid from both communist and non-communist governments. He refused to join in Western military alliances, and he established friendly relations with the communist nations.

Nasser seized control of the vital Suez Canal in 1956, taking it over from its British and French owners. In retaliation, British, French, and Israeli troops attacked Egypt, but were forced to withdraw in the face of opposition to the action by both Russia and the United States.

Nasser seemed to be achieving his dream of drawing together the Arab countries under his leadership when in 1958 he proclaimed the formation of the United Arab Republic and announced that Syria was giving up its independence to become part of the U.A.R. However, the union lasted only until 1961, when Syria seceded. The small Arab country of Yemen also associated itself with Nasser from 1958 to 1961 in what was called the United Arab States, but this organization also fell apart. In the mid-1960's Nasser's troops and planes intervened in Yemen to help republican forces overthrow Yemen's monarchy. But generally the rulers of the other Arab countries of the Near East mistrusted Nasser and he was unable to convince them that they should unify under his leadership.

Nasser repeatedly urged other Arab nations to join with him in attacking Israel and returning the area of that Jewish nation to Arab control. But the humiliating defeat of Egypt's army in the six-day Arab-Israeli War of 1967 brought an even further drop in his prestige.

Egyptian President Abdel Gamal Nasser, Yugoslav President Marshal Tito, and Indian Prime Minister Jawaharlal Nehru (left to right) at the Brione meeting of the neutral "Big Three" July 19, 1956. (UPI PHOTO)

V. K. Wellington Koo of China, Georges Bidault of France, E. R. Stettinius, Jr. of the United States, V. M. Molotov of the U.S.S.R., and Clement Attlee of Great Britain, after a discussion at the Fairmont Hotel at the time of the UN Conference in San Francisco. (UPI PHOTO)

The United Nations

The organization founded at the end of World War II to help the world stay at peace saw three changes of leadership in its chief executive office, the position of secretary-general. The men who held this job were Trygve Lie of Norway, Dag Hammarskjöld of Sweden, and U Thant of Burma.

Trygve Lie

Trygve Lie was chosen as first secretary-general of the UN in February, 1946. He was a compromise candidate, agreed upon after Russia had vetoed Western efforts to place Canada's Lester Pearson in the position. Before entering his government career, Lie had been a successful labor lawyer in Norway. At the age of 38 he had joined Norway's cabinet as minister of justice and later held other cabinet offices. After Germany captured Norway in 1940, Lie went to London with the Norwegian government in exile, where he served as foreign minister. He headed Norway's delegation to the UN organizational meeting at San Francisco, and to the first UN General Assembly meeting in London, where at the age of 48 he was chosen secretary-general.

During the seven years that he served in the UN's highest executive office, Lie exhibited great executive ability and diplomatic skill in attending to the many details of setting up the new organization, attending to the demands of the delegates from many nations, and supervising the construction of the permanent headquarters in New York City.

The greatest international crisis during Lie's term came with the outbreak of the Korean War in 1950. Lie became the target for bitter attacks by Russia for his part in calling the emergency meeting of the Security Council that urged members to intervene in the war to halt the aggression of the North Korean communists. Lie made many efforts to bring peace in the war, but finally felt that he had become a liability to the UN because of Russia's attitude toward him and resigned to make room for someone who might be able to ease international tensions.

Dag Hammarskjöld

The son of a former premier of Sweden, Dag Hammarskjöld brought a wealth of diplomatic and political experience with him when he accepted appointment as UN secretary-general in April, 1953. He was 47 at the time—the first chief executive of the UN to have been born in the twentieth century. After graduating from college, he taught political science for a time at the University of Stockholm. Then he became an official of the Bank of Sweden and served as its chairman throughout most of the 1940's. After World War II he headed Swedish delegations to various international conferences and became his country's deputy foreign minister.

During his first several years in office as secretary-general, the slim, self-effacing Hammarskjöld won universal respect for his efforts to turn the United Nations from being an international debating society into an effective instrument for maintaining world peace. Then, as had happened to his predecessor, he incurred the wrath of Russia because he had supported the sending of United Nations troops into the Congo to try to end a civil

Aerial photographs showing missile sites in Cuba were displayed at a special session of the UN Security Council October 25, 1962. Adlai Stevenson is shown watching the proceedings, at far right. (UPI PHOTO)

war in that nation. The world had watched on television as the dictator of Russia, Nikita Khrushchev, had pounded his shoe on a desk at the United Nations and angrily demanded Hammarskjöld's resignation. But Hammarskjöld refused to be intimidated. On September 18, 1961, while on a trip to the Congo in an effort to arrange a cease-fire, Hammarskjöld's plane crashed, and he was killed. In recognition of his peacemaking efforts, Hammarskjöld was awarded after his death the 1961 Nobel Peace Prize.

U Thant

U Thant, a 52-year-old Burmese diplomat, became the acting secretary-general of the United Nations in 1961. Before entering government service he had been a teacher and then headmaster of a high school in his birthplace, Patanaw, Burma. After Burma won its independence in 1948, Thant became a government official, serving first as director of broadcasting and then in other administrative positions. He was appointed as his country's permanent representative to the UN in 1957, and at the time of Hammarskjöld's death was chairman of the UN commission seeking peace in the Congo. He served more than a year as acting secretary-general before being appointed secretary-general in 1962 to fill out a five-year term.

In the years that followed, Thant won admiration for his dedication to peace and his ability to end conflicts in the world's trouble spots. He helped bring an end to the fighting in the Congo, aided the settlement of the Cuban missile crisis in 1962, helped restore peace on Cyprus in 1964, and aided in the negotiation of a cease-fire in the Arab-Israeli War in 1967. However, Thant was discouraged because despite his best efforts he could not bring the fighting in the Vietnam War to an end. He announced in 1966 that he would not accept reappointment to another term as secretary-general, but he later was persuaded to remain in office by a unanimous vote of confidence by the UN General Assembly.

This early morning session of the United Nations Security Council, June 10, 1967, was held for the purpose of discussing the Mid-East crisis. (UPI PHOTO)

THE COLD WAR BETWEEN EAST and WEST

American and Russian soldiers meeting at the Oder River, Germany. (UPI PHOTO)

The guns of World War II had hardly been stilled in Europe before it became apparent that Communist Russia and the Western Allies were not going to see eye to eye with each other in the postwar world.

Two years before the war was over the Big Three had decided on the boundary lines for the zones of military occupation of Germany when the war would be won. But when V-E did come, the British and American armies had advanced much farther east than the line agreed to.

British Prime Minister Winston Churchill had long been uneasy and worried about the powerful position that Russia was staking out for itself in Eastern Europe. He particularly hated to see the American and British armies give up large parts of Germany and Czechoslovakia to Russia when he had the feeling that Russia was unlikely to live up to its agreements that people in occupied areas would be allowed to freely choose their own governments.

So on June 4, 1945, Churchill cabled President

Truman urging him not to order the American and British withdrawal from 20,000 square miles of European territory—an action that he said would bring "Soviet Russian power into the heart of Western Europe and the descent of an iron curtain between us and everything to the eastward." Churchill suggested that the decision be delayed until the Big Three could meet at Potsdam and tie the withdrawal into the settlement of other problems with Russia.

However, Truman replied that he felt obliged to carry out the commitment that had been made by President Roosevelt, and that his advisors believed that if the withdrawal was delayed it might hurt relations with Russia. So on July 1 American and British troops that had been within a few miles of Berlin withdrew more than a hundred miles to the West. Thousands of German refugees who did not wish to live under communist rule went with them.

In July and August, 1945, President Truman met at Potsdam, Germany, with Stalin, Churchill, and Churchill's successor, Attlee. Truman wrote later of this conference: "It was clear that the Russian foreign policy was based on the conclusion that we were heading for a major depression, and that they were already planning to take advantage of our setback. . . . Force is the only thing the Russians understand."

The Iron Curtain Clangs Down in Europe

In the months after the war most Americans did not pay much attention to what was going on in Europe. They were much more concerned with converting the American economy to peacetime and relocating in civilian life the millions of servicemen who were returning home. But during this time Russian-sponsored communist governments were taking over the countries occupied by Soviet troops.

The first of the Russian-occupied countries of Eastern Europe to become communist was Yugoslavia. Marshal Tito, whose communist guerrillas had helped Russian troops conquer the Germans, became dictator of Yugoslavia, which was proclaimed a communist republic on November 29, 1945, ending the monarchy. The communists established a police state, abolishing all other political parties.

Albania, Yugoslavia's small neighbor to the south, likewise became a communist country on January 11, 1946. Its communist dictator, Enver Hoxha, had, like Tito, led communist guerrillas in fighting the Germans during World War II.

Russian dictator Stalin signaled the beginning of the Cold War with a speech in Moscow in February, 1946, in which he stated flatly that there would continue to be major wars as long as there were capitalist nations. He then went on to say that Russian communism was superior to any other social order, and claimed sole credit to the Red Army for the victory over Germany.

Stalin Signals Beginning of Cold War

—from speech by Joseph Stalin at Election Rally in Moscow, February 9, 1946

. . . It would be wrong to think that the Second World War was a casual occurrence or the result of mistakes of any particular statesmen, though mistakes undoubtedly were made. Actually, the war was the inevitable result of the development of world economic and political forces on the basis of modern monopoly capitalism. Marxists have declared more than once that the capitalist system of world economy harbors elements of general crises and armed conflicts and that, hence, the development of world capitalism in our time proceeds not in the form of smooth and even progress but through crises and military catastrophes.

Marshal Joseph Stalin, seated, with Vyacheslav Molotov and Averell Harriman (left to right) standing behind him at Yalta in 1945. (UPI PHOTO)

The fact is, that the unevenness of development of the capitalist countries usually leads in time to violent disturbance of equilibrium in the world system of capitalism, that group of capitalist countries which considers itself worse provided than others with raw materials and markets usually making attempts to alter the situation and changing the "spheres of influence" in its favor by armed force. The result is a splitting of the capitalist world into two hostile camps and war between them.

Perhaps military catastrophes might be avoided if it were possible for raw materials and markets to be periodically redistributed among the various countries in accordance with their economic importance, by agreement and peaceable settlement. But that is impossible to do under present capitalist conditions of the development of world economy. . . .

And so, what are the results of the war? . . .

Our victory means, first of all, that our Soviet social order has triumphed, that the Soviet social order has successfully passed the ordeal in the fire of war and has proved its unquestionable vitality.

As you know, it was claimed more than once in the foreign press that the Soviet social order was a "risky experiment" doomed to failure, that the Soviet order was a "house of cards" which had no roots in real life and had been imposed upon the people by the Cheka (secret police), and that a slight push from without was enough for this "house of cards" to collapse.

Now we can say that the war refuted all these claims of the foreign press as groundless. The war showed that the Soviet social order is a truly popular order springing from the depths of the people and enjoying their mighty support, that the Soviet social order is a form of organization of society which is perfectly stable and capable of enduring. . . .

The point now is that the Soviet social order has shown itself more stable and capable of enduring than a non-Soviet social order, that the Soviet social order is a form of organization, a society superior to any non-Soviet social order.

Second, our victory means that our Soviet state system has triumphed, that our multinational Soviet State has stood all the trials of war and has proved its vitality. . . . the point now is that the Soviet state system has proved itself a model for a multinational state, has proved that the Soviet state system is a system of state organization in which the national question and the problem of collaboration among nations has been settled better than in any other multinational state.

Third, our victory means that the Soviet armed forces have triumphed, that our Red Army has triumphed, that the Red Army bore up heroically under all the trials of war, utterly routed the armies of our enemies and came out of the war as a victor. . . . It must not be forgotten that the Red Army is the army that utterly routed the German army which but yesterday was striking terror into the armies of the European states. . . .

Americans first became fully aware of the growing split with Russia from a speech made by Winston Churchill at Fulton, Missouri, on March 5, 1946. Churchill warned that a communist "iron curtain has descended" across Europe, cutting off Eastern Europe from the western democracies. He cautioned that no one knew "what are the limits" of Russian plans for expansion and that the West should strengthen itself militarily "while time remains."

Churchill's Iron Curtain Warning

—from Winston Churchill's address at Westminster College, Fulton, Missouri, March 5, 1946.

. . . The United States stands at this time at the pinnacle of world power. It is a solemn moment for the American democracy. With primacy in power is also joined an awe-inspiring accountability to the future. As you look around, you must feel not only the sense of duty done but also feel anxiety lest you fall below the level of achievement. Opportunity is here now, clear and shining, for both our countries. To reject it or ignore it or fritter it away will bring upon us all the long reproaches of the aftertime. . . .

When I stand here this quiet afternoon I shudder to visualize what is actually happening to millions now and what is going to happen in

An informal photograph of Sir Winston Churchill and President Harry Truman at their historic meeting in Fulton, Missouri, in 1946, when Churchill spoke about the dangers of Communism. (UPI PHOTO)

this period when famine stalks the earth. None can compute what has been called "the unestimated sum of human pain." Our supreme task and duty is to guard the homes of the common people from the horrors and miseries of another war. We are all agreed on that. . . .

A shadow has fallen upon the scenes so lately lighted by the Allied victory. Nobody knows what Soviet Russia and its Communist international organization intends to do in the immediate future, or what are the limits, if any, to their expansive and proselytizing tendencies. . . .

From Stettin in the Baltic to Trieste in the Adriatic, an iron curtain has descended across the Continent. Behind that line lie all the capitals of the ancient states of central and eastern Europe. Warsaw, Berlin, Prague, Vienna, Budapest, Belgrade, Bucharest, and Sofia, all these famous cities and the populations around them lie in the Soviet sphere and all are subject in one form or another, not only to Soviet influence but to a very high and increasing measure of control from Moscow. Athens alone, with its immortal glories, is free to decide its future at an election under British, American, and French observation. The Russian-dominated Polish government has been encouraged to make enormous and wrongful inroads upon Germany, and mass expulsions of millions of Germans on a scale grievous and undreamed of are now taking place. The Communist parties, which were very small in all these eastern states of Europe, have been raised to pre-eminence and power far beyond their numbers and are seeking everywhere to obtain totalitarian control. Police governments are prevailing in nearly every case, and so far, except in Czechoslovakia, there is no true democracy. Turkey and Persia are both profoundly alarmed and disturbed at the claims which are made upon them and at the pressure being exerted by the Moscow government. An attempt is being made by the Russians in Berlin to build up a quasi-Communist party in their zone of occupied Germany by showing special favors to groups of left-wing German leaders. At the end of the fighting last June, the American and British armies withdrew westward, in accordance with an earlier agreement, to a depth at some points 150 miles on a front of nearly 400 miles, to allow the Russians to occupy this vast expanse of territory which the western democracies had conquered. If now the Soviet government tries, by separate action, to build up a pro-Communist Germany in their areas this will cause new serious difficulties in the British and American zones, and will give the defeated Germans the power of putting themselves up to auction between the Soviets and western democracies. Whatever conclusions may be drawn from these facts—and facts they are—this is certainly not the liberated Europe we fought to build up. Nor is it one which contains the essentials of permanent peace. . . .

In front of the iron curtain which lies across Europe are other causes for anxiety. In Italy the Communist party is seriously hampered by having to support the Communist-trained Marshal Tito's claims to former Italian territory at the head of the Adriatic. Nevertheless the future of Italy hangs in the balance. . . . In a great number of countries, far from the Russian frontiers and throughout the world, Communist fifth columns are established and work in complete unity and absolute obedience to the directions they receive from the Communist center. Except in the British Commonwealth and in the United States, where Communism is in its infancy, the Communist parties or fifth columns constitute a growing challenge and peril to Christian civilization. . . .

The outlook is also anxious in the Far East and especially in Manchuria. The agreement which was made at Yalta, to which I was a party, was extremely favorable to Soviet Russia, but it was made at a time when no one could say that the German war might not extend all through the summer and autumn of 1945 and when the Japanese war was expected to last for a further eighteen months from the end of the German war. In this country you are all so well informed about the Far East, and such devoted friends of China, that I do not need to expatiate on the situation there. . . .

I do not believe that Soviet Russia desires war. What they desire is the fruits of war and the indefinite expansion of their power and doctrines. But what we have to consider here today while time remains, is the permanent prevention of war and the establishment of conditions of freedom and democracy as rapidly as possible in all countries. . . . From what I have seen of our Russian friends and allies during the war, I am convinced that there is nothing they admire so much as strength, and there is nothing for which they have less respect than for military weakness. For that reason the old doctrine of a balance of power is unsound. We cannot afford, if we can help it, to work on narrow margins, offering temptations to a trial of strength. . . .

Stalin replied to Churchill a few days later with an interview in the communist newspaper *Pravda*. The Russian dictator compared Churchill to Hitler, called him a "firebrand of war," and said the speech was a "dangerous act." Stalin said, "What can be surprising in the fact that the Soviet

The dedication ceremony in Philadelphia preceding a large relief shipment, in 1951, of dried milk, wheat, corn syrup and cereals, destined for India, Italy, Austria and Lebanon, from the farms of America. (UPI PHOTO)

East Berliners awoke November 14, 1961 to discover that the statue of the late Soviet dictator, Joseph Stalin, had been removed during the night. Picture-taking was forbidden, but an artist retouched a photograph to show the scene before and after. (UPI PHOTO)

Union, in a desire to ensure its security for the future, tries to ensure that these countries should have governments whose relations to the Soviet Union are loyal? How can one, without having lost one's reason, qualify these peaceful aspirations of the Soviet Union as expansionist tendencies of our Government? . . . I do not know whether Mr. Churchill and his friends will succeed in organizing . . . a new crusade against 'Eastern Europe.' But if they succeed in this . . . then one may confidently say they will be beaten . . ."

The first major dispute of the Cold War came in Iran, and the United States won. The first complaint brought before the United Nations Security Council in January 19, 1946, was a charge by Iran that Russia was interfering in its internal affairs. Russian troops had been stationed in northern Iran during World War II to protect a supply route for lend-lease aid from the United States, while American and British troops had been in southern Iran. The government of Iran charged that the Russians were encouraging communists to organize a rebellion in the part of the country they were occupying. Earlier, at a foreign ministers' meeting of the Big Three in September, 1945, it had been agreed that Russian, American, and British troops would be withdrawn from Iran by March 2, 1946. In the UN Security council, Russia walked out in protest of any consideration of the Iranian charges. Then the deadline for Russian troop withdrawal passed. On March 6 the United States sent a diplomatic note to Russia politely asking that Russia make good on its promise to withdraw its troops. The Russians ignored the note. American intelligence reported to President Truman that, instead of withdrawing, Russian troops were on the march toward Iran's capital, Teheran. President Truman had a "blunt" message, some called it an ultimatum, sent to Stalin. On March 24 Stalin reacted by announcing that Russian troops would be withdrawn, and by the end of May all the Russian troops had left.

Before the year was out two more Eastern European countries had new communist governments. On September 8, 1946, the communist-controlled government of Bulgaria held a vote which abolished the monarchy and established a republic. Elections were scheduled for October, and Russia blocked American efforts to see that outside observers insure that the elections were free. After the election on October 27, the communist leader George Dimitrov became prime minister, and in the next several months had opposition political leaders arrested, tried, and executed or imprisoned. A similar pattern was going on in Romania, where in an election on November 9, the communists won full control of the government, despite protests by the United States that the elections were unfair and did not represent the true desires of the Romanian people. A year later, on December 30, 1947, the communists forced King Michael of Romania to abdicate and the country became another Russian-dominated "people's republic."

The United States was virtually helpless to do anything to aid the non-communist people of the countries in which Russia had occupation armies without risking war with Russia. Moreover, the United States was not in a position to risk such a war, having withdrawn the largest part of its troops from Europe.

But when the communists attempted to take over the government of Greece, the United States reacted strongly and forcefully. On September 1, 1946, the Greek people voted in a national plebiscite, supervised by American and British observers, to restore Greek King George II to power. Almost immediately a civil war broke out in Greece with communist guerrillas supported by Yugoslavia, Bulgaria, and Albania. On March 3, 1947, the Greek government appealed to the United States for help. On March 12, President Truman went before a joint session of Congress to urge that economic aid and military supplies be sent to Greece to help the people there maintain their freedom. His proposals became known as the "Truman Doctrine," establishing a pattern for U.S. foreign policy in which the United States would aid any government in its efforts to preserve its freedom from communist attack or communist subversion. In May, 1947, Congress approved the Truman Doctrine, authorizing $400 million in aid to Greece and Turkey, which also was threatened by Russia, and approved the use of U.S. civil and military personnel as advisers in Greece. By November American army officers were aiding Greek troops in the field in their fight against the communist guerrillas. The fighting in Greece continued until late in 1949 when the government announced that all communist resistance had been destroyed.

The Truman Doctrine

—from President Truman's address to Congress, March 12, 1947

I believe that it must be the policy of the United States to support free peoples who are resisting attempted subjugation by armed minorities or by outside pressures.

I believe that we must assist free peoples to work out their own destinies in their own way.

I believe that our help should be primarily through economic and financial aid which is essential to economic stability and orderly political processes.

One way of life is based upon the will of the majority, and is distinguished by free institutions, representative government, free elections, guarantees of individual liberty, freedom of speech and religion and freedom from political oppression.

The second way of life is based upon the will of a minority forcibly imposed upon the majority. It relies upon terror and oppression, a controlled press and radio, fixed elections, and the suppression of personal freedoms. . . .

The seeds of totalitarian regimes are nurtured by misery and want. They spread and grow in the evil soil of poverty and strife. They reach their full growth when the hope of a people for a better life has died.

We must keep that hope alive.

The free peoples of the world look to us for support in maintaining their freedoms.

If we falter in our leadership, we may endanger the peace of the world—and we shall surely endanger the welfare of our own nation.

A wooden cross in front of the Berlin Wall—one of the many memorials to the East Berliners who have been killed trying to escape. (UPI PHOTO)

On hearing the official announcement of the lifting of the Russian blockade, in May, 1949, these residents of Berlin are shown here waving to an American airlift plane. (UPI PHOTO)

The most shocking communist takeover to Americans took place in Czechoslovakia. In elections in 1946 the communist party had won about 35 percent of the vote, and the communist party leader, Klement Gottwald, had formed a coalition government. But non-communist Eduard Benès had been elected president, and the foreign minister was non-communist Jan Masaryk, son of the country's founder. New elections were planned in 1948, and President Benès had told Prime Minister Gottwald, "I insist on parliamentary democracy." But in February, 1948, armed communists, with the encouragement of the communist head of the police, took over the headquarters of opposition parties. On February 25 the communists seized all the key ministries in the government, and on March 10 Masaryk was found dead below an open window from which he had jumped or been pushed. On June 7 Benès was forced to resign, and he died in September. Gottwald took over the presidency, and became dictator of the country.

Poland, which had been governed by the communists since Russia had liberated it from the Germans in 1945, had seemingly docilely followed Russian policy since the end of World War II. But in 1949 Russia dropped all pretense in its control of Poland by appointing Russian Marshal Konstantine Rokossovsky as minister of Poland's national defense and as commander in chief of the Polish army.

With Russian support the communists took over the government of Hungary in 1947 after receiving only 22 percent of the vote in an election held in August. The communists forced the resignation of Hungary's President Zoltan Tildy of the Smallerholders' party, who had been president since the country declared itself a republic in 1946.

The Berlin Airlift and the Berlin Wall

The first major confrontation between Russia and the United States in the Cold War came in Berlin, the former capital of Germany. At the end of World War II this city of four million persons had been divided into Russian, American, British, and French zones of occupation, but the entire city lay deep inside the Russian occupation zone of Germany. From June, 1945, to March, 1948, Berlin had been governed by a council made up

A forty-yard section of the Berlin Wall was moved three yards closer to West Berlin one night by East German border guards working under floodlights in the pre-dawn darkness. (UPI PHOTO)

of the Allied commandants of the four zones. On March 20, 1948, the Russian commander had walked out of the council meeting and refused to return. The Russians were disturbed because the Western Allies were rebuilding and strengthening their zones to provide a free economy, while the Russians had stripped factories in their zone to send machinery to Russia and had done little rebuilding of the war-torn city. The comparison between living under communist rule and under democratic government in Berlin was doing Russia no good with the German population and the Russians were determined to force the Allies out of Berlin.

Up to 1948 all four zones of Berlin used the same kind of currency, but the Russians had been manufacturing this money in huge quantities and sending it into the Western zones in an effort to create inflation and destroy the economy. On June 18, a new type of currency was announced for use in the western zones—currency that the Russians could not duplicate. In retaliation for the currency reform, Russia cut off all land travel through East Germany to West Berlin—stopping all supplies of food, fuel, clothing, and other necessities.

The Berlin blockade began on June 24, and four days later United States and British planes started flying supplies into West Berlin in what became called the Berlin Airlift. During the next fifteen months this airlift delivered more than two million tons of food, coal, and other materials to the people of West Berlin. More than anything else up to this point in the Cold War, the Berlin Airlift dramatized the American determination not to back down in the face of Russian efforts to dominate Europe.

In August, 1948, armed communist groups broke up a meeting of the Berlin city council, which up to this time had been holding its sessions in the Russian zone. After communists broke up two more attempts by the city council to meet in September, the city government transferred itself to the British zone. Elections for a new city council were held in the western zones in December, but were prohibited in the Russian zone. The Social Democratic party, which was friendly to the West, won the election, and its leader, Ernst Reuter, became mayor of West Berlin, splitting the city.

In September the United States brought the Berlin issue before the United Nations Security Council, charging that the Russian blockade of Berlin was "a threat to the peace." Russia vetoed discussion of the matter in the UN.

By the spring of 1949 it had become apparent to the Russians that the Berlin Airlift had successfully overcome the blockade, and that as long as it continued they were likely to look worse and worse. So on May 12 the Russians ended the blockade. President Truman later commented, "When we refused to be forced out of the city of Berlin, we demonstrated to the people of Europe that with their co-operation we would act, and act resolutely, when their freedom was threatened."

In the years that followed, West Berlin became more and more a showcase for western democracy easily visible to the communist-ruled Germans of East Berlin and East Germany. The economy of West Berlin prospered while that of East Berlin remained static. An estimated three million Germans escaped from East Berlin into West Berlin in the fifteen years after the war, despite armed guards posted by the communists with orders to shoot to kill any refugees. On June 17, 1953, the people of East Berlin revolted against their communist rulers, but Russian troops and tanks restored order.

In 1958 Russia made new demands that the western powers withdraw from Berlin and turn it into a demilitarized zone. But the Allies rejected the demands.

Then, in an effort to prevent further escapes to the West, the communists built a 26-mile long wall topped with barbed wire along the entire boundary between East and West Berlin. The Berlin Wall started as a barbed wire barricade built by the communists on August 13, 1961, and in the following weeks was replaced by a high concrete wall, with only a few guarded gates left open for traffic. To Western eyes, the Berlin Wall became a symbol of the communists' inability to satisfy their people and govern them without force.

The North Atlantic Treaty Organization (NATO)

In the face of the aggressive communist policies, the countries of Western Europe became increasingly fearful that someday the huge Russian armies might suddenly roll out and engulf them just as Hitler had done in World War II. In the spring of 1948 the foreign minister of Belgium, Paul Henri Spaak, suggested that all the countries of Western Europe should band together in a military alliance. In the summer of 1948, while Berlin was being blockaded, the United States took the initiative in trying to get the European nations to agree on an alliance. Details of the North Atlantic Treaty were worked out by January, 1949, and on April 4 it was signed in Washington—the first peacetime military alliance that the United States had ever entered into. In July the United States Senate voted approval of the treaty and it went into effect on August 24, 1949. On December 18, 1950, President Truman appointed General Dwight D. Eisenhower as supreme commander of the NATO military forces. In the years that followed, a strong defense force was built in Western Europe.

The original members of NATO included Great Britain, France, Belgium, the Netherlands, Luxembourg, the United States, Canada, Portugal, Denmark, Norway, Italy, and Iceland. Later Greece, Turkey, and West Germany also joined the alliance.

North Atlantic Treaty Organization (NATO) Flag raised over first German troops. (UPI PHOTO)

Part of the first shipment of American arms to reach France under the terms of the North Atlantic Pact. Artillery pieces are shown being loaded onto flatcars at a dock in Cherbourg in April, 1950. (UPI PHOTO)

A general view of the conference room as NATO's fifteen foreign ministers met in Bonn, Germany in 1957.
(UPI PHOTO)

The North Atlantic Treaty
—signed April 4, 1949

PREAMBLE. The parties to this treaty reaffirm their faith in the purposes and principles of the Charter of the United Nations and their desire to live in peace with all peoples and all governments.

They are determined to safeguard the freedom, common heritage and civilization of their peoples, founded on the principles of democracy, individual liberty and the rule of law.

They seek to promote stability and well-being in the North Atlantic area.

They are resolved to unite their efforts for collective defense and for the preservation of peace and security.

They therefore agree to this North Atlantic Treaty:

Article 1. The parties undertake, as set forth in the Charter of the United Nations, to settle any international disputes in which they may be involved by peaceful means in such a manner that international peace and security, and justice are not endangered, and to refrain in their international relations from the threat or use of force in any manner inconsistent with the purposes of the United Nations.

Article 2. The parties will contribute toward the further development of peaceful and friendly international relations by strengthening their free institutions, by bringing about a better understanding of the principles upon which these institutions are founded, and by promoting conditions of stability and well-being. They will seek to eliminate conflict in their international economic policies and will encourage economic collaboration between any or all of them.

Article 3. In order more effectively to achieve the objectives of this treaty, the parties, separately and jointly by means of continuous and effective self-help and mutual aid, will maintain and develop their individual and collective capacity to resist armed attack.

Article 4. The parties will consult together whenever, in the opinion of any of them, the territorial integrity, political independence or security of any of the parties is threatened.

Article 5. The parties agree that an armed attack against one or more of them in Europe or North America shall be considered an attack against them all; and consequently they agree that, if such an armed attack occurs, each of them, in exercise of the right of individual or collective self-defense recognized by Article 51 of the Charter of the United Nations, will assist the party or parties so attacked by taking forthwith, individually and in concert with the other parties, such action as it deems necessary, including the use of armed force, to restore and maintain the security of the North Atlantic area.

Any such armed attack and all measures taken as a result thereof shall immediately be reported to the Security Council. Such measures shall be terminated when the Security Council has taken the measures necessary to restore and maintain international peace and security.

Article 6. For the purpose of Article 5 an armed attack on one or more of the parties is deemed to include an armed attack on the territory of any of the parties in Europe or North America, on the Algerian Departments of France, on the occupation forces of any party in Europe, on the islands under the jurisdiction of any party in the North Atlantic area north of the Tropic of Cancer or on the vessels or aircraft in this area of any of the parties.

Article 7. This treaty does not affect, and shall not be interpreted as affecting, in any way the rights and obligations under the Charter of the parties which are members of the United Nations, or the primary responsibility of the Security Council for the maintenance of international peace and security.

Article 8. Each party declares that none of the international engagements now in force between it and any other of the parties or any third state is in conflict with the provisions of this treaty, and undertakes not to enter into any international engagement in conflict with this treaty.

General Matthew B. Ridgway (seated, in center) met members of the North Atlantic Treaty Organization Military Committee in Washington, D.C., in May, 1952, shortly before he succeeded General Dwight D. Eisenhower as Supreme Commander of Allied forces in Europe. (UPI PHOTO)

Article 9. The parties hereby establish a Council, on which each of them shall be represented, to consider matters concerning the implementation of this treaty. The Council shall be so organized as to be able to meet promptly at any time. The Council shall set up such subsidiary bodies as may be necessary; in particular it shall establish immediately a defense committee which shall recommend measures for the implementation of Articles 3 and 5.

Article 10. The parties may, by unanimous agreement, invite any other European state in a position to further the principles of this treaty and to contribute to the security of the North Atlantic area to accede to this treaty. Any state so invited may become a party to the treaty by depositing its instrument of accession with the Government of the United States of America. The Government of the United States of America will inform each of the parties of the deposit of each such instrument of accession.

Article 11. This treaty shall be ratified and its provisions carried out by the parties in accordance with their respective constitutional processes. The instruments of ratification shall be deposited as soon as possible with the Government of the United States of America, which will notify all the other signatories of each deposit. The treaty shall enter into force between the states which have ratified it as soon as the ratifications of the majority of the signatories, including the ratifications of Belgium, Canada, France, Luxembourg, the Netherlands, the United Kingdom and the United States, have been deposited and shall come into effect with respect to other states on the date of the deposit of their ratifications.

Article 12. After the treaty has been in force for ten years, or at any time thereafter, the parties shall, if any of them so requests, consult together for the purpose of reviewing the treaty, having regard for the factors then affecting peace and security in the North Atlantic area, including the development of universal as well as regional arrangements under the Charter of the United Nations for the maintenance of international peace and security.

Article 13. After the treaty has been in force for twenty years, any party may cease to be a party one year after its notice of denunciation has been given to the Government of the United States of America, which will inform the Governments of the other parties of the deposit of each notice of denunciation.

Article 14. This treaty, of which the English and French texts are equally authentic, shall be deposited in the archives of the Government of the United States of America. Duly certified copies thereof will be transmitted by that Government to the Governments of the other signatories.

Troubles Behind the Iron Curtain

The Russians succeeded in imposing communist dictatorships on all the countries which they had occupied, with the exception of Austria which was freed by a peace treaty in 1955. But the Russians had many troubles in maintaining control over their satellites.

The first major split in communist ranks came in June, 1948, when the Cominform, the international communist organization, expelled Yugoslavia for deviating from the communist line. The next year saw most of the communist countries of Eastern Europe break their treaties of friendship and alliance with Yugoslavia. In 1950 Marshal Tito denounced Stalin's Russian government as a kind of state capitalism instead of true communism. After Stalin's death and the de-Stalinization program launched by Nikita Khrushchev, Yugoslavia and Russia resumed more friendly relations, but Marshal Tito continued to pursue policies independent of Moscow.

On June 28, 1956, a riot by an estimated 50,000 workers broke in Poznán, Poland, calling for an end to communist rule and Russian occupation. Communist troops put down the riot, killing and wounding many of the workers. But the Russians eased their restraints on Poland. The Polish communist leader Wladyslaw Gomulka, who had been dismissed from the communist party as an anti-Stalinist and then imprisoned, was permitted again to head the country's communist party. Russian Marshal Rokossovsky was removed as director of national defense and commander in chief of the Polish army. Poland also negotiated to receive economic aid from the United States.

A Russian tank firing in a street in Budapest, Hungary, in front of the Palace Hotel, in 1956. (UPI PHOTO)

But the greatest explosion to shake the communist world came in Hungary in October, 1956. Students stormed the Budapest radio station on October 23, asking that their demands for the ouster of Stalinist Premier Erno Gero be broadcast. Police fired on the demonstrators, but later that day the communist leadership replaced Gero as premier with Imre Nagy, a former premier considered less devoted to Russia. The next day the demonstrations against Gero continued, even though ten thousand Russian troops had entered Budapest to put down the riots. The communists gave in further to the rioters by removing Gero from his post as head of the Hungarian communist party.

Because of Hungary's isolated position in central Europe, President Eisenhower decided the United States could not risk war by sending military forces to aid the Hungarian Freedom Fighters. On October 25, he issued a statement saying:

"The United States considers the development in Hungary as being a renewed expression of the intense desire for freedom long held by the Hungarian people. . . . The United States deplores the intervention of Soviet military forces which under the treaty of peace should have been withdrawn and the presence of which in Hungary, as is now demonstrated, is not to protect Hungary against armed aggression from without, but rather to continue an occupation of Hungary by the forces of an alien government for its own purposes."

By October 27 the Hungarian revolution had continued to spread, much of western Hungary

Residents of battered Budapest crowded the rubble-strewn streets to see the scars left by the Hungarian fight for freedom against the Russians in 1956. (UPI PHOTO)

was under control of the rebels and many soldiers of the Hungarian army had joined the revolution. That day Premier Nagy announced that he was forming a new coalition government that would include non-communist political leaders, including former President Zoltan Tildy.

On November 1, Premier Nagy announced that Hungary was ending its military alliances with other communist states and he appealed to the United Nations to help defend his country's neutrality.

Early on the morning of November 4, the United Nations Security Council met to consider the Hungarian question and Russia used its veto power to kill an American resolution calling for the withdrawal of Russian forces from Hungary. Later that same day Russia moved an army of about 200,000 men and 4,000 tanks into Hungary and crushed the rebellion, killing thousands of Hungarians. Premier Nagy took asylum in the embassy of Yugoslavia and the Roman Catholic cardinal of Hungary, Joseph Mindszenty, who had been released from prison by the rebels, was given refuge in the American legation. A new communist government was formed under Premier Janos Kadar. Later that month, after Nagy had been lured out of the Yugoslavian embassy by a pledge of safe conduct, he was seized by the Russians, tried in secret and executed.

An estimated 150,000 Hungarians fled from their country after the crushing of the rebellion. Thousands of these Hungarian refugees were admitted to the United States, Canada, and other western nations.

A roaming Soviet tank, with its big gun threatening, in the heart of Budapest, Hungary, in 1956. (UPI PHOTO)

The Bamboo Curtain in Asia

At the end of World War II, Russian troops had marched into Japanese-held Manchuria, the northern part of China. Instead of turning Manchuria over to the Chinese government and leaving when the war was over, the Russian troops stayed on through 1946. During this time the Russians dismantled and sent to Russia nearly a billion dollars worth of factory machinery, and at the same time armed and helped train Chinese communist armies.

President Truman had sent General George C. Marshall to China as his personal representative in an effort to end the fighting between Chinese nationalists and communists. Marshall served as mediator in peace talks between Nationalist Generalissimo Chiang Kai-shek and Communist Chou En-Lai. These peace talks dragged on throughout 1946. Marshall succeeded in arranging several cease-fires, but they were always of short duration, being broken either by the nationalists or by the communists. Marshall finally gave up and returned to the United States in January, 1947, after condemning extremists on both sides for continuing the civil war.

On March 19, 1947, Chinese nationalist forces captured Yenan, the Chinese communist capital. But the communists continued to hold most of northern China, and Russia refused to withdraw from the Chinese ports of Darien and Port Arthur. The United States sent Lt. Gen. Albert C. Wedemeyer to China on a fact-finding mission, but he, like Marshall, was as critical of the nationalists as he was of the communists and could find no practical solution to bring the civil war to an end.

By the end of 1948 the Chinese communist forces had taken nearly one-third of China and had extended their lines to within a few miles of the Chinese capital of Nanking. In April, 1948, the U.S. Congress voted $463 million dollars in aid to Nationalist China, but Chiang Kai-shek complained that this was not enough and that military supplies from America were not being delivered quickly.

From January through April, 1949, the Chinese nationalists and the communists bargained and negotiated for a peace settlement. The communists demanded that the government be turned over to them with Mao Tse-tung as chairman and that a list of "war criminals" headed by Chiang Kai-shek be handed over to them for punishment. The nationalists rejected the terms on April 19, and five days later the communist armies captured Nanking. As the communists drove south many of the nationalist armies not only surrendered but joined the communists in attacking their former comrades. In December Chiang Kai-shek gave up the struggle and fled to the island of Formosa with the remnants of his army.

The loss of China's more than 700 million people to communism was by far the Free World's biggest defeat in the Cold War. With the Chinese communist victory a bamboo curtain descended across Asia that was as impenetrable as the iron curtain in Europe. America withheld recognition of the Chinese communist government, continuing diplomatic relations with the Chinese nationalists on Formosa as the legitimate government of China. In the years that followed, the U.S. fleet protected Formosa from attack by the Chinese communists, but at the same time neutralized Chiang Kai-shek, preventing him from making any invasion attempt against the Chinese mainland.

Chinese Nationalist troops comprising the garrison of Shanghai marched along the bund past part of the British compound (right) as they prepared to man defenses of the city against the onslaught of Communist forces in 1949. (UPI PHOTO)

The Sugar Cane Curtain in Cuba

When the bearded young revolutionary Fidel Castro succeeded in overthrowing Cuba's dictator Fulgencio Batista early in 1959, he had considerable sympathy in the United States, because Batista's government had been notably corrupt. But soon the United States began to view Castro with apprehension. With police state tactics he brutally executed thousands of his opponents. Instead of giving Cubans the democracy that he had promised, he made himself dictator of the country. Tens of thousands of Cubans fled into exile.

A year after coming to power, Castro began in 1960 to confiscate most property belonging to Americans, other foreigners, and wealthy Cubans. In March, 1960, President Eisenhower, who had become convinced through secret intelligence reports that Castro was a communist, ordered the Central Intelligence Agency to help train Cuban exiles in Guatemala for a prospective invasion to overthrow Castro. Eisenhower also exerted economic pressure on Castro by cutting American sugar imports from the island.

On January 2, 1961, Castro charged that eighty percent of the U.S. embassy staff in Havana were spies, and ordered the United States to drastically cut its embassy staff. President Eisenhower replied by breaking off diplomatic relations with Cuba.

President Kennedy, who took office in January, 1961, ordered preparations to continue for the Cuban exiles' invasion of Cuba. With American help, a force of about 1,200 exiles landed at Cuba's Bay of Pigs on April 17, 1961, but at the last minute Kennedy refused to give the landing any support by U.S. aircraft. Castro's forces quickly captured the invaders and tried them for treason. A year later the United States bought freedom for the Bay of Pigs prisoners by sending Cuba $54 million in food, drugs, and other civilian supplies.

The inept defeat of the Cuban exiles at the Bay of Pigs made the United States a laughingstock for the time. Kennedy took full responsibility for

Fidel Castro, with a shaggy beard and wearing glasses, writing a letter at the rebel hideout in the Sierra Maestra foothills in 1958, the year before he seized control of Cuba after dictator Batista suddenly fled. (UPI PHOTO)

An aerial reconnaissance photograph showing a missile base at San Cristobal, Cuba, in late October, 1962.
(UPI PHOTO)

the failure of the project.

On December 2, 1961, Castro publicly announced for the first time that he was a Marxist-Leninist communist, and that he was turning Cuba into a communist country. The next month the Organization of American States expelled Cuba and condemned Castro's regime.

In October, 1962, the world approached the brink of a new World War over Cuba. On October 22, President Kennedy revealed in a nationwide telecast that Cuba had been armed with medium range missiles that had a range that would cover the entire southern United States. He showed enlarged photographs taken by U.S. spy planes to substantiate his charges. Then he warned Russia that if Cuba launched an atomic missile against any nation of the Western Hemisphere, the United States would regard it as an attack by Russia against the United States. President Kennedy also ordered a blockade of Cuba, giving the U.S. Navy orders to stop and search any ships bound for the island.

More than two dozen Russian ships were known to be on their way to Cuba, and the world waited tensely, fearing that Russia would regard it as an act of war if one of her ships was stopped and searched. The American armed forces began making obvious preparations for an invasion of Cuba.

In the face of American determination, Russian dictator Khrushchev announced on October 28 that he was ordering the missile bases in Cuba dismantled and the missiles returned to Russia. By November 2, President Kennedy was able to report that air photographs showed that the bases were being dismantled, and by November 10 the missiles had been loaded aboard ships for return to Russia. On November 20, the U.S. blockade was ended, and the world breathed a sigh of relief.

Efforts to End the Cold War

After the death of Russian Dictator Joseph Stalin in 1953, the world hoped that the change in leadership might lead to an end to the Cold War. Russian Premier Khrushchev had announced that he believed that capitalism and communism could live together in the world in "peaceful coexistence."

In an effort to end the Cold War, President Eisenhower attended a "summit meeting" in Geneva in July, 1955, with the leaders of Great Britain, France, and Russia. At this meeting, Eisenhower proposed an "open skies" plan that would enable the United States to inspect Russian military bases from the air and would in turn permit Russia to do the same with American bases. However, the idea fell on deaf ears.

In September, 1959, Khrushchev visited the United States. In a speech before the United Nations General Assembly he called for worldwide disarmament, but in the months and years

Soviet Premier Nikita Khrushchev gesturing angrily as he launched a bitter tirade against the United States and President Eisenhower, to whom he referred as "a thief caught red-handed in his theft" in reference to the American photo reconnaissance flights over Russia, in 1960. (UPI PHOTO)

that followed, Russian diplomats blocked all efforts by UN committees to work out a practical disarmament plan that provided for any sort of inspection to insure that the disarmament was actually carried out. During his visit to the United States, Khrushchev also met several times with President Eisenhower, but their conversations bore little fruit except for an invitation for Eisenhower to visit Russia and agreement that there should be another "summit meeting" the following year.

As Eisenhower was preparing to go to the "summit meeting" in Paris that was scheduled to open on May 15, 1960, a new international crisis developed. On May 5 Khrushchev announced that a United States U-2 photo spy plane had been shot down deep inside Russia. At first the United States claimed that the plane was on a weather observation mission and had accidentally flown into Russia. Then the next day Khrushchev announced that the American pilot of the plane, Francis Gary Powers, had been captured alive, and had confessed he had been on a spying mission. On May 9, Eisenhower publicly took responsibility for the U-2 flight and explained it was part of the necessary espionage activities of the United States.

When the "summit meeting" convened in Paris on May 15, Khrushchev took the floor first and in a long speech demanded that Eisenhower apologize for the U-2 flight and agree to punish those responsible for it. Eisenhower replied briefly that the United States felt that the flight had been necessary and that in fact the United Nations should sponsor such flights to help protect the world from surprise military attacks. Khrushchev walked out of the meeting and did not come back. He and Eisenhower did not meet again.

In June, 1961, President Kennedy met with Khrushchev in Vienna to discuss problems of the Cold War and particularly the repeated Russian demands that the Allies remove their troops from Berlin. The Cold War reached its climax with the "eyeball-to-eyeball" confrontation of Russia and the United States in the Cuban missile crisis in 1962. But tensions eased in 1963 after the first step toward world disarmament was taken with the signing on August 5 of a treaty that banned nuclear explosive tests in the atmosphere, outer space, and under water. The treaty was ratified by Great Britain, the United States, and Russia. However, two nuclear powers, Communist China and France, refused to approve the treaty.

Under President Johnson the United States made new efforts at a "bridge-building" policy of friendship with Russia. Progress was made slowly, but in June, 1964, the United States and Russia signed their first bi-lateral treaty of the Cold War —a treaty providing for the resumption of consular relations that had been severed in 1948. Nearly three years later, in March, 1967, the U.S. Senate approved the treaty.

President Johnson and Russian Premier Kosygin held two meetings in Glassboro, New Jersey, in June, 1967, to discuss international problems. Largely as a result of their meetings, American and Russian diplomats agreed two months later to a draft treaty for the control of atomic weapons. However, the draft treaty did not include a paragraph on the most critical issue . . . the problem of international inspection and enforcement of the treaty.

THE REBIRTH of WESTERN EUROPE

At the end of World War II much of Europe lay in ruins. Millions of civilians had been killed. Other millions had fled their homes as refugees. New governments had to be formed in many countries. And plans had to be made to rebuild industries that had been destroyed and to reconvert to peacetime production those that still existed.

The Allied armies and the United Nations Relief and Rehabilitation Administration (UNRRA), an organization that had been created in 1943, set up camps in Germany and France for about 8 million refugees, displaced persons, and war prisoners. Other such camps on a smaller scale were established in the other war-torn countries of Europe. Various service and religious organizations sent volunteers to work in these camps and helped gather food, clothing, and medicine to care for the people.

By 1946 the number of displaced persons in the UNRRA camps had been reduced to about 3 million as the others were repatriated to their

Reconstructed after war damage, Amsterdam's shipyards became busy with orders from many countries. Here crowds are gathering at the harbor to watch the launching of the "Oslofjord," built for the Norwegian-American Line. (UPI PHOTO)

home countries or to new countries that agreed to take them. In 1948 UNRRA was replaced by a new United Nations agency called the International Refugee Organization (IRO), which took over the task of caring for the 1.5 million refugees who still had no homes to go to.

Although nearly 800,000 of the refugees were resettled in the United States, Australia, Canada, and other countries by 1950, additional hundreds of thousands had joined the ranks of displaced persons, largely fleeing from communist-dominated countries. The United Nations ended the IRO agency in 1951, replacing it with the Office of the UN High Commissioner for Refugees, which continued to coordinate the work of volunteer organizations caring for displaced persons in the 1950's.

Changed Borders and Peace Treaties

The major changes in the map of Europe came in Russian-dominated East Europe. Russia incorporated within its own borders the former countries of Estonia, Lithuania, and Latvia. In addition Russia took over part of East Prussia, the entire eastern part of Poland, and part of northeastern Romania.

Despite protests by the United States and Great Britain, Russia turned over a huge section of eastern Germany to the communist-controlled government of Poland. This moved the eastern border of Germany to the line of the Oder and Neisse rivers. In the years that followed, Russian insistence on the Oder-Neisse line as the German-Polish border became a major stumbling block in efforts to prepare a German peace treaty.

Although the Western Allies and Russia could not reach agreement on a peace treaty for Germany, they were able to draw up treaties for Italy, Bulgaria, Finland, Hungary, and Romania. These treaties were signed on February 10, 1947, and became effective the following September 15.

Under the Italian peace treaty, Italy was forced to give up some small border areas to France and Yugoslavia as well as turn the Dodecanese Islands over to Greece. Italy also gave up its former African colonies of Eritrea, Libya, and Somaliland, and recognized the independence of Ethiopia. In addition, Italy agreed to pay $360 million of reparations to Russia, Ethiopia, Albania, Greece, and Yugoslavia.

The Bulgarian treaty called for the payment of $70 million in reparations to Greece and Yugoslavia, while Russia was given most of the German property in the country. Bulgaria was allowed to keep the area of Dobruja that had been taken from Romania in 1940.

The Finnish treaty called for the payment of $300 million in reparations to Russia. In addition Finland gave up to Russia territory that it had lost in the Russo-Finnish War of 1939-1940 as well as the province of Petsamo.

The treaty with Hungary caused that country to give up a small area to Czechoslovakia and pay $300 million in reparations to Russia, Czechoslovakia, and Yugoslavia.

The Romanian treaty gave up the areas of

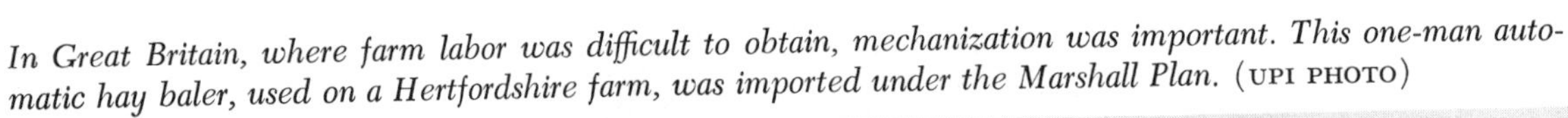

In Great Britain, where farm labor was difficult to obtain, mechanization was important. This one-man automatic hay baler, used on a Hertfordshire farm, was imported under the Marshall Plan. (UPI PHOTO)

Bessarabia and northern Bucovina to Russia and southern Dobruja to Bulgaria. Romania also agreed to pay $300 million in reparations to Russia.

Almost ten years after the end of World War II in Europe, Russia agreed to work with the Western Allies in preparing a peace treaty for Austria. The treaty was signed on May 15, 1955, and went into effect on July 27 that year. Austria agreed to remain neutral in the international dispute between Russia and the West. Austria was forced to pay $150 million reparations to Russia and turn over a substantial amount of German-owned property to Russia.

The inability of Russia and the Western Allies to agree on a peace treaty for Germany resulted in that country being divided on a *de facto* basis into two countries, East Germany and West Germany. West Germany, which consisted of the military occupation zones of the United States, Great Britain, and France, came into being as the Federal Republic of Germany on May 23, 1949, with the ratification of its constitution by the various German states. Later that same year, on October 7, East Germany, called the German Democratic Republic, was formed in the Russian zone of occupation. The Russians recognized East Germany as a fully sovereign nation in March, 1954, but continued to keep Russian troops on duty in the country. The Western Allies formally ended their military occupation of West Germany in May, 1955, but American and other Allied troops continued to serve in West Germany as part of the NATO military alliance.

The Punishment of War Criminals

One of the major unfinished pieces of business for the Allies at the end of World War II was the punishment of enemy war criminals. Throughout the war the world had been shocked by the acts of Nazi Germany and Japan that had included torture, murder, and mass extermination of persons for political, racial, and religious motives. As early as 1942 President Roosevelt had stated as one of the objectives of the war "the intention to apprehend and punish war criminals, as well as to create an agency to investigate war crimes." When the war ended, the Allies held more than eleven thousand suspected war criminals as prisoners.

At the request of General Eisenhower these leaders of the American press were sent to Germany to observe, at first hand, the evidence of maltreatment of prisoners in Nazi camps. From the top down, right to left, are Julius Ochs Adler, ***New York Times;*** *L. K. Nicholson,* ***New Orleans Times-Picayune;*** *Stanley High,* ***The Reader's Digest;*** *William Nichols,* ***This Week;*** *Norman Chandler,* ***Los Angeles Times;*** *Amon Carter,* ***Fort Worth Star-Telegram;*** *John Randolph Hearst,* ***Hearst Newspapers;*** *B. W. Smith, Jr.,* ***American Magazine;*** *Gideon Seymour,* ***Minneapolis Star-Journal;*** *Ben Hibbs,* ***Saturday Evening Post;*** *Joseph Pulitzer,* ***St. Louis Post-Dispatch;*** *Ben McKelway,* ***Washington Post;*** *Walker Stone,* ***Scripps Howard Newspaper Alliance;*** *M. E. Walter,* ***Houston Chronicle;*** *Malcolm Bingay,* ***Detroit Free Press;*** *Duke Shoop,* ***Kansas City Star;*** *E. C. Dimitman,* ***Chicago Sun;*** *and William Chenery,* ***Collier's Magazine.***

(AIR TRANSPORT COMMAND PHOTO FROM ACME)

In France Marshal Henri Pétain, who had headed the German-controlled Vichy government of France during the war, was tried and convicted of aiding the enemy and on August, 15, 1945, was sentenced to death. But his sentence was commuted to life imprisonment. Pierre Laval, who had served under Pétain with dictatorial powers and had carried out many atrocities for the Germans, was tried in Paris, sentenced to death, and shot by a firing squad on October 15, 1945. In like manner, Vidkun Quisling, who had been the puppet premier of German-occupied Norway, was found guilty of treason and shot by a firing squad in Oslo on October 24, 1945.

But world attention focused on the trial of the leading Nazi war criminals that was held at Nuremberg, Germany, before an International Military Tribunal. Twenty-one of the top German

As liberated slave laborers waved and cheered, the Nazi commandant of the camp at Altendorn, Germany, was led away to answer for the atrocities that occurred in his camp. (SIGNAL CORPS—ACME)

Statement made Voluntarily at Gaol
by Rudolf Hoess former Commandant of
Auschwitz Concentration Camp on 16th day of March 1946

I personally arranged on orders received from Himmler in May 1941 the gassing of two million persons between June/July 1941 and the end of 1943 during which time I was commandant of Auschwitz.

signed.
Rudolf Höß
SS-Ostubaf.
E. Kdt. v. Auschwitz-Birkenau

LEFT: *A photograph of the actual confession signed by Rudolph Hess admitting that he supervised the death by gas of about two million people while he was in charge of the Auschwitz extermination camp.* (UPI PHOTO)

RIGHT: *The Nuremberg War Crimes Trials with the main defendants on the third day. In front row left to right: Hermann Goering; Joachim von Ribbentrop; General Wilhelm Keitel; Alfred Rosenberg. In back row left to right: Admirals Karl Doenitz and Erich Raeder; Von Schirach; Fritz Sauckel; General Jodl.*
(U.S. SIGNAL CORPS—ACME)

BELOW: *A general view of the court room on the second day of the Nuremberg trials.*
(UPI PHOTO)

Three former Nazis being sentenced to prison terms in February 1967 in Munich after being convicted of sending fifteen-year-old Anne Frank and 83,000 other Jews to their deaths during World War II. (UPI CABLEPHOTO)

leaders were brought to court in a trial that lasted from November 20, 1945, to October 1, 1946. Among them were such figures as Herman Goering, who had been named by Hitler as his successor in the event of his death, and Joachim von Ribbentrop, Hitler's foreign minister. Three of the defendants were acquitted, three were sentenced to life imprisonment, four were given sentences of from 10 to 20 years, and the rest, including Goering and von Ribbentrop, were sentenced to death by hanging. Goering killed himself by poison a few hours before he was to be hanged. The sentences were carried out on the others.

Because of the huge number of persons involved in carrying out the war atrocities, war crime trials continued in Europe well into the 1960's. One of the most sensational of these latter trials took place in Israel. In May, 1960, Israeli agents had discovered former Gestapo Lieutenant Colonel Adolf Eichmann living in hiding in Argentina. They kidnapped him and took him to Israel, where he was tried from April 11, to December 15, 1961. He was found guilty of being largely responsible for the extermination of Germany's Jews and he was executed in 1962.

The Beginning of the Marshall Plan

—from a speech by Secretary of State George C. Marshall at Harvard University, June 5, 1947.

I need not tell you gentlemen that the world situation is very serious. . . .

It is logical that the United States should do whatever it is able to do to assist in the return of normal economic health in the world, without which there can be no political stability and no assured peace. Our policy is directed not against any country or doctrine but against hunger, poverty, desperation and chaos. Its purpose should be the revival of a working economy in the world so as to permit the emergence of political and social conditions in which free institutions can exist. Such assistance, I am convinced, must not be on a piecemeal basis as various crises develop. Any assistance that this Government may render in the future should provide a cure rather than a mere palliative. Any government that is willing to assist in the task of recovery will find full cooperation, I am sure, on the part of the United States Government. Any government which maneuvers to block the recovery of other countries cannot expect help from us. Furthermore, governments, political parties or groups which seek to perpetuate human misery in order to profit therefrom politically or otherwise will encounter the opposition of the United States.

It is already evident that, before the United States Government can proceed much further in its efforts to alleviate the situation and help start the European world on its way to recovery, there must be some agreement among the countries of Europe as to the requirements of the situation and the part those countries themselves will take in order to give proper effect to whatever action might be undertaken by this Government. It would be neither fitting nor efficacious for this Government to undertake to draw up unilaterally a program designed to place Europe on its feet economically. This is the business of the Europeans. The initiative, I think, must come from Europe. The role of this country should consist of friendly aid in the drafting of a European program and of later support of such a program so far as it may be practical for us to do so. The program should be a joint one, agreed to by a number, if not all European nations.

An essential part of any successful action on the part of the United States is an understanding on the part of the people of America of the character of the problem and the remedies to be applied. Political passion and prejudice should have no part. With foresight, and a willingness on the part of our people to face up to the vast responsibility which history has clearly placed upon our country, the difficulties I have outlined can and will be overcome.

Rebuilding from Rubble

Of more immediate importance to the future of Western Europe were the vast problems faced in rebuilding the war-torn industries and establishing an economic system that would again bring prosperity to the people. Most of the Western European countries, including Great Britain, adopted forms of socialism in which the governments took over the basic industries, while leaving light industries and small businesses in the hands of private owners.

From the outset of the postwar period the United States recognized an obligation to help its

The ruins of Whitfield Tabernacle in London in World War II. (UPI PHOTO)

The ruins of a church in southern England in World War II. (UPI PHOTO)

wartime allies get back on their feet. In 1946 the United States loaned Britain $4.4 billion to aid in its recovery and at the same time loaned $1.37 billion to France for its reconstruction.

Soon, however, it became apparent that these initial loans were a mere drop in the bucket compared to what was needed. Moreover, as economic conditions showed only slight improvement in Europe, communist parties seemed to be making gains. It was feared that if countries such as France or Italy once admitted communists into their cabinet governments they, too, might fall into the sphere of Russian influence.

In June, 1947, United States Secretary of State George C. Marshall proposed a solution that became known as the "Marshall Plan"—a program directed against "hunger, poverty, desperation and chaos." He suggested that the countries of Europe must work together to determine what were their needs and that the United States would then work with them to help solve their economic problems. Marshall made it clear that he believed aid should be provided for any European country, including Russia and its satellites, but that all who did participate must work together.

Late in June, 1947, the foreign ministers of Great Britain, France, and Russia met in Paris to consider the Marshall proposal. Russia objected to drawing up an all-European program, but Britain and France insisted on going ahead. They issued invitations to all European nations to attend a conference in Paris on July 12. Several of the Russian-occupied nations at first indicated they would attend and then withdrew. Altogether sixteen countries attended the meeting: Austria, Belgium, Denmark, France, Great Britain, Greece, Iceland, Ireland, Italy, Luxembourg, Netherlands, Norway, Portugal, Sweden, Switzerland, and Turkey. They formed a group known as the Committee of European Economic Cooperation, and estimated that in the next four years they would need about $20 billion in aid.

In December, 1947, President Truman called upon Congress to approve Marshall Plan aid of $17 billion for the next four years. The following month Marshall bluntly warned, "If we decide that the United States is unable or unwilling effectively to assist in the reconstruction of Western Europe, we must accept the consequences of its collapse into a dictatorship of police states." After considerable debate, in which many Representatives and Senators objected to sending financial support to socialist governments, Congress finally appropriated in June, 1948, $4.875 billion of Marshall Plan aid for European recovery.

Meanwhile, in Europe the 16 countries that had agreed to participate in the plan established the Organization for European Economic Cooperation (O.E.E.C.) to determine the allocation of money from the United States. The United States set up a new agency called the Economic Cooperation Administration (ECA) to administer the U.S. aid, and President Truman appointed as its director Paul G. Hoffman, former president of the Studebaker Corporation. By the time Marshall Plan aid ended in 1951, the United States had sent more than $11 billion in food, machinery, and other goods to Europe as well as making additional loans and direct military aid.

The Marshall Plan enabled all the countries of Western Europe to recover and rebuild, but perhaps the most remarkable recovery was experienced by West Germany. Its heavy industrial plants shattered by Allied bombings and its manpower greatly reduced by war casualties and by the division into two countries, it seemed unlikely at the end of the war that Germany ever again would be an important factor in Europe. In 1947 West Germany's industrial output represented only about one-third of its prewar level.

But the United States and the countries of Western Europe realized that a healthy Germany would be necessary to stand as a buffer state against the growing power of Russia. So Germany was admitted to receive Marshall Plan help. The country's manpower shortage was ended by the influx of refugees from Communist East Germany, so that by 1948 the population of West Germany was nearly 6 million larger than before World War II. The Germans vigorously went to work rebuilding their cities and their industries, and by 1951 West Germany alone was exceeding the previous prewar output of all of Germany.

Moves Toward Western European Unity

In the face of a common threat by Communist East Europe, the countries of Western Europe began to work together more closely than ever before in their history. The ancient feud between France and Germany was ended. For a time some statesmen were even hopeful that they might create a United States of Europe—a federation of all the Western European countries. But in the 1960's a revival of nationalism under de Gaulle in France began to hinder moves toward Western European unity.

Great Britain and France had agreed to a military alliance in 1947 called the treaty of Dunkirk. The next year British Foreign Minister Ernest Bevin suggested that "the time is ripe for a consolidation of Western Europe." He called for other European countries to join the British-French alliance. A conference was called in Brussels, Belgium, in March, 1948, and there a treaty establishing a Western European Union was signed by Britain, France, Belgium, Netherlands, and Luxembourg. The Treaty of Brussels called for mutual assistance in case any member was attacked.

Foreign Minister Ernest Bevin making a point during an address at the Labor Party conference in Margate, England, in October 1950. (ACME)

An even more important step toward European unity was taken in 1949 with the formation of the Council of Europe, a non-military organization of ten nations: Belgium, Britain, Denmark, France, Luxembourg, Netherlands, Ireland, Italy, Norway, and Sweden. Later eight other nations joined: Austria, Cyprus, Greece, Iceland, Malta, Switzerland, Turkey, and West Germany. At the first meeting of the Council in August, 1949, at Strasbourg, France, Winston Churchill, an honorary president of the Council, told the delegates:

> "We have met in this ancient and war-scarred city to set up an assembly which we hope will one day become the Parliament of Europe. The first step has been taken, and it is the first step that counts. We are not here as the representatives of our countries or parties, but as Europeans walking forward hand in hand, and if need be, shoulder to shoulder."

The first major contribution of the Council of Europe was the adoption of the European Convention for the Protection of Human Rights and Fundamental Freedoms, which was signed by member nations on November 4, 1950, and became effective on September 3, 1953. This convention spelled out the rights and freedoms that the people of Western Europe should expect from their governments and established a European Commission of Human Rights to study complaints and attempt to settle them. In addition the convention called for the setting up of a Court of Human Rights which came into being on January 21, 1959. The court judges complaints brought by citizens against their governments.

The next important European organization to be formed was the European Coal and Steel Community (ESC). It was first proposed in 1950 by French Foreign Minister Robert Schuman as a means to make available on an equal basis the two most important raw materials for heavy industry by removing all trade barriers on coal,

A new fertilizer plant in the Netherlands was made possible through the Marshall Plan, one of its primary tasks being to help the European chemical industry. (UPI PHOTO)

iron, and steel among the member countries. The organization began functioning in 1953 with Belgium, France, Italy, Luxembourg, Netherlands, and West Germany. Great Britain refused to join.

The nations of Western Europe drew even closer together with the formation of the European Economic Community (EEC), usually called the European Common Market. The organization was formed by the Treaty of Rome signed in March, 1958, and became effective on January 1, 1958. The original members were Belgium, France, Italy, Luxembourg, Netherlands, and West Germany. Greece, Turkey, and a dozen newly independent African countries later were admitted to associate membership. Under terms of the agreement the members slowly reduced all trade restrictions on goods flowing from one member nation to another and agreed to establish common tariffs on the importation of goods from other nations. The members of EEC also formed the European Atomic Energy Community (Euratom) simultaneously with the common market—an organization planned to provide an equitable development of peacetime atomic power for the member nations.

Seven European countries which were not members of the European Common Market formed their own economic organization, the European Free Trade Association (EFTA), on June 26, 1961. The members were Austria, Denmark, Great Britain, Norway, Portugal, Sweden, and Switzerland. Later Finland became an associate member. This organization also was planned to eliminate tariffs and quota restrictions between the member nations.

In 1961 the members of EFTA applied for membership in the European Economic Community, but President de Gaulle of France blocked the formation of the larger organization, mostly to protect French farmers and industries from competition with Great Britain.

Ten European countries formed the European Space Research Organization (ESRO) in 1962 to coordinate space research. The original members were Austria, Belgium, France, Great Britain, Italy, Netherlands, Spain, Sweden, Switzerland, and West Germany.

SHOOTING WARS

While Russia and the United States did not fight each other directly during the period of the Cold War, there were many shooting wars in which one or the other or both were involved. Although any of these wars could have touched off a world-wide conflagration, Russia and the United States cautiously maneuvered to hold the fighting to "limited objectives" and prevent situations arising that would require either to resort to the use of the devastating power of their atomic weapons. In most cases the United Nations brought these wars to an end either through diplomacy or by armed intervention. One war—that in Vietnam—continued throughout most of the two-decade period, except for a brief respite in the mid-1950's.

The Arab-Israeli War

The region at the eastern end of the Mediterranean Sea called the Holy Land, the Bible Land, or Palestine, was the scene of the first major war of the era. Ever since this area had been liberated from Turkey in World War I, it had been governed by Great Britain under a mandate approved by the League of Nations. Jewish Zionist organizations laid claim to Palestine as the historic

Shortly after an Arab bomb spread death and terror through the Jewish Agency Building in Jerusalem in March 1948, this sports car was used as an ambulance to rush victims to the hospital. (UPI PHOTO)

homeland of the Jews, while the huge Arab population of the area was equally forceful in believing they should control any government that might be set up. Before World War II thousands of Jews had emigrated to Palestine to escape Nazi anti-Semitism in Europe. In 1939 Britain had announced the intention of establishing an independent government in Palestine in ten years, with Arabs and Jews having an equal voice in its affairs. Both Arabs and Jews denounced the plan. World War II brought a truce in the argument.

After World War II ended in Europe, many displaced Jews wanted to go to Palestine to live, but the British would not issue them certificates of immigration because of Arab objections. On August 31, 1945, President Truman wrote a letter to British Prime Minister Attlee, appealing to him to open up Palestine to Jewish immigrants:

". . . no other single matter is so important for those who have known the horrors of concentration camps for over a decade as is the future of immigration possibilities into Palestine . . . future peace in Europe depends in large measure upon our finding sound solutions of problems confronting the displaced and formerly persecuted groups of people. No claim is more meritorious than that of the groups who for so many years have known persecution and enslavement. The main solution appears to lie in the quick evacuation of as many as possible of the non-repatriable Jews, who wish it, to Palestine. If it is to be effective, such action should not be long delayed."

The British delayed taking action in 1945, and instead asked for a joint American and British committee to investigate the Palestine problem and recommend a solution. Early in 1946 the committee reported that relations between the Jews and Arabs were so strained that an independent government could not be set up and that the area should continue to be ruled as a mandate.

Meanwhile, the Jews were taking matters into their own hands. By the summer of 1946 the extremist Jewish Irgun Zvai Leumi and the Stern group were attacking British military installations in Palestine in an effort to drive out the British. Thousands of Jewish immigrants were entering Palestine illegally with the help of the Haganah, a Jewish secret military society. The British retaliated by intercepting shiploads of Jewish immigrants and sending the refugees to camps on Cyprus.

In July, 1946, the British government proposed to divide Palestine into a Jewish state and an Arab state to be ruled over by a British-appointed high commissioner, and to admit 100,000 additional Jewish immigrants. Both Jews and Arabs opposed the plan. President Truman also told the British he opposed the partition of Palestine, but urged that the 100,000 immigration certificates be issued at once. But the British decided to do nothing.

Britain brought world-wide public opinion down on its head in July, 1947, when it forced 4,500 Jewish refugees aboard the ship *Exodus 1947* to sail back to Germany under miserable living conditions and be interred there in a displaced persons camp. That same month Jewish terrorists hanged two British sergeants in Palestine.

On August 31, 1947, a United Nations special committee recommended that Palestine should be divided into two independent countries, one Arab and the other Jewish, and that Jerusalem be given the status of an international city. A month later, on September 26, the British announced that they soon would withdraw their military forces from Palestine. Two months later, on November 29, the UN General Assembly, with both American and Russian agreement, approved the plan to partition Palestine, setting October 1, 1948, as the date by which the independent Arab and Jewish countries should be established. Arabs greeted the plan with anger while the Jews hailed it with joy. In December the British said they would have nothing to do with the plan, since the Arabs and Jews were not in agreement, and that they intended to give up their mandate and withdraw their troops on May 15, 1948.

Wide-scale fighting between Arabs and Jews began in the winter of 1947-1948. When British troops began leaving Palestine in March, 1948, Arabs cut off the Jewish city of Tel Aviv from Jerusalem. Almost at once the Jewish Haganah called to arms all men and women between the ages of 17 to 45. By April Jewish troops had driven back the Arabs from their positions and were attacking the Arab city of Jaffa.

On May 15, 1948, the day the British gave up their mandate, the Jews announced the independence of the new country of Israel with David

Troopers of the 1st Cavalry Division (airmobile) leave their helicopter to conduct a search and destroy mission near Duc Pho, Vietnam. (UPI–OFFICIAL U.S. ARMY PHOTO)

A North Vietnamese Mig-17 as photographed by a U.S. Air Force F 4 C Phantom jet during a dog-fight May 1, 1967. (UPI–U.S. AIR FORCE PHOTO)

United States Marines at Con Thien relax during a lull in the fighting the week of September 25, 1967. (UPI–USMC PHOTO)

Infantrymen of the 1st Cavalry Division (airmobile) direct artillery fire on an enemy position near Duc Pho in Quang Ngai Province, Vietnam. (UPI–OFFICIAL U.S. ARMY PHOTO)

Marines helping their wounded buddies on a slope leading to Hill 881, April 30, 1967. (UPI–USMC PHOTO)

Israeli soldiers pass Arab prisoners in the Arab-Israeli War of 1967. (UPI PHOTO)

Inside the walls of Old Jerusalem, Israeli troops congregate near the Damascus Gate during the 1967 Arab-Israeli War. (UPI PHOTO)

Men of the Haganah, formerly the "underground" force of Palestine Jews, rallied to help beat off Arab terrorists. (UPI PHOTO)

This convoy of trucks crashed through Arab-infested territory to bring a thousand tons of food from Tel Aviv to Jerusalem in April 1948. (UPI PHOTO)

Ben-Gurion as prime minister. Eleven minutes after Israel's announcement, President Truman recognized the sovereignty of the new state. The United Nations at once appointed Count Folke Bernadotte of Sweden to act as mediator to try to bring peace between the Arabs and the Jews.

Arab armies from Jordan, Iraq, Lebanon, Syria, and Egypt advanced into Palestine to attack the Jews. The Arab forces were well-equipped with British arms and were supported by Egyptian air force planes and artillery. But the Jewish forces fought back desperately, largely with small arms.

Bernadotte succeeded in arranging a truce from June 11 to July 8, during which time the Israeli army imported large quantities of arms and ammunition. When fighting resumed in July the Israelis succeeded in putting the Arabs to flight in most of the northern part of the country.

A new truce was arranged by Bernadotte beginning on July 18, but it was more ignored than observed in the weeks that followed. On September 17 Bernadotte was assassinated in the Jewish section of Jerusalem, and the following month Israel forces launched a major attack against the Arabs capturing most of the territory to be included in the state of Israel. Fighting continued into 1949, until Ralph J. Bunche, who had replaced Bernadotte as UN mediator, succeeded in arranging a cease-fire between Israel and Egypt on January 6. In the next several weeks Bunche arranged armistice agreements between Israel and all its Arab neighbors.

More than 900,000 Arab refugees had fled from Palestine to escape the Israeli army. After the war Israel refused to readmit these refugees on grounds that they had left the country voluntarily. These refugees continued to live in desolate camps in neighboring Arab countries throughout the 1950's, being supported with food supplied by the United Nations, and causing continuing friction between Israel and the Arab countries of the Near East.

At the time of its declaration of independence Israel had a population of only about 600,000 Jews, but immigration swelled the population to nearly four times that size by the mid-1960's. Through hard work Israel quickly developed both its farming and manufacturing industries, becoming one of the most modern countries of the Near East region. See also the later sections in this chapter on "The Suez Canal War" and "The Second Arab-Israeli War."

The Indonesian-Netherlands War

Borneo, Java, Sumatra, and hundreds of other tropical islands lying between Southeast Asia and Australia were known for hundreds of years as the East Indies—an important source for valuable spices much sought by European traders. The Netherlands controlled the islands for nearly three and a half centuries, first as the preserve of the Dutch East India Company, and later as a Dutch colony.

During the 1920's a young engineer called Sukarno, who had been born on Java, began demanding independence for his people. The Dutch threw him in jail. But, when the Japanese invaded the islands in 1942 and took over from the Dutch, they released Sukarno because he agreed to help them. Immediately after Japan announced its surrender in World War II, Sukarno, on Agust 17, 1945, proclaimed the formation of an independent Indonesian republic.

The Dutch refused to recognize Sukarno's government, but did not have military forces of their own to re-occupy the islands. Therefore, the Dutch persuaded the British to help them, and in September, 1945, the British began landing troops on the islands. Sukarno's forces, armed with bamboo spears and guns supplied by the Japanese, began fighting the Dutch-British occupation forces almost as soon as they had gone ashore. The fighting continued until a truce was agreed to on October 14, 1946, and the next month the Dutch and Indonesians agreed to form a temporary commonwealth under the Dutch crown that would give way to an independent Indonesian republic in 1949.

When Sukarno refused to allow his troops on Java to become part of a joint Dutch-Indonesian force, the Dutch in July, 1947, launched an attack on Sukarno's troops on Java, Sumatra, and other islands, and met little resistance except in central Java. On August 1, the UN Security Council called for an end to hostilities. After months of discussion and investigation, a UN commission began discussions with the Dutch and the Indonesians aboard the U.S. ship *Renville* in the harbor of Djakarta, then called Batavia. A

Lend-Lease in action in 1943. U.S. officers, in foreground, are inspecting the work of surfacing the taxi ramp of an airfield in India. (UPI PHOTO)

new truce agreement was signed in January, 1948, while negotiations for a final settlement continued.

Now Indonesia began to become a focal point of the Cold War. In May and June, 1948, Russia and other communist countries recognized the independence of Sukarno's government. As a result, the Dutch angrily broke off negotiations with Sukarno, and established a naval blockade of Java and Sumatra to prevent Sukarno from receiving arms from the communists. In December, 1948, Dutch troops attacked Java and Sumatra and captured Sukarno and other members of his government.

The UN Security Council protested the action by the Dutch, and on January 28, 1949, passed a resolution sponsored by the United States which called for the Dutch to withdraw from Java and Sumatra and restore Sukarno to power. Under threat that U.S. aid to the Netherlands might be cut off, the Dutch began withdrawing troops from Java in May, and Sukarno was restored to power on July 6. A new cease-fire agreement was signed in August, and late that month a conference began in The Hague, Netherlands, among the Dutch, the Indonesians, and UN representatives. Agreement for Indonesian independence was reached in November, and on December 27, 1949, President Sukarno took over complete sovereignty from the former Dutch high commissioner to the islands.

For the next fifteen years Sukarno ruled as a dictator, generally favoring the communists in international disputes. Throughout most of this period Sukarno was unfriendly to the United States, but his government contained both conservatives and communists. In September, 1965, with Sukarno's secret support, the communists conspired to purge the conservatives from the government. They murdered six leading generals, but failed to eliminate the most important Lieutenant, General Suharto. In the days that followed General Suharto unleashed the army against communists in Indonesia, killing between 150,000 and 500,000 in one of the greatest massacres of all time. Because of President Sukarno's implication in the attempted communist coup, the Indonesian congress removed the 65-year-old president from office in March, 1967, replacing him with General Suharto.

Viet Minh President Ho Chi Minh (left) discussed the division of Vietnam with Sir M. J. Desai of India (right) before Ho's Communist forces took over the Tonkin capital October 9, 1954. (UPI PHOTO)

The French-Indochina War

Before World War II, Indochina was France's most valuable colony because of its rich supplies of coal, rice, and rubber. France had conquered the region in the 1880's, but the people had never given up struggling to regain their independence. In the 1930's the communist leader Ho Chi Minh had organized guerrilla attacks against the French which continued until the Japanese took over the region in 1940.

After Japan's defeat in World War II, Ho Chi Minh on September 2, 1945, proclaimed the independence of the Democratic Republic of Vietnam with himself as president. The Allies ignored Ho's proclamation and proceeded to help France regain control with Chinese troops occupying the northern part of Vietnam while British forces took over the southern part of Indochina. But Ho Chi Minh's guerrilla forces began a struggle against colonial rule that would continue with increased intensity over the next nine years.

France made several efforts to assuage the nationalistic feelings of the people while still retaining control of Indochina. In January, 1946, France granted internal self-rule to Cambodia under King Norodom Sihanouk. Two months later, on March 6, France recognized internal self-rule for Vietnam under Ho Chi Minh. And when nationalist demonstrations broke out in and around Saigon, France agreed to the setting up of an independent republic of Cochin-China centered on Saigon. However, this last move was violently opposed by Ho Chi Minh who wanted the area of Cochin-China included in Vietnam. Although negotiations continued throughout most of 1946, no substantive agreement was reached.

Then on December 19, 1946, Ho Chi Minh, who had become suspicious that the French were merely stalling for time in which to build up their military forces, launched a full-scale surprise attack on French troops and bases. During 1947 the French poured 100,000 troops into Vietnam and regained many of the towns and cities held by Ho's forces, but the communist guerrillas took to the countryside and continued their attacks against the French.

In an effort to rally anti-communist Vietnamese to their side, the French in 1949 restored to power the former emperor of Vietnam, Bao Dai, and recognized his government as independent within the French Union, incorporating within it the short-lived republic of Cochin-China. Also in 1949 France recognized the independence within the French Union of the Indochinese country of

Laos under its King Sisavang Vong.

During the early 1950's Ho Chi Minh spread the war to Cambodia and Laos, while France with American economic aid continued to pour more men and arms into Indochina in a losing effort to root out the guerrillas.

The French-Indochina War reached its climax in 1954 with the siege of Dien Bien Phu. French paratroopers had captured this town near the border of Laos in northern Vietnam in November, 1953, and the French had strongly fortified it and garrisoned it with 10,000 troops. On March 13, 1954, Ho Chi Minh's soldiers laid siege to the town with a force of about 40,000 men. The battle continued for 55 days with the steadily weakening French forces being supplied by parachute drops. Finally, on May 7, 1954, the French were forced to surrender.

The loss of Dien Bien Phu broke the will of the French government to continue the struggle. A conference was called at Geneva, Switzerland, where on July 21, 1954, an armistice was signed ending the war. Vietnam was split into two countries approximately at the 17th parallel. North Vietnam was turned over to the communist government of Ho Chi Minh, and South Vietnam became a monarchy under Emperor Bao Dai. As French troops were pulled out of North Vietnam, some 800,000 Vietnamese refugees fled to South Vietnam. The government of South Vietnam protested the division of the country and proposed that the United Nations should administer the entire country until free elections could be held; however, the French and Ho Chi Minh rejected the proposal. Although the Geneva agreement enabled the French to get out of a trouble spot which was costing them a great deal in men and money, the main issue of whether the communists or the anticommunists were to govern the country remained unsettled and would soon cause the outbreak of the Vietnam War to be discussed later in this chapter.

French and Vietnamese prisoners of war in 1954, marching from the battlefields of Dien Bien Phu, the fallen French fortress, under the guard of Communist Viet Minh troops. (UPI PHOTO)

The Malayan War

Another target for communist subversion in Southeast Asia was Malaya, the southernmost tip of the continent that extends almost to the equator. This region is rich in rubber, tin, and petroleum. Portugal was the first European nation to win control of the region in the 1500's. The Dutch threw out the Portuguese in the mid-1600's, and then the British won possession of the area in the early 1800's. The Japanese took possession of Malaya in 1942, but the British returned immediately after the end of World War II.

In 1946 the British organized the area into two political divisions, the Malayan Union and the colony of Singapore. However, there was considerable unrest among the people who hoped for a greater voice in their government. The situation was made even more complicated because the population was divided into three main groups, Chinese (40 percent), Malays (40 percent), and Indians (20 percent). Each of these groups feared that the others might win dominance in any new government.

In 1948 the British agreed to reconstitute the government into a federation with a strong central government, and the country's first central parliament began meeting in February. Singapore was maintained as a separate colony and most of its 750,000 Chinese residents were excluded from the right to vote.

Then in June, 1948, communist guerrillas began terrorist attacks against the British. The following month the British outlawed the communist party and rushed in troops from Hong Kong and Palestine. In the years of struggle that followed the British successfully fought the terrorists by drawing the people together from their scattered homes in the countryside into concentrated villages that could be protected by local troops. In the first five years of the war the British killed more than 4,000 communist guerrillas while another 2,000 were captured or surrendered. By 1957 the communists had been thoroughly beaten and the Federation of Malaya was granted independence within the British Commonwealth of Nations.

The Korean War

In 1950 the communists demonstrated clearly their intent to take all of Asia by a reckless attack on American-supported South Korea. Since the end of World War II, Korea—a country about

Malaysian soldiers with one of the howitzers they received under an agreement with Britain in exchange for the privilege of maintaining troops and military and naval bases in Malaya. (UPI PHOTO)

United States Marine Corps retreating from Changjin Reservoir area in northeast Korea in December 1950.
(UPI PHOTO)

twice the size of Tennessee—had been a focal point of trouble in the Cold War. Shortly before the Japanese surrender in 1945, Russian troops had invaded northern Korea and a few weeks later American troops had occupied southern Korea. The United Nations had called for free elections to be held throughout Korea to let the people choose what kind of government they wanted, but the Russians refused permission to hold elections in the part of the country they held. Then in 1948 the United States encouraged the UN to supervise free elections in South Korea which resulted in the establishment of an independent republic on August 15, with Syngman Rhee as the elected president. American troops then withdrew from South Korea. In turn the Russians set up a communist dictatorship in North Korea and announced that they, too, were withdrawing their occupation troops. The 38th parallel, which had been the dividing line between the Russian and American zones of occupation of Korea, became the political boundary between the two new countries, although each claimed itself the rightful government for the entire country.

Without warning on June 25, 1950, a North Korean army equipped with Russian tanks and artillery invaded South Korea. A hastily called meeting of the UN Security Council—which was being boycotted by Russia—unanimously condemned North Korea and called for an end to the fighting. Then, as the North Koreans continued their attack, the UN on June 27 adopted a U.S. resolution that called on all UN members to go to the aid of South Korea. At once President Truman ordered U.S. air and navy units into action, and on June 30 threw the U.S. army into the fight. General Douglas MacArthur was placed in command of UN forces in South Korea.

The well disciplined troops of North Korea, supported by Russian and Chinese arms and advisers, drove swiftly through South Korea, cap-

Troops of the 25th Infantry Division watching for movements of enemy forces, as UN forces dropped white phosphorus on a Red concentration in the Korean foothills in February 1951. (UPI PHOTO)

turing the capital city, Seoul. By August 5 they had pushed UN forces into the southeast corner of the country surrounding the port of Pusan. Here the U.S. 8th Army under Lt. Gen. Walton H. Walker waged a heroic fight to keep from being driven into the sea before reenforcements could arrive.

The tide of war suddenly turned in favor of the UN on September 15 when, in one of the most brilliant maneuvers of modern warfare, General MacArthur landed U.S. marines and soldiers far behind enemy lines at the port of Inchon on Korea's west coast. The North Korean army was demoralized by the turn of events and began surrendering by the tens of thousands, while UN troops drove across the 38th parallel into North Korea, capturing that country's capital of Pyongyang.

In mid-October General MacArthur and President Truman met on Wake Island, where MacArthur gave assurances that he believed the war would be over by Thanksgiving and that U.S. troops would be on their way home by Christmas. He said he was sure the Chinese communists would not enter the war. By this time nineteen other UN nations besides the United States had sent or were sending fighting forces to aid South Korea, and twenty-three other UN nations had offered help.

But unbeknownst to the UN, the Chinese communists had already begun in October to move hundreds of thousands of troops into northwest Korea. On November 6, MacArthur asked for and got permission to bomb the Korean end of bridges leading over the Yalu River to China, but was forbidden to bomb on the Chinese side of the Yalu for fear this might draw Russia into the war on the side of the Chinese and North Koreans.

In November General MacArthur began a general offensive intended to bring the war to a close. By November 21 some UN troops had reached the Yalu River. But almost simultaneously the Chinese had launched a drive to cut behind the UN forces and trap them. The Chinese were supported by Russian made MIG jet fighters, leading to the first jet dogfights in history between the MIGs and U.S. F-86 Sabre jets. During the last days of November huge numbers of Chinese troops began pushing the UN forces back toward the 38th parallel. The U.S. 10th Corps in northeast Korea was forced to retreat to the port of Hungnam where over 200,000 troops were rescued by ship. In January, 1951, the Chinese drove south across the 38th parallel and captured the South Korean capital of Seoul, but the UN forces soon regrouped and by mid-March again took Seoul from the enemy.

Meanwhile, General MacArthur had publicly criticized the limits that had been placed upon his forces, particularly denouncing the orders that prevented his planes from bombing supply bases

"Bloody Ridge," a battleground secured by UN troops after a terrific pounding by artillery, mortar bombs, and napalm. (UPI PHOTO)

General MacArthur and President Truman meeting on Wake Island in October 1950. (UPI PHOTO)

in China. On April 5, a particularly strong letter by MacArthur was released by Republican Representative Joseph W. Martin, Jr., in which the general said, ". . . we must win. There is no substitute for victory." In addition he indicated that President Truman's administration was wrong in not allowing Chiang Kai-Shek's Chinese Nationalist army to attack Communist China. As a result, the American joint chiefs of staff recommended unanimously to President Truman that MacArthur should be relieved of his command, and on April 11 the President issued orders replacing MacArthur with General Matthew B. Ridgway.

By June, 1951, UN forces had pushed the Chinese and North Koreans back to the 38th parallel. For the next two years heavy fighting went on all along a line north of the 38th parallel as UN and communist forces contested for tactically important but economically unimportant mountains and hills that were given such names as Pork Chop Hill and Old Baldy.

At the suggestion of Russia, talks aimed at achieving a ceasefire went on from July 10, 1951, to October 8, 1952, when they were broken off because the UN refused to agree to force Chinese and North Korean prisoners of war to return to their homeland against their will.

After Dwight D. Eisenhower became President, truce talks were resumed on April 26, 1953. Despite many interruptions in this new series of talks, a formal truce agreement was signed on July 27, 1953, providing that only prisoners who wished to return home would be exchanged. In all the UN forces held more than 130,000 Chinese and North Korean prisoners at the end of the war. Over 50,000 American servicemen were listed as dead or missing and more than 100,000 were wounded. The South Korean army had more than 1,300,000 casualties with more than 400,000 killed, while Chinese and North Korean casualties were estimated at more than 2,000,000. The United States later charged that 6,000 Americans who had been taken prisoner had been tortured and killed in communist prison camps.

Although a truce had been achieved in the Korean fighting, a true peace agreement was never reached. Troops continued to patrol the buffer zone established along the 38th parallel, and Korea continued to be a divided country. However, the United States and the United Nations had proven that they were willing at huge cost to come to the aid of any nation threatened by communist aggression.

The Suez Canal War

One of the shortest wars of the period came in the autumn of 1956 over the issue of control of the Suez Canal, a vital link in the shortest ocean trade route between Europe and the Far East.

The crisis first began to develop in May, 1956, when Egypt's President Abdel Gamal Nasser angered the United States by granting diplomatic recognition to Communist China. On July 19 United States Secretary of State John Foster Dulles notified Egypt that the United States was withdrawing an offer it had made the previous year to loan Egypt money to help build the huge Aswan Dam hydroelectric project. In retaliation, on July 26, Nasser denounced the United States and seized control of the Suez Canal, which until then had been the property of a private company controlled by Britain and France. Nasser announced that he would use revenues from the Canal to pay for the Aswan Dam project.

Because for more than half a century the Suez Canal had stood as a symbol of French and British power in the Near East, the governments of both those countries were very upset by Egypt's action. Although President Eisenhower urged Britain and France to show moderation, both began to prepare for military action to regain their control of the Canal. But they agreed to the calling of a 22-nation conference in London in mid-August, at which a proposal was made to Egypt that the Canal be placed under international control. Early in September Nasser rejected the proposal. Britain and France then brought the matter before the United Nations, where the matter was debated at length during early October, but no solution acceptable to all parties could be reached. On October 23 world attention was diverted from the Suez problem by the outbreak of the short-lived Hungarian revolution that was crushed in less than two weeks by Russian troops and tanks.

United Arab Republic President Gamal Abdel Nasser bidding farewell to Soviet Premier Nikita Khrushchev at the end of Khrushchev's state visit in the UAR in May 1964. (UPI RADIOTELEPHOTO)

Then without warning on October 29 Israel attacked Egypt, sending armored columns racing across the desert toward the Suez Canal while paratroops landed to capture strategic Egyptian positions. Britain and France viewed Israel's attack on Egypt as justified, because since the end of the Arab-Israeli War the Arab countries had ringed Israel with armies and continually threatened to crush the Jewish nation. But President Eisenhower took the position that Israel was an aggressor nation and should be stopped by UN action.

On October 31 Britain and France bombed Egyptian cities, while Egypt sank ships in the Suez Canal to block anyone from using it. Two days later the UN General Assembly voted approval of a U.S. resolution calling for a cease-fire in Egypt and of a Canadian proposal to create a special UN force to supervise a truce. On November 5 British and French paratroops captured Port Said at the northern end of the Suez Canal, and that same day Russia threatened to join the war on the side of the Egyptians. On November 7 the fighting stopped in Egypt as the combatants accepted the UN cease-fire. By the end of December the British and French had withdrawn from Egypt, turning peace-keeping operations over to a UN military force. Altogether in the fighting about 1,000 Egyptians had been killed while about 250 British, French, and Israeli soldiers had died. See also the later section in this chapter, "The Second Arab-Israeli War."

General Charles de Gaulle speaking in Algiers in 1944. (UPI PHOTO)

The Algerian War

A little over three months after France had lost the Indochina War in 1954, a rebellion broke out in Algeria that was to continue to drain French resources for the next seven years. This huge North African country—more than three times as large as Texas—had been ruled by France since the 1830's. French settlers and their descendants, who made up less than 10 percent of Algeria's population, lived on the fertile coastal lands along the Mediterranean Sea and dominated the government. The other 90 percent of the population—made up of Arabs and Berbers—were for the most part excluded from the government and barely eked out a living by subsistence farming or by nomadic livestock herding. The tough devil-may-care troops of the French Foreign Legion had repeatedly put down lesser rebellions in the more than a century of French rule of Algeria, but they were vastly outnumbered in the new wave of nationalism that swept the country in the late 1950's.

The Algerian War began with an outbreak of guerrilla warfare in November, 1954, with attacks on Foreign Legion outposts. Fighting temporarily died down during the early part of 1955 and then flared anew in August of that year under leadership of an Arab nationalist organization called the FLN. Soon France had more than 500,000 troops fighting in Algeria in an attempt to restore order, but the nationalist forces adopted hit-and-run tactics, slipping away to hide in the rugged terrain of Algeria's mountains.

In October, 1956, the French captured FLN leader Ahmed Ben Bella and four of his aides. They were held prisoner throughout the rest of the war, but the FLN guerrillas continued the fighting.

With a weak national government in power in France, the French population of Algeria became apprehensive in 1958 that France was about to give in to the rebels, as had happened in Indochina. So French Algerians and the leaders of the French army in Algeria rebelled against the French government and insisted that General Charles de Gaulle be returned to power as premier. The French parliament gave in to the demands and made De Gaulle premier with almost dictatorial powers. He drew up a new constitution, and in 1959 became president of France. But De Gaulle was not able to bring the Algerian War under control.

De Gaulle announced in September, 1959, that he was planning to allow the people of Algeria to decide what kind of government they wanted. Fearing that the Arab majority would dominate under De Gaulle's plan, the French Algerians, supported by French troops, staged a short-lived revolt against De Gaulle's government in January, 1960. Then in January, 1961, French voters approved Algerian self-determination in a nationwide referendum.

In April, 1961, four former French generals led by Raoul Salan started a mutiny and formed a secret terrorist organization called the OAS with the object of preserving French control over Algeria. The OAS carried on bombings and outbreaks of violence both in Algeria and France, including an attempted assassination of De Gaulle in September, 1961. Salan and the other generals later were captured and imprisoned.

Meanwhile, De Gaulle's government had been conducting long negotiations with Arab nationalist leaders that finally resulted in a cease-fire in the Algerian War on March 19, 1962. It was estimated that during the seven-year struggle about 250,000 French, Arab, and Berber soldiers and civilians had been killed. As an aftermath of the war most of the million French Algerians left the country to go live in France.

Released from prison by the French as soon as the fighting was over, FLN leader Ahmed Ben Bella was elected as the first president of the independent republic of Algeria in 1963. He established a socialist government and made many overtures of friendship to the Russian and Chinese communists. But in June, 1965, Ben Bella was overthrown and imprisoned in a military coup carried out by the leading officers of the Algerian army.

The Congo War

From the time it gained independence in 1960 into the late 1960's, the Congo, Africa's second largest country, suffered war and bloodshed. Much of the trouble was stirred up as local leaders struggled for power. But behind much of the fighting was a contest between the forces of communism and anticommunism for control of the land's rich mineral resources, including uranium—the basic material for atomic bombs.

The Congo had been ruled by Belgium since 1885, first as a private possession of the Belgian king and later as a colony. Throughout the period of Belgian control the country was exploited for its mineral riches. Until 1957 the people were given no voice in the government and so few were educated that in the 1960's only about 2 out of every 10 Congolese could read and write.

After riots by the Congolese in 1959 demanding political freedom, Belgium suddenly decided to grant the country its liberty. Although only a handful of Congolese had more than an elementary school education, they were confronted with having to form their own government on independence day, June 30, 1960. Adopting a parliamentary form of government, Joseph Kasavubu was elected as the first president, and his main political opponent, Patrice Lumumba, a leftist, became premier.

Within a few days Congolese soldiers mutinied against their Belgian officers. This started riots throughout the country, and Belgian soldiers were unable to preserve order. Belgian residents of the Congo hurriedly began to leave for Europe.

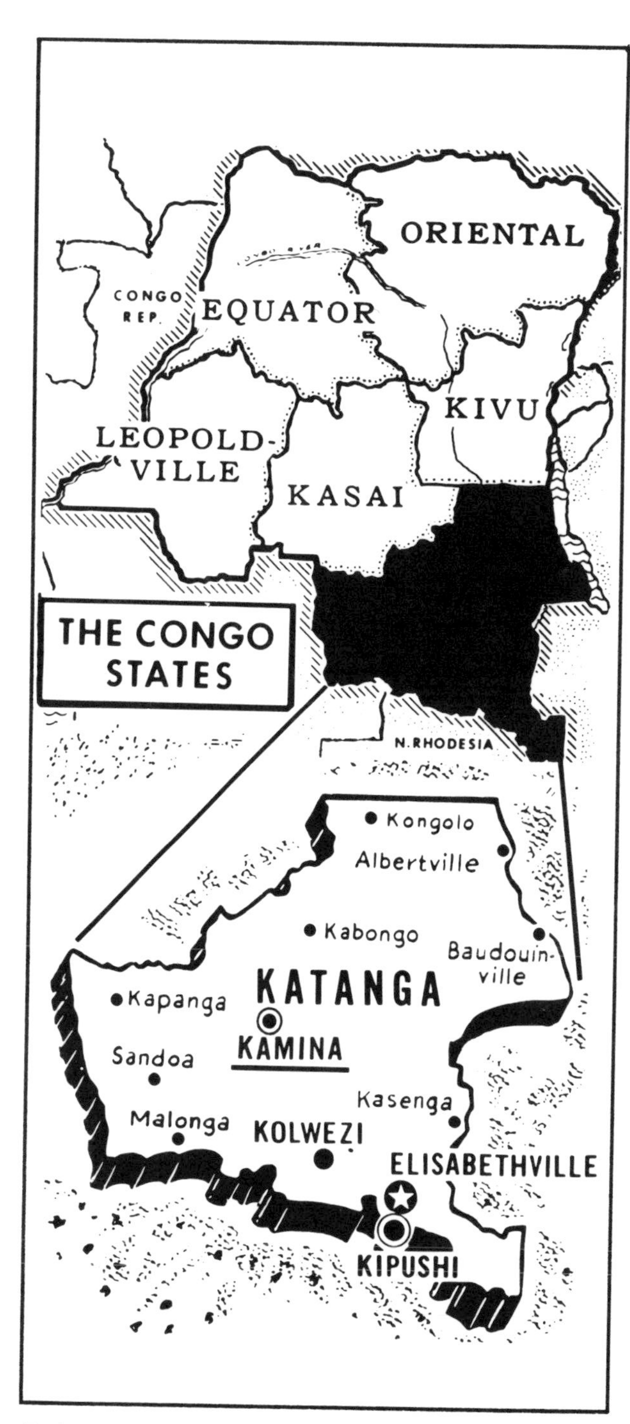

Fighting erupted between the United Nations and Katangese troops around Kamina Air Base, December 31, 1962. News map shows Katanga's position in the Congo. (UPI TELEPHOTO)

A Soviet pamphlet, discarded following the dismissal of Communist diplomatic delegations from the Congo in September 1960. The slogan under the picture of Khrushchev means "Hands off the Congo!" (UPI PHOTO)

RIGHT: *Seated alone at conference table, Adlai Stevenson, U.S. Ambassador to the UN, held a press conference at UN headquarters December 21, 1962, regarding the Cuban crisis and the situation in the Congo.* (UPI PHOTO)

Fighting broke out between Congo tribes, and on July 9, the Congo's mineral-rich southeastern province of Katanga declared itself an independent country with Moise Tshombe as president. At the same time the southern province of Kasai also declared its independence under the tribal leader Albert Kalonji.

Congo Premier Lumumba appealed to the United Nations for help in restoring order and in having Belgium remove its troops from the country. On July 14 the UN Security Council voted to send a UN military force to the Congo—a force that eventually amounted to 20,000 troops mostly drawn from other African nations.

As tribal fighting continued, the head of the Congo army, Colonel Joseph Mobutu, arrested the pro-communist Premier Lumumba and threw him in prison in Katanga where, it was later revealed, he was killed in January, 1961. Meanwhile, Antoine Gizenga, a Lumumba follower, set up a pro-communist independent country in Orientale province around the city of Stanleyville.

An armored car leading a convoy of UN troops in the Jadotville area of the break-away province of Katanga, preparatory to a showdown between UN forces and the remnants of Katanga's secessionist army in 1963.

(UPI PHOTO)

On February 21, the UN Security Council approved a resolution permitting the UN troops in Congo to use force to prevent a civil war. Full-scale fighting broke out in September between UN troops and Tshombe's 11,000-man Katanga army led by European soldiers-of-fortune. UN Secretary General Dag Hammarskjöld was killed that month in a plane crash in the Congo while on a mission to try to bring an end to the fighting. A cease-fire finally was agreed to between the UN and Katanga on December 18, 1961.

After many unsuccessful efforts to bring Katanga back into a union with the Congo, fighting again broke out in late December, 1962, and UN troops captured Elisabethville, Katanga's capital. Tshombe fled into exile, and Katanga was rejoined to the Congo.

Although fighting continued in many parts of the country in 1963 between tribes and the Congo army, United Nations Secretary General U Thant withdrew most UN troops from the Congo. The next year President Kasavubu invited Tshombe to return from Spain, where he had been living, and in July appointed him premier of the Congo in hopes that he might restore order. But bloodshed and revolt continued. On September 7, 1964, a new rebel regime, believed to be supported by Communist China and Cuba, established a "Congolese People's Republic," at Stanleyville. The rebels held about 1,500 American and European prisoners and threatened to execute them if the Congolese army attacked. In November, U.S. planes flew 600 Belgian paratroopers to Stanleyville and rescued most of the hostages, although the rebels executed 18 men, women, and children.

In April, 1965, Tshombe declared that the Congolese army had finally succeeded in suppressing the rebellion and that all rebels had fled from the country. However, guerrilla warfare continued in the country's tropical jungles. In October President Kasavubu dismissed Tshombe from the government, and the next month Joseph Mobutu, now a major general of the Congo army, seized power in a coup. Mobutu declared himself president with the powers of a dictator. Tshombe again went into exile, and in 1966 was accused of treason by Mobutu for plotting further revolts.

Helmeted United Nations troops moving along in a truck convoy, nearing the battle area around Jadotville, the Katangese town captured by UN forces. Katangese civilians looked on as the UN soldiers rolled by. (UPI PHOTO)

The presence of armored cars and trucks underlined the determination of United Nations forces to wipe out the remaining power of Katangese President Moise Tshombe's secessionist army. Silent natives are watching the troops. (UPI PHOTO)

BELOW: *A crowd of 5000, including 2500 armed gendarmes and troops, gathered at the Kolwezi market place to hear Katanga President Moise Tshombe give his emotion-packed "finale" speech, in which he thanked his men for their loyalty. Here he appears to be turning away to regain his composure.* (UPI PHOTO)

An agreement regarding the treatment of minorities was signed in New Delhi April 8, 1950 by Prime Minister Jawaharlal Nehru of India and Prime Minister Liaquat Ali Khan of Pakistan (UPI PHOTO)

Wars in India

When British India was divided into the two independent countries of Moslem Pakistan and Hindu India, a smouldering feud was lighted between the two that occasionally burst into the flames of war during the next two decades. In addition, India was threatened in the northeast by the menacing power of Communist China which launched one aggressive attack during the period to demonstrate its power to crush India anytime it chose.

In October, 1947, only two months after India and Pakistan had become independent, fighting broke out in the northern state of Kashmir where a Hindu maharaja ruled a mostly illiterate Moslem population. Moslem tribesmen from Pakistan's northwest frontier province invaded Kashmir to claim the state for their country. The maharaja of Kashmir declared himself in favor of union with India and appealed to that country for help. India immediately sent an army of 15,000 troops into Kashmir and saved the state's capital of Srinagar from being captured by the Pakistanis.

While fighting continued throughout 1948, India appealed to the United Nations for help. The UN Security Council appointed a five-man commission to go to Kashmir and restore order. In August, the UN called for a cease-fire, and finally India and Pakistan accepted a truce effective January 1, 1949.

In the years that followed, the United Nations made many fruitless efforts to settle the Kashmir dispute. Pakistan insisted that a plebiscite should be held, knowing that the large Moslem population likely would vote for union with Pakistan. But India insisted that the maharaja had been within his rights in joining Kashmir to India, and that no plebiscite was necessary. Flare-ups of border fighting in Kashmir continued through the 1950's.

For several years China and India had disputed the exact location of India's northeastern border.

At the ceremony unfurling the new flag signifying Alaska statehood, President Eisenhower talks with Interior Secretary Seaton and Senators Ernest Gruening and El Bartlett of Alaska, July 7, 1958. (UPI PHOTO)

President Eisenhower, Vice President Nixon (left) and Speaker of the House Sam Rayburn (right), with interested legislators at the ceremony formally making Hawaii the 50th State, August 21, 1959. (UPI PHOTO)

A peaceful scene during the Chinese New Year, Tet, celebration in South Vietnam showing worshippers at a temple in Saigon before the serious American involvement in the war with North Vietnam. (UPI PHOTO)

Since 1959 there had been a number of border clashes between Chinese and Indian border guards. But India was entirely unprepared for the full-scale attack that China launched at several points along the Indian border on October 20, 1962. India, which until this communist attack had endeavored to remain neutral in the Cold War, quickly called upon the United States and Great Britain for aid, and these nations answered by sending a stream of war supplies by airlift.

In four weeks of fighting, the Chinese captured about 5,000 square miles of India's territory and took about 10,000 Indian troops prisoner.

Then, as suddenly as they had started the war, the Chinese called a cease-fire on November 21 and offered to negotiate the dispute. Prime Minister Jawaharlal Nehru proudly refused to negotiate, but the Chinese had made their message amply clear that they had the power to back up their claims to the border regions.

In the spring of 1965 the uneasy truce between India and Pakistan was ended with open warfare that began in April in the desolate Rann of Kutch area near the Arabian Sea. Britain interceded and successfully negotiated a cease-fire signed on June 30.

Then, two months later, on August 5, 1965, Pakistan began moving about 5,000 troops into Kashmir. On August 16, Indian troops attacked Pakistan positions across the 1949 cease-fire line and began a drive toward the Pakistan capital of Karachi. In turn the Pakistan army invaded the Indian states of Punjab and Rajasthan. The two sides fought bitterly with planes, tanks, and ground troops for about a month. But on September 20, the UN Security Council called for an immediate cease-fire, with both the United States and Russia supporting the resolution. Three days later both India and Pakistan accepted the truce, but troops were not withdrawn to their lines of the previous August until February, 1966. The Kashmir dispute remained unsettled and minor border incidents continued into the late 1960's.

The Cyprus War

The third largest island in the Mediterranean Sea, Cyprus, was the scene of a war in which the opposing sides were backed by Greece and Turkey. Because both were allies of the United States, the American government was unable to satisfy either by attempting to mediate the fighting, while Russia used the situation to stir up anti-American feelings in Turkey.

After 82 years of British rule, Cyprus had become an independent republic in the British Commonwealth of Nations on August 16, 1960. The British had granted the island self-rule only after five years of guerrilla warfare by the underground Cypriote nationalist organization EOKA. With four-fifths of the island's population of Greek descent and the other fifth of Turkish descent, the island's independence was guaranteed by international treaties signed by Great Britain, Greece, and Turkey. The constitution of Cyprus was drawn up to provide the Turkish minority with a much larger voice in the government than would have been proportionate to the size of the Turkish population of the island. The Greek majority was particularly galled by the constitutional provision that permitted the Turkish Cypriotes to elect a vice-president who had veto power over any action of the government.

In November, 1963, the president of Cyprus, Archbishop Makarios III, proposed a plan to eliminate the Turkish veto power and generally reduce the influence of the Turkish Cypriotes in the government. Speaking for the Turkish minority, Turkey rejected the proposals on December 16. Five days later violent rioting broke out between Greek and Turkish Cypriotes and more than a hundred people had been killed by Christmas.

During 1964 the fighting swiftly intensified with from 20,000 to 40,000 armed Greek Cypriotes slowly driving the Turks into one small corner of the island. Turkey threatened to intervene directly in the conflict, so the United Nations Security Council on March 4 authorized Secretary General U Thant to establish a military peacekeeping force on the island. Member nations of the UN contributed more than 6,000 troops, but because the UN soldiers were ordered to fire only if fired upon they were relatively ineffective in halting the spreading civil war. On August 7, Turkish jet fighters began bombing and strafing the Greek Cypriotes as Turkey claimed the Greeks were trying to massacre the Turkish people of the island. The UN called for an immediate cease-fire, and on August 10 both Turkey and Cyprus agreed to the truce.

Outbreaks of violence continued on Cyprus in the late 1960's, as the Turkish government and the pro-Greek Cyprus government were unable to reach agreement on any long-term settlement despite the efforts of UN mediators. Largely to cause trouble between Turkey and the United States, Russia supported Turkey's demands that separate Turkish and Greek states be set up on Cyprus, while the United States endeavored to maintain neutrality and friendship with both Greece and Turkey.

The Yemen War

During the 1960's an undeclared war flared intermittently between Egypt and Saudi Arabia with the fighting going on in the tiny Arab country of Yemen, across the Arabian Sea from Ethiopia. The fighting started on September 27, 1962, when a military coup supported by Egypt overthrew Yemen's King Mohamed al-Badr. The leader of the uprising, Abdullah al-Salal, declared Yemen a republic with himself as president.

Yemen tribesmen in the northern and eastern parts of the country rallied to the king's aid, and supported by money and troops from Saudi Arabia began a guerrilla warfare against the forces of the republic. Egypt came to the aid of al-Salal, sending about 65,000 troops into the country.

Violent desert warfare continued for about three years, and then King Faisal of Saudi Arabia and President Nasser of Egypt signed a cease-fire agreement on August 24, 1965, with al-Salal going into exile in Cairo. Egypt withdrew some of its forces, but continued to hold about one-third of the country south of the capital of Sana, while royalist troops held the northern and eastern two-thirds of the country.

During 1966 and 1967 both Saudi Arabia and Egypt continued to build up military forces in Yemen for a possible resumption of open warfare, while in September, 1966, al-Salal returned from exile to resume the offices of president and premier. His new government executed many of the officials of the acting government set up after the cease-fire of 1965, including the former acting president. Western observers believed Egypt's army in Yemen was preparing to take the South Arabian port of Aden if British forces withdrew from that British protectorate.

The Vietnam War

The Vietnam War was the biggest war of the period after the Korean War. Like that earlier conflict of the 1950's, the Vietnam War was a fierce fight between communists and anticommunists for control of a small Asian nation. And, as in the Korean War, the United States led the western powers in helping the South Vietnamese resist being overrun by communist aggressors, while Russia and Communist China aided the communist North Vietnamese.

Unlike the Korean War, however, the Vietnam War did not begin by a mass attack of communist troops. Instead, it began in 1957 with sporadic guerrilla fighting and night attacks by communist irregulars, called the Viet Cong, on undefended villages. For several years the small-scale fighting went on almost unnoticed by the world, being regarded as an internal problem that was an aftermath of the nine-year French-Indochina War of 1945-1954.

The first American military involvement in Vietnam came during the French-Indochina War when on June 27, 1950, President Truman announced that he was sending a 35-man military advisory group to Vietnam to aid French and Vietnamese forces fighting the communists. But Truman's announcement went almost unnoticed at the time because on that same day he first ordered U.S. air and sea forces to go to the aid of South Korea, which had been attacked by North Korea two days earlier. The next year, on September 7, 1951, the United States signed a mutual defense treaty with Vietnam.

By the time the French-Indochina War drew to a close in 1954, the United States was supplying nearly half the financing for the French and anti-communist Vietnamese. But the United States had not greatly expanded the number of its military advisers assigned to the conflict. The United States and South Vietnam refused to sign the settlement of the French-Indochina War which divided Vietnam, giving the most heavily populated part of the country to the communists. In

ON FACING PAGE: *In July 1954 a truce agreement was signed at Geneva by the French and Communist negotiators, the French agreeing to surrender to the Communists all of northern Vietnam above the 17th parallel.* (UPI PHOTO)

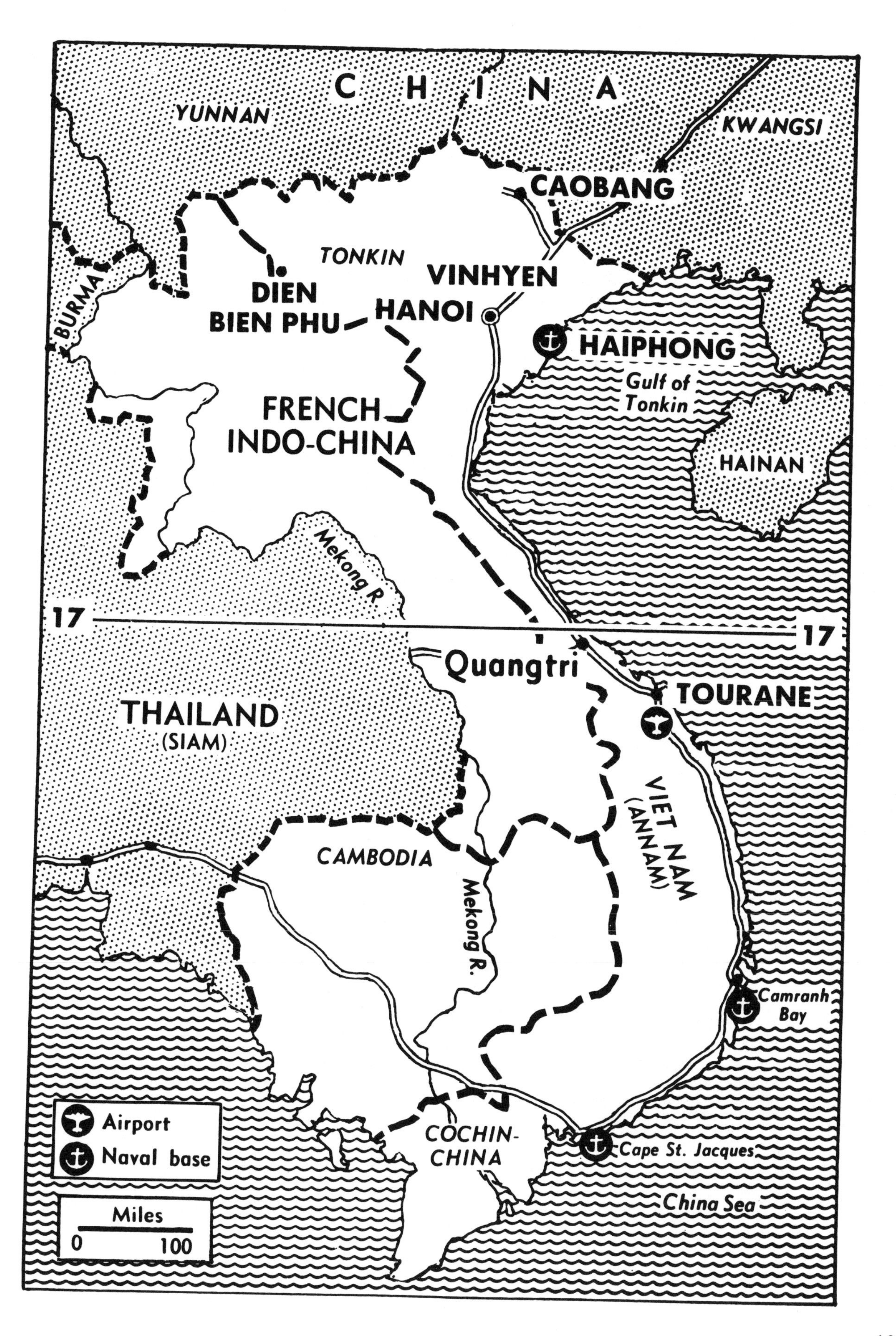
C H I N A
YUNNAN
KWANGSI
CAOBANG
TONKIN
VINHYEN
DIEN
BIEN PHU
HANOI
HAIPHONG
BURMA
Gulf of
Tonkin
FRENCH
INDO-CHINA
HAINAN
Mekong R.
17
17
Quangtri
TOURANE
THAILAND
(SIAM)
VIET NAM
(ANNAM)
CAMBODIA
Mekong R.
Camranh
Bay
Airport
Naval base
COCHIN-
CHINA
Cape St. Jacques
China Sea
Miles
0
100

American Naval men aboard the USS Montague at Haiphong "clocking in" a Vietnamese refugee and her two children shortly before the Communists took over control of Hanoi in 1954.
(OFFICIAL NAVY PHOTO FROM UPI)

1955, President Eisenhower extended further military aid to South Vietnam, sending an increased number of U.S. military personnel to help build and train a modern South Vietnamese army.

In a national election in October, 1955, the people of South Vietnam decided to depose their emperor, Bao Dai. The country became a republic headed by Ngo Dinh Diem as president. The next year Diem's government refused to take part in a referendum that had been scheduled in July to let the people of North and South Vietnam decide what kind of government they wanted for a re-unified Vietnam. Diem's government declared that such elections would not be free and would be dominated by the communists. The United States supported Diem's views, and the elections were not held. The communist Viet Cong organization soon began making terrorist attacks on South Vietnam government officials and started guerrilla activities in the countryside.

U.S. military advisers helping train the South Vietnam army went along with their units to help suppress the communist guerrillas. The first American soldiers were wounded in October, 1957, and the first were killed on July 8, 1959. The Viet Cong steadily increased their forces as men and supplies were smuggled into the country from North Vietnam.

In 1960 attention was diverted to South Vietnam's neighbor Laos, where communist guerrillas called the Pathet Lao, aided by North Vietnamese forces, overran about two-thirds of that country. A force of 300 U.S. military advisers were sent to aid Laos. A cease-fire was arranged in Laos in May, 1961, but the communists continued to hold much of the country.

By 1961, the Viet Cong had built their guerrilla forces in Vietnam to about 20,000 troops and had disrupted most rural life with their terror attacks. To demonstrate American determination to preserve South Vietnam's independence, President Kennedy signed a friendship treaty with that country in April, 1961, and sent Vice President Lyndon Johnson to visit South Vietnam in May. American military forces in Vietnam were increased to about 11,000 men, including armed helicopter units that supported the South Vietnam army of more than 200,000 troops.

Despite the increased American support, the communists continued to hold much of South Vietnam. Believing that dictatorial President Diem was unable to unify his people in the war, President Kennedy indicated his lack of confidence in Diem and threatened to withdraw American economic aid unless the South Vietnamese government was improved. Consequently, in November, 1963, the commanding generals of the South Vietnamese armies overthrew Diem, executed him, and took over the government. The number of American troops in South Vietnam was increased to 16,000 in 1963, and they began to take a larger role in combat leadership. Wide-scale fighting between the communists and government forces also raged in Laos during 1963, particularly in the area of the Plaine des Jarres.

Under President Johnson the United States became even more deeply involved in Vietnam in 1964. On August 2 and 4, U.S. destroyers in the Gulf of Tonkin were attacked by North Vietnamese torpedo boats. The United States retaliated on August 5 by bombing North Vietnam, and two days later Congress passed a resolution giving the President authority "to take all necessary meas-

Chinese Minister Chou En-lai (second from the left), and Viet Minh delegate, Pham Van Dong (third from the left), at the Geneva Conference in July 1954. (UPI PHOTO)

The Geneva peace settlement of 1954, which left northern Indochina under Red Viet Minh control, started a steady stream of refugees fleeing their homeland in voluntary exile. (UPI PHOTO)

ures to repel any armed attack against the forces of the United States and to prevent further aggression." This resolution, passed unanimously by the House and with only two dissenting votes in the Senate, was to become the key that enabled President Johnson to send ever-increasing military forces to Vietnam without a formal declaration of war. By the end of 1964 the United States had increased the number of its armed forces in South Vietnam to more than 20,000, while the communist and North Vietnam forces who held about two-thirds of the country were estimated at a strength of about 50,000. In all, 243 American servicemen had been killed in Vietnam from 1961 through 1964.

The war increased in intensity in 1965. At least twelve North Vietnamese army regiments were believed operating in South Vietnam, and the total communist forces, including the Viet Cong guerrillas were estimated to have a strength of about 200,000 men. More than 170,000 U.S. troops, including army and marine divisions, were sent to Vietnam, and by July were beginning to search for and destroy the communist forces. U.S. Air Force and Navy bombers and fighters carried on daily sorties against the communist forces, and bombed the Ho Chi Minh trail that led through Laos to North Vietnam—the supply route by which North Vietnam, Russia, and Communist China moved men and equipment to support their forces. In May and again in December President Johnson ordered the bombing of North Vietnam to halt temporarily in an effort to get the communists to agree to truce talks—but each time North Vietnam's dictator, Ho Chi Minh, insisted that he would discuss a truce only on condition that the United States withdraw all of its military forces from South Vietnam.

The government of South Vietnam had been quite unstable since the fall of Ngo Dinh Diem, undergoing a dozen changes in leadership. But in June, 1965, a more stable government finally was

Hungry, weary and frightened, these women and children, found hiding along the river banks, were questioned by Vietnamese paratroopers about Viet Cong activity in September 1962. (UPI PHOTO)

organized under the leadership of the commander of the South Vietnamese air force, Nguyen Cao Ky. He won support from both major religious groups of the Vietnamese people—the Roman Catholics and the Buddhists, and plans were set underway to draw up a new constitution that eventually could return the government to democratic civilian control.

The war continued to escalate in 1966 and 1967 with more and more American troops committed to the war until more than half a million U.S. fighting men were taking part. In addition, South Korea, Australia, New Zealand, the Philippines, and Thailand all sent forces to aid in the fight against the communists. By mid-1967 more than 10,000 American servicemen had been killed in Vietnam and more than 50,000 had been wounded. The communists and the South Vietnamese suffered many times more casualties than these, and it was difficult to tell who was winning the war because of the constantly shifting battle lines in the overgrown tropical forests of the region.

In the United States the Vietnam War became the most important political issue of the times. There were many public demonstrations by people who felt that the United States should pull its troops out of Vietnam and let the people of that country settle their own problems. These were countered by parades and demonstrations by persons supporting the war. Some young Americans burned their draft cards and refused to be taken into the army to fight in a war of which they disapproved. But the majority of young men willingly joined the armed services when drafted, and fought bravely in Vietnam when called upon to do so. President Johnson suffered a drop in popularity in public opinion polls because of his role in escalating the war, but his Democratic party retained its control of both houses of Congress in the 1966 elections. The majority of Americans seemed to feel that it was unfortunate that U.S. forces had to fight in Vietnam, but that it was necessary to continue the fight to prevent the communists from taking the country and to demonstrate that the United States would not back down on its promises to an ally.

On the international scene, the United States did not have the wholehearted support of Great Britain in Vietnam, and was actively opposed on the diplomatic front by France. President Johnson repeatedly offered to meet with the communists to try to negotiate a cease-fire, but Ho Chi Minh rejected these offers with demands that the United States unconditionally stop bombing North Vietnam. The United States was unwilling to stop the bombing unconditionally for fear that the communists would proceed to build up their forces while dragging out the truce talks for months—as had been done in the Korean War truce talks.

A weary, wounded United States Marine in Saigon, awaiting evacuation in July 1966. (UPI PHOTO)

As the fighting continued to escalate in 1967, United Nations Secretary-General U Thant, who had tried unsuccessfully for several years to bring peace to Vietnam, expressed his fears that the Vietnam War might continue to grow until it generated World War III.

President Johnson's Proposal for Vietnam Truce Talks

—letter to Ho Chi Minh of February 2, 1967

Dear Mr. President:

I am writing to you in the hope that the conflict in Vietnam can be brought to an end. That conflict has already taken a heavy toll—in lives lost, in wounds inflicted, in property destroyed and in simple human misery. If we fail to find a just and peaceful solution, history will judge us harshly.

Therefore, I believe that we both have a heavy obligation to seek earnestly the path to peace. It is in response to that obligation that I am writing directly to you.

We have tried over the past several years, in a variety of ways and through a number of channels, to convey to you and your colleagues our desire to achieve a peaceful settlement. For whatever reasons, these efforts have not achieved any results.

It may be that our thoughts and yours, our attitudes and yours, have been distorted or misinterpreted as they passed through these various channels. Certainly that is always a danger in indirect communication.

There is one good way to overcome this problem and to move forward in search for a peaceful settlement. That is for us to arrange for direct talks between trusted representatives in a secure setting and away from the glare of publicity. Such talks should not be used as a propaganda exercise, but should be a serious effort to find a workable and mutually acceptable solution.

In the past two weeks, I have noted public statements by representatives of your Government suggesting that you would be prepared to enter into direct bilateral talks with representatives of the U.S. Government, provided that we ceased "unconditionally" and permanently our bombing operations against your country and all military actions against it. In the last day, serious and responsible parties have assured us indirectly that this is in fact your proposal.

Let me frankly state that I see two great difficulties with this proposal. In view of your public position, such action on our part would inevitably produce worldwide speculation that discussions were under way and would impair the privacy and secrecy of those discussions. Secondly, there would inevitably be grave concern on our part whether your Government would make use of such action by us to improve its military position.

With these problems in mind, I am prepared to move even further toward an ending of hostilities than your Government has proposed in either public statements or through private diplomatic channels. I am prepared to order a cessation of bombing against your country and the stopping of further augmentation of United States forces in South Vietnam as soon as I am assured that infiltration into South Vietnam by land and by sea has stopped. These acts of restraint on both sides would I believe, make it possible for us to conduct serious and private discussions leading toward an early peace.

I make this proposal to you now with a specific sense of urgency arising from the imminent new year holidays in Vietnam. If you are able to accept this proposal I see no reason why it could not take effect at the end of the new year, or Tet, holidays. The proposal I have made would be greatly strengthened if your military authorities and those of the Government of South Vietnam could promptly negotiate an extension of the Tet truce.

As to the site of the bilateral discussions I propose, there are several possibilities. We could, for example, have our representatives meet in Moscow where contacts have already occurred. They could meet in some other country such as Burma. You may have other arrangements or sites in mind, and I would try to meet your suggestions.

The important thing is to end a conflict that has brought burdens to both our peoples, and above all to the people of South Vietnam. If you have any thoughts about the actions I propose, it would be most important that I receive them as soon as possible.

Ho Chi Minh's Rejection of Truce Talks

—letter to President Johnson of February 15, 1967

Your Excellency,

On 10 February 1967, I received your message. This is my reply.

Vietnam is thousands of miles away from the United States. The Vietnamese people have never done any harm to the United States. But contrary to the pledges made by its representative at the 1954 Geneva conference, the U.S. Government has ceaselessly intervened in Vietnam; it has unleashed and intensified the war of aggression in South Vietnam with a view to prolonging the partition of Vietnam and turning South Vietnam into a neocolony and a military base of the United States. For over two years now, the U.S. Government has with its air and naval forces carried the war to the Democratic Republic of Vietnam, an independent and sovereign country.

The U.S. Government has committed war crimes, crimes against peace and against mankind. In South Vietnam, half a million U.S. and satellite troops have resorted to the most inhuman weapons and the most barbarous methods of warfare, such as napalm, toxic chemicals and gases, to massacre our compatriots, destroy crops and raze villages to the ground.

In North Vietnam, thousands of U.S. aircraft have dropped hundreds of thousands of tons of bombs, destroying towns, villages, factories, roads, bridges, dikes, dams and even churches, pagodas, hospitals, schools. In your message, you apparently deplored the sufferings and destructions in Vietnam. May I ask you: Who has perpetrated these monstrous crimes? It is the U.S. and the satellite troops. The U.S. Government is entirely responsible for the extremely serious situation in Vietnam.

The U.S. war of aggression against the Vietnamese people constitutes a challenge to the countries of the Socialist camp, a threat to the national independence movement and a serious danger to peace in Asia and the world.

The Vietnamese people deeply love independence, freedom and peace. But in the face of the U.S. aggression, they have risen up, united as one man. Fearless of sacrifices and hardships, they are determined to carry on their resistance until they have won genuine independence and freedom and true peace. Our just cause enjoys strong sympathy and support from the peoples of the whole world, including broad sections of the American people.

The U.S. Government has unleashed the war of aggression in Vietnam. It must cease this aggression. That is the only way to the restoration of peace. The U.S. Government must stop definitively and unconditionally its bombing raids and all other acts of war against the Democratic Republic of Vietnam, withdraw from South Vietnam all U.S. and satellite troops, and let the Vietnamese people settle themselves their own affairs. Such is the content of the four-point stand of the Government of the D.R.V., which embodies the essential principles and provisions of the 1954 Geneva agreements on Vietnam. It is the basis of a correct political solution to the Vietnam problem.

In your message, you suggested direct talks between the D.R.V. and the United States. If the U.S. Government really wants these talks, it must first of all stop unconditionally its bombing raids and all other acts of war against the D.R.V. It is only after the unconditional cessation of the U.S. bombing raids and all other acts of war against the D.R.V. that the D.R.V. and the United States would enter into talks and discuss questions concerning the two sides.

The Vietnamese people will never submit to force, they will never accept talks under the threat of bombs.

Our cause is absolutely just. It is to be hoped that the U.S. Government will act in accordance with reason.

Trucks, tanks and armored cars of the United Arab Republic Army preparing to take up positions in the Sinai Peninsula desert at the start of the United Arab Republic-Israel confrontation in 1967. (UAR VIA UPI)

The Second Arab-Israeli War

For the third time in the two decades a major war broke out between Israel and its Arab neighbors in the spring of 1967. Led by Egypt, the Arab countries had continued to refuse to recognize Israel as an independent nation and had made repeated threats to wipe the Jewish country off the map. During the 1960's Egypt had received substantial military aid from Russia, equipping its army with Russian tanks and jet fighters.

Then on May 19, 1967, responding to a request from the Egyptian government, UN Secretary General U Thant withdrew the UN Emergency Force that had for 10 years patrolled the armistice line between Egypt and Israel and maintained peace between the two countries. Fearing that Egypt was preparing to attack, the Israel government began all-out preparations for war. Egypt stepped up pressure on Israel by blockading the Israeli port of Aqaba, cutting off access to shipping on the Persian Gulf.

On the morning of June 5, Israel claimed to have observed Egyptian tanks moving toward the Israeli border and picked up radar signals of Egyptian planes heading toward Israel. About 8 a.m. Israel launched an air attack on Arab air bases in Egypt, Syria, Jordan, and Iraq, destroying almost the entire Arab air force on the ground. By the end of the first day Israel's air force held unchallenged command of the skies in the Middle East.

The closing of the Gulf of Aqaba to Israeli shipping was an immediate cause of the outbreak of the Arab-Israeli War in June 1967. (UPI PHOTO)

Israeli tanks rolling into a border position May 24, 1967, as tension in the Middle East continued. (UPI RADIOPHOTO)

An Israeli soldier, armed with a machine-gun carbine, watching Arab refugees returning across the war-wrecked Allenby Bridge in July 1967. (UPI PHOTO)

Jordan's King Hussein (center) and the United Arab Republic's President Gamal Abdel Nasser (right), after signing mutual defense treaty against Israel May 30, 1967. Chairman Ahmed Shukairy of the Palestine Liberation Organization is at the left. (UAR–UPI)

Egyptian prisoners removing their shoes and stockings prior to boarding trucks, and barefoot Egyptian prisoners lying face down with their hands on their heads near El Arish, U.A.R. in June 1967. (UPI PHOTOS)

An Arab woman weeping in despair as she prepared to leave her home. (UPI PHOTO)

A historic Pentecostal pilgrimage at the Wailing Wall in the old city of Jerusalem, from which Jews had been barred since 1948. (UPI PHOTO)

Israel's Defense Minister Moshe Dayan, architect of Israel's victories in the 1956 and 1967 Middle East wars. (UPI PHOTO)

A long column of Jews proceeding up the hill after praying at the Wailing Wall in June 1967. Behind the Wall is the dome of the Mosque of the Holy Rock. (UPI PHOTO)

Almost at the same time that Israel launched its air attack on June 5, the Israeli army sent three divisions into action against Egyptian forces in the Sinai peninsula. By the early morning hours of June 9, less than four days after the war began, the Israeli army had fought its way to the eastern bank of the Suez Canal and had captured the entire Sinai peninsula. An estimated 20,000 Egyptians had been killed in the fighting and tens of thousands had been captured, while Israel had only a few hundred casualties. At the same time, fighting on the borders with Jordan and Syria, Israeli forces took all of the city of Jerusalem, all of Jordan's land west of the Jordan River, and high ground along the Syrian border that had been used for Syrian artillery positions.

By Saturday, June 10, the war was over—both sides accepting United Nations demands for a cease-fire. Taking the side of Egypt and the Arabs, Russia called upon the United Nations to denounce Israel as an aggressor and make it give up the territory it had won. But the United States supported Israel's demands that the Arab nations must finally recognize Israel as an independent country and negotiate peace terms.

Russian Premier Aleksei Kosygin and President Johnson held summit conferences on June 23 and 25 at Glassboro, New Jersey, in an effort to reconcile their opposing views on the Arab-Israeli conflict. But neither would change his opinion. As a result, the United Nations was unable to reach agreement on any solution to the Middle East crisis. Israel held onto the land it had won, nearly doubling its area. And Egypt began a new build-up of its military forces with Russian assistance.

EMERGING NATIONS

The break-up of the British and French colonial empires in the years after World War II brought the greatest upsurge in the number of independent nations in history. Altogether sixty-four countries became sovereign powers in a little more than two decades. Most were admitted to membership in the United Nations, more than doubling the size of the world organization from fifty-one at the beginning to one-hundred-and-twenty-one by 1967.

Thirty-one of the newly independent countries had been ruled by Britain before attaining their freedom, and twenty-four had been French territories and possessions. Africa saw the greatest upswing of nationalism as thirty-six countries attained their freedom, but Asia was not far

A general view of the signing of the North Atlantic Treaty Organization agreement, in Paris in 1954, providing for the entry of the West German Government into NATO. John Foster Dulles, U.S. Secretary of State, is in the process of signing. (UPI PHOTO)

behind with twenty-one nations achieving sovereignty.

Because most of the new nations had been colonies for many years before winning independence, they often had unbalanced economies. Most were dependent on the production and export of a few agricultural or mineral products that were important to world commerce, while little had been done to develop diversified manufacturing and processing industries to serve the needs of the people. In most of the new countries the majority of people lived hand-to-mouth existences, making a subsistence living by primitive farming methods.

In many of the new countries relatively few people had ever learned to read and write, and even fewer had received enough education to perform the kinds of professional and skilled work demanded of modern government and industry. As a result, almost all the new countries were faced with the huge problem of trying to educate their people quickly to take important positions in government and industry.

Because so many of the people in the new countries could not read and write, it was often difficult, if not impossible, to establish any sort of truly democratic representative government. Often the new governments began with carefully phrased democratic constitutions and then within a short time fell prey to coups and intrigues that turned them into military or one-party dictatorships.

The United States and Russia as the leaders of the opposing forces in the Cold War set about wooing the new nations with economic and military aid. Some of the emerging nations, such as India, tried to remain neutral in the Cold War struggle, accepting aid from both western and communist powers. Other new nations chose one side or the other. Many former British and French possessions retained close political and economic ties with their colonial rulers by becoming members of the British Commonwealth of Nations or of the French Community.

Altogether the United States has spent more than $100 billion on aid to other countries in the years since 1945, about a third of which was in the form of military aid. Of the approximately $67 billion in non-military foreign aid by the United States, about $30 billion went to Europe, about $14 billion to the nations of the Middle East, another $14 billion to the Far East, about $5 billion to Latin America, and about $4 billion to the emerging nations of Africa. Much of this money went to finance the building of roads, hydroelectric power plants, and other capital projects that the countries otherwise could not have financed.

Perhaps the most dramatic aid program for the emerging nations sponsored by the United States was the Peace Corps. In this organization young Americans volunteered to work for two years in other countries at nominal salaries in order to help teach the people how to help themselves. The idea for a peace corps had been suggested as early as 1959 in Congress, but it was not until John Kennedy made it a campaign issue in the presidential election of 1960 that it began to capture the imagination of youth. Less than two months after he became President, Kennedy established the Peace Corps on March 1, 1961, and named his brother-in-law, Robert Sargent Shriver, Jr., as its first director. The first group of Peace Corps volunteers went overseas to the African nation of Ghana in September, 1961. In the years since then thousands of young Americans have served in the Peace Corps helping the peoples of more than 50 nations.

The United Nations through its specialized agencies also was an important force in helping get the new countries on their feet economically. The Food and Agriculture Organization (FAO) sent advisers to assist in improving farm production and in managing soil and forest conservation. The International Bank for Reconstruction and Development, the International Finance Corporation, and the International Development Association, all were set up by the UN to loan money to countries to finance important capital works projects. The UN's International Labor Organization helped the new nations train skilled workers and establish fair labor laws. The International Monetary Fund aided new countries in the establishment of their monetary systems. The UN Educational, Scientific, and Cultural Organization (UNESCO) took an active role in organizing schools and educational systems in the underdeveloped nations. And the World Health Organization helped fight disease and set health standards in the new countries.

The following countries all won their independence since the end of World War II:

ALGERIA, formerly a French colony, was granted its independence on July 3, 1962. This North African republic is more than three times as large as Texas. Its most important natural resource is petroleum. Most of its people are Arabs and Berbers who believe in the Islamic religion. Its independence was won only after a hard fought war with France summarized in the chapter "Shooting Wars."

BARBADOS, formerly a British colony, received its independence on November 30, 1966. The farthest east of the islands of the West Indies, it is one of the most densely populated countries in the world. Most of the people are Negroes, and nearly all can read and write English. Most worship in the Anglican church. The island's main products are sugar, cotton, rum, and molasses.

BOTSWANA, formerly the British protectorate of Bechuanaland, became independent on September 30, 1966. This land-locked republic in southern Africa is just slightly larger than Texas. Much of the country is covered by the Kalahari Desert. The main industry is cattle raising. Most of the people are Negroes, and the country's constitution forbids all racial discrimination.

French troops patrolling Moslem quarter in Algiers in January 1962, when exceptional security measures were enforced to cope with outbreaks of violence. (UPI PHOTO)

In February 1962, the French government shuffled its forces in an effort to stem the wave of terrorism by the outlawed Secret Army Organization, which was waging a war to keep Algeria in French hands. (UPI PHOTO)

Buddhist monks in procession during a protest demonstration in Rangoon, Burma, September 8, 1963, against the suppression of Buddhists in South Vietnam. (UPI PHOTO)

BURMA, a former British colony, became independent on January 4, 1948. This Southeastern Asia country is slightly smaller than Texas. Most of the Burmese people are Buddhists. The country has many mineral resources, including petroleum. The most important export product is rice. Burma pursued a policy of neutrality in the Cold War. The country's constitutional government was overthrown in 1962 by a military coup, and from then on the country was ruled as a military dictatorship by the commander of the armed forces, General Ne Win.

BURUNDI, the former Belgian trust territory of Urundi, became an independent monarchy on July 1, 1962. A land-locked country in central Africa, Burundi is somewhat larger than the state of Maryland. The people belong to several Negro tribes, with the Bahutu making up the majority, although historically the physically taller Batutsi tribe dominated the Bahutus. About half the people are Roman Catholics and the rest worship tribal religions. The local language, Kirundi, and French both are official languages. The people largely earn their livings by farming and livestock raising. Coffee is the main export crop.

CAMBODIA, a former French colony in Southeast Asia, became an independent monarchy on November 9, 1953. Slightly larger than the state of Utah, Cambodia is mostly covered with tropical forests. Most of the people are Buddhists. The main products of Cambodia are rice and rubber. Lying west of South Vietnam and south of Laos, Cambodia has repeatedly been charged during the Vietnam War with allowing communist forces to cross the Cambodian border for refuge. In turn Cambodia broke off diplomatic relations with the United States in 1965 after an attack by South Vietnam planes on a Cambodian border village.

CAMEROON, a republic on the west coast of Africa, won its independence on January 1, 1960. Before World War I the country had been the German protectorate of Kamerun, and after that war, had been divided into British and French administered territories. The French granted independence to their part of the region in 1960, and the next year the British permitted their part of Cameroon to join the independent country. Somewhat larger than California, Cameroon is mostly an agricultural country. Its chief export products include bananas, cacao, coffee, cotton, and lumber. The people belong to several hundred Negro tribes.

CENTRAL AFRICAN REPUBLIC, formerly the French colony of Ubangi-Shari in French Equatorial Africa, became independent on August 13, 1960. Somewhat smaller than Texas, the country lies in the middle of Africa. Diamonds are the country's most important export product, followed by coffee and cotton. The government had grown progressively more friendly toward Communist China until it was overthrown on December 31, 1965, by the army. Col. Jean-Bedel Bokassa, the former army chief of staff, began ruling as a dictator, broke off relations with Communist China, and ordered all Chinese to leave the country.

CEYLON, a former British crown colony, became an independent dominion in the British Commonwealth of Nations on February 4, 1948. A little larger than the state of West Virginia, Ceylon is an island off the southeastern tip of India. Its chief export is tea. The United States had cut off economic aid to Ceylon after a leftist government seized western oil companies in 1962. But in 1965 a new government more friendly to the West won control of parliament, and the United States resumed sending economic aid to Ceylon.

CHAD, a former colony in French Equatorial Africa, was granted independence on August 11, 1960. It is almost twice as large as Texas. Chad has few natural resources other than farmland, and its chief export product is cotton. The majority of people are Arabs who believe in the Islamic religion and live in the northern part of Chad, which is a desert region. Negro peoples who believe in tribal religions live in the wooded southern part of the country. The country keeps close ties to France, which provides substantial economic aid.

CONGO (Brazzaville), the former territory of Middle Congo in French Equatorial Africa, became independent on August 15, 1960. Somewhat larger than the state of New Mexico, this tropical country is hot and rainy and much of the land is covered with dense jungles. Most of the people are Negroes who live in primitive tribal villages. Only about 2 of every 10 persons can read and write. The country's chief exports are diamonds and lumber. The country maintains ties with France, although it is controlled by a leftist government friendly to Russia, Cuba, and Communist China.

CONGO (Kinshasa), formerly the Belgian Congo colony, was granted independence on June 30, 1960. More than three times as large as Texas, this republic is especially rich in mineral resources with large deposits of copper, manganese, zinc, tin, diamonds, and uranium. The country has had a turbulent existence since gaining its freedom, as summarized in the chapter "Shooting Wars."

The strong threat of a food shortage was at its brink in the Congo when this "bread line" formed outside a Leopoldville bakery in 1963. (UPI PHOTO)

CYPRUS, a former British crown colony, became independent on August 16, 1960. This island republic, smaller than the state of Connecticut, lies in the Mediterranean Sea south of Turkey. Conflicts between the Greek majority and the Turkish minority gripped the island throughout the 1960's, as summarized in the chapter "Shooting Wars."

DAHOMEY, a former territory in French West Africa, won independence on August 1, 1960. Somewhat larger than the state of Tennessee, this Negro republic is one of the poorest countries of Africa. Its chief export products are palm oil and palm kernels used to make soap, while most of its people eke out an existence by growing vegetables for their own consumption. Only about 5 of every 100 persons can read and write. Gen. Christophe Soglo, the head of the country's army, took over the government in 1965, and made himself dictator. Soglo broke off diplomatic relations with Communist China, whose representatives had a strong influence on the previous government.

Canadians of the U.N. peace force guarding well near Kyrenia, Cyprus, in March 1964. (UPI PHOTO)

GABON, a former territory in French Equatorial Africa, became independent on August 17, 1960. Slightly smaller than the state of Colorado, Gabon was best known as the site of the jungle hospital of Dr. Albert Schweitzer. This Negro nation has a healthy economy with exports substantially larger than imports. It has many natural resources, its chief exports being manganese, lumber, petroleum, and uranium. The country maintains close ties to France, which has helped finance modern industrial improvements in Gabon.

GAMBIA, a former British Colony and protectorate, became an independent country in the British Commonwealth of Nations on February 18, 1965. About twice the size of Delaware, Gambia is the smallest country of Africa. Most of the people belong to five main tribes and believe in the Islamic religion. Peanuts and peanut oil are the main products exported. The country has so few natural resources that it is quite poor, and can afford to maintain diplomatic representatives only in neighboring Senegal and in Great Britain.

GHANA, formerly a British colony called the Gold Coast, became an independent country in the British Commonwealth of Nations on March 6, 1957. Somewhat smaller than the state of Oregon, Ghana is a hot, wet country with many tropical forests. Its most important export is cacao, used to make chocolate and cocoa. But the country also has many mineral resources, including diamonds, manganese, gold, and bauxite. The majority of people follow tribal religions, but about a fourth are Christians. The first British Commonwealth nation to be governed by Negroes, Ghana was ruled for its first nine years of independence by Kwame Nkrumah, who gradually established a one-party dictatorship that became increasingly friendly to Russia and Communist China. A military coup overthrew Nkrumah's government in 1966 and the new pro-western government ejected many Russian and Chinese diplomats and technicians.

GUINEA, formerly a territory in French West Africa, became an independent republic outside

Accra, Ghana, showing the Ambassador Hotel. (UPI PHOTO)

the French Community on October 2, 1958. About the same size as Ghana, Guinea also is a hot, wet country on the west coast of Africa. Guinea has important mineral deposits of bauxite, iron ore, and diamonds. Its most important agricultural crop is bananas. The people belong to more than a dozen Negro tribes, and the majority follow the Islamic religion. The country has followed a policy of neutrality in the Cold War, receiving aid from Russia and Communist China as well as from the United States and other western nations. After the pro-communist Kwame Nkrumah was overthrown in Ghana, he was granted asylum by Guinea, whose President Sékou Touré named Nkrumah to the honorary post of co-president of Guinea.

GUYANA, the former colony of British Guiana, became an independent country in the British Commonwealth of Nations on May 26, 1966. This country on the northeast coast of South America is about the size of Idaho. Most of the country is covered by tropical forests with only a small percentage of land along the coast used for farming. The chief exports are bauxite and diamonds. The population is about evenly divided between Negroes and East Indians. About a third of the people are Christians and another third are Hindus.

India's Prime Minister Nehru astride a horse, on the way through a narrow Himalayan pass on the Tibet-Sikkim border in June 1952. (UPI PHOTO)

INDIA, formerly the British Indian Empire, became an independent country in the British Commonwealth of Nations on August 15, 1947. Compared to the United States, India has about 2½ times as many people crowded into less than half as much area. Most of the people belong to the Hindu religion, and only about 3 out of 10 can read and write. Although the country has many resources, its problems of over-population and under-education have thwarted the efforts of its government to move ahead toward a modern industrial economy. India's wars with its neighbors are summarized in the chapter "Shooting Wars."

INDONESIA, formerly the Dutch colony of the Netherlands Indies, declared its independence on August 17, 1945, but was not recognized as a sovereign nation by the Dutch until 1949. The Indonesian-Netherlands War is summarized in the chapter "Shooting Wars."

ISRAEL, formerly part of the British Palestine mandate, declared its independence on May 15, 1948. The Arab-Israeli War with which the country achieved its freedom is summarized in the chapter "Shooting Wars."

IVORY COAST, formerly a territory of French West Africa, became an independent republic outside the French Community on August 7, 1960. Somewhat larger than the state of New Mexico, the Ivory Coast is covered by tropical rain forests in the south and by grasslands in the north. Coffee, lumber, and cacao are the country's chief export products. Most of the people belong to six chief Negro tribes and worship tribal religions, but nearly a fourth of the people belong to the Islamic faith. A pro-western government headed by President Felix Houphouët-Boigny has ruled the country since its independence, and in 1966 threatened to call for help from the French army if its neighbor Guinea tried to help Kwame Nkrumah regain his dictatorship in Ghana.

JAMAICA, formerly part of the British West Indies Federation, became an independent country in the British Commonwealth on August 6, 1962. This island country is not quite as large as the state of Connecticut. Its chief export products are bauxite and sugar. Most of the population are Negroes. The island has a high level of education with 8 out of 10 persons able to read and write.

JORDAN, formerly part of the British Palestine mandate, was granted its independence by Britain on March 22, 1946. This Arab kingdom is a little larger than the state of Indiana. Its most important natural resource is its farmland along the valley of the Jordan River, but most of the eastern part of the country is covered by a rocky desert. Because the country has few mineral resources it must depend on agriculture for its main products, which include wheat, tomatoes, and olives. Since gaining its independence Jordan has had to rely heavily on economic assistance from the western countries.

KENYA, formerly a British colony and protectorate, became an independent dominion in the British Commonwealth on December 12, 1963,

Jewish orphans from the British Zone of Germany arriving at Marseille, France, en route to Palestine.

(UPI PHOTOS)

An Arab refugee riding down the road in Jerusalem on his donkey with a laden camel following, in 1967.

Prince Souvanna Phouma, neutralist Premier of the new coalition government of Laos, met with President Kennedy at the White House July 27, 1962 to discuss American aid and other issues of vital concern to his country. (UPI PHOTO)

and a year later became a republic. This east African country is nearly as large as Texas. Although it lies on the equator much of the country is mountainous with a cool climate. The country has few mineral resources, so the people depend largely on farming for their livings. The chief export products are coffee and tea. Most of the people are Negroes, millions of whom live primitive lives on tribal reserves. Only a small percentage of the people can read and write. The country has been ruled since its independence by President Jomo Kenyatta, who had been imprisoned by the British throughout the 1950's as a leader of the terrorist Mau Mau movement that sought freedom from British rule.

KUWAIT, formerly a British protectorate, became independent on June 19, 1961. An Arab monarchy somewhat larger than Connecticut, Kuwait lies at the northern end of the Persian Gulf. It is the fourth most important oil producing country in the world, and as a result is one of the world's richest countries for its size. Its people have the highest average income of any nation. Oil revenues supply the government with substantially more income than its expenses, so, as well as providing new schools and ample public welfare for its people, Kuwait has become one of the few new independent countries to afford economic aid and loans to less fortunate countries. Because Kuwait's wealth attracts people from many other nations, almost half its 470,000 population are not citizens.

LAOS, formerly a colony in French Indochina, became an independent monarchy on July 19, 1949, but did not win world-wide diplomatic recognition as a sovereign state until after the Geneva peace conference in 1954 that settled the French-Indochina War. Somewhat smaller than the state of Oregon, this mountainous country has few natural resources and depends heavily on economic aid from the United States. Laos has been deeply involved in the Vietnam War, and the communist guerrilla forces, called the Pathet Lao, and North Vietnamese troops hold much of the countryside. See the chapter "Shooting Wars."

LEBANON, a former French mandate under the League of Nations, declared its independence on November 26, 1941, but did not realize full sovereignty until the last French troops had been withdrawn in December, 1946. Not quite twice as large as the state of Delaware, this small country lies at the eastern end of the Mediterranean Sea. Although most of the people of Lebanon are Arabs, about half of them are Christians and only about a third are Muslims. In ancient times Lebanon was the homeland of the seafaring

Phoenicians, and today shipping, trade, and tourism are still the country's main sources of income. In 1958 President Eisenhower sent 6,000 U.S. marines to Lebanon to help protect the government from being overthrown by pro-communist rebels. Lebanon was the first Arab country to establish a democratic parliamentary government with a legislature elected every four years.

LESOTHO, formerly the British protectorate of Basutoland, became an independent monarchy in the British Commonwealth of Nations on October 4, 1966. About the size of the state of Maryland, Lesotho is completely surrounded by the country of South Africa. Lesotho is dry and mountainous with few natural resources. Its Negro peoples make their livings by primitive agriculture or by working in the mines in neighboring South Africa.

LIBYA, formerly ruled by Italy as four separate provinces, became an independent monarchy on December 24, 1951. About two-and-a-half times as large as Texas, this North African Arab country is almost entirely covered by desert, has little farmland, and few water resources. About half the people are nomads who move from oasis to oasis with their flocks of sheep, camels, and goats. Only about three people out of ten can read and write. At the time it gained independence Libya seemed doomed always to be one of the poorer nations of the world. But an American company discovered petroleum in the Libyan desert in 1957, bringing the country oil riches that caused the national economy to soar 1,000 percent in the next ten years. Today petroleum accounts for about 80 percent of Libya's income and 98 percent of its exports. Libya has permitted Great Britain to maintain military bases near the Egyptian border since the end of World War II.

MALAGASY, formerly the French territory of Madagascar, became an independent republic in the French Community on June 26, 1960. This island nation off the southeastern coast of Africa is about half again as large as the state of California. The people of Malagasy came to the island about two thousand years ago from the East Indies, now Indonesia. Over the years they have intermarried with Negroes from the African continent, but still speak a language similar to

The three rival princes of Laos held their own summit conference in Zurich, Switzerland, in 1962. From left to right are: Premier Prince Boun Oum (Western-backed), Prince Souvanna Phouma (neutralist) and Prince Souphanouvong (Communist-supported). (UPI PHOTO)

that spoken on the island of Borneo. The island has few important natural resources other than its soil, so the people depend largely on farming for their income. The chief export crop is coffee. The country depends on economic aid from the United States, France, and West Germany.

MALAWI, formerly the British protectorate of Nyasaland, became an independent country in the British Commonwealth on July 6, 1964. From 1953 through 1963 the country had been part of the Federation of Rhodesia and Nyasaland, but the Negro people of Nyasaland resented the white domination of Rhodesia and finally seceded from the federation. In 1966, two years after gaining independence, Malawi became a republic, electing as its first president, Hastings K. Banda, who had led its struggle for independence. About the size of Pennsylvania, this southeastern African country has a wide range of scenery and climate from snow-capped mountains to hot, humid valleys. It has few mineral resources, so its economy is based on agriculture. Its chief exports are tobacco and tea. The country depends on economic aid from the United States, Britain, and other western countries for nearly a fourth of its national budget.

MALAYSIA, formerly the British governed Federated Malay States, became an independent monarchy within the British Commonwealth on August 31, 1957, as the Federation of Malaya. It was reconstituted on September 16, 1963, as the Federation of Malaysia. This southeastern Asian country covers the tip of the Malay peninsula and the northern part of the island of Borneo. Altogether it has an area about the size of New Mexico. About half the people belong to the Islamic faith. During the Malayan War from 1948 to 1957 communist guerrillas unsuccessfully tried to take over the country. See chapter "Shooting Wars." From 1963 to 1966 Indonesian guerrillas attacked the Malaysian part of Borneo, but this fighting ended after the overthrow of Indonesia's President Sukarno. Malaysia produces more tin and more rubber than any other country in the world. In addition it has major deposits of iron, bauxite, and titanium.

MALDIVE ISLANDS, formerly a British protectorate, became an independent sultanate on

A few of the hundreds of small vessels which arrived at Brunei Town, Brunei, carrying Brunei citizens from the Malaysian state of Sarawak to their homeland, in November 1964. (UPI PHOTO)

July 26, 1965. This group of more than a thousand islands off the southwest tip of India has a land area only about twice the size of the city of Washington, D.C. Most of the people are Muslims and make their livings by fishing or raising coconuts. Britain provides the islands economic aid and maintains an air base there.

MALI, formerly the territory of French Sudan in French West Africa, became an independent republic outside the French Community on September 22, 1960. Almost twice as large as Texas, Mali is a land-locked country in western Africa. The northern part of the country is a hot, dry desert, while the southern part has substantial rain and fertile soil. Most of the people are Negroes who live in tribes in the southern part of the country, but about a fifth of the people are Berbers and Tauregs who live in the northern desert. About two-thirds of the people follow the Islamic faith, and most of the rest worship tribal religions. The country has few natural resources and must import about three times as much goods as it exports. Its main exports are fish caught in the Niger River, cotton, and peanuts. The country is ruled by a one-party dictatorship headed by Modibo Keita who holds both the offices of president and premier. The country receives economic aid from France, Russia, Communist China, and North Vietnam.

MALTA, a former British colony, became an independent country within the British Commonwealth on September 21, 1964. This small island midway between Sicily and Africa in the Mediterranean Sea has an area about twice the size of Washington, D.C. Most of the people speak Maltese, a language similar to Arabic, but many also speak English. Almost all the people are Roman Catholics. Much of the island's income comes from tourists and from the military bases Britain maintains.

MAURITANIA, a former territory in French West Africa, became an independent republic outside the French Community on November 28, 1960. About half again as large as Texas, this nation in northwest Africa has had much unrest between the Arab and Berber majority that live in the north and the Negro minority that live in the south. The Islamic religion is the official state religion and Arabic is taught in the schools, despite opposition by the Negroes. Mauritania is very poor, with the average person having an income equivalent to only $10 a year. The country's main resource is iron ore, which accounts for most of Mauritania's exports.

MONGOLIA, a country formerly claimed by China, became an independent communist nation on January 5, 1946, when China recognized its sovereignty. Covering an area more than twice as large as Texas, Mongolia lies between Russia and China and is governed by a one-party communist dictatorship. Most of the land is covered by deserts and plains. Many of the people are nomads. Almost all the country's foreign trade is with Russia, the chief exports being agricultural products, including cattle, horses, and wool. Almost all the people are Buddhists.

MOROCCO, formerly a French protectorate, won its independence on March 2, 1956. This North African Arab monarchy is somewhat larger than the state of California. Since 1965 Morocco's King Hassan II has ruled as an absolute monarch holding both the titles of king and premier. The rugged Atlas Mountains cover most of the country. Morocco's most important natural resource is phosphate, which provides about a fourth of the country's export revenue. Morocco's most important export crop is oranges. The country has attempted to remain neutral in the Cold War, receiving economic aid both from the western and the communist nations.

NIGER, formerly a territory in French West Africa, became an independent republic outside the French Community on August 3, 1960. Almost twice as large as Texas, Niger is a poor country, most of which is covered by the Sahara desert. Arabs live in the north and Negroes in the south. Almost all the people belong to the Islamic faith. The country has few resources of any consequence and depends on economic aid from the western powers, particularly France. The people lead primitive lives with fewer than one person in 100 being able to read and write. The country's chief export crop is peanuts.

NIGERIA, formerly a British colony and protectorate, became an independent country in the British Commonwealth on October 1, 1960. More than twice as large as California, Nigeria is the most heavily populated country in Africa, with nearly 60 million people. A hot, tropical country, Nigeria is chiefly an agricultural country,

A massive traffic jam in Lagos, Nigeria, as federal troops and civil defense personnel attempted to trap rebel soldiers in September 1967. (UPI PHOTO)

but it also has important mineral resources, including petroleum, coal, and most of the world's supply of columbium, that is used in making stainless steel. Petroleum, peanuts, and cacao provide the bulk of the country's export revenues. Almost all the people of Nigeria are Negroes who are divided into more than 250 tribes. Since winning its independence the country has suffered much internal violence as the various tribes have contested for power. The people of the eastern part of Nigeria declared their independence as the Republic of Biafra on May 30, 1967, but the Nigerian government refused to recognize the new state and a civil war erupted.

NORTH KOREA, formerly ruled by Japan, was proclaimed as an independent communist republic on September 9, 1948. A little larger than the state of Pennsylvania, North Korea is a mountainous country rich in mineral resources. Most of its trade is with Russia, the chief exports being coal, graphite, magnesite, pyrite, silver, and gold. For a summation of the Korean War of the 1950's, see the chapter "Shooting Wars."

NORTH VIETNAM, formerly the French protectorate of Tonkin in French-Indochina, proclaimed its independence on September 2, 1945, under the rule of communist leader Ho Chi Minh. This led to the French-Indochina War and the Vietnam War, both of which are summarized in the chapter, "Shooting Wars." A little smaller than the state of Washington, North Vietnam has rich farmland as well as many mineral resources, including coal, iron, copper, gold, and silver. Its chief crop is rice.

PAKISTAN, formerly part of the British India Empire, became an independent dominion within the British Commonwealth on August 15, 1947, and later became a republic in 1956. About three

Trucks of the Viet Minh 308th Division paraded through the streets as Viet Minh forces took official possession of Hanoi after the departure of the French forces in 1954. (UPI PHOTO)

Signs reading "Independence or Death" were attached to the backs of bicycle rickshaws in Hanoi as part of the demonstration against partition at the time of the Geneva Conference in 1954. (UPI PHOTO)

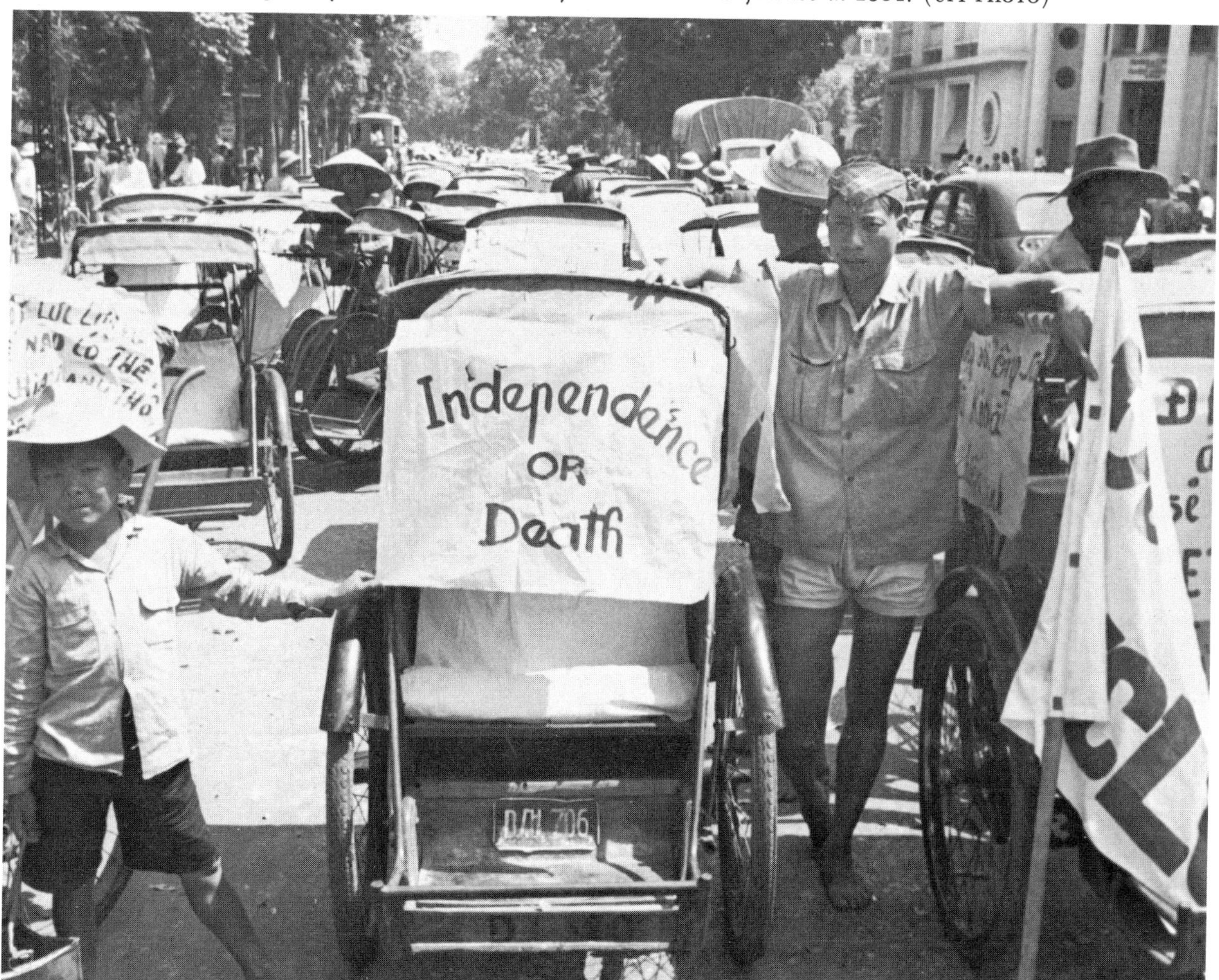

times the size of New Mexico, Pakistan is divided into two parts widely separated by India. Most of the people worship the Islamic faith. Pakistan has some mineral resources, including coal, iron, and petroleum, but agriculture is the main industry. About four-fifths of the people earn their livings by farming, using primitive methods and barely growing enough food to keep from starving. Pakistan has obtained economic and military assistance both from the western and communist nations. For a summary of Pakistan's wars with India, see the chapter "Shooting Wars."

PHILIPPINES, formerly a commonwealth of the United States, became an independent republic on July 4, 1946. For ten years after the end of World War II the Philippine army fought bands of communist guerrillas called Hukbalahaps who sought to overthrow the government and set up a communist regime, but the Huks finally gave up their fight and surrendered in 1954. The Philippines includes more than 7,000 islands southeast of Asia with a land area a little larger than the state of Arizona. The islands have some mineral resources, including coal and iron, but most people earn their livings from agriculture. The chief exports are coconut products. Most of the people are Roman Catholics. English is taught in the schools, and about three-fourths of the people can read and write. The country depends heavily on economic aid from the United States.

RHODESIA, formerly the British protectorate of Southern Rhodesia, declared itself an independent republic outside the British Commonwealth on November 11, 1965, but was refused recognition of its sovereignty by Britain and other nations of the world. Almost the size of California, Rhodesia was regarded as an outlaw nation because the white government of Prime Minister Ian D. Smith represented only 5 percent of Rhodesia's population and denied rights to the more than 4 million Negroes in the country. Only South Africa and Portuguese Mozambique, which have followed similar policies of racial discrimination, maintained relations with Rhodesia. On December 16, 1966, the United Nations Security Council ordered all its members to refuse to purchase exports from Rhodesia and to refuse to supply it with petroleum. The Negro nations of Africa felt these economic sanctions were not strong enough and urged that force be used to make Rhodesia change its government. Rhodesia has ample natural resources of such minerals as coal, iron, asbestos, copper, gold, and lithium, but lacks petroleum. Its main exports are tobacco and asbestos.

RWANDA, formerly part of the Belgian trusteeship of Ruanda-Urundi, became an independent republic on July 1, 1962. About one-fourth larger than the state of Massachusetts, Rwanda is a poor country whose economy is based on agriculture. Most of the people are members of three Negro tribal groups, the Watusis, the Bahutus, and the Batwas. The country formerly was governed by the Watusi tribe, but in 1960 the Bahutus, who represent about 80 percent of the people, rebelled and drove the Watusi king and many of his followers into exile. Ruled by a one-party government, Rwanda maintains friendly relations with both western and communist nations.

SENEGAL, formerly a territory in French West Africa, became an independent republic within the French Community on August 20, 1960. About the size of South Dakota, Senegal lies on the western hump of Africa surrounding the small country of Gambia. The country's economy is based on agriculture, with peanuts being the main export crop. The country is ruled by a one-party government headed by President Leopold Senghor, a poet. Most of the people are Negroes, and most worship the Islamic faith. Only about 6 persons out of 100 can read and write. The country depends heavily on economic aid from France and the United States.

SIERRA LEONE, formerly a British colony and protectorate, became an independent country within the British Commonwealth on April 27, 1961. Somewhat larger than the state of West Virginia, this Negro nation has valuable mineral resources although most of the people make their livings from farming. The country's main exports are diamonds and iron ore. Because it must import most of its manufactured goods, Sierra Leone depends on western nations for economic aid.

SINGAPORE, formerly a British colony, became an independent republic within the British Commonwealth on August 9, 1965. From 1963 to 1965 it had been part of Malaysia. Only about one-fifth the size of Rhode Island, Singa-

Typical government houses which provided homes for one fifth of Singapore's 1.8 million population in 1965, at rents ranging from $10 to $25 a month. (UPI PHOTO)

pore is an island at the very tip of the Malay peninsula south of Malaysia. About three-fourths of the people are Chinese and most follow the Buddhist religion. Most of the people live in the port city of Singapore and depend on trade for their livings. Following a policy of neutrality in the Cold War, Singapore has trade and economic agreements with both western and communist nations.

SOMALIA, formerly the Italian and British protectorates of Somaliland, became an independent republic on July 1, 1960. The easternmost country in Africa, Somalia lies across the Gulf of Aden from the Arabian peninsula. Most of the people are members of the dark-skinned Somali tribes and follow the Islamic religion. The majority of people are nomads who move with their flocks from place to place, and as a consequence their children seldom have an opportunity to go to school. Only about 1 person in 10 can read and write. The country has few mineral resources. Its chief export product is bananas. Remaining neutral in the Cold War, Somalia receives economic aid from both western and communist powers, but its armed forces have largely been equipped by Russia.

SOUTH KOREA, formerly ruled by Japan, became an independent republic on August 15, 1948. Somewhat smaller than the state of Indiana, South Korea is a mountainous country with few natural resources, other than large forests. Its chief export product is plywood. Most of the people make their livings growing rice for their families to eat. The majority of Koreans do not belong to an organized religion. Because the value of South Korea's imports are more than twice as much as its exports, it must depend heavily on economic aid from the United States.

A part of the immense crowd that cheered the United Nations forces in Seoul, Korea, in 1950, in a great demonstration of gratitude after the tide of war had ebbed. (UPI PHOTO)

Secretary of State John Foster Dulles pointing out the 17th parallel in Indochina to Senator Alexander Wiley, Wisconsin Republican, after speaking at a Foreign Relations Committee meeting in July 1954. (UPI PHOTO)

The Korean War of the 1950's is summarized in the chapter "Shooting Wars."

SOUTH VIETNAM, formerly the French territories of Annam and Cochin China in French-Indochina, became an independent empire on July 1, 1949, and later became a republic in 1955. Somewhat smaller than the state of Washington, South Vietnam has few natural resources other than its fertile soil. Its chief export is rubber, although most of its farmland is devoted to raising rice to feed the country's people. South Vietnam imports ten times as much as it exports, with the difference being made up in economic aid from the United States. For a summary of the Vietnam War see the chapter "Shooting Wars."

SUDAN, formerly the British condominium of Anglo-Egyptian Sudan, became an independent republic on January 1, 1956. The largest country in Africa in area, Sudan is more than a fourth as large as the United States. The northern part of the country is a desert and the southern part has wet, tropical marshes. About two-thirds of the people live in the northern part of the country and are Muslim Arabs. Negro tribes live in the southern part of the country and follow tribal religions. The people are very poor with an average income of less than $100 a year, and only about 12 percent can read and write. The country has few mineral resources and depends on farm products to support its economy. Its chief exports are cotton and gum arabic, used in making perfume. The country relies on aid from the United States and other nations to make up the deficit in its foreign trade.

SYRIA, formerly a French mandate, declared itself an independent republic on January 1, 1944, but did not become fully sovereign until French troops left the country in 1946. An Arab country about the size of North Dakota, Syria lies at the eastern end of the Mediterranean Sea just south of Turkey. It has few mineral resources and is mainly a farming country. Syria's chief export products are cotton, barley, and wool. From 1958 to 1961 Syria gave up its independence to join with Egypt in the United Arab Republic, then it resumed its sovereignty. Syria has undergone many changes of government since its independence. In the 1960's it maintained close relations with Egypt and Russia. There were repeated armed clashes with Israel.

TANZANIA, formerly the British-ruled states of Tanganyika and Zanzibar, became an independent unified republic on April 26, 1964. About three times the size of New Mexico, Tanzania lies on the east coast of Africa and includes the two offshore islands of Zanzibar. The majority of the people of Tanzania belong to various Negro tribes and worship tribal religions; however, there are large Christian and Muslim minorities. The country's economy is based on agriculture, with its chief export products being sisal, cotton, and coffee. The country also mines diamonds and several other minerals. Tanzania's President Julius K. Nyerere claimed to be leading his country in a policy of nonalignment in foreign affairs, but his relations with Russia and Communist China were much friendlier than with the United States and Great Britain. Russia, Communist China, and other communist nations supplied Tanzania with substantial economic aid as well as military weapons.

Important men of the Zanzibar Nationalist Party met Sheik Abdul Rahman Babu after his release from jail, in April 1963.
(UPI PHOTO)

TOGO, the former UN trust territory of French Togoland, became an independent republic outside the French Community on April 27, 1960. Somewhat smaller than West Virginia, Togo lies on the west coast of Africa between Ghana and Dahomey. Togo has a hot, damp climate and much of the land is covered with tropical jungles. Most of the people belong to various Negro tribes and grow food for their own subsistence. The chief export crops are cacao and coffee. Togo also mines phosphate rock for export. The country has had many changes of government by coups and revolts since its independence.

TRINIDAD AND TOBAGO, formerly part of the British West Indies, became an independent country in the British Commonwealth on August 31, 1962. These two islands off the northeast coast of South America have a land area only slightly smaller than the state of Delaware. The people are predominantly Negroes, but about a fourth of the population is made up of Hindus from India. About 8 out of 10 people can read and write—a major factor in giving the country a stable, democractic government. Petroleum mining and processing is the most important industry, providing more than three-fourths of the country's export revenues.

TUNISIA, a former French protectorate, became an independent constitutional monarchy on April 13, 1956, and a republic a year later. Somewhat larger than the state of Georgia, this North African country has a dry, sunny climate with good farmlands along the Mediterranean coast and a desert inland. Most of the people are Arabs and Berbers who follow the Islamic religion. Most make their livings from agriculture, with olives being the most important crop. The country's most important mineral resource is phosphate rock, which accounts for about a third of its export revenue. However, petroleum was discovered in the mid-1960's and the country placed great hopes on becoming an important oil-producing center. Since its independence Tunisia has been ruled as a one-party government under Habib Bourguiba, first as premier and later as president. Tunisia has consistently maintained

On January 1, 1962, Western Samoa was granted independence by New Zealand. (UPI PHOTO)

friendly relations with the western powers while refusing to support Egypt's President Nasser as leader of the Arab world.

UGANDA, formerly a British protectorate, became an independent nation within the British Commonwealth on October 9, 1962, and became a republic a year later. Somewhat larger than the state of Utah, this mountainous central African country lies on the equator but has temperate temperatures because of the altitude. The country's main export products are coffee, cotton, and copper. The country depends on economic aid from the United States and Great Britain to develop its economy. Most of the people belong to nearly thirty Negro tribes. More than half are Christians, being about evenly divided between Roman Catholicism and Protestantism. The country became a one-party dictatorship in 1966 when Milton A. Obote, who had been premier, took over the office of president, forcing the former president and king of Uganda to flee into exile.

UPPER VOLTA, formerly a French territory, became an independent republic outside the French Community on August 5, 1960. Somewhat larger than the state of Colorado, Upper Volta is a land-locked nation in western Africa. Grasslands cover most of the country and most of the people make their livings by raising livestock. The country's chief exports are cattle, sheep, hides, and other livestock products. But the value of the country's imports is about three times that of its exports, so the country must depend heavily on economic aid from France and the other western powers. Most of the people belong to Negro tribes and worship tribal religions, but about a fourth of the population are Muslims. Relatively few people can read and write and less than 10 percent of the children attend school. In 1966 the army's commander, Lt. Col. Sangoulé Lamizana, overthrew the government, proclaimed himself as president, and set up a military dictatorship.

WESTERN SAMOA, formerly a New Zealand trust territory, became an independent country on January 1, 1962. The four Pacific islands that make up this country have a land area slightly smaller than the state of Rhode Island. The country's chief products are coconuts, cacao, and bananas. Most of the Polynesian people of the islands are Christians. The country is ruled by a chief and a one-house parliament. Western Samoa depends on economic aid from New Zealand and other western nations.

Ethiopia's Haile Selassie inspecting an honor guard with Zambia's President Kenneth Kaunda (in robes) after the Emperor's arrival in Lusaka, Zambia, July 29, 1965, for a state visit (UPI PHOTO)

ZAMBIA, formerly the British protectorate of Northern Rhodesia, became an independent republic within the British Commonwealth on October 24, 1964. Nearly twice as large as the state of California, Zambia is surrounded by eight other countries in south-central Africa. Most of the people belong to the more than 70 Negro tribes and make their livings by primitive subsistence farming. However, Zambia is the third most important copper-mining nation of the world, with copper providing four-fifths of the country's export revenues. Zambia is one of the few countries of Africa with a favorable balance of trade—its exports far exceeding its imports. The country has been governed since its independence by President Kenneth Kaunda.

EXPANDING AMERICAN PROSPERITY

A line patiently waiting to buy nylon stockings in New York during World War II. (UPI PHOTO)

The United States had never before had it so good as in the years the Space Age generation was growing up. The economy soared to new heights in the amount of goods produced each year, the numbers of people employed, and the average of salaries earned. Of course prices and taxes rose, too, but not so much that almost everyone wasn't better off than ever before. There were slight dips in the economy in 1946, 1949, and 1958, but they were such minor readjustments that they were quickly forgotten. So the Space Age generation grew up without experiencing a financial panic or depression such as had been visited upon every American generation in the past. In the minds of their parents, who had lived through the Great Depression of the early 1930's, there remained the lingering fear that something might happen to end the increasing prosperity.

The End of Price Controls and Rationing

Throughout World War II the government had imposed tight controls on prices and wages and had rationed such products as gasoline and sugar. Almost all of American industry had been turned to war production, so there developed a scarcity of civilian products. But the war workers in the defense plants were working overtime and earning more money than ever before. Much of this money was saved anticipating the end of the war when new cars, refrigerators, and other products would again be available. And some of the money was spent in the black market in which some unscrupulous businessmen managed to lay their hands on scarce commodities and then sold them to consumers at illegal high prices.

Price controls were due to expire on June 30, 1946, and many special interest groups felt they should be allowed to expire at that time so that the nation could return to a free economy. However, the majority of consumers feared that prices would skyrocket upward, and President Truman urged Congress to pass new legislation to extend the controls. At the last minute Congress passed a bill extending the measures, but weakening the powers of the Office of Price Administration (OPA). On June 29 President Truman vetoed the bill, hoping by this action to force Congress to pass a stronger measure. But Congress allowed price controls to expire as scheduled.

Although some responsible businessmen attempted to hold price increases to reasonable levels, most did not. Within a few weeks prices shot up an average of 25 percent. As a huge outcry arose from consumers unable and unwilling to pay the new prices, Congress reluctantly passed new legislation restoring most controls and President Truman signed it. On July 25 prices on most products were rolled back to their June 30 levels, but the new law did not permit the resumption of price controls on meat until at least August

An orderly line of customers waiting to purchase meat during rationing in World War II, in Jackson Heights, New York. (UPI PHOTO)

In Greensboro, North Carolina, the line formed at five o'clock in the morning for the sale of 5000 pairs of nylon stockings seized by the government from black market operators in 1944. (UPI PHOTO)

20. So during the next few weeks farmers rushed young and unfattened livestock to market to take advantage of the prevailing high prices. When meat controls were restored in August most available livestock already had been slaughtered, so that during the next several months a severe meat shortage developed. By October 14 meat was so scarce that President Truman decided to end all controls on meat pricing, announcing his decision in a nationwide radio talk. Three weeks later, on November 9, 1946, after the Republicans had won the mid-term Congressional elections, the President gave in to pressures from the business community and removed most remaining controls on wages and prices, retaining for the most part only sugar rationing and rent controls. In doing so he pointed out that so many businesses and industries were withholding goods from the market in anticipation of higher decontrolled prices that the hoarding was causing false scarcities. With the end of price controls, meat prices shot up an average of 65 percent by the end of 1946, and manufacturers of consumer goods, such as the General Electric Company, increased their prices by 30 percent.

The black market in scarce goods was so prevalent in 1946 that the OPA investigated more than 125,000 cases of black market operations, bringing more than 40,000 to court and collecting more than $17 million in fines and settlements. With the end of most price controls a "gray market" replaced the black market. In the "gray market" speculators bought up scarce materials, such as special kinds of steel, and held them to force prices even higher. The "gray market" ultimately was brought to an end when industry reached full-scale peacetime production capacity.

Sugar rationing to consumers finally was ended on June 11, 1947. Rent controls were maintained in areas with housing shortages, although landlords were allowed to make modest rent increases. After 1949 the continuation of rent controls was made optional to local governments, and in some areas, such as New York City, rent controls were continued into the late 1960's.

Throughout the two decades after World War II prices continued to spiral higher and higher. By 1948 food prices had climbed an average of 40 percent since the end of price controls, while clothing and other prices were up about 25 percent. By the mid-1950's the cost of living had risen an additional 15 percent, and another 20 percent was added to prices and the cost of living in the period from 1955 to 1967. Economists estimated that the trend would continue with an additional 25 percent rise in the cost of living over the next ten years.

Labor

In the two decades since World War II American labor has made the greatest gains in its history in raising the level of wages, in improving working conditions, and in securing a variety of fringe benefits. But in many cases these gains were obtained only after strikes that at their least seriously inconvenienced the public and at their worst threatened to set back the nation's entire economy. Average wages rose from $40 a week in 1946 to $112 in 1966—an increase of 180 percent.

As soon as World War II was over the Congress of Industrial Organizations (CIO) led the way in demanding a 30 percent increase in wages to make up for the loss of overtime work during wartime. Industry's resistance to these demands caused 1946 to become the year that saw the greatest number of strikes in history. Some 4,985 strikes took place involving 4.6 million workers and resulting in 116 million man-days of labor lost. Strikes were called in almost every major industry, including automobiles, coal-mining, meat-packing, oil, railroads, steel, and telephones. Ultimately most of these strikes were settled on formulas that amounted to an 18 percent increase in wages—about equal to the rise in the cost of living with the discontinuation of price controls.

The general public was angered by the product shortages and inconveniences caused by the widespread strikes. An outcry rose that the government had gone too far in encouraging the growth of labor unions and had given them too much power. However, when Congress passed the Case bill in 1946 that imposed restrictions on unions, President Truman vetoed the measure and was upheld by the House of Representatives. Political observers believed that the Republican victory in the Congressional elections of 1946 was largely a result of the public dissatisfaction with the Democratic administration's "soft" attitude toward labor unions.

As the American economy began to pick up steam in 1947, the labor unions demanded another round of wage increases that were generally settled for about 15 percent raises. But during this year there were fewer strikes. The Republican-controlled Congress passed the Taft-Hartley Act over President Truman's veto, restricting the rights of labor unions by outlawing the closed shop that required an employer to hire union members, imposing tighter controls on unions, and expanding the rights of employers.

Since the 1930's the labor movement in the United States had been divided by the conflicting policies of the CIO and the American Federation of Labor (AFL). The CIO believed that its union should represent all the workers in a specific industry, such as all automobile workers. The AFL on the other hand believed its unions should be organized to include all the workers with a specific skill, such as carpenters, regardless of the industry in which they worked. Union leaders, feeling that this division in labor had contributed to the passage of the Taft-Hartley Act, began talks in the late 1940's concerning merger of the two organizations. Finally, on December 5, 1955, the AFL, under leadership of its president George Meany, and the CIO, led by its president Walter Reuther, merged into a single organization called the American Federation of Labor and Congress of Industrial Organizations (AFL-CIO). In the 1960's AFL-CIO unions represented about one-fifth of the more than 80 million work force of the United States.

President Truman's Veto of Taft-Hartley Bill

—from radio address by President Truman, June 20, 1947

At noon today I sent to Congress a message vetoing the Taft-Hartley Labor Bill. I vetoed this bill because I am convinced it is a bad bill. It is bad for labor, bad for management and bad for the country. . . .

The bill is deliberately designed to weaken labor unions. When the sponsors of the bill claim that by weakening unions, they are giving rights back to the individual working men, they ignore the basic reason why unions are important to our democracy. Unions exist so that laboring men can bargain with their employers on a basis of equality. Because of unions, the living standards of our working people have increased steadily until they are today the highest in the world. . . .

This bill would again expose workers to the abuses of labor injunctions.

It would make unions liable for damage suits for actions which have long been considered lawful. . . .

The bill would soon upset security clauses in thousands of existing agreements between labor and management. . . .

One of the basic errors of this bill is that it ignores the fact that over the years we have been making real progress in labor-management relations. We have been achieving slow but steady improvement in cooperation between employers and workers. . . .

Automation, Computers, and Copying Machines

The greatest technological changes in American industry came in the development of automation, computers, copying machines, and other new devices that helped increase the productivity of workers. These machines and systems contributed to greater efficiency and greater per worker production as evidenced by the fact that from 1946 to 1967 the American work force increased only about 60 percent while the gross national product rose about 300 percent. In other words, while the average worker produced only about $3,400 in goods in 1946, the average worker of the mid-1960's produced about $8,750 in goods each year.

Information from weather stations all over the world is received at the National Meteorological Center in Suitland, Maryland, via teletype machines. This IBM computer is part of the mechanical genius that helps to process the reports. (UPI PHOTO)

The nation's first full-scale privately financed nuclear power station, built by General Electric at Joliet, Illinois, produces enough electricity to meet the needs of a city with a population of more than 200,000. (UPI PHOTO)

Automation was a new extension of the Industrial Revolution in which machines began to be used to replace the work of men. With automation, machines now began to be used to control other machines. One of the first major automation installations was in a Ford Motor Company automobile engine factory in 1948. This system utilized machines to control more than 500 machining operations, signalling an operator whenever a tool became worn and needed to be replaced. Automation quickly spread to other industries, especially to the petroleum and chemical industries. Automated petroleum refineries were built in which machines automatically performed hundreds of operations that previously had to be supervised by men, and some chemical plants were built in which one man at a switchboard could control all manufacturing production.

At the same time the development of computers, or electronic calculating machines, began to relieve white collar workers in business offices, banks, and government of such clerical chores as lengthy calculations, filing, and preparation of statistical reports. The first large electronic computer using vacuum tubes was the ENIAC developed at the University of Pennsylvania in 1946 and installed at Aberdeen Proving Ground in 1947. Most of the early computers were built for government use, and the first computer was not installed for use by a business firm until 1954.

From the mid-1950's to the mid-1960's the use of computers proliferated rapidly in business, and at the same time the computers themselves were made more efficient by the use of transistors instead of vacuum tubes. A small desk-size computer of the late 1960's was more efficient, could operate more rapidly, and could store more data than could the early models that were so large that they would take up an entire floor of an office building.

As the use of computers expanded, new professions were created of personnel especially trained to work with these sophisticated machines. The most important of these new jobs was that of a computer programmer—a person who could work out the complicated mathematical programs needed to tell the computers what to do. The shortage of persons trained in this field handicapped industries from moving ahead faster in the use of computers—by 1967 it was estimated there were only 200,000 trained computer programmers in the United States.

Another new type of office machine also contributed to making life easier for office workers. This was the copying machine that could duplicate exact copies of a typewritten page without the necessity of retyping it on special stencils. The first of these machines to become widely used depended on photographic techniques with light-sensitive paper and liquid developers. Then machines were produced using paper sensitive to heat. Finally, machines using a dry electrostatic reproduction process called xerography became the most popular, enabling an office worker to place an ordinary typewritten sheet in a machine and receive back copies within a few seconds.

Agriculture

The story of American agriculture in the years since World War II is told in two statistics: Farm income almost doubled in the years from 1946 to 1967, increasing from about $27 billion to about $50 billion. But during the same period the number of farm workers dropped by fifty percent —from 10 million farm workers in 1946 to only 5 million in 1967. In other words, American agriculture continued to produce more efficiently, requiring less labor, and receiving higher income. The average farm worker of 1946 produced about $2,700 in crops each year, while his counterpart of the late 1960's produced about $10,000 worth annually.

At the same time that the number of farm workers fell, the number of farms also was reduced from nearly 6 million at the end of World War II to about 3.4 million. This came about as more efficient farm machinery made it possible for farmers to manage larger acreages. By 1967 about one-third of the nation's farms—the largest —produced more than four-fifths of all the farm income.

But all was not rosy for American farmers. Almost half of the farms—about 1.5 million—produced barely enough to keep starvation away from the door for the farmer and his family. These small farms produced an average income of

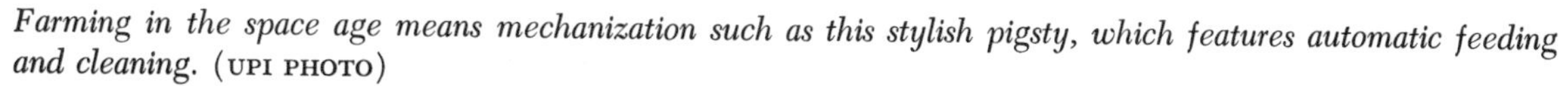

Farming in the space age means mechanization such as this stylish pigsty, which features automatic feeding and cleaning. (UPI PHOTO)

only about $1,200 a year, and little of this was in cash.

Farmers also justifiably complained that farm prices had not risen comparably to the prices of manufactured goods. In fact, twenty years after World War II many important farm commodities were selling for less than they had in 1945—these included chickens, turkeys, eggs, wheat, corn, oats, barley, sorghum, cottonseed, potatoes, and apples. The farmer complained that while housewives were paying substantially more for food in the grocery stores it was the middleman rather than the farmer who was benefiting.

Of course the reason that farm prices did not rise was because farmers could produce far more food than the United States could consume or than the rest of the world could afford to buy. The federal government endeavored to aid the farmers with a variety of legislation throughout the period aimed at keeping farm prices up and preventing over-production. By 1966 the government was paying $3.4 billion a year directly to farmers to attain these objectives as well as providing farmers with government loans to keep them from going bankrupt. Under a "food for peace" law passed in 1954, the federal government sends abroad about $1.5 billion in surplus food each year to aid the world's emerging nations.

Manufacturing

Beset by shortages of materials, labor strikes, and retooling for peace, the manufacturing industries of the United States did not get into full peacetime production until 1947, when with 14.3 million workers they produced goods with an added manufacturing value of $74.4 billion. Twenty years later the number of manufacturing employees had climbed 35 percent to about 19.2 million while the annual added value of manufactured products had risen an astounding 220 percent to about $240 billion. Thus, the average manufacturing worker who had produced about $5,200 in goods each year in the 1940's was able in the 1960's to produce about $13,000 per year.

Outside of automation and computers one of the major factors leading to the tremendous expansion of manufacturing was industrial and government investment in research. The large automobile, chemical, and electrical industries led the way in research, but other industries joined the race for new products and new ways of using old products. By the mid-1950's annual expenditures on research had reached a level of about $5 billion a year. Ten years later in the mid-1960's the amount spent for research had risen 300 percent to more than $20 billion spent each year,

This industrial complex shows part of the Standard Oil Company of Indiana refinery in Whiting, Indiana. (UPI PHOTO)

of which the federal government was spending about $14 billion. Nearly $6 billion a year of the government's research money was being used to develop the space program, guided missiles, and aircraft.

Critics of American manufacturing industries claimed that the manufacturers designed their products for "planned obsolescence"—that they deliberately produced consumer goods that would wear out quickly and that they designed new models that were no better than the old models but were sold on the basis of being up-to-date. Most American consumers ignored these criticisms of industry, feeling that the competition between companies would in the long run insure them of their dollar's worth.

Mining

Like farming, the mining industry saw the number of workers it employed decline while its production increased. In the two decades after World War II, mining employment fell from 784 thousand workers to 632 thousand, a drop of about 20 percent. In the same period the value of products mined each year rose from $6.2 billion to $21.4 billion, an increase of 235 percent.

As natural gas, petroleum, atomic energy, and hydroelectric power increased in importance as power sources in the United States, the use of coal remained about constant. Improved methods of mining coal reduced the number of coal mine employes from 370 thousand to 142 thousand, a decrease of 62 percent.

In the 1950's considerable alarm began to be expressed that the economy was expanding so rapidly that the United States was in danger of using up its natural resources within the next few decades. But the discovery of new mineral deposits and new methods of recovering minerals from low-quality ores allayed these fears by the 1960's.

The petroleum and natural gas industries showed the most rapid growth in the two decades. The value of crude oil produced annually rose from $2.1 billion to $8.2 billion—an increase of nearly 300 percent. At the same time natural gas production expanded from $191 million to $2.5 billion—an amazing rise of more than 1200 percent!

Present-day mechanized mining at the Bingham Mine, Ogden, Utah, showing a giant shovel scooping up copper ore. (UPI PHOTO)

The New York Stock Exchange celebrated its 175th anniversary May 17, 1967. This fisheye lens view (180 degrees) shows the floor of the Exchange on a typical day. (UPI PHOTO)

Business and Finance

As the average American became more affluent, he had more money to spend on things other than food and manufactured goods. As a result employment opportunities expanded most rapidly in other industries than manufacturing. Service occupations catering to hobbies and leisuretime activities doubled their employes during the two decades—increasing from 4.5 million persons working in service jobs to more than 9.1 million. Likewise the number of persons employed in finance, insurance, and real estate doubled, from 1.5 million in 1946 to 3 million in 1965. Federal, state, and local government employes increased by 80 percent, from 5.6 million to over 10 million. And persons working in retail and wholesale trade rose by 47 percent, from 8.5 million to 12.6 million.

While Americans were earning more, they also were saving more. Total deposits in banks increased from $151 billion in 1945 to $385 billion in 1966—a rise of more than 150 percent. At the same time the amount of life insurance held by American families increased by 440 percent, from $182 billion in 1946 to $985 billion in 1966.

Although the stock market proved to be a generally unreliable barometer of business trends during the two decades, investors who held onto their securities for the longrun increase in values made out very well, particularly those who bought stock in electronic and business machine companies. In 1945 the value of all the stocks traded on the New York Stock Exchange was $69.5 billion. By 1966 the stocks on this market had zoomed upward by more than 670 percent to reach a total value of $537.4 billion.

Poverty

Despite the fact that most Americans had better jobs with more money to spend and more money to save, the nation still had more than 5 million families trying to exist on incomes of less than $2,000 a year. The heads of many of these families were women whose husbands had deserted them and others were men so badly educated that they could not find any steady employment.

In his State of the Union message in 1964, President Johnson called for a "War on Poverty" to root out its causes. In August of that year Congress passed anti-poverty legislation called the Economic Opportunity Act and implemented it with an appropriation of $800 million for the first year's operation. An additional $1.5 billion was appropriated for the second year, and $1.6 billion more for the third. President Johnson appointed Sargent Shriver, President Kennedy's brother-in-law, as director of the anti-poverty program.

During the next several years the Office of Economic Opportunity launched attacks on poverty on many fronts. Community action programs were financed in more than 1,000 local communities designed to have local people work with the poor. A "Head Start" program was begun for preschool children to try to bring them up to a level of learning readiness comparable to that of children from less deprived homes. A Volunteers in Service to America (VISTA) program was modeled after the Peace Corps which Shriver also had headed; this "domestic peace corps" called for young volunteers to serve in poverty-stricken communities to help teach the people how to help themselves. Thousands of high school dropouts were enrolled in a Job Corps program designed to teach them skills that would enable them to fill jobs in government and industry. And a Neighborhood Youth Corps program found part-time jobs for poor high school students to enable them to remain in school. For the most part, everyone was in agreement that only through education could the people living in poverty be turned into useful citizens who could win their own way in America's expanding prosperity.

This view of a rubble and garbage littered street in Newark, New Jersey, shows the results of four nights of violence in July 1967. (UPI PHOTO)

President Johnson Calls for a War on Poverty

—from State of the Union address, January 8, 1964

. . . This budget, and this year's legislative program, are designed to help each and every American citizen fulfill his basic hopes:

His hopes for a fair chance to make good.

His hopes for fair play from the law.

His hopes for a full-time job on full-time pay.

His hopes for a decent home for his family in a decent community.

His hopes for a good school for his children with good teachers.

And his hopes for security when faced with sickness or unemployment or old age.

Unfortunately, many Americans live on the outskirts of hope, some because of their poverty and some because of their color, and all too many because of both.

Our task is to help replace their despair with opportunity.

And this Administration today, here and now, declares unconditional war on poverty in America, and I urge this Congress and all Americans to join with me in that effort.

It will not be a short or easy struggle, no single weapon or strategy will suffice, but we shall not rest until that war is won.

The richest nation on earth can afford to win it.

We cannot afford to lose it.

One thousand dollars invested in salvaging an unemployable youth today can return $40,000 or more in his lifetime.

Poverty is a national problem, requiring improved national organization and support. But this attack, to be effective, must also be organized at the state and the local level, and must be supported and directed by state and local efforts.

For the war against poverty will not be won here in Washington. It must be won in the field, in every private home, in every public office, from the courthouse to the White House.

The program I shall propose will emphasize this cooperative approach. To help that one-fifth of all American families with income too small to even meet their basic needs, our chief weapons in a more pinpointed attack will be better schools and better health and better homes and better training and better job opportunities to help more Americans, especially young Americans, escape from squalor and misery and unemployment rolls, where other citizens help to carry them.

Very often a lack of jobs and money is not the cause of poverty, but the symptom.

The cause may lie deeper in our failure to give our fellow citizens a fair chance to develop their own capabilities, in a lack of education and training, in a lack of medical care and housing, in a lack of decent communities in which to live and bring up their children. But whatever the cause, our joint federal-local effort must pursue poverty, pursue it wherever it exists. In city slums, in small towns, in sharecroppers' shacks or in migrant worker camps, on Indian reservations, among whites as well as Negroes, among the young as well as the aged, in the boom towns and in the depressed areas.

Our aim is not only to relieve the symptom of poverty, but to cure it, and, above all, to prevent it. . . .

ATOMIC ENERGY—POWER for GOOD and EVIL

A panorama of the ruins in Hiroshima, Japan, after an atomic bomb was dropped on the city in World War II.
(UPI PHOTO)

The Era of Atomic Energy burst forth upon the world with the mushroom cloud rising over Hiroshima, bringing with it such power for both good and evil as had never before been known. Although the world's statesmen and military leaders could not fail to understand that they held in their hands weapons that could bring destruction to all mankind, they were unwilling or unable to adjust their thinking or their actions to such a revolutionary concept. Russia and the United States, the two most powerful nations, could not reach agreement on means to outlaw atomic weapons and convert all atomic energy to peaceful uses. As a result, Russia and the United States began the costliest armaments race in the world's history, later being joined by Great Britain, France, and China as the knowledge to construct atomic weapons spread. While hundreds of billions of dollars were poured into building atomic weapons, relatively small amounts were spent in developing the peaceful potential of atomic energy. But the awesome destruction of atomic warfare did not break out, leaving the solution to the problem, if there ever was to be one, in the hands of the Space Age generation.

President Truman's Plans for Atomic Energy

—from message to Congress, October 3, 1945

Almost two months have passed since the atomic bomb was used against Japan. That bomb did not win the war, but it certainly shortened the war. We know that it saved the lives of untold thousands of American and Allied soldiers who would otherwise have been killed in battle.

The discovery of the means of releasing atomic energy began a new era in the history of civilization. The scientific and industrial knowledge on which this discovery rests does not relate merely to another weapon. It may someday prove to be more revolutionary in the development of human society than the invention of the wheel, the use of metals, or steam or internal combustion engines.

Never in history has society been confronted with a power so full of potential danger and at the same time so full of promise for the future of man and for the peace of the world. I think I express the faith of the American people when I say that we can use the knowledge we have won, not for the devastation of war, but for the future welfare of humanity.

To accomplish that objective we must proceed along two fronts—the domestic and the international.

The first and the most urgent step is the determination of our domestic policy for the control, use and development of atomic energy within the United States.

We cannot postpone decisions in this field. The enormous investment which we have made to produce the bomb has given us the two vast industrial plants in Washington and Tennessee and the many associated works throughout the country. It has brought together a vast organization of scientists, executives, industrial engineers and skilled workers—a national asset of inestimable value.

The powers which the Congress wisely gave to the Government to wage war were adequate to permit the creation and development of this enterprise as a war project. Now that our enemies have surrendered, we should take immediate action to provide for the future use of this huge investment in brains and plants. I am informed that many of the people on whom depend the continued successful operation of the plants and the further development of atomic knowledge are getting ready to return to their normal pursuits. In many cases these people are considering leaving the project largely because of uncertainty concerning future national policy in this field. Prompt action to establish national policy will go a long way toward keeping a strong organization intact.

It is equally necessary to direct future research and to establish control of the basic raw materials essential to the development of this power whether it is to be used for purposes of peace or war. Atomic force in ignorant or evil hands could inflict untold disaster upon the nation and the world. Society cannot hope even to protect itself—much less to realize the benefits of the discovery—unless prompt action is taken to guard against the hazards of misuse.

I therefore urge, as a first measure in a program of utilizing our knowledge for the benefit of society, that the Congress enact legislation to fix a policy with respect to our existing plants, and to control all sources of atomic energy and all activities connected with its development and use in the United States.

The legislation should give jurisdiction for these purposes to an Atomic Energy Commission with members appointed by the President with the advice and consent of the Senate. . . .

The other phase of the problem is the question of the international control and development of this newly discovered energy.

In international relations as in domestic affairs, the release of atomic energy constitutes a new force too revolutionary to consider in the framework of old ideas. We can no longer rely on the slow progress of time to develop a program of control among nations. Civilization demands that we shall reach at the earliest possible date a satisfactory arrangement for the control of this discovery in order that it may become a powerful and forceful influence towards the maintenance of world peace instead of an instrument of destruction.

Scientific opinion appears to be practically unanimous that the essential theoretical knowledge upon which the discovery is based is already widely known. There is also substantial agreement that foreign research can come abreast of our present theoretical knowledge in time.

The hope of civilization lies in international arrangements looking, if possible, to the renun-

RIGHT: *Honolulu, Hawaii, July 8, 1962, at the time of the detonation of a rocket-borne nuclear device, about 800 miles from the detonation at eleven P.M., showing the brilliant flash and unusual hue of the sky at night.* (UPI PHOTO)

BELOW: *The unusual sky pattern at eleven P.M. after the detonation of a thermonuclear device code-named Mike, which caused the greatest destructive effects ever noted from a single explosion.* (UPI PHOTO)

China exploded its first Atomic Bomb on October 16, 1964. (UPI PHOTO)

An episode in the confrontation of the U.S.S.R. and the United States of America over the installation of Soviet missiles in Cuba, showing the USS Barry (left) about to inspect the cargo of the Soviet freighter Anosov.
(UPI PHOTO)

Another view of the massive destruction in Hiroshima after the explosion of the atomic bomb, August 6, 1945.
(UPI PHOTO)

The "Little Boy" atom bomb, the type detonated over Hiroshima was 120 inches long, 28 inches in diameter, weighed about 9000 pounds, and had a yield equivalent to approximately 20,000 tons of high explosive.
(UPI PHOTO FROM AEC)

One of the atomic bomb tests at Bikini in the Pacific Ocean during the summer of 1946. (UPI PHOTO)

ciation of the use and development of the atomic bomb, and directing and encouraging the use of atomic energy and all future scientific information toward peaceful and humanitarian ends. The difficulties in working out such arrangements are great. The alternative to overcoming these difficulties, however, may be a desperate armament race which might well end in disaster. . . .

The Bikini A-Bomb Tests

The surrender of Japan had not yet been signed ending World War II when the American admirals and generals began making plans for testing the new atomic bombs to learn their potential and to determine just how much they would have to change the rules of warfare. A joint army-navy task force was created to carry out the tests, called "Operation Crossroads," in the summer of 1946 at Bikini atoll in the Pacific Ocean. Vice Admiral William H. P. Blandy was named commander of the operation. The task force included more than 40,000 men and 200 ships as well as many airplanes.

The task force anchored 75 American, Japanese, and German warships in the 20-mile-long Bikini lagoon, placing them about 1,000 yards apart. Live animals, including goats, pigs, and rats, as well as many scientific measuring instruments, were stationed aboard the ships to determine the effect of the bombs on personnel if the ships were manned.

On the first test, July 1, 1946, an atomic bomb was dropped from a B-29 to explode in the air over the battleship *Nevada* in the center of the target formation. Seconds after the explosion a fireball three-miles-wide spread out over the target area, and then during the next several minutes a mushroom atomic cloud climbed five miles into the sky. A Japanese cruiser, two destroyers, and two transports were damaged so badly that they sank immediately or within the next 24 hours. All the ships within a half mile of the explosion, including several battleships and aircraft carriers, were judged to be so badly damaged they would have been put out of action. If the ships had been manned by their crews, only some of those below decks would have survived.

On the second Bikini test, on July 25, the bomb was exploded underwater, suspended from a landing ship near the center of the target fleet. Instantly after the explosion a huge balloon of water vapor rose into the air, then disappeared as a column of water almost a half a mile wide and a mile high briefly carried the 26,000-ton battleship *Arkansas* into the air. This explosion sank about ten ships, including the *Arkansas*, and the aircraft carrier *Saratoga*. The Japanese battleship *Nagato* sank five days later. Most of the ships still afloat suffered damage and were badly contaminated by radioactivity.

The conclusions drawn from the Bikini tests were obvious. The use of massive fleets of ships to carry out amphibious operations, as the United States had successfully pioneered in Europe and the Pacific in World War II, was done. Moreover, any enemy using atomic weapons could successfully knock out a major ship such as a battleship or an aircraft carrier with a single bomb dropped even as close as a half a mile to its target.

Domestic Control of Atomic Energy

While the admirals and the generals planned for and carried out the Bikini tests with their new war toy, the United States Congress was engaged in a great debate as to whether civilians or military officials should be given control of the future development of atomic energy. On October 3, 1945, President Truman sent a message to Congress outlining the necessity of new legislation to control and develop atomic energy. That same day the May-Johnson bill for the control of atomic energy was introduced in the House by Rep. Andrew J. May of Kentucky, chairman of the House Military Affairs committee. This bill provided for atomic energy to be under control of military authorities and had the approval of Secretary of War Robert Patterson. For a time everyone assumed that the bill also had the support of President Truman. Then late in November he circulated a memorandum to various Washington officials indicating that he believed the bill should be amended to provide for ultimate control of atomic energy by a civilian board. A few days later he called Patterson and Secretary of the Navy James Forrestal to his office and insisted that they accept civilian control of atomic energy. On December 20, Senator Brien McMahon of Connecticut, chairman of the Senate Atomic Energy committee, introduced a new bill calling for a civilian Atomic Energy Commission. A week later Secretary Patterson issued a statement opposing the McMahon bill. Finally, early in February President Truman publicly endorsed the McMahon bill.

By this time many prominent scientists had issued statements warning that continued military control of the development of atomic energy

The bevatron at the University of California at Berkeley. (UPI PHOTO)

would lead to a disastrous armaments race. In March Republican Senator Arthur Vandenberg proposed an amendment to the bill that would set up a military committee given the right to veto actions of the civilian Atomic Energy Commission. Truman immediately spoke out in opposition to the Vandenberg amendment.

Then, after much more debate and many more attempts to give the army and navy complete control of the atomic program, Congress finally passed the McMahon bill, and on August 1, 1946, President Truman signed it into law as the Atomic Energy Act. As the first chairman of the all-civilian Atomic Energy Commission established by the act, President Truman appointed David E. Lilienthal, who previously had directed the Tennessee Valley Authority.

For the next eight years the Atomic Energy Commission controlled all phases of atomic energy research and development as a government monopoly. Then in 1954, under President Eisenhower, Congress passed a new Atomic Energy Act which enabled private industry to own atomic facilities and lease nuclear materials from the government. The Atomic Energy Act was modified again in 1964, under President Johnson, requiring the Atomic Energy Commission to begin selling fissionable materials to private companies and to stop all its leasing arrangements by 1973—thus ending the government monopoly that had been created in 1946.

International Control of Atomic Energy

The United States recognized the need to establish international controls over the use and development of atomic energy if there was ever to be security from the threat of atomic war. At the outset of the Era of Atomic Energy the United States alone knew how to make atomic weapons. Some persons suggested that the United States should use the threat of the atomic bomb to force other nations—especially Russia—to agree to international controls. However, to threaten another nation with war ran counter to American principles; besides, American scientists and engineers were confident that Russia was so

An atomic power station at Novo-Voronezh, U.S.S.R. (UPI PHOTO FROM SOVIET NEWS AGENCY TASS)

backward that it would take it many years to solve the technical problems of making atomic weapons.

The first international conference on the control of atomic energy took place early in November, 1945, in Washington among President Truman, Prime Minister Attlee of Great Britain, and Prime Minister King of Canada. At the end of the conference the three leaders agreed to an exchange of scientific information about atomic energy, but they also agreed that the United States should not disclose basic information for the application of atomic energy until adequate international controls had been established. They called for the creation of a commission by the United Nations to prepare proposals for the international control of atomic weapons and the development of peaceful uses of atomic energy.

At a conference of the foreign ministers of the United States, Great Britain, and Russia in Moscow in December, 1945, the three powers agreed to the creation of an Atomic Energy Commission by the United Nations. The next month, when the United Nations General Assembly held its first meeting in London, the UN Atomic Energy Commission was established on January 24, 1946. After lengthy hearings, this commission issued a report in December, 1946, which called for the establishment of an international control agency with the power to manage any atomic installations that might be dangerous to world peace and to be able to make inspections in any country to insure that atomic weapons were not being created.

Russia refused to accept the report of the UN Atomic Energy Commission. Instead the communist leaders demanded that as a first step atomic bombs should be outlawed and the United States should destroy its stockpile of the weapons. After that had been accomplished, said the Russians, they would then discuss the idea of international inspections. Of course, the United States would not agree to such a suggestion.

The atomic armaments race began in earnest after President Truman announced on September 23, 1949, that Russia had recently exploded its first atomic bomb. The United States immediately went to work on the problems of building a much larger hydrogen bomb, and on November 1, 1952, successfully tested an H-bomb at Eniwetok atoll in the Pacific Ocean. This bomb registered an explosive force of 14 megatons—the equivalent of 14 million tons of TNT, 700 times more powerful than the bombs dropped on Japan seven years earlier.

The "Davy Crockett" nuclear weapons system, portable by jeep, and giving small units a volume of firepower obtained previously only from massed heavy artillery. (UPI PHOTO)

Meanwhile, Great Britain had joined the atomic armaments race, exploding its first atomic bomb on October 3, 1952. The next year, Russia exploded its first hydrogen bomb on August 13, 1953. Again Great Britain caught up by exploding its first hydrogen bomb on May 15, 1957.

As each of the atomic powers exploded dozens of nuclear weapons in their testing programs, the level of radiation in the atmosphere began to rise. Both scientists and the general public began to be more and more concerned that the fallout of radioactive materials from the air would begin to affect the health of all the people of the world. Then, in 1958 the United States, Russia, and Great Britain agreed informally to suspend the testing of nuclear weapons in the atmosphere while a formal treaty to that effect was being written. But in the months and years that followed, Russia dragged its feet in the negotiations concerned with the exact wording of such a treaty.

France, which had not agreed to the moratorium on atomic bomb tests, joined the nuclear armaments race with the explosion of its first A-bomb in the Sahara desert in Algeria, on February 13, 1960.

Without warning on September 1, 1961, Russia broke the ban on atomic bomb tests with a series of explosions. Five days later President Kennedy announced that the United States, too, would resume testing. On October 30, 1961, Russia exploded the most powerful nuclear device tested to date, causing an explosion equivalent to nearly 60 million tons of TNT, or about 3,000 times more powerful than the bomb that destroyed Hiroshima.

Then in 1963 the world's hopes brightened when the United States, Russia, and Great Britain announced that they had signed a treaty banning the testing of atomic weapons in the air, underwater, or in space. The treaty was quickly ratified and became effective on October 10, 1963, ending the threat to mankind's health of nuclear pollution of the air. Dozens of other nations subscribed to the treaty, but France refused to do so, preferring to continue testing its new atomic arsenal.

The Nuclear Test Ban Treaty

—became effective October 10, 1963

The Governments of the United States of America, the United Kingdom of Great Britain and Northern Ireland, and the Union of Soviet Socialist Republics, hereinafter referred to as the "Original Parties,"

Proclaiming as their principal aim the speediest possible achievement of an agreement on general and complete disarmament under strict international control in accordance with the objectives of the United Nations which would put an end to the armaments race and eliminate the incentive to the production and testing of all kinds of weapons, including nuclear weapons,

Seeking to achieve the discontinuance of all test explosions of nuclear weapons for all time, determined to continue negotiations to this end, and desiring to put an end to the contamination of man's environment by radioactive substances,

Have agreed as follows:

ARTICLE I

1. Each of the Parties to this Treaty undertakes to prohibit, to prevent, and not to carry out any nuclear weapon test explosion, or any other nuclear explosion, at any place under its jurisdiction or control:

(a) in the atmosphere; beyond its limits, including outer space; or underwater, including territorial waters or high seas; or

(b) in any other environment if such explosion causes radioactive debris to be present outside the territorial limits of the State under whose jurisdiction or control such explosion is conducted. It is understood in this connection that the provisions of this subparagraph are without prejudice to the conclusion of a treaty resulting in the permanent banning of all nuclear test explosions, including all such explosions underground, the conclusion of which, as the Parties have stated in the Preamble to this Treaty, they seek to achieve.

2. Each of the Parties to this Treaty undertakes furthermore to refrain from causing, encouraging, or in any way participating in, the carrying out of any nuclear weapon test explosion, or any other nuclear explosion, anywhere which would take place in any of the environments described, or have the effect referred to, in paragraph 1 of this Article.

ARTICLE II

1. Any Party may propose amendments to this Treaty. The text of any proposed amendment shall be submitted to the Depositary Governments which shall circulate it to all Parties

In Moscow in the summer of 1963, the Nuclear Test Ban Treaty was signed by U.S. Secretary of State Dean Rusk (left), Soviet Foreign Minister Andrei Gromyko (center), and British Foreign Secretary, Lord Home (right). Standing just behind Gromyko, from left to right, are Senator Hubert Humphrey; U.S. Ambassador to the UN, Adlai Stevenson; UN Secretary-General U Thant; and Soviet Premier Nikita Khrushchev. (UPI PHOTO)

to this Treaty. Thereafter, if requested to do so by one-third or more of the Parties, the Depositary Governments shall convene a conference, to which they shall invite all the Parties, to consider such amendment.

2. Any amendment to this Treaty must be approved by a majority of the votes of all the Parties to this Treaty, including the votes of all of the Original Parties. The amendment shall enter into force for all Parties upon the deposit of instruments of ratification by a majority of all the Parties, including the instruments of ratification of all of the Original Parties.

ARTICLE III

1. This Treaty shall be open to all States for signature. Any State which does not sign this Treaty before its entry into force in accordance with paragraph 3 of this Article may accede to it at any time.

2. This Treaty shall be subject to ratification by signatory States. Instruments of ratification and instruments of accession shall be deposited with the Governments of the Original Parties—the United States of America, the United Kingdom of Great Britain and Northern Ireland, and the Union of Soviet Socialist

The graphs at which the Reverend J. Joseph Lynch, director of Fordham University's Seismic Observatory, is pointing indicated the explosion of Communist China's first atom bomb in 1964. (UPI PHOTO)

Republics—which are hereby designated the Depositary Governments.

3. This Treaty shall enter into force after its ratification by all the Original Parties and the deposit of their instruments of ratification.

4. For States whose instruments of ratification or accession are deposited subsequent to the entry into force of this Treaty, it shall enter into force on the date of the deposit of their instruments of ratification or accession.

5. The Depositary Government shall promptly inform all signatory and acceding States of the date of each signature, the date of deposit of each instrument of ratification of and accession to this Treaty, the date of its entry into force, and the date of receipt of any requests for conferences or other notices.

6. This Treaty shall be registered by the Depositary Governments pursuant to Article 102 of the Charter of the United Nations.

ARTICLE IV

This Treaty shall be of unlimited duration.

Each Party shall in exercising its national sovereignty have the right to withdraw from the Treaty if it decides that extraordinary events, related to the subject matter of this Treaty, have jeopardized the supreme interests of its country. It shall give notice of such withdrawal to all other Parties to the Treaty three months in advance.

ARTICLE V

This Treaty, of which the English and Russian texts are equally authentic, shall be deposited in the archives of the Depositary Governments. Duly certified copies of this Treaty shall be transmitted by the Depositary Governments to the Governments of the signatory and acceding States.

Communist China, which also had refused to sign the nuclear test ban treaty, became the fifth nation to join the atomic armaments race when it exploded its first atomic bomb on October 16, 1964, in a desert area near the Russian border. And on June 17, 1967, China exploded its first hydrogen bomb.

For twenty years Russian and American diplomats held discussions in an attempt to reach agreement on a treaty outlawing atomic weapons. Finally, on August 24, 1967, Russia and the United States made public the text of a draft treaty to prevent the further spread of nuclear weapons. Although the treaty left blank the critical article on inspections needed to enforce the agreement, world leaders hailed the treaty as the greatest step forward toward international control of atomic energy that had yet been made.

President Johnson said of the draft treaty:

"For more than 20 years, the world has watched with growing fear as nuclear weapons have spread. . . . Today, for the first time, we have within our reach an instrument which permits us to make a choice. . . . Failure to complete our work will be interpreted by our children and grandchildren as a betrayal of conscience, in a world that needs all of its resources and talents to serve life, not death."

Another important step toward the international control of nuclear weapons was taken in 1967 when both the United States and Russia ratified a treaty governing activities in space. The treaty prohibits the carrying of nuclear weapons into space beyond the earth's atmosphere. It is discussed more fully in the chapter "Space—Man's Greatest Adventure."

The Developing Uses of Atomic Energy

At the same time the devastating power of atomic energy revolutionized warfare, the statesmen of the world promised mankind that it also brought with it the ability to erase poverty and hunger and make the deserts bloom. Although the atomic armaments race took much greater precedence in the allocation of government budgets and scientific know-how, some progress was made toward peacetime uses of atomic energy.

Within a year after the first bomb had been dropped on Hiroshima, radioactive isotopes produced from the uranium piles of the A-bomb project began to be delivered to medical researchers. Although radioactive isotopes had been produced in tiny quantities by cyclotrons before the advent of the Era of Atomic Energy, they now began to be manufactured in great quantities. During the next two decades radioisotopes found many uses in medicine, industry, and scientific research—playing an important part in the detection and treatment of cancer and as tracers in various industrial and biological processes.

The first experimental production of electric power by using atomic energy took place in December, 1951, at Arco, Idaho, and four years later some electricity from this plant was switched into public power lines. However, the British moved ahead of the United States in the development of electricity from atomic power, opening the first large atomic power station for producing electricity in October, 1956, at Calder Hall in western England. The next year, the United States opened its first large nuclear plant for electric power at Shippingport, Pennsylvania, to supply some of the power needs of Pittsburgh. By 1967 Great Britain was producing about 7 percent of its electric power by the use of nuclear energy, while the United States was filling only about 1 percent of its electric power needs from nuclear plants. Many other countries around the world built relatively small-scale nuclear power plants, but two decades after the dawn of the Era of Atomic Energy a real solution for producing *low-cost* electric power by the use of atomic energy had not been achieved.

The United States Navy in a joint project with the Atomic Energy Commission took the lead in developing nuclear power plants for the propulsion of ships. In 1954 the atomic-powered submarine *Nautilus* was launched, and by the mid-1960's the U.S. Navy had about a hundred atomic warships, including cruisers and aircraft

Downtown Pittsburgh at night illuminated by electric power from the atomic plant at Shippingport, Pennsylvania—a glowing symbol of peacetime atomic power. (UPI PHOTO)

carriers as well as many submarines. Russia also developed nuclear-powered warships. On the other hand, because there was less urgency from a military standpoint, the use of atomic power for merchant ships evolved more slowly. The United States placed the first atomic-powered merchant ship, the *Savannah*, in service in 1962.

Although substantial amounts of money were spent endeavoring to build atomic engines for aircraft, no practical method was evolved to compensate for the heavy shielding needed to protect passengers and crew from the effects of radiation. However, in 1965, a 210-pound nuclear reactor called SNAP 10-A was successfully orbited in space as a source of auxiliary electric power in the Snapshot satellite. The device operated for 43 days in space before quitting. Similar small atomic power generators were planned as equipment for the first American astronauts to be sent to the moon.

Another application of atomic energy that was beginning to be used in many parts of the world by the mid-1960's was the irradiation of food by atomic energy. In this process food, such as fish or grain, is exposed to low radiation and as a result is preserved from spoiling without refrigeration.

Looking to the future, researchers hoped to develop practical atomic energy plants that could be used to remove salt from ocean water, thus providing a supply of fresh water for irrigating desert areas. But many scientists believed that widespread use of nuclear energy for extremely large-scale power projects depended on an ultimate discovery of some practical method of controlling the power of thermonuclear reaction as released by the hydrogen bomb.

At a research center in Trombay, India, a steel shell covers the Canada-India $20,000,000 reactor, for which Canada supplied equipment and foreign exchange. It is said by Indian experts to be one of the world's largest producers of radioisotopes. (UPI PHOTO)

Draft Treaty on Control of Atomic Weapons

—Issued by the United States and Russia at Geneva, Switzerland, August 24, 1967

The states concluding this treaty, hereinafter referred to as the "parties to the treaty,"

Considering the devastation that would be visited upon all mankind by a nuclear war and the consequent need to make every effort to avert the danger of such a war and to take measures to safeguard the security of peoples,

Believing that the proliferation of nuclear weapons would seriously enhance the danger of nuclear war,

In conformity with resolutions of the United Nations General Assembly calling for the conclusion of an agreement on the prevention of wider dissemination of nuclear weapons,

Undertaking to cooperate in facilitating the application of International Atomic Energy Agency safeguards on peaceful nuclear activities,

Expressing their support for research, development and other efforts to further the application, within the framework of the International Atomic Energy Agency safeguards system, of the principle of safeguarding effectively the flow of source and special fissionable materials by use of instruments and other techniques at certain strategic points,

Affirming the principle that the benefits of peaceful applications of nuclear technology, including any technological by-products which may be derived by nuclear-weapon states from the development of nuclear-explosive devices, should be available for peaceful purposes to all parties to the treaty, whether nuclear-weapon or nonnuclear-weapon states,

Convinced that in furtherance of this principle, all parties to this treaty are entitled to participate in the fullest possible exchange of scientific information for, and to contribute, alone or in cooperation with other states, to the further development of the applications of atomic energy for peaceful purposes,

Declaring their intention that potential benefits from any peaceful applications of nuclear explosions should be available through appropriate international procedures to nonnuclear-weapon states party to this treaty on a nondiscriminatory basis and that the charge to such parties for the explosive devices used should be as low as possible and exclude any charge for research and development,

Declaring their intention to achieve at the earliest possible date the cessation of the nuclear arms race,

Urging the cooperation of all states in the attainment of this objective,

Desiring to further the easing of international tension and the strengthening of trust between states in order to facilitate the cessation of the manufacture of nuclear weapons, the liquidation of all their existing stockpiles, and the elimination from national arsenals of nuclear weapons and the means of their delivery pursuant to a Treaty on General and Complete Disarmament under strict and effective international control,

Noting that nothing in this treaty affects the right of any group of states to conclude regional treaties in order to assure the total absence of nuclear weapons in their respective territories,

Have agreed as follows:

ARTICLE I

Each nuclear-weapon state party to this treaty undertakes not to transfer to any recipient whatsoever nuclear weapons or other nuclear explosive devices or control over such weapons or explosive devices directly, or indirectly; and not in any way to assist, encourage, or induce any nonnuclear-weapon state to manufacture or otherwise acquire nuclear weapons or other nuclear explosive devices, or control over such weapons or explosive devices.

ARTICLE II

Each nonnuclear-weapon state party to this treaty undertakes not to receive the transfer from any transferor whatsoever of nuclear weapons or other nuclear explosive devices or of control over such weapons or explosive devices directly, or indirectly; not to manufacture or otherwise acquire nuclear weapons or other nuclear explosive devices; and not to seek or receive any assistance in the manufacture of

The 11th Airborne Division troops watch an atomic explosion at close range at the Atomic Energy Commission's testing grounds in the desert. (UPI PHOTO)

nuclear weapons or other nuclear explosive devices.

ARTICLE III

(This article was left blank in the draft treaty because Russia and the United States had not reached complete agreement on the wording to be used concerning international inspection and control for enforcement of the treaty.)

ARTICLE IV

Nothing in this treaty shall be interpreted as affecting the inalienable right of all the parties to the treaty to develop research, production and use of nuclear energy for peaceful purposes without discrimination and in conformity with Article I and II of this treaty, as well as the right of the parties to participate in the fullest possible exchange of information for, and to contribute alone or in cooperation with other states to, the further development of the applications of nuclear energy for peaceful purposes.

ARTICLE V

1. Any party to this treaty may propose amendments to this treaty. The text of any proposed amendment shall be submitted to the depositary government which shall circulate it to all parties to the treaty. Thereupon, if requested to do so by one-third or more of the parties to the treaty, the depositary governments shall convene a conference, to which they shall invite all the parties to the treaty, to consider such an amendment.

2. Any amendment to this treaty must be approved by a majority of the votes of all the parties to the treaty, including the votes of all nuclear-weapon states party to this treaty and all other parties which, on the date the amendment is circulated, are members of the Board of Governors of the International Atomic Energy Agency. The amendment shall enter into force for all parties upon the deposit of instruments of ratification by a majority of all the parties, including the instruments of ratification of all nuclear-weapon states party to this treaty and all other parties which, on the date the amendment is circulated, are members of the Board of Governors of the International Atomic Energy Agency.

3. Five years after the entry into force of this treaty, a conference of parties to the treaty shall be held in Geneva, Switzerland, in order to review the operation of this treaty with a view to assuring that the purposes and provisions of the treaty are being realized.

ARTICLE VI

1. This treaty shall be open to all states for signature. Any state which does not sign the treaty before its entry into force in accordance with Paragraph 3 of this article may accede to it at any time.

2. This treaty shall be subject to ratification by signatory states. Instruments of ratification and instruments of accession shall be deposited with the Governments of. . . . ., which are hereby designated the depositary governments.

3. This treaty shall enter into force after its ratification by all nuclear-weapon states signatory to this treaty, and. . . . . other states signatory to this treaty, and the deposit of their instruments of ratification. For the purposes of this treaty, a nuclear-weapon state is one which has manufactured and exploded a nuclear weapon or other nuclear explosive device prior to January 1, 1967.

The first privately financed nuclear power station, Commonwealth Edison's Dresden Station, located near Joliet, Illinois, at the time of dedication, October 12, 1960. (UPI PHOTO)

4. For states whose instruments of ratification or accession are deposited subsequent to the entry into force of this treaty, it shall enter into force on the date of the deposit of their instruments of ratification or accession.

5. The depositary governments shall promptly inform all signatory and acceding states of the date of each signature, the date of deposit of each instrument of ratification or of accession, the date of the entry into force of this treaty, and the date of receipt of any requests for convening a conference or other notices.

6. This treaty shall be registered by the depositary governments pursuant to Article 102 of the Charter of the United Nations.

ARTICLE VII

This treaty shall be of unlimited duration.

Each party shall in exercising its national sovereignty have the right to withdraw from the treaty if it decides that extraordinary events, related to the subject matter of this treaty, have jeopardized the supreme interests of its country. It shall give notice of such withdrawal to all other parties to the treaty and to the United Nations Security Council three months in advance. Such notice shall include a statement of the extraordinary events it regards as having jeopardized its supreme interests.

ARTICLE VIII

This treaty, the English, Russian, French, Spanish and Chinese texts of which are equally authentic, shall be deposited in the archives of the depositary governments. Duly certified copies of this treaty shall be transmitted by the depositary governments to the governments of the signatory and acceding states.

In witness whereof the undersigned, duly authorized, have signed this treaty.

A historic view of the housing, at Idaho Falls, Idaho, for the prototype nuclear reactors for the atomic engines which power the Navy's first atomic surface ships—the guided missile cruiser Long Beach and the aircraft carrier Enterprise. (UPI PHOTO)

NATIONAL and CIVIL DEFENSE

Shocked by the realization in 1949 that Russia possessed the atomic bomb, the people of the United States suddenly became aware that a city such as New York or Chicago could suffer greater bomb damage in a few minutes than London or Berlin had experienced in all of World War II. To meet the public demands that something be done to protect the civilian population, Congress soon passed the Federal Civil Defense Act of 1950 to provide federal funds and guidance to states and local governments.

During the early 1950's white-helmeted civil defense teams were set up in every community. School children were taught to huddle under their desks in the event of an air raid alarm and cautioned not to look up if a bomb went off because to look at an A-bomb blast could cause blindness. Air raid shelters were marked in the basements of buildings, and some well-to-do homeowners built bomb shelters of their own. Air raid drills were carried out in many communities with the population being timed to see how quickly they could get to designated shelters. And the civil defense organizations prepared lists of emergency supplies that every homeowner should keep on hand. In all, more than half a billion dollars was spent in civil defense preparations in the 1950's.

After Russia exploded its first hydrogen bomb in 1953, it became apparent that much of the earlier preparation for civil defense had been futile, because now one or two bombs could completely destroy any large city and its suburbs, killing all or most of its people. Feeling that there was no place to run in the event of an H-bomb attack, the public became apathetic about civil defense.

Then on July 25, 1961, a few days after the federal civil defense organization had been transferred to the responsibility of the Department of Defense, President Kennedy in a nationwide television address said he was asking Congress for more than $200 million to survey factory and office buildings for the use of shelters and to develop new types of radiation detectors that would warn homeowners of dangerous radiation fallouts. He called for a civil defense program that would ". . . let every citizen know what steps he can take . . . to protect *his family* in case of attack."

Because at the time of President Kennedy's remarks the Cold War had reached one of its various crises over Berlin, many people interpreted the President's talk as a warning that atomic war might be fast approaching. Many families again began building fallout shelters and stocking emergency food and water supplies. When Russia exploded the largest H-bomb so far in history at the end of October, 1961, the drive by homeowners for fallout shelters was heightened. Public debates arose over the question of whether a man would be justified in barring his neighbors who had not built shelters from entering his own shelter that had only been stocked with enough supplies for his own family. Groups formed that ran newspaper advertisements denouncing the building of private fallout shelters as a trick to delude the public into accepting the inevitability of atomic war.

The fallout shelter building fever subsided by mid-1962, partly because Congress drastically cut President Kennedy's civil defense budget requests by nearly 80 percent. Businesses that had been formed to sell pre-fabricated home fallout shelters went bankrupt. Although about $100 million a year continued to be spent by the federal government for civil defense, most Americans lost interest in the program, relying on the world's statesmen to find some way to prevent the outbreak of total war.

Unification of the Military Services

Within a week after Japan had surrendered, President Truman recommended that the army and navy begin studying the possibility of reorganizing the postwar structure of the military

Russia's nuclear-powered icebreaker "Lenin" operating in the ice of the Baltic Sea. (UPI PHOTO)

services. Truman had long felt that the separation of the army and the navy into separate departments resulted in great inefficiencies and needless duplication of expenditures. In September, 1945, an army committee recommended that the army and navy should be combined into a single department. But when the plan came before the joint chiefs of staff the navy admirals vehemently opposed the idea of unification. In October the Senate's committee on military affairs began hearings on legislation for military unification.

In December, 1945, President Truman sent a message to Congress outlining a plan that called for creation of a single Department of Defense with three branches for the army, navy, and air force. He also called for a chief of staff to head the three services.

Throughout 1946 the question of military unification was a matter of public debate with army generals speaking out for the plan and navy admirals opposing it. Finally, in January, 1947, the secretaries of the army and navy submitted to Truman a compromise unification plan that preserved the marine corps as part of the navy. The President submitted new unification legislation to Congress, and in July, the National Security Act of 1947 was passed by Congress and signed into law.

In September, James V. Forrestal, formerly Secretary of the Navy, was sworn into office as the nation's first Secretary of Defense. For the next year and a half Forrestal worked tirelessly to coordinate the armed forces, preparing for a war that he feared was inevitable with Russia. Resigning in March, 1949, because his overwork had affected his health, Forrestal killed himself three months later by jumping from the window of his room in a naval hospital.

Before 1949 was out the controversy between the admirals and the generals once more was made a matter of public debate when the new Secretary of Defense, Louis A. Johnson, stopped construction on a new super aircraft carrier that the navy wanted. The admirals protested that the navy was not being given its fair share under the new unified defense establishment, and Secretary

In the Exhibition Hall of the National Archives, Washington, D. C. a guard keeps constant watch while visitors view the Constitution and the Declaration of Independence. Sealed in bronze and glass cases filled with helium and screened from harmful rays of light by special filters, the precious parchments can be lowered at a moment's notice into a large fireproof and shockproof safe. Many other historical documents are stored in this same building. (UPI PHOTO)

The crowd of civil-rights marchers, estimated at 200,000, gathered before the Lincoln Memorial in Washington, D. C., August 28, 1963. (UPI PHOTO)

of the Navy John L. Sullivan resigned as a protest. President Truman rebuffed the admirals by removing the navy's chief of naval operations, Louis E. Denfeld. But the prestige of the unified Department of Defense was not fully established until 1950 to 1951, during the Korean War, when President Truman appointed as Secretary of Defense George C. Marshall, who had been the army's chief of staff during World War II and later had served as Truman's Secretary of State from 1947 to 1949.

Universal Military Training and the Draft

Although Truman was successful in bringing the military services together under a Department of Defense, he met defeat on a second measure that he believed was of equal importance to the long-term security of the United States—a system of Universal Military Training in which all young men would receive training in the armed services to provide a huge reserve force for national emergencies. President Truman proposed such a program to Congress late in 1945, but received little support because at that time most Americans only were interested in getting their sons and husbands out of the army or navy.

During 1946 there was considerable pressure on Congress to end the selective service system and the draft—to let the armed forces go back to depending on volunteers to fill their ranks. Congress extended the selective service system to March 31, 1947, and then allowed it to expire, ending the draft that had inducted millions of young men into the services during World War II.

An American artillery team pouring 105 mm. fire into the South Korean hills, which greatly hampered the Red drive on the city of Taegu in 1950. (ACME PHOTO BY STAFF CORRESPONDENT NORMAN WILLIAMS)

President Truman appointed an advisory committee under the chairmanship of Dr. Karl T. Compton, president of the Massachusetts Institute of Technology, to study Universal Military Training. This committee reported in June, 1947, that it favored a system that would give at least six months' training to every man in the United States. But opponents of UMT claimed that it would turn the United States into a military nation, and Congress failed to act on the recommendation.

U.S. troops crossing a floating bridge spanning the Han River, as UN forces abandoned Seoul, Korea, to the Communists. (UPI PHOTO)

U.S. Marines retreating from Changjin Reservoir the winter of 1950. (UPI PHOTO)

As the Cold War heated up in 1948 with the Russian blockade of Berlin, Congress reinstituted the draft with a selective service act that made 19- to 25-year-olds eligible for 21 months of military service. However, reduced military appropriations resulted in only about 30,000 men being called up under this act prior to the outbreak of the Korean War in 1950.

In June, 1951, Congress passed and President Truman signed a new Universal Military Training and Service Act that lowered the draft age to 18½ and reduced physical and mental standards to widen the pool of men eligible for military service. Although the law carried "Universal Military Training" in its title, it was in effect merely a continuation of the earlier selective service laws and did not provide for training all men nor obligate those who were trained to long service in the military reserve. Because the United States had not adopted a system of UMT, hundreds of thousands of World War II veterans had to be called to duty in the Korean War. Less than a third of the 3½ million men who served in the Korean War were drafted by selective service.

In the 1960's the selective service draft continued to operate with little change. As the buildup of the armed forces for the Vietnam War continued, mental standards for inductees again were lowered in 1966 by executive order. Opponents of the Vietnam War criticized the selective service system as being undemocratic because its student deferments tended to increase the proportion of draftees who were high school drop-outs, including a large percentage of Negroes, while not drafting college students who were in good standing in their classes. At demonstrations opposing the selective service system, some college students in the 1960's burned their draft cards. This led Congress to make draft-card burning a crime, resulting in some students being sent to prison.

The Atlas-Centaur space vehicle, poised on launch complex, undergoing one of the numerous preflight tests at Cape Kennedy, Florida. (UPI PHOTO)

Guided Missiles

Of almost equal importance to the atomic bomb in its effect on national defense, the development of guided missiles as a means of carrying the atomic weapons radically changed military planning.

Nine months before the end of World War II in Europe, German engineers under the direction of Wernher von Braun perfected the rocket-propelled V-2 guided missile. These huge rockets could carry a ton of conventional explosives about 200 miles. Because they flew faster than the speed of sound, they plunged noiselessly into their targets before exploding.

Although Germany developed the V-2 too late to win World War II, military authorities realized that such rockets carrying atomic warheads would be formidable weapons in any future total war. Von Braun was brought to the United States to aid in the production of rockets and guided missiles for the U.S. army, and other German engineers were taken to Russia to help that country design similar weapons.

By the early 1950's several types of operational guided missiles had been developed by the United States military services, but at that time all details were kept secret. In those years manned bombers were the only method of delivering the atomic bomb to a target, so the defense systems were geared to detect and destroy enemy bombers.

But a dozen years later, by the mid-1960's, both the United States and Russia had successfully developed a huge arsenal of guided missiles of various sizes and for various purposes. The most frightening of these missiles were the huge Intercontinental Ballistic Missiles (ICBMs) that could travel 6,000 to 7,000 miles to a target in two hours or less. There were also air-to-air missiles launched by airplanes to shoot down enemy aircraft, ground-to-ground missiles used as anti-aircraft weapons, air-to-ground missiles used by aircraft against ground targets, and ground-to-ground missiles to attack enemy targets at a distance. In addition anti-missiles and anti-anti-missiles were developed as counteroffensive weapons. By 1966 the United States had about 60 different kinds of missiles in development, production, and operation.

One of the most effective missiles developed by the United States was the Polaris, first tested in 1960. The Polaris could be launched from a submerged submarine to carry an atomic warhead to a target 2,500 miles away. More than 40 American submarines were built in the next several years that could carry these missiles and fire them from underwater. Deployed in various parts of the world, these Polaris submarines provided missile launching platforms that an enemy could not possibly hope to find and destroy if he were inclined to order a surprise attack against the United States.

The United States also built and installed about 800 Minuteman ICBMs in underground launching sites throughout the United States. Again, it was believed that an enemy could not conceive of knocking out all these installations in a single surprise attack, thus leaving himself open to a devastating counterattack that would insure that neither side could "win" a total atomic war.

By the mid-1960's the Air Defense Command of the U.S. Air Force had developed a worldwide network of radar and computer stations that could keep track of all objects in space and in the air to insure that an enemy could not attack the United States without warning. The Air Defense Command established its headquarters inside a mountain near Colorado Springs, Colorado, to protect itself from possible attack.

In November, 1966, Secretary of Defense Robert McNamara announced that Russia was beginning to install a large anti-missile system to defend its major cities. Congress began exerting pressure on the United States to set up a similar system of Nike-X anti-missiles even though this installation might cost as much as $50 billion to complete.

A U.S. Air Force HH-53B helicopter refuels in flight from HC-310P tanker plane, a technique permitting unlimited range for aircraft. (UPI PHOTO)

SPIES and EXTREMISM

Former Under Secretary of State Sumner Welles (center) is shown in 1948 telling the House Committee on Un-American Activities that disclosure of documents involved in the Hiss-Chambers case might enable other nations to break the secret code of the U.S. State Department. (UPI PHOTO)

Fear of a surprise atomic bomb attack and the repeated crises of the Cold War brought a suspicion of Russia, of communist spying, and of communist subversion that sometimes reached the point of public hysteria. Nor were the suspicions unjustified. Throughout the two decades communist spy plots were uncovered and the spies sent to jail or deported to Russia. But the anticommunist hysteria was inflamed by political demagogues who used it to attack honest Americans who disagreed with their policies, and it spawned "hate" organizations which spread undemocratic ideas under the patriotic banner of anticommunism.

The CIA

As one of the world's two super powers, the United States found it necessary to build a worldwide spy network of its own to keep informed of what the communists were planning and plotting in various areas. President Truman created a

Central Intelligence Group by an executive order on January 20, 1946, with the purpose of bringing together the various intelligence or spy activities of the military services and the state and justice departments. In 1947, when the National Security Council was created, the spy organization was renamed the Central Intelligence Agency (CIA), and it was made responsible to the National Security Council.

Because the work of the CIA must be secret to be effective little information about CIA activities is disclosed to the public. From time to time the CIA has been said to have been responsible for the overthrow of governments unfriendly to the United States and for the bribery of officials of other governments. Even the budgets of the CIA are not made public, with funds being hidden as appropriations for innocent activities. In the late 1960's it was disclosed that for nearly two decades the CIA had financed the expenses of delegates by student and labor organizations to international conferences to insure that the American viewpoint would be expressed at communist-dominated gatherings.

Many persons have expressed disapproval of the CIA and its activities, fearing that it is becoming a secret police organization of the sort used by totalitarian states. But it has been defended as a necessary evil in a world in which the very survival of the United States depends upon gathering information by any means possible of the plans and actions of its enemies.

The Communist Party in the United States

The communist party in the United States always had represented only a tiny minority of the people. But during World War II it had changed its policies so consistently to match those of the Soviet Union that even intellectuals who believed in the communist theory of the government providing the individual's needs regardless of his productivity had realized that the communist party of the United States was primarily a propaganda organ of Russia.

In 1947 figures published in Russia showed the claimed membership of the communist party of the United States was 74,000. The previous year, on January 14, 1946, the communists had expelled Earl Browder, the former leader of the American communist party, on charges of "betraying the principles of Marxism-Leninism."

On July 20, 1948, the 12 top communists in the United States were indicted by a federal grand jury on the charges of teaching and advocating the overthrow of the government of the United States. William Z. Foster, who had succeeded Browder as secretary of the party, was excused from the subsequent trial because of ill health. But the eleven others were tried in a nine-month trial that lasted from January 17 to October 14, 1949. Ten were sentenced to five years in prison and one to three years. All received fines of $10,000 each. The convictions were made under the Alien Registration Act of 1940. Although the convictions were appealed, they were upheld by the Supreme Court.

In 1954 Congress passed the Communist Control Act which outlawed the communist party and required its members to register as foreign agents. Communist-controlled labor unions were deprived of all privileges of collective bargaining. During the next decade the communist party had little influence in the United States and its membership steadily declined.

The first national convention of the communist party of the United States since the 1950's was held in New York City in 1966. By this time the party claimed only 12,000 members, and many persons half-jokingly said that half of those claimed as members actually were FBI agents. In the late 1960's, the American communist party still closely followed Russian foreign policy, primarily opposing the United States' participation in the Vietnam War, but most Americans discounted it as a threat to their way of life.

Atomic-Bomb Spies

The greatest revulsion of Americans against the communist party came with the disclosure that members of the American communist party had been key figures in a spy ring that had turned over to Russia secrets of the atomic bomb.

Shortly before it was announced that Russia had exploded its first atomic bomb in 1949, the FBI had learned that A-bomb secrets had been stolen. The first arrest in the case came in February, 1950, by British officials who took into custody Dr. Klaus Fuchs, a German-born physicist who had worked on the atomic bomb project. Fuchs confessed taking part in a spy ring, leading to the arrest three months later of Harry Gold, a chemist in Philadelphia. The next month, on June 16, 1950, David Greenglass, who had been an army sergeant assigned to the atomic project at Los Alamos, New Mexico, was arrested. Greenglass, in turn, implicated his brother-in-law and sister, Julius and Ethel Rosenberg, as members of the American communist party who had persuaded him to turn over to them atomic secrets. Another member of the spy ring, Morton Sobell, fled to Mexico, but was extradited. The A-bomb secrets had been turned over to a Russian consular official in New York City, Anatoli Yakovlev, who had returned to Russia in December, 1946.

The American atomic spies were tried for espionage. Gold and Sobell each were sentenced to 30 years in prison. Greenglass became the state's chief witness against the Rosenbergs, and received a sentence of 15 years in prison. The Rosenbergs were sentenced to death in 1951, and, after many pleas to the Supreme Court and the President had been turned down, they were electrocuted on June 19, 1953.

Harry Gold (right), an admitted courier for a Soviet atomic spy ring, as he appeared before Senate Internal Security Subcommittee with (left to right) U.S. Marshal Joseph G. Oreto; David Greenglass, brother of Mrs. Rosenberg; and U.S. Marshal W. O. Collins, in April 1956. (UPI PHOTO)

Whittaker Chambers vs. Alger Hiss

Of equal public sensation to the trials of the communist party leaders and of the atomic-bomb spies was the case of Whittaker Chambers vs. Alger Hiss. In testimony before the House Committee on Un-American Activities in August, 1948, Whittaker Chambers, a senior editor for *Time* magazine, testified that he had once been part of a communist spy ring in Washington, D.C., and that one of the other members of the ring had been Alger Hiss, who had been acting secretary-general of the United Nations at its founding conference in San Francisco. At first Hiss testified that he could not remember having ever known Chambers. Later he admitted having known Chambers in 1935 by the name of George Crosley and that he had rented him an apartment. But Hiss denied he had ever been a communist or a member of a spy ring.

Some members of the House Committee on Un-American Activities favored dropping the matter, but Richard Nixon, then a Representative from California and a member of the committee, insisted on pursuing the case. Nixon, who later became Vice-President under Eisenhower, and an

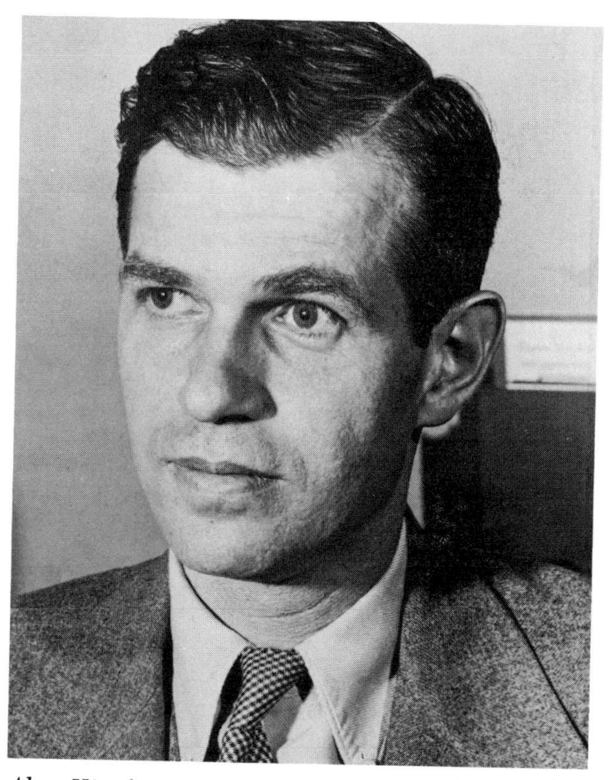

Alger Hiss, former official in the State Department, named by Whittaker Chambers as being a member of a Washington spy ring. (UPI PHOTO)

Whittaker Chambers after testifying before the Federal Grand Jury in New York in 1948 about the microfilms of state documents he had kept hidden in a hollowed-out pumpkin on his Maryland farm. (UPI PHOTO)

unsuccessful candidate for President against John Kennedy, believed Chambers and felt that the committee's investigation was demonstrating that many communists had infiltrated the government and influenced its policies. Moreover, Nixon felt that the "communists-in-government" issue would help defeat President Truman in the 1948 election.

Hiss, who had resigned from the government in 1946 to become president of the Carnegie Endowment for International Peace, challenged Chambers to repeat his charges when not under the cloak of Congressional immunity. When Chambers accepted the challenge, Hiss brought suit for libel.

In December, 1948, the Congressional committee released testimony by Chambers that Hiss had supplied the communist spy ring with secret state department documents. To substantiate his charges, Chambers took the Congressional investigators to his farm in Maryland where he dramatically produced microfilms of the documents from a pumpkin where he had concealed them. On December 15, a federal grand jury indicted Hiss for perjury for denying Chambers' accusations.

Hiss was first brought to trial in 1949, but the jury was unable to agree on a verdict. At his second trial he was found guilty on January 21, 1950, and was sentenced to five years in prison. Hiss continued to deny his guilt, and after he had served his sentence wrote a book defending himself.

The House Committee on Un-American Activities made public in 1948 testimony in which Whittaker Chambers, former Communist agent, accused Alger Hiss of securing important U.S. Government documents, which were turned over to a Russian agent. Richard Nixon (center) is speaking. (UPI PHOTO)

The committee room as Senator Joseph McCarthy questioned Senator Arthur Watkins of Utah (right, with back to camera), chairman of the special Senate committee that recommended censure of McCarthy. (UPI PHOTO)

McCarthyism

At the time Alger Hiss was sentenced to prison, Joseph McCarthy was a little-known Republican Senator from Wisconsin who faced the difficult task of getting re-elected in 1952. But he had decided to make himself prominent on the issue of "communists-in-government." Accordingly, on February 9, 1950, in a speech in Wheeling, West Virginia, he said:

"While I cannot take the time to name all of the men in the State Department who have been named as members of the Communist Party and members of a spy ring, I have here in my hand a list of 205 that were known to the Secretary of State as being members of the Communist Party and who nevertheless are still working and shaping the policy of the State Department."

In subsequent speeches within the next few days he changed the number of communists on his "list" from 205 to 57. Then on February 20 he

Senator Joseph McCarthy, seated, and Army Secretary Robert Stevens, leaving the committee table on his way to the witness stand. (UPI PHOTO)

Senator Joseph McCarthy at the witness table (lower left), as Senate hearings on charges of misconduct began against him. (UPI PHOTO)

spoke to the U.S. Senate for about six hours in a rambling discourse filled with double-talk. He did not produce the "list"—and never did in the following years in which he became the acknowledged leader of the radical anticommunist movement in the United States that became generally labeled as "McCarthyism."

A Senate subcommittee under Senator Millard Tydings of Maryland was set up to investigate McCarthy's charges. In the subsequent highly-publicized sessions of the Tydings committee, McCarthy began to name names of people he claimed were bad "security risks," but he was unable to produce enough evidence to bring any formal charges. In July the Tydings committee issued a report saying that McCarthy's claims had been a "fraud and hoax." In retaliation McCarthy worked hard to defeat Tydings in his campaign for re-election in 1950—a campaign in which thousands of circulars were distributed with a faked picture of Tydings and Earl Browder, former head of the communist party, carrying a caption claiming that Tydings was thanking Browder for testifying that some of the people McCarthy had accused really never had been communists. Tydings was defeated and McCarthyism continued to hold sway.

McCarthy called for the impeachment of President Truman and claimed that the United States had suffered "20 years of treason" under Presidents Roosevelt and Truman. He called Secretary of State Dean Acheson a friend of communism and demanded his resignation. And he called General George Marshall "an instrument of the Soviet conspiracy." Contributions rolled in to McCarthy from anti-communist admirers, and he used the money both for his investigations and his own expenses.

In the 1952 presidential election Dwight Eisenhower accepted McCarthy's support and toured Wisconsin with the anti-communist Senator. Later, McCarthy was to say that the United States had suffered "21 years of treason" under Roosevelt, Truman, *and Eisenhower*.

With Republican victory in the 1952 election, McCarthy became chairman of the Senate Committee on Government Operations. He then appointed himself chairman of the committee's investigative subcommittee, employed two young assistants, Roy Cohn and David Shine, and launched one investigation after another hunting for former communists. As well as exposing some communists and former communists, the McCarthy committee also besmirched the names of innocent persons whose names were added to "blacklists" that often frightened employers from hiring them.

McCarthyism reached its crescendo in 1954. McCarthy's subcommittee had been investigating the possibility that communists had infiltrated the U.S. Army. The army charged in turn that the McCarthy investigation merely was retaliation for the army having drafted Shine, and that McCarthy and Cohn were guilty of improper conduct in asking special favors for Shine.

Senate Resolution Condemning McCarthy

—approved 67 to 22 on December 2, 1954

Section 1: Resolved, that the Senator from Wisconsin, Mr. McCarthy, failed to cooperate with the Subcommittee on Privileges and Elections of the Senate Committee on Rules and Administration in clearing up matters referred to that subcommittee which concerned his conduct as a Senator, and affected the honor of the Senate and instead, repeatedly abused the members who were trying to carry out assigned duties, thereby obstructing the constitutional processes of the Senate, and that the conduct of the Senator from Wisconsin, Mr. McCarthy, is contrary to Senatorial traditions and is hereby condemned.

Section 2. The Senator from Wisconsin (Mr. McCarthy) in writing to the chairman of the Select Committee to study censure charges (Mr. Watkins) after the Select Committee had issued its report and before the report was presented to the Senate charging three members of the Select Committee with "deliberate deception" and "fraud" for failure to disqualify themselves; in stating to the press on November 4, 1954, that the special Senate session that was to begin November 8, 1954, was a "lynch party;" in repeatedly describing this special Senate session as a "lynch bee" in a nationwide television-radio show on November 7, 1954; in stating to the public press on November 13, 1954, that the chairman of the Select Committee (Mr. Watkins) was guilty of "the most unusual, the most cowardly thing I've ever heard of" and stating further: "I expected he would be afraid to answer the questions but didn't think he'd be stupid enough to make a public statement;" and in characterizing the said committee as the "unwitting handmaiden," "involuntary agent," and "attorneys in fact" of the Communist Party and in charging that the said committee in writing its report "imitated Communist methods—that it distorted, misrepresented, and omitted, in its effort to manufacture a plausible rationalization" in support of its recommendations to the Senate, which characterizations and charges were contained in a statement released to the press and inserted in the *Congressional Record* of November 10, 1954, acted contrary to Senatorial ethics and tended to bring the Senate into dishonor and disrepute, to obstruct the constitutional processes of the Senate, and to impair its dignity; and such conduct is hereby condemned.

With Senator Karl Mundt presiding, televised hearings were held in the spring of 1954, and for the first time the American people got a filling-look at the innuendo and demagoguery with which McCarthy flourished. The army appointed as its special counsel a Boston trial lawyer named Joseph L. Welch, whose courtesy and dry humor seemed to bring out the worst in McCarthy. The hearings were officially inconclusive (the mem-

Senator Joseph McCarthy scanning a presidential directive ordering government employees not to tell hearings investigators about conversations within the executive branch of government. (UPI PHOTO)

Republican candidate for President, Senator Barry Goldwater, flanked by avid supporters, as he arrived at a reception in San Francisco, July 13, 1964. (UPI PHOTO)

bers of the subcommittee eventually issuing four conflicting reports), but McCarthyism had been exposed for what it was.

In August, 1954, the Senate by a vote of 75 to 12 set up a special committee to consider charges that "the conduct of the Senator from Wisconsin, Mr. McCarthy, is unbecoming a member of the United States Senate, is contrary to Senatorial traditions, and tends to bring the Senate into disrepute." Lengthy hearings were held, and on December 2, 1954, the Senate by a vote of 67 to 22 condemned McCarthy. McCarthyism was dead, and McCarthy himself died three years later in 1957.

Many of McCarthy's followers tried to carry on in his footsteps, but none attained his renown. On December 9, 1958, a year and a half after McCarthy's death, Robert Welch, a retired candy manufacturer, founded the John Birch Society, an organization devoted to anticommunist activities. It carried on the McCarthy tradition with accusations that Presidents Roosevelt, Truman, and Eisenhower had acted as agents of communism. Further, the society called for the impeachment of Chief Justice Earl Warren. For a few years it gained many right-wing adherents. Its members adopted communist tactics to infiltrate civic bodies such as school boards to put across the society's views.

In the presidential election of 1964 the John Birch Society became a public issue. The national convention of the Democratic party condemned "extremist" groups of both the right and left, naming both the John Birch Society and the Communist party. But at the Republican national convention supporters of Senator Barry Goldwater, who was to win the GOP presidential nomination, voted down similar resolutions. In his acceptance speech to the convention, Goldwater stated "extremism in the defense of liberty is no vice," and "moderation in the pursuit of justice is no virtue." After Goldwater's defeat by President Johnson in the 1964 election, the John Birch Society slowly became less prominent in the news.

SPACE—MAN'S GREATEST ADVENTURE

The giant 363-foot Saturn V moon rocket with its three-man Apollo spacecraft being moved from the assembly plant to the launch pad at Cape Kennedy, Florida, prior to its successful launching and perfect orbital flight and splash-down in the Pacific ten miles from its target, November 9, 1967. (UPI PHOTO)

Men of many nations dreamed of traveling to the moon and to the other planets for hundreds of years before the dawn of the Space Age. Scores of science fiction tales about space exploration had been written by famous scientists and writers, including Johannes Kepler, Cyrano de Bergerac, Voltaire, Christian Huygens, Emanuel Swedenborg, Jules Verne, and H. G. Wells. Rockets, which were to provide the engines for space flight, had been invented and used for more than a thousand years. And the laws of motion that would determine the flight patterns of space vehicles had been known by physicists for hundreds of years.

Two scientists, the Russian Konstantin Tsiolkovsky and the American Robert Goddard, independently in the early 1900's developed the necessary scientific theories for the construction of practical space vehicles. Both said they were influenced by the science-fiction stories of Jules Verne.

In the 1920's and 1930's groups of space enthusiasts formed interplanetary societies to investigate the use of rockets for space travel.

These groups in the United States, Germany, Russia, France, and Great Britain began to receive some support from their governments which were interested in the development of military guided missiles. The most successful of the government-financed projects was that in Germany in which the V-2 guided missile was developed under the direction of Wernher von Braun.

Beginnings of the Space Age

Immediately after World War II the United States and Russia began intensive development of rocket programs for vehicles to be used as guided missiles. The United States brought Von Braun and dozens of other leading German rocket scientists and engineers to the United States, while Russia took others to work on its rockets. At first the United States military services concentrated on the development of relatively short-range rocket vehicles while the Russians began designing much larger rockets that could carry heavy loads for long distances.

The United States had captured a large number of unused German V-2 rockets, and these were brought to the United States for testing. On February 24, 1949, the United States launched its first rocket into space from White Sands Proving Ground in New Mexico. On this flight a Wac Corporal rocket was mounted on top of a V-2 and soared to a height of 244 miles.

On November 3, 1957, Russia launched Sputnik II, carrying the dog, Laika, the first animal to travel in space (UPI PHOTO)

On July 29, 1955, President Eisenhower announced that the United States planned as part of its contribution to the International Geophysical Year to launch "small unmanned earth-circling satellites." In order not to interfere with the development of military guided missiles by the army and the air force, the project was turned over to the navy. Work was begun to develop a three-stage rocket called Vanguard to be based on Viking rockets that had been built for high altitude research.

Then on October 4, 1957, Russia surprised the world by launching the first artificial satellite into orbit around the earth—Sputnik I. A month later, on November 3, 1957, the Russians sent a second satellite, Sputnik II, into orbit, this time carrying a dog called Laika, the first living thing to orbit the earth.

The Russian achievement caused consternation in the United States because the weight of the Sputnik satellites was much greater than anything the United States even planned to send into orbit. Obviously the Russians were much further ahead than the United States not only in the development of space vehicles but also in the building of military guided missiles. On top of this, the first American attempts in late 1957 and early 1958 to launch a satellite by means of the Vanguard rocket were failures.

In order to save face, the government authorized the army to send some satellites into orbit using ballistic missiles developed with the aid of Von Braun at the Redstone Arsenal in Huntsville, Alabama. Using a Jupiter C three-stage rocket topped by a fourth stage called Juno 1, the army successfully launched the first American earth-orbiting satellite, Explorer I, on January 31, 1958. About six weeks later the navy succeeded in launching its first successful satellite, Vanguard I, on March 17, 1958.

The First Men in Space

Russia and the United States now joined in a race to see which could first put a manned space

Ceremonies in Moscow, April 14, 1961, honoring Cosmonaut Yuri Gagarin, first man to orbit the earth. Shown from left to right are: K. E. Voroshilov, Yuri Gagarin, Soviet Premier Nikita Khrushchev, F. R. Kozlov and L. I. Brezhnev. (UPI PHOTO)

A summing up of Astronaut John Glenn's "Project Mercury" flight in Friendship 7. (NASA)

vehicle in orbit around the earth. The United States called its plans for manned space flight Project Mercury, and on April 9, 1959, announced the selection of the first seven astronauts to begin training as space pilots.

Again Russia beat the United States to the punch. The Russian cosmonaut Yuri Gagarin made a single orbit around the earth on April 12, 1961, that lasted 1 hour and 48 minutes. He flew in a 10,400-pound Vostok I space vehicle that was more than twice as large as the planned Mercury spacecraft.

Less than a month later, on May 5, the United States launched its first manned flight in a spacecraft. The 15-minute suborbital flight carried Astronaut Alan B. Shepard out over the Atlantic Ocean before he safely landed and was picked up at sea. To help buoy up lagging American spirits, President Kennedy in a message to Congress on May 25 declared that the United States intended to beat Russia in landing a man on the moon. He said, "Now is the time to take longer strides—time for a great new American enterprise—time for this nation to take a clearly leading role in space achievement, which in many ways may hold the key to our future on earth."

On July 21, 1961, the United States launched Astronaut Virgil I. Grissom on another 15 minute suborbital flight over the Atlantic Ocean.

But before the United States could get its first astronaut into orbit, Russia produced another space spectacular. This time Russian Cosmonaut Gherman S. Titov orbited the earth 17 times on August 6, 1961, staying aloft 25 hours and 11 minutes.

Finally, on February 20, 1962, the United States launched its first successful manned space flight in orbit. Astronaut John Glenn Jr. circled the earth three times in the space craft Friendship 7, staying aloft 4 hours and 55 minutes. Three months later, on May 24, 1962, American Astronaut M. Scott Carpenter duplicated Glenn's flight in the spacecraft Aurora 7.

In the years that followed both Russia and the United States sent many successful manned spacecraft into orbit around the earth. But in 1967 both countries suffered their first serious space accidents. Three American astronauts were killed when an electric spark ignited oxygen in the Apollo spacecraft they were testing on its launchpad. And that same year a Russian cosmonaut was killed when the parachute on his space vehicle became tangled during reentry into the earth's atmosphere.

Soviet Cosmonauts Pavel Popovich (left) and Andrian Nikolayev (center) at a reception given at the Kremlin in their honor August 18, 1962. Premier Khrushchev looks on. (TASS PHOTO FROM UPI RADIOTELEPHOTO)

A Marine helicopter recovers Freedom 7, the Mercury capsule carrying Alan Shepard, after the historic first manned U. S. space flight.

THE PICTORIAL RECORD of the AMERICAN SPACE EXPLORATIONS

Here, on this and succeeding pages, are the highlights of the step by step progress toward putting Americans on the moon, and possibly other celestial bodies, in the coming decades.

All photos by courtesy of National Aeronautics and Space Administration.

Alan Shepard, the first American in space, was launched in a Mercury capsule atop a Redstone rocket. (Left)

President Kennedy congratulates Astronaut Alan B. Shepard, Jr., first U. S. man in space, on his historic ride in the Freedom 7 spacecraft, May 5, 1961.

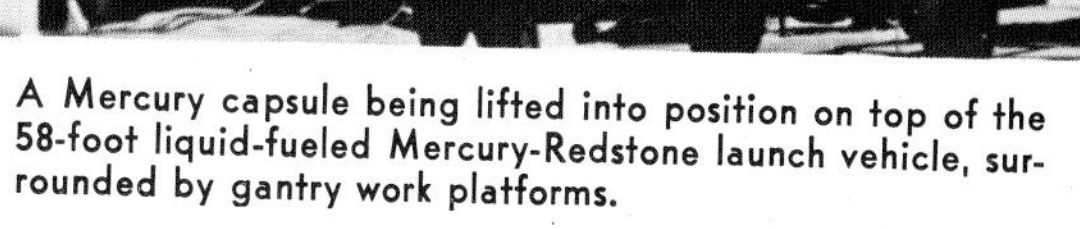

A Mercury capsule being lifted into position on top of the 58-foot liquid-fueled Mercury-Redstone launch vehicle, surrounded by gantry work platforms.

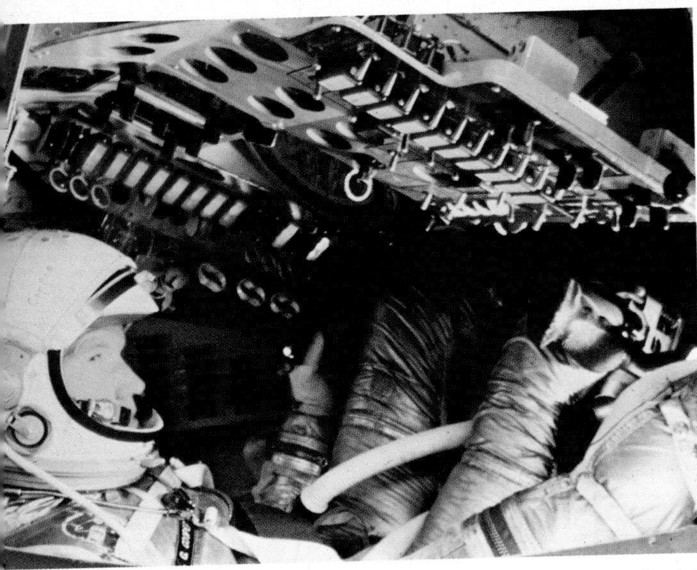

Astronaut L. Gordon Cooper checking out procedures prior to Faith 7 flight of 22 orbits May 15, 1963.

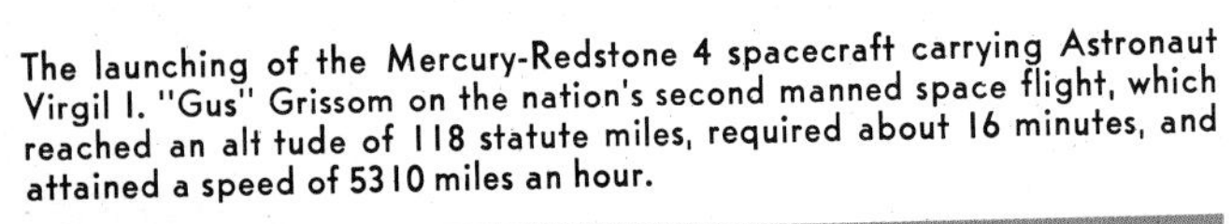

The launching of the Mercury-Redstone 4 spacecraft carrying Astronaut Virgil I. "Gus" Grissom on the nation's second manned space flight, which reached an alt tude of 118 statute miles, required about 16 minutes, and attained a speed of 5310 miles an hour.

One of the five Mercury-Atlas 5 flight animals (chimpanzee) poses in his netted flight suit with his technician handler. The flight couch at the bottom right is where the chimp was harnessed in a pressure-tight container with a window dome.

The X-15 number 2 showing its external flight tanks designed to carry 13,500 lbs. of propellant (anhydrous ammonia and liquid oxygen). The tanks, which are jettisoned at 69,000 feet and a speed of 1400 m.p.h., make it possible for the aircraft to attain a speed of about 5000 m.p.h. and an altitude of more than 50 miles.

Astronaut M. Scott Carpenter just after the recovery of Aurora 7 in the second three-orbit flight by an American on May 24, 1962.

Liftoff of Gemini 3, the first United States two-man spacecraft, March 23, 1965, carrying command pilot Virgil I. "Gus" Grissom and pilot John W. Young in a three-orbit flight.

Astronauts James A. McDivitt, command pilot, and Edward H. White II a few minutes after entering the Gemini 4 spacecraft June 3, 1965 for their 62-orbit flight.

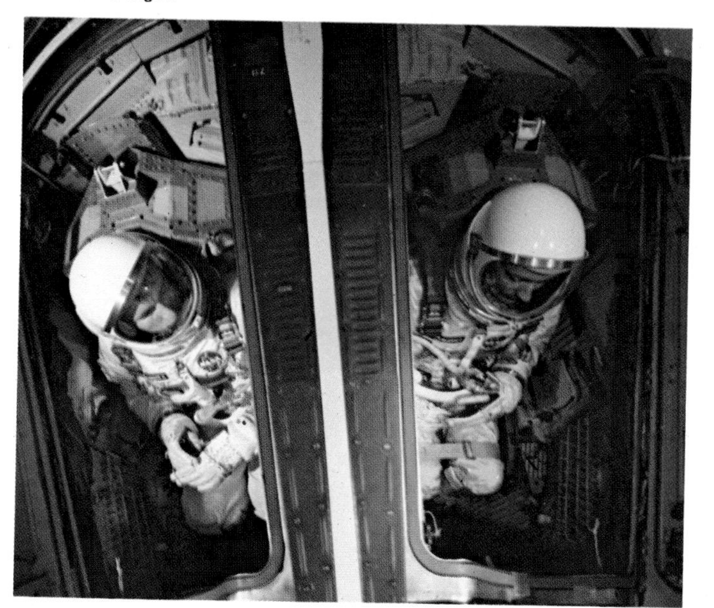

L. Gordon Cooper in Faith 7 as it swings under its 65-foot ringsail parachute before splashing down 7000 yards from the USS Kearsarge May 16, 1963, after a 22-orbit flight of 34 hours and 20 minutes.

The launch of Pegasus III, the final flight of the Saturn I launch vehicle prior to the development of Saturn I-B of the Apollo/Saturn series, which is directed at a successful manned landing on the moon.

Mercury spacecraft Faith 7 showing interior after Astronaut L. Gordon Cooper's successful 22-orbit mission.

Launch Complex 39 where Apollo/Saturn V vehicles will be prepared, transported to the firing site, and launched on their epochal journeys. The Apollo/Saturn V will be assembled within the VAB on a structure known as a Mobile Launcher and then transported to the launch site by a huge tracked vehicle known as the Crawler Transporter.

Frogmen recover Gemini 4 after its 62-orbit flight covering more than 1,600,000 miles.

Astronaut Edward H. White II performing his spectacular space feat during the third orbit of the Gemini 4, June 3, 1965 flight. This was the first American space walk, during which White remained outside the spacecraft for 21 minutes.

Photograph taken by Gemini 6 of spacecraft Gemini 7 during rendezvous and station keeping maneuvers at an altitude of approximately 160 miles on December 15, 1965, the first such rendezvous in history.

Gemini 5 astronauts Charles Conrad Jr. and L. Gordon Cooper Jr. aboard the USS Lake Champlain after splashdown August 29, 1965.

(above) The Augmented Target Docking Adapter with fiber glass cover still attached, as seen from Gemini 9 orbiting over the Caribbean Sea, with Caracas, Venezuela, below the cloud cover at the right.

(right) Gemini 9A, carrying Astronauts Thomas P. Stafford and Eugene A. Cernan, as it descended by parachute into the Atlantic Ocean 345 miles east of Cape Kennedy at 9 a.m. Eastern Standard Time, June 6, 1966.

(below) Astronauts Eugene A. Cernan and Thomas P. Stafford show their appreciation to crewmen aboard the aircraft carrier USS Wasp as they emerge from Gemini 9A at the completion of the seventh manned Gemini mission.

(below) A moon rock six inches high and eighteen inches long, photographed by Surveyor's television camera at a distance of about twelve feet above the center of the rock.

From a rescue helicopter a photographer catches the major elements in the recovery of Gemini 12 Astronauts James Lovell and Edwin Aldrin, November 15, 1966, in the Western Atlantic, more than 600 miles southeast of Cape Kennedy.

(left) India and Ceylon, with the Bay of Bengal to the right and the Arabian Sea to the left, as photographed from a distance of 540 nautical miles above the surface of the earth by the crew of Gemini 11, Astronauts Charles Conrad and Richard Gordon.

(left) Pilot Edwin Aldrin being hoisted aboard a helicopter following the 94½-hour orbital flight of Gemini 12, during which he conducted three extravehicular activities—two standups and one umbilical.

(below) Astronauts Edwin Aldrin and James Lovell after their flawless automatic reentry, as they arrive via helicopter on the USS Wasp for a "red carpet" welcome, greeting NASA officials and military personnel.

ABOVE: *Regulus I was launched at sea off Hawaii from the USS Halibut on April 4, 1960, marking the first firing of a missile from a nuclear-powered submarine. The total flight covered about 277 miles.* (UPI PHOTO)

RIGHT: *The launching of the "Lafayette," Polaris submarine, on May 8, 1962.* (UPI PHOTO)

BELOW: *The Navy's first nuclear-powered cruiser, the USS Long Beach.* (UPI PHOTO)

The historic meeting of the nuclear-powered submarines, USS Skate and USS Seadragon, at the North Pole after voyages under the polar ice pack, August 22, 1962. (UPI PHOTO)

Little America, Antarctica, during "Operation Deepfreeze" 1957–1958. (UPI PHOTO)

The Exploration and Use of Space

Public interest in the Space Age largely was captured by the various manned space flights because these were given complete coverage on television. Families watched breathlessly by their TV sets as the countdown progressed minute-by-minute and second-by-second to blastoff. Then messages from the astronauts were relayed to the waiting audience as the spacecrafts circled the earth. Finally, there was the tension of waiting for the reentry, which by 1966 was itself broadcast live over television. Afterwards there were motion pictures taken by the astronauts in space.

The drama of the manned flights overshadowed the importance of the hundreds of unmanned satellites and space probes that were launched in the first decade of the Space Age. Many of the satellites launched by Russia and the United States were clouded in secrecy because they were used for military experimentation and information. But others were of great significance to science and communication.

Explorer I, the first successful satellite launched by the United States in 1958, carried instruments that discovered the Van Allen radiation belts in space surrounding the earth. And the second U.S. satellite, Vanguard I, relayed back information that showed that the earth was not perfectly round but was slightly pear-shaped.

Beginning in 1960 a series of Tiros satellites was launched by the United States which relayed back thousands of pictures of the earth that were used to improve weather forecasting. Vastly improved weather satellites began to be orbited in 1966 by the Environmental Science Services Administration.

Also beginning in 1960 the United States sent into orbit a series of navigation satellites that carried the name Transit. These satellites were used to provide information to improve the navigation of spacecraft.

Another important use of satellites has been to improve communications. The Echo I satellite launched on August 12, 1960, was what was called a passive communications satellite because radio signals sent from the ground could be bounced off of it to distant locations. Telstar I orbited on July 10, 1962, made it possible to relay live television programs between the United States and Europe. By 1963 communications satellites were in use that permitted the broadcast of television between the United States and Japan. In 1962 Congress established the Communications Satellite Corporation (Comsat) as a profit-making corporation to control the future development of communications satellites. The corporation's first satellite, Early Bird, was sent into orbit on April 6, 1965. It flew in a nearly stationary position above the Atlantic Ocean to provide television, telephone, and telegraph relays between the United States and Europe.

India and Ceylon, with the Bay of Bengal to the right and the Arabian Sea to the left, as photographed by the crew of Gemini 11 Astronauts Charles Conrad and Richard Gordon. (NASA)

As the Space Age progressed more and more satellites were sent into orbit every year, to the point that it was almost impossible for the average person to keep track of the scores of different types. In 1966 alone more than 70 satellites were successfully launched.

Another important aspect of space exploration was the use of unmanned space vehicles to explore the moon, the sun, and other planets. Russia launched the first such space probe, Lunik I, on January 2, 1959. This spacecraft missed the moon, but became the first artificial satellite to go into orbit around the sun. Later the same year, Russia launched Lunik II, the first space probe to strike the moon. And on October 4, 1959, Russia's Lunik III was sent toward the moon, relaying back the first picture of the side of the moon hidden from the earth.

The United States experienced a series of failures with its early attempts to explore the moon, but on July 28, 1964, Ranger 7 was sent toward the moon and it successfully sent back more than 4,000 pictures of the moon's surface. In February, 1965, Ranger 8 took more than 7,000 moon pictures, and the following month Ranger 9 sent back more than 6,000 moon pictures, some of which were broadcast live over commercial television stations.

On February 3, 1966, Russia achieved the first "soft" landing on the moon with the spacecraft Luna 9, which transmitted pictures back to earth showing the moon's surface at close range. The Russians also were the first to place an artificial satellite in orbit around the moon with Luna 10, which was launched on March 31, 1966.

The United States achieved its first "soft" landing on the moon with an unmanned vehicle on June 2, 1966, with Surveyor 1, which sent thousands of closeup pictures of the moon back to earth.

After several unsuccessful attempts by both Russia and the United States to send spacecraft to distant planets, the United States won the first success with Mariner 2 which passed within 22,000 miles of Venus on December 14, 1962, and relayed back information that the planet was completely obscured by clouds but seemed to have a surface temperature of about 700° F.

An even more spectacular space probe was performed by Mariner 4, which in July, 1965, came within about 6,000 miles of Mars and took 22 photographs of the planet which revealed a cratered surface similar to that of the moon.

One of the most spectacular of the space accomplishments was the soft landing on the planet Venus by a Russian space vehicle, 2400-pound Venus 4. On October 18, 1967, after a four-month journey from Russia, the mission was hailed as an important success because of the data that it transmitted from within the planet's atmosphere.

It broadcast for ninety minutes during its parachute trip through the Venus atmosphere, registering temperature, atmospheric pressure, analysis of the composition of atmosphere, and other scientific data.

The Russian spaceship entered Venus' atmosphere at a speed equal to that required for an escape from the earth's atmosphere. After aerodynamic braking, a parachute was released allowing a gradual descent to the surface. During the descent of more than fifteen miles, which took more than ninety minutes, the space laboratory transmitted data about the composition of the atmosphere. It was found to be composed primarily of carbon dioxide, although oxygen and water vapors accounted for one and one-half percent.

The atmospheric pressure was found to be fifteen times that of the earth's 14.7 pounds per square inch at sea level, and the temperature, as high as 536° Fahrenheit.

Mariner 5, the American space vehicle, flew within 2500 miles of Venus on October 19, 1967, generally confirming the data provided by the Russian scientists. Flight controllers said Mariner 5's instruments performed flawlessly during the 19,000 miles per hour trip.

After passing Venus, Mariner 5 went into orbit around the sun. Instruments aboard the craft included devices to measure ultraviolet-ray content of the atmosphere of Venus, which would give some idea of the oxygen, hydrogen, and radiation content.

Meanwhile, the people of the world awaited the first attempt by man to land on the moon. Russian plans for such a voyage were kept shrouded in secrecy. But the United States had been at work on its $20 billion Apollo project since 1961 and hoped to execute a moon landing by 1970 or 1971.

But perhaps of even more significance than any of the space flights and space probes of the first ten years of the Space Age was the conclusion of an international treaty among the United States, Russia, Great Britain, and 76 other nations governing the exploration and use of space. The treaty, which was signed on January 27, 1967, prohibited the use or installation of atomic weapons in space and set up rules to insure that no nation would claim the moon or any other celestial body as its own possession.

The guided missile cruiser USS Albany firing three surface-to-air test missiles simultaneously from forward, aft, and one side of the vessel, January 30, 1963. (UPI PHOTO)

Treaty on the Exploration and Use of Space

—signed January 27, 1967

The states parties to this treaty,

Inspired by the great prospects opening up before mankind as a result of man's entry into outer space,

Recognizing the common interest of all mankind in the progress of the exploration and use of outer space for peaceful purposes,

Believing that the exploration and use of outer space should be carried on for the benefit of all peoples irrespective of the degree of their economic or scientific development,

Desiring to contribute to broad international cooperation in the scientific as well as the legal aspects of the exploration and use of outer space for peaceful purposes,

Believing that such cooperation will contribute to the development of mutual understanding and to the strengthening of friendly relations between states and peoples,

Recalling Resolution 1962 (XVIII), entitled "Declaration of Legal Principles Governing the Activities of States in the Exploration and Use of Outer Space," which was adopted unanimously by the United Nations General Assembly on Dec. 13, 1963,

Recalling Resolution 1884 (XVIII), calling upon states to refrain from placing in orbit around the earth any objects carrying nuclear weapons or any other kinds of weapons of mass destruction or from installing such weapons on celestial bodies, which was adopted unanimously by the United Nations General Assembly on Oct. 17, 1963,

Taking account of United Nations General Assembly Resolution 110 (II) of Nov. 3, 1947, which condemned propaganda designed or likely to provoke or encourage any threat to the peace, breach of the peace or act of aggression, and considering that the aforementioned resolution is applicable to outer space,

Convinced that a treaty on principles governing the activities of states in the exploration and use of outer space, including the moon and other celestial bodies, will further the purposes and principles of the Charter of the United Nations,

Have agreed on the following:

ARTICLE 1

The exploration and use of outer space, including the moon and other celestial bodies, shall be carried out for the benefit and in the interests of all countries, irrespective of their degree of economic or scientific development, and shall be the province of all mankind.

Outer space, including the moon and other celestial bodies, shall be free for exploration and use by all states without discrimination of any kind, on a basis of equality and in accordance with international law, and there shall be free access to all areas of celestial bodies.

There shall be freedom of scientific investigation in outer space, including the moon and other celestial bodies, and states shall facilitate and encourage international cooperation in such investigation.

ARTICLE 2

Outer space, including the moon and other celestial bodies, is not subject to national appropriation by claim of sovereignty, by means of use or occupation, or by any other means.

ARTICLE 3

States parties to the treaty shall carry on activities in the exploration and use of outer space, including the moon and other celestial bodies, in accordance with international law, including the Charter of the United Nations, in the interest of maintaining international peace and security and promoting international cooperation and understanding.

ARTICLE 4

States parties to the treaty undertake not to place in orbit around the earth any objects carrying nuclear weapons or any other kinds of weapons of mass destruction, install such weapons on celestial bodies, or station such weapons in outer space in any other manner.

The moon and other celestial bodies shall be used by all states parties to the treaty exclusively for peaceful purposes. The establishment of military bases, installations and fortifications, the testing of any type of weapons and the conduct of military maneuvers on celestial bodies shall be forbidden. The use of military personnel for scientific research or for any other peaceful purposes shall not be prohibited. The use of any equipment or facility necessary for peaceful exploration of the moon and other celestial bodies shall also not be prohibited.

ARTICLE 5

States parties to the treaty shall regard astronauts as envoys of mankind in outer space and shall render to them all possible assistance in the event of accident, distress, or emergency landing on the territory of another state party or on the high seas. When astronauts make such a landing, they shall be safely and promptly returned to the state of registry of their space vehicle.

In carrying on activities in outer space and on celestial bodies, the astronauts of one state party shall render all possible assistance to the astronauts of other states parties.

States parties to the treaty shall immediately inform the other states parties to the treaty or the Secretary General of the United Nations of any phenomena they discover in outer space, including the moon and other celestial bodies, which could constitute a danger to the life or health of astronauts.

ARTICLE 6

States parties to the treaty shall bear international responsibility for national activities in outer space, including the moon and other celestial bodies, whether such activities are carried on by governmental agencies or by nongovernmental entities, and for assuring that national activities are carried out in conformity with the provisions set forth in the present treaty. The activities of nongovernmental entities in outer space, including the moon and other celestial bodies, shall require authorization and continuing supervision by the state concerned. When activities are carried on in outer space, including the moon and other celestial bodies, by an international organization, responsibility for compliance with this treaty shall be borne both by the international organization and by the states parties to the treaty participating in such organization.

ARTICLE 7

Each state party to the treaty that launches or procures the launching of an object into outer space, including the moon and other celestial bodies, and each state party from whose territory or facility an object is launched, is internationally liable for damage to another state party to the treaty or to its natural or juridical persons by such object or its component parts on the earth, in air space or in outer space, including the moon and other celestial bodies.

ARTICLE 8

A state party to the treaty on whose registry an object launched into outer space is carried shall retain jurisdiction and control over such object, and over any personnel thereof, while in outer space or on a celestial body. Ownership of objects launched into outer space, including objects landed or constructed on a celestial body, and of their component parts, is not affected by their presence in outer space, including the body or by their return to the earth. Such objects or component parts found beyond the limits of the state party to the treaty on whose registry they are carried shall be returned to that state, which shall, upon request, furnish identifying data prior to their return.

ARTICLE 9

In the exploration and use of outer space, including the moon and other celestial bodies, states parties to the treaty shall be guided by the principle of cooperation and mutual assistance and shall conduct all their activities in outer space, including the moon and other celestial bodies, with due regard to the corresponding interests of all other states parties to the treaty. States parties to the treaty shall pursue studies of outer space, including the moon and other celestial bodies, and conduct exploration of them so as to avoid their harmful contamination and also adverse changes in the environment of the earth resulting from the introduction of extraterrestrial matter and, where necessary, shall adopt appropriate measures for this purpose. If a state party to the treaty has reason to believe that an activity or experiment planned by it or its nationals in outer space, including the moon and other celestial bodies, would cause potentially harmful interference with activities of other states parties in the peaceful exploration and use of outer space, including the moon and other celestial bodies, it shall undertake appropriate international consultations before proceeding with any such activity or experiment. A state party to the treaty which has reason to believe that an activity or experiment planned by another state party in outer space, including the moon and other celestial bodies, would cause potentially harmful interference with activities in the peaceful exploration and use of outer space, including the moon and other celestial bodies, may request consultation concerning the activity or experiment.

ARTICLE 10

In order to promote international cooperation in the exploration and use of outer space, including the moon and other celestial bodies, in conformity with the purposes of this treaty, the states parties to the treaty shall consider on a basis of equality any requests by other states parties to the treaty to be afforded an opportunity to observe the flight of space objects launched by those states.

The nature of such an opportunity for observation and the conditions under which it could be afforded shall be determined by agreement between the states concerned.

ARTICLE 11

In order to promote international cooperation in the peaceful exploration and use of outer space, states parties to the treaty conducting activities in outer space, including the moon and other celestial bodies, agree to inform the Secretary General of the United Nations as well as the public and the international scientific community, to the greatest extent feasible and practicable, of the nature, conduct, locations and results of such activities. On receiving the said information, the Secretary General of the United Nations should be prepared to disseminate it immediately and effectively.

ARTICLE 12

All stations, installations, equipment and space vehicles on the moon and other celestial bodies shall be open to representatives of other states parties to the treaty on a basis of reciprocity. Such representatives shall give reasonable advance notice of a projected visit, in order that appropriate consultations may be held and that maximum precautions may be taken to assure safety and to avoid interference with normal operations in the facility to be visited.

ARTICLE 13

The provisions of this treaty shall apply to the activities of states parties to the treaty in the exploration and use of outer space, including the moon and other celestial bodies, whether such activities are carried on by a single state party to the treaty or jointly with other states, including cases where they are carried on within the framework of international intergovernmental organizations.

Any practical questions arising in connection with activities carried on by international intergovernmental organizations in the exploration and use of outer space, including the moon and other celestial bodies, shall be resolved by the states parties to the treaty either with appropriate international organization or with one or more state members of that international organization, which are parties to this treaty.

ARTICLE 14

1. This treaty shall be open to all states for signature. Any state which does not sign this treaty before its entry into force in accordance with Paragraph 3 of this article may accede to it at any time.

2. This treaty shall be subject to ratification by signatory states. Instruments of ratification and instruments of accession shall be deposited with the Governments of the Union of Soviet Socialist Republics, the United Kingdom of Great Britain and Northern Ireland and the United States of America, which are hereby designated the depositary governments.

3. This treaty shall enter into force upon the deposit of instruments of ratification by five Governments including the Governments designated as Depositary Governments under this treaty.

4. For states whose instruments of ratification or accession are deposited subsequent to the entry into force of this treaty, it shall enter into force on the date of the deposit of their instruments of ratification or accession.

5. The Depositary Governments shall promptly inform all signatory and acceding states of the date of each signature, the date of deposit of each instrument of ratification of and accession to this treaty, the date of its entry into force and other notices.

6. This treaty shall be registered by the Depositary Governments pursuant to Article 102 of the Charter of the United Nations.

ARTICLE 15

Any state party to the treaty may propose amendments to this treaty. Amendments shall enter into force for each state party to the treaty accepting the amendments upon their acceptance by a majority of the states parties to the treaty and thereafter for each remaining state party to the treaty on the date of acceptance by it.

ARTICLE 16

Any state party to the treaty may give notice of its withdrawal from the treaty one year after its entry into force by written notification to the Depositary Governments. Such withdrawal shall take effect one year from the date of receipt of this notification.

ARTICLE 17

This treaty, of which the Chinese, English, French, Russian and Spanish texts are equally authentic, shall be deposited in the archives of the Depositary Governments. Duly certified copies of this treaty shall be transmitted by the Depositary Governments to the Governments of the signatory and acceding states.

EXPLORING the WORLD

Although man stood on the threshold of traveling to the moon and beyond, there remained much that was still unknown about the world he lived on. So, throughout the growing-up decades of the Space Age generation, many men risked their lives to explore the natural challenges of the earth itself—to climb higher, to dive lower, and to go where no man had gone before.

Climbing the Highest Mountain

The world's highest mountain, Mount Everest, towers more than 29,000 feet on the border between Tibet and Nepal in the Himalaya range. It had presented the greatest challenge to mountain climbers and had defeated expedition after expedition that had tried to conquer it over the years.

Sir Edmund Hillary leading a Sherpa (not Tenzing Norgay) over broken and very dangerous ground, in an icefall at about 19,000 feet. The snow is knee-deep and almost hides huge crevices. (UPI PHOTO)

Hillary and Tenzing relaxing at Camp 4, the day after their victorious ascent to the top of the world's highest mountain—29,028-foot Mount Everest. (UPI PHOTO)

But in the early 1950's Edmund Hillary, a beekeeper from New Zealand, became determined that he would scale the peak. In 1951 and 1952 he and other mountaineers explored the southern face of the mountain, plotting a path by which it might be possible to climb up its rocky, snow and ice covered surface.

On March 10, 1953, Hillary set out with an expedition under the leadership of Colonel John Hunt for the final assault on the mountain. The expedition moved slowly up the mountain establishing a series of camps at increasingly higher levels. Then on May 29, Hillary and Tenzing Norgay, a Sherpa tribesman, climbed the last few hundred feet to the summit wearing oxygen masks to enable them to breathe in the thin air. Hillary described his sensation as one of "vague astonishment that I should have been the lucky one to attain the ambition of so many brave and determined climbers." Hillary and Hunt were knighted by Queen Elizabeth for the achievement.

Swiss mountaineers climbed Mount Everest twice in 1956. On May 1, 1963, James Whittaker became the first American to reach the top of Everest, and three weeks later two other American mountain-climbing teams reached the summit, having climbed up by different routes to meet at the top.

Gold medals, the highest award for civilians given by the Indian Government, were awarded to the conquerors of Mt. Everest in 1953. On their way to the Moghul gardens after the ceremonies are (left to right) Madame Nehru, Prime Minister Nehru, Tenzing Norgay, Colonel John Hunt, and Sir Edmund Hillary. (UPI PHOTO)

Cousteau's "diving saucer" was transported by air from Marseille, France, to San Diego, California, for use in submarine experiments in 1964. (UPI PHOTO)

To the Bottom of the Sea

Although the American zoologist William Beebe had descended a little over 3,000 feet in the ocean in an iron ball called a bathysphere in 1934, it was not until the 1950's and 1960's that men began to dive to really great ocean depths to explore the almost unknown world under the seas. Oceanography began to develop as an important branch of the sciences.

In 1948 the aqualung, a compressed air tank and breathing mask that could be worn by a swimmer began to be used in Europe. Invented by a French naval officer, Jacques-Yves Cousteau, and an associate, Emile Gagnan, the aqualung freed ocean divers from the necessity of wearing heavy diving helmets and led to the sport of skin-diving. For the first time many swimmers were able to move freely along the ocean floors in shallow areas observing marine life.

Auguste Piccard, a Swiss physicist, who in the 1930's had made high altitude balloon flights to explore the upper atmosphere, began exploring the ocean depths in an underwater balloon called a bathyscaph, which he had invented. In 1953 Piccard descended almost two miles into the ocean in a bathyscaph, a distance of 10,300 feet. Seven years later, in 1960, Piccard and his son Jacques made a dive in a bathyscaph of 35,800 feet in the Pacific Ocean.

Cousteau, the co-inventor of the aqualung, also developed bathyscaph exploration machines and conducted extensive investigations of the ocean depths. In 1966 Cousteau led a team of divers who lived for three weeks on the floor of the Mediterranean Sea at a depth of 330 feet using a large sphere as a base. Cousteau's team wore aqualungs to leave the sphere and work on the sea's floor, building an oil well.

Astronaut Scott Carpenter (right) and Boatswain's Mate, Bill Meeks, preparing to dive into the Gulf of Mexico, while training for the Navy's "Man in the Sea" project at Panama City, Florida, in May, 1965. (U.S. NAVY PHOTO VIA UPI TELEPHOTO)

The International Geophysical Year

Scientists and explorers of 66 nations joined in an 18-month concerted effort to learn more about the earth in the International Geophysical Year (IGY) from July 1, 1957, to December 31, 1958. The launching of the earth's first artificial satellites by Russia and the United States took place under the auspices of IGY.

Working in the many areas of study of geophysics the scientists and explorers learned much that was new about the earth, its atmosphere, and the space around the earth. It was discovered that ionized particles of high energy surround the earth in what became called the Van Allen radiation belts. It was learned that for as far as 14,000 miles out into space from earth the space was not "empty" but contained hundreds of ion particles in every cubic centimeter of space.

Scientists determined that the earth seems to be in a period of slowly warming up, discovering this by the careful measurement of dozens of glaciers throughout the period of IGY.

New ocean currents were found in both the Atlantic and Pacific Oceans. In the Atlantic it was found that there was an ocean current at the depth of about 9,000 feet that flows in the opposite direction of the Gulf Stream. In the Pacific another deep current was discovered that runs all the way across the Pacific from Asia to the area of the Galpagos Islands.

The North Pole and the Arctic

The North Pole and the region of Arctic Ocean and continuous cold surrounding it was the scene of extensive exploration throughout the two decades.

In 1946 a huge United States and Canadian army expedition, accompanied by representatives of seven other nations, conducted operation "Musk Ox." This expedition traveled about 3,000 miles by snowmobile and caterpillar tractor through unmapped territory that extended north to Cambridge Bay on Victoria Island. The journey lasted from February 15 to May 6. During most of the trip temperatures were more than 40 degrees below zero. Supplies for the expedition were dropped by parachute and by glider.

Also during 1946 a Russian airplane expedition commanded by M. A. Titlov made the first map of the arctic ice pack. Russia also established a network of drifting radio-weather stations in the arctic to aid in weather forecasting.

In 1958, as part of the International Geophysical Year, the United States atomic submarine *Nautilus* made an 1,800 mile trip under the arctic ice pack to the North Pole. Also during the IGY several drifting observation stations were established on arctic ice floes. These stations reported that although there appeared to be little life near the floor of the Arctic Ocean there were substantial numbers of fish and other sea life at a depth of about 8,000 feet.

From 1952 to the late 1960's the United States maintained a floating observation station on what was called Fletcher's Ice Island. During its first 15 years of existence this manned-station twice drifted in a huge circle around the Arctic Ocean on the Canadian side of the North Pole. A similar floating ice island manned by the University of Alaska had floated 1,500 miles from 1961 to 1965 when it had to be abandoned as it neared Iceland. Russia regularly maintains two such floating observation islands in the arctic ice pack.

The South Pole and Antarctica

But the most extensive and far-reaching explorations on earth during the two decades took place in Antarctica surrounding the South Pole. Here also international cooperation led to the establishment of treaties that prepared guidelines for the treaty banning the miliary use of outerspace and might set the pattern for a treaty establishing international controls over atomic weapons.

Operation "High Jump," one of the largest exploration expeditions of all time, set out for Antarctica from Norfolk, Virginia, on December 2, 1946. Under command of Rear Admiral Richard E. Byrd, the expedition included 4,000 men, 13 ships ranging from a large aircraft carrier to a submarine, and numerous aircraft. The expedition returned to the United States four months later after having mapped more than 300,000 square miles of never-before-seen land and discovered ten new mountain ranges.

A much smaller antarctic expedition under Commander Finn Ronne spent a year in Antarctica from March, 1947, to April, 1948. With one ship and an airplane, the Ronne expedition mapped about 460,000 square miles of land. An area west of Weddell Sea was named Edith Ronne Land in honor of the commander's wife, who accompanied the expedition and was the first woman to have set foot on Antarctica.

Admiral Byrd, who in 1929 had been the first person to fly to the South Pole, again flew over the South Pole during a new expedition that he led to Antarctica in 1955 and 1956. He was working on plans for another expedition to be undertaken as part of the IGY when he died in 1957.

Twelve nations including the United States sent expeditions to Antarctica as part of IGY. The

The two-man submarine "Asherah" was transferred from the General Dynamics research vessel "Sea Surveyor" to the Smithsonian Institution's ship "Phykos" to study coralline algae growth off the coast of Nova Scotia, in 1965. (UPI TELEPHOTO)

A watertight observation chamber allowing scientists to view underwater happenings, commissioned by the National Science Foundation for its studies of Antarctica, being lowered as a blast of ice explodes, in January 1966. (U.S. NAVY-UPI)

American endeavor under command of Admiral George J. Dufek was called operation "Deep Freeze." On October 31, 1956, Dufek landed at the South Pole in a twin-engine DC-3, becoming the first man to set foot on the South Pole since the historic race to the pole of Roald Amundsen of Norway and Robert Scott of Great Britain in 1911. In the days that followed the United States established a base at the South Pole supplying it by air. During the IGY this base was directed by Paul Siple, who had been a Boy Scout with Admiral Byrd's first Antarctic expedition in 1928.

In December, 1957, Sir Edmund Hillary, the conquerer of Mount Everest, led a New Zealand expedition that traveled overland by tractor from Ross Island to the South Pole. At the same time Sir Vivian Fuchs led a British expedition equipped with tractors overland from the Weddell Sea to the South Pole. Fuchs arrived at the South Pole on January 20, 1958, and was greeted there by Hillary and Dufek. Fuchs, accompanied by Hillary, then continued on across Antarctica, arriving at Ross Island on March 2, 1958. Thus, Fuchs became the first man to make a transcontinental land crossing of Antarctica, a distance of 2,158 miles.

The most important single event growing out of the IGY was the signing on December 1, 1959, of the Antarctica Pact by the 12 nations that had conducted expeditions to the continent during the period. This pact insured the continued use of Antarctica for peaceful purposes, forbidding the establishment of military bases or the use of the continent for military purposes. In this regard it was a forerunner of the international Space Treaty signed in 1967 that assured the peaceful exploration of space. The Antarctica Pact, signed both by the United States and Russia, provided for inspection of the activities of the various expeditions in Antarctica to insure their non-military character, thus possibly laying the groundwork for an international inspection system that ultimately could insure the peaceful use of atomic energy.

The Antarctica Pact

—signed December 1, 1959

The Governments of Argentina, Australia, Belgium, Chile, the French Republic, Japan, New Zealand, Norway, the Union of Soviet Socialist Republics, the United Kingdom of Great Britain and Northern Ireland, and the United States of America,

Recognizing that it is in the interest of all mankind that Antarctica shall continue forever to be used exclusively for peaceful purposes and shall not become the scene or object of international discord;

Acknowledging the substantial contributions to scientific knowledge resulting from international cooperation in scientific investigation in Antarctica;

Convinced that the establishment of a firm foundation for the continuation and development of such cooperation on the basis of freedom of scientific investigation in Antarctica as applied during the International Geophysical Year accords with the interests of science and the progress of all mankind;

Convinced also that a treaty ensuring the use of Antarctica for peaceful purposes only and the continuance of international harmony in Antarctica will further the purposes and principles embodied in the charter of the United Nations;

Have agreed as follows:

ARTICLE I

1. Antarctica shall be used for peaceful purposes only. There shall be prohibited, inter alia, any measure of a military nature, such as the establishment of military bases and fortifications, the carrying out of military maneuvers, as well as the testing of any type of weapons.

Three U.S. Navy icebreakers, from left to right, USS Burton Island (AGB-10); USS Atka (AGB-3); and USS Glacier (AGB-4), teaming up to move a mountain of ice which closed the shipping channel to McMurdo Station, Antarctica, in January 1966. (UPI PHOTO)

2. The present treaty shall not prevent the use of military personnel or equipment for scientific research or for any other peaceful purpose.

ARTICLE II

Freedom of scientific investigation in Antarctica and cooperation toward that end, as applied during the International Geophysical Year, shall continue, subject to the provisions of the present treaty.

ARTICLE III

1. In order to promote international cooperation in scientific investigation in Antarctica, as provided for in Article II of the present treaty, the contracting parties agree that, to the greatest extent feasible and practicable:

(A) Information regarding plans for scientific programs in Antarctica shall be exchanged to permit maximum economy and efficiency of operations;

(B) Scientific personnel shall be exchanged in Antarctica between expeditions and stations;

(C) Scientific observations and results from Antarctica shall be exchanged and made freely available.

2. In implementing this article, every encouragement shall be given to the establishment of cooperative working relations with those specialized agencies of the United Nations and other international organizations having a scientific or technical interest in Antarctica.

ARTICLE IV

1. Nothing contained in the present treaty shall be interpreted as:

(A) A renunciation by any contracting party of previously asserted rights of or claims to territorial sovereignty in Antarctica;

(B) A renunciation or diminution by any contracting party of any basis of claim to territorial sovereignty in Antarctica which it may have whether as a result of its activities or those of its nationals in Antarctica, or otherwise;

(C) Prejudicing the position of any contracting party as regards its recognition or nonrecognition of any other state's right of or claim to territorial sovereignty in Antarctica.

2. No acts or activities taking place while the present treaty is in force shall constitute a basis for asserting, supporting or denying a claim to territorial sovereignty in Antarctica or create any rights of sovereignty in Antarctica. No new claim, or enlargement of an existing claim, to territorial sovereignty in Antarctica shall be asserted while the present treaty is in force.

ARTICLE V

1. Any nuclear explosions in Antarctica and the disposal there of radioactive waste material shall be prohibited.

2. In the event of the conclusion of international agreements concerning the use of nuclear energy, including nuclear explosions and the disposal of radioactive waste material, to which all of the contracting parties whose representatives are entitled to participate in the meetings provided for under Article IX are parties, the rules established under such agreements shall apply in Antarctica.

ARTICLE VI

The provisions of the present treaty shall apply to the area south of 60 Degrees South Latitude, including all ice shelves, but nothing in the present treaty shall prejudice or in any way affect the rights, or the exercise of the rights, of any state under international law with regard to the high seas within that area.

ARTICLE VII

1. In order to promote the objectives and ensure the observance of the provisions of the present treaty, each contracting party whose representatives are entitled to participate in the meeting referred to in Article IX of the treaty shall have the right to designate observers to carry out any inspection provided for by the present article. Observers shall be nationals of the contracting parties which designate them. The names of observers shall be communicated to every other contracting party having the right to designate observers and like notice shall be given of the termination of their appointment(s).

The U.S. Navy icebreaker, USS Burton Island, plowing through the thick ice of the Ross Sea in Antarctica, opening channels to permit cargo ships to reach the American base at McMurdo Sound. (UPI PHOTO)

2. Each observer designated in accordance with the provisions of Paragraph 1 of this article shall have complete freedom of access at any time to any or all areas of Antarctica.

3. All areas of Antarctica, including all stations, installations and equipment within those areas, and all ships and aircraft at points of discharging or embarking cargoes or personnel in Antarctica, shall be open at all times to inspection by any observers designated in accordance with Paragraph 1 of this article.

4. Aerial observation may be carried out at any time over any or all areas of Antarctica by any of the contracting parties having the right to designate observers.

5. Each contracting party shall, at the time when the present treaty enters into force for it, inform the other contracting parties, and thereafter shall give them notice in advance, of

(A) All expeditions to and within Antarctica, on the part of its ships or nationals and all expeditions to Antarctica organized in or proceeding from its territory;

(B) All stations in Antarctica occupied by its nationals; and

(C) Any military personnel or equipment intended to be introduced by it into Antarctica subject to the conditions prescribed in Paragraph 2 of Article I of the present treaty.

ARTICLE VIII

1. In order to facilitate the exercise of their functions under the present treaty, and without prejudice to the respective positions of the contracting parties relating to jurisdiction over all other persons in Antarctica, observers designated under Paragraph 1 of Article VII and scientific personnel exchanged under Subparagraph 1(B) of Article III of the treaty, and members of the staffs accompanying any such persons, shall be subject only to the jurisdiction of the contracting party of which they are nationals in respect of all acts or omissions occurring while they are in Antarctica for the purpose of exercising their functions.

2. Without prejudice to the provisions of

Paragraph 1 of this article, and pending the adoption of measures in pursuance of Subparagraph 1(E) of Article IX, the contracting parties concerned in any case of dispute with regard to the exercise of jurisdiction in Antarctica shall immediately consult together with a view to reaching a mutually acceptable solution.

ARTICLE IX

1. Representatives of the contracting parties named in the preamble to the present treaty shall meet at the city of Canberra within two months after the date of entry into force of the treaty, and thereafter at suitable intervals and places, for the purpose of exchanging information, consulting together on matters of common interest pertaining to Antarctica, and formulating and considering, and recommending to their governments measures in furtherance of the principles and objectives of the treaty, including measures regarding:

(A) Use of Antarctica for peaceful purposes only;

(B) Facilitation of scientific research in Antarctica;

(C) Facilitation of international scientific cooperation in Antarctica;

(D) Facilitation of the exercise of the rights of inspection provided for in Article VII of the treaty;

(E) Questions relating to the exercise of jurisdiction in Antarctica;

(F) Preservation and conservation of living resources in Antarctica.

2. Each contracting party which has become a party to the present treaty by accession under Article XIII shall be entitled to appoint representatives to participate in the meetings referred to in Paragraph 1 of the present article, during such time as that contracting party demonstrates its interest in Antarctica by conducting substantial scientific research activity there, such as the establishment of a scientific station or the dispatch of a scientific expedition.

3. Reports from the observers referred to in Article VII of the present treaty shall be transmitted to the representatives of the contracting parties participating in the meetings referred to in Paragraph 1 of the present article.

4. The measures referred to in Paragraph 1 of this article shall become effective when approved by all contracting parties whose representatives were entitled to participate in the meetings held to consider those measures.

5. Any or all of the rights established in the present treaty may be exercised as from the date of entry into force of the treaty whether or not any measures facilitating the exercise of such rights have been proposed, considered or approved as provided in this article.

ARTICLE X

Each of the contracting parties undertakes to exert appropriate efforts, consistent with the Charter of the United Nations, to the end that no one engages in any activity in Antarctica contrary to the principles or purposes of the present treaty.

ARTICLE XI

1. If any dispute arises between two or more of the contracting parties concerning the interpretation or application of the present treaty, those contracting parties shall consult among themselves with a view to having the dispute resolved by negotiation, inquiry, mediation, conciliation, arbitration, judicial settlement or other peaceful means of their own choice.

2. Any dispute of this character not so resolved shall, with the consent, in each case, of all parties to the dispute, be referred to the International Court of Justice for settlement; but failure to reach agreement on reference to the International Court shall not absolve parties to the dispute from the responsibility of continuing to seek to resolve it by any of the various peaceful means referred to in Paragraph 1 of this article.

ARTICLE XII

1. (A) The present treaty may be modified or amended at any time by unanimous agreement of the contracting parties whose representatives are entitled to participate in the meeting provided for under Article IX. Any such modification or amendment shall enter into force when the depositary government has received notice from all such contracting parties that they have ratified it.

Street scene at McMurdo Sound. At the right is the mess hall for the 1000 scientists and sailors who man the station in summer. In the background is Observation Hill, the site of a cross in memory of Robert F. Scott, the British explorer who lost his life there in 1903. (UPI PHOTO)

(B) Such modification or amendment shall therafter enter into force as to any other contracting party when notice of ratification by it has been received by the depositary government. Any such contracting party from which no notice of ratification is received within a period of two years from the date of entry into force of the modification or amendment in accordance with the provisions of Subparagraph 8(A) of this article shall be deemed to have withdrawn from the present treaty on the date of the expiration of such period.

2. (A) If after the expiration of thirty years from the date of entry into force of the present treaty, any of the contracting parties whose representatives are entitled to participate in the meetings provided for under Article

Living in huts built in this tunnel, scientists study everything from Seismology to Glaciology. Here a Navy man is collecting food cases inside the tunnel, which is a natural refrigerator. (UPI PHOTO)

IX so requests by a communication addressed to the depositary government, a conference of all the contracting parties shall be held as soon as practicable to review the operation of the treaty.

(B) Any modification or amendment to the present treaty which is approved at such a conference by a majority of the contracting parties there represented including a majority of those whose representatives are entitled to participate in the meetings provided for under Article IX shall be communicated by the depositary government to all the contracting parties immediately after the termination of the conference and shall enter into force in accordance with the provisions of Paragraph 1 of the present article.

(C) If any such modification or amendment has not entered into force in accordance with the provisions of Subparagraph 1 (A) of this article within a period of two years after the date of its communication to all the contracting parties, any contracting party may at any time after the expiration of that period give notice to the depositary government of its withdrawal from the present treaty; and such withdrawal shall take effect two years after the receipt of the notice by the depositary government.

ARTICLE XIII

1. The present treaty shall be subject to ratification by the signatory states. It shall be open for accession by any state which is a member of the United Nations, or by any other state which may be invited to accede to the treaty with the consent of all the contracting parties whose representatives are entitled to participate in the meetings provided for under Article IX of the treaty.

2. Ratification of or accession to the present treaty shall be effected by each state in accordance with its constitutional processes.

3. Instruments of ratification and instruments of accession shall be deposited with the Government of the United States of America, hereby designated as the depositary government.

4. The depositary government shall inform all signatory and acceding states of the date of each deposit of an instrument of ratification or accession, and the date of entry into force of the treaty and of any modification or amendment thereto.

5. Upon the deposit of instruments of ratification by all the signatory states, the present treaty shall enter into force for those states and for states which have deposited instruments of accession. Thereafter the treaty shall enter into force for any acceding state upon the deposit of its instrument of accession.

6. The present treaty shall be registered by the depositary government pursuant to Article 102 of the Charter of the United Nations.

ARTICLE XIV

The present treaty, done in the English, French, Russian and Spanish languages, each version being equally authentic, shall be deposited in the archives of the Government of the United States of America, which shall transmit duly certified copies thereof to the governments of the signatory and acceding states.

FASTER TRANSPORTATION SHRINKS the WORLD

Against a background of the Hong Kong skyline, an estimated 200 swimmers plowed their way across Hong Kong harbor during the 55th annual harbor swim in September 1967. (UPI PHOTO)

Speed was the key word for transportation in the two decades after World War II. Men learned how to fly faster than the speed of sound and speedy jets replaced slower propeller-driven airplanes. Automobiles were made bigger, faster, and safer, and multi-lane expressways and turnpikes were built to accommodate them. As a result airplanes and automobiles took over a larger and larger share of passenger transportation, leaving railroads and ships largely as haulers of freight. But the expanding population constantly strained the transportation facilities, calling for even greater improvements in the years ahead.

Aviation Comes of Age

Developments in aviation followed a consistent pattern. First, research planes were built to test new designs. Next, several years later these

The big "bird," the China Clipper, in Manila Bay, Philippine Islands, after completing its inaugural Air Mail trans-Pacific flight in December 1935, is a historic contrast to the jet marvels that streak across the skies of the world today. (UPI PHOTO)

designs were used to build military aircraft. And finally, after several more years, the designs were incorporated into commercial airliners.

Immediately after World War II the airlines depended largely on twin-engine Douglas DC-3 transports and DC-4's. Both of these planes had been designed before World War II, the DC-3 having been introduced in 1936. And they had been workhorses for the armed forces during the war, in which they were designated as C-47's and C-54's. These planes were slow but dependable, flying at about 200 miles an hour and carrying 30 to 40 passengers.

The first postwar airliners introduced in 1946 and 1947 were larger four-engine craft, including the Douglas DC-6, the Lockheed Constellation, and the Boeing Stratocruiser. These planes could carry from 50 to 60 passengers and had cruising speeds of 270 to 300 miles an hour. All these were propeller-driven planes.

Meanwhile, the air force, recognizing that the jet fighters developed by Germany during the later part of World War II would revolutionize air warfare, rushed to convert its air fleets to jet power. American military aircraft recaptured world leadership in 1947 when a Lockheed Shooting Star won the world speed record at 623.8 miles an hour. But it was not until ten years later that the U.S. Air Force took out of service the last of its propeller-driven fighter planes.

Aircraft researchers and engineers already were looking far ahead. The rocket-powered Bell X-1 had been built to test aircraft design for even greater speeds. And on October 14, 1947, Air Force Captain Charles E. Yeager flying the X-1 became the first man to travel faster than the speed of sound. Six years later Yeager flew an improved version, the X-1A at a speed 2½ times the speed of sound.

Airlines did not begin to use jet-propelled aircraft until the 1950's. In 1952 British Overseas Airways started the first regular passenger service using British-made De Haviland Comets on the run from London to South Africa. The next year Trans World Airlines began the first nonstop coast-to-coast airline service in the United States. Using turbo-prop Lockheed Super Constellations, the flights between New York and California took about 8 hours of flying. Five years later, on December 10, 1958, the first American jet airliner, the four-engine Boeing 707, with a cruising speed of about 500 miles an hour, was placed in regular service by National Airlines between New York and Miami. A month later, in January, 1959, American Airlines began using the Boeing 707 jet for its transcontinental service, cutting the flying time between California and New York to less than 5 hours.

The big new jet airliners flew so much faster than the older propeller-driven airplanes and carried so many more passengers that they were much more efficient for airlines to operate. In 1960 a Boeing 707 set a record for a flight from New York to London in 5 hours and 25 minutes. The same year a Douglas DC-8 jet flew 4,300 miles from Honolulu to Chicago in a record 7 hours and 52 minutes. By the mid-1960's the airlines were replacing propeller-driven airplanes on even their short-haul routes, using such smaller jet airliners as the Boeing 727 and 737 and the Douglas DC-9. The aircraft companies were planning on deliveries of even larger jet airliners before the end of the 1960's, such as the 490-passenger Boeing 747 and the 250-passenger Douglas DC-8-60.

Throughout the two decades the airlines constantly increased their business as they won

A photographer captured this odd angle of the Concorde, which is equipped to carry hundreds of people thousands of miles. (UPI PHOTO)

A full-scale mockup of the Sleek Concorde supersonic airliner being towed from its hangar at Paris' Le Bourget Airport, May 25, 1967, to go on public display at the press preview of the 27th Paris International Air Show. The jetliner is a joint British-French undertaking. (UPI PHOTO)

In 1965 two external propellant tanks were added to the X-15 airplane of the U.S. Air Force in order to increase its speed to about 5000 mph. (NASA)

Major William Knight inspecting the connection between one of the external tanks and X-15 No. 2 experimental aircraft, at the NASA Flight Research Center preparatory to an attempt to fly it at approximately 4500 mph. in September 1967. (UPI–NASA)

greater and greater public acceptance for their reliability. In 1945 the airlines flew only 7 million passengers. But 20 years later the number of passengers had increased by an astounding 1350 percent to include nearly 95 million passengers flown in 1965.

Research in aircraft design continued to seek craft that could fly faster and faster. The X-15 research plane, a successor to the X-1, had been redesigned to achieve speeds from 7 to 8 times the speed of sound. But the problem had now become one of finding materials and designs that could withstand the extreme temperatures caused by air friction at these high speeds. Military fighter and reconnaissance planes by the late 1960's were flying at speeds of more than 2,000 miles an hour in level flight.

An international race developed to build

airline transports that could fly at supersonic speeds. Britain and France worked together to produce the Concorde, a plane designed to fly at about 1,500 mph, that was expected to be available to airlines by 1971. Russia was at work on the TU-144, also planned to fly at about 1,500 mph, with which it hoped to beat the Concorde into production. And in the United States the Boeing company was chosen in 1966 to produce a moveable-wing supersonic airliner that would carry 300 passengers at a speed of about 1,800 mph. The American supersonic transport (SST) was planned for production in 1974. This plane is expected to be able to carry passengers from New York to Paris in 2 hours or less.

As airplanes became bigger and faster, carrying more anu more passengers between cities, the airports became crowded. Throughout the two decades, larger and larger airports were constructed. And to find space, the new airports usually were built farther and farther away from the metropolitan centers. As a result, passengers had to take more time to get from the airport into the city of their destination than it took them to fly from airport to airport. Beginning in the 1950's helicopter airlines began to be used to shuttle passengers between various airports within a metropolitan area, and by the 1960's some helicopter services were operating from downtown areas to outlying metropolitan airports. At the same time, the number of planes using the airports was increasing so that there was heavier traffic in the air in and around airports. Thus, there were major traffic problems to be solved both in the air and on the ground, and for both airline passengers and for the aircraft.

The first pure jet aircraft to land in Antarctica, and also the first of its type to land on an ice runway—the U.S. Air Force Starlifter transport. (U.S. NAVY–UPI)

The Growing Automobile Industry

The automobile industry got off to a slow start after World War II. Most automobile plants had built tanks, airplanes, or other war equipment throughout the war, so in getting back into peacetime production they for the most part revived their 1941 model designs with slight modifications. A strike against General Motors that lasted from November, 1945, to April, 1946, prevented the country's largest automaker from achieving full-scale output.

Henry J. Kaiser, an industrialist who had amassed a fortune mass-producing ships during the war, joined with Joseph W. Frazer to found the Kaiser-Frazer Corporation in an effort to build automobiles starting in 1946. The first car produced by the new company was the Frazer, introduced in 1946, and the second was the Kaiser, first shown in 1947. The cars were more streamlined than the refurbished pre-war models of other companies, having fenders that extended the full length of the car from front to back. However, the Kaiser-Frazer organization was unable to compete successfully with the Big Three automobile makers dealers' organizations and discontinued making passenger cars in the early 1950's.

Altogether in 1946 the American automobile industry produced only about 2 million cars and about 740 thousand trucks and buses. This brought the total number of automobiles registered in the United States to about 27 million and the number of trucks and buses to a little over 5 million. But the year's total automobile sales were little more than had been produced a quarter of a century earlier in 1920.

During the next two decades there were many improvements and changes in automobiles. In 1948 "hard-top" convertibles, tubeless tires, and higher-compression engines were introduced. In 1951 some automobiles began to have power steering, and tinted glass was added to windshields to reduce glare. Automobile air-conditioners became available in 1953, and the same year power brakes became an optional feature. New cars in 1954 featured the first curved windshields that gave the driver a wider vision of the road. Safety belts and padded dashboards were introduced in 1956, and the same year push-button transmissions became available, moving the gear-changing lever off the steering column to the dashboard. In 1957 fuel injection systems became available to replace carburetors and some cars were designed with dual headlights. American automakers introduced smaller "compact" styles in 1960 in order to compete with small, less expensive cars being imported from Europe. In 1962 luxury sports cars with bucket seats, wire wheels, and manual transmission with four forward speeds became popular—a trend that continued into the late 1960's. Under the pressure of public opinion automobile makers emphasized safety equipment with turn signals, backup lights, front and rear seat belts, and windshield washers, all of which became standard equipment on 1966 models.

By 1966 American automobile companies were producing about 9 million cars a year, about 4½ times as many as in 1946. The number of automobiles registered in the United States had tripled to a total of more than 75 million.

Throughout the two decades as the number of motor vehicles on the road increased so did the number of deaths from auto accidents. In 1946 33,000 people died from automobile accidents, and by 1966 the annual number of auto accident deaths had increased to more than 52,000. In other words, almost 3 persons out of every 1,000 died in automobile accidents every year.

Concern with the climbing highway death toll caused Congress to pass in September, 1966, the National Traffic and Motor Vehicle Safety Act and the National Highway Safety Act. The first established safety standards for both American-made cars and foreign cars imported for sale in the United States. The second authorized federal aid of about $100 million a year to the states to improve highway safety. President Johnson named Dr. William J. Haddon, Jr. as the first director of the National Traffic Safety Agency established to supervise the automobile safety standards. In January, 1967, 20 standards were issued by Haddon which would be required on all 1968 model cars.

Another important aspect of the changes in transportation brought about by the automobile since World War II was the rapid growth of bus and truck transportation. During the two decades the number of buses and trucks on the highways tripled from about 5 million to more than 15

A typical aerial view of a metropolitan area (Los Angeles) showing the complicated traffic lanes during the late 1950's, which, by comparison with those of a decade later, were relatively simple. (UPI PHOTO)

An unusual view of Queens Boulevard, New York, showing the complex traffic, business and apartment pattern at the time of the historic visit of Pope Paul VI, October 4, 1965. (UPI PHOTO)

million. The trucking industry grew to an $11 billion a year industry while the number of passengers carried each year by intercity buses rose to more than 450 million.

With the tremendous increase in the number of automobiles, trucks, and buses on the highways, the roads that had been built before World War II proved inadequate to carry the traffic. Even the best highways were two-lane and were dangerous because of the many intersections of side roads. The first modern four-lane toll road, the Pennsylvania Turnpike, had been started in 1938, but was not completed to the Ohio border until 1951. It served as a model for other toll roads and expressways that began to be built in the 1950's and 1960's, with cloverleaf intersections that allowed other roads access to the turnpike without dangerous crossings.

Recognizing the need for a better system of four-lane roads throughout the United States, Congress in 1956 authorized the establishment and construction of a National Interstate Highway System. The 41,000-mile network of high-speed roads was to be built with the federal government providing 90 percent of the funds and the states paying the other 10 percent. The total cost for this huge highway program was estimated at $51 billion. By 1966 about 23,000 miles of the roads had been completed and opened to traffic. The system was expected to be completed by 1972.

To meet the problems of congested traffic in city streets, most metropolitan areas, such as New York, Chicago, and Los Angeles, also undertook huge programs to build limited access multi-lane expressways that enabled automobile drivers to travel into and out of the cities without the interference of stoplights.

Britisher Stirling Moss, whose driving career ended abruptly after a serious accident.

Decline of the Railroads

The railroads, which had been the backbone of America's transportation system from the mid-1800's to the 1930's, declined in importance in the two decades since World War II.

The most significant decline lay in the numbers of passengers carried. In 1945 the nation's railroads had nearly 900 million paying passengers, but twenty years later the annual number of passengers was only about a third of that amount—just a little more than 300 million passengers a year. Part of these passengers were lost to the airlines and part to automobiles and buses.

Generally, the railroads did little to discourage the loss of passengers. Most railroads regarded their passenger business as not very profitable. So throughout the period many passenger trains were discontinued, and about 14,000 miles of railroad track were abandoned.

Although the nation's economy was expanding rapidly, the railroads also suffered a decline in the amount of freight carried. In 1945 the railroads carried 2.9 billion tons of freight, but twenty years later this had fallen to 2.6 billion tons. The railroad industry's annual operating revenues rose from $8.9 billion in 1945 to $10 billion twenty years later. But in 1965 they were surpassed for the first time by the trucking industry whose annual income in that year exceeded $10.2 billion.

To maintain their economic position, the railroads spent large sums to improve their equipment. During the two decades nearly all the huge coal-burning steam engines were replaced by diesel engines, and the low throated sound of the steam engine whistles was replaced by the blaring honk of the diesel horns. Many smaller railroads merged with larger lines for greater operating efficiency. And the railroads made efforts to obtain freight revenues from the growing trucking industry itself by hauling loaded truck vans on railroad flat cars in what became called "piggy-backing."

Recognizing that if the railroads were to be preserved as an important element in the nation's passenger transportation system, the federal government in 1966 established a three-year $90 million research and development program to provide high-speed train service from Washington, D.C., to Boston. By welding the rails together in a continuous line for a smoother riding surface, the new train service was expected to achieve average speeds of 110 miles an hour. Some authorities believed the railroads eventually would have to be completely reconstructed and replaced with high-speed monorail systems, such as were built experimentally at various world fairs in the 1960's.

The Twentieth Century Limited speeding along the Hudson River on a special trial run September 9, 1948. (UPI PHOTO)

The Queen Mary, grand old super liner of the Cunard Line, leaving New York en route to Southampton, England, September 22, 1967, prior to retirement and conversion into a hotel and maritime museum at Long Beach, California. (UPI PHOTO)

Ships and Shipping

At the end of World War II the United States was by far the world's leading maritime nation—operating about two-thirds of all the merchant ships in the world. But in the years that followed, despite government subsidies, U.S. shipping companies found it difficult to compete with those of other nations which paid their seamen lower than American wages. By the end of the two-decade period, the active U.S. merchant fleet had fallen into fourth place behind the shipping fleets of Great Britain, Liberia, and Norway. In 1965 U.S. merchant ships accounted for only one-sixth of the total of 209 million tons of cargo vessels entering American ports during the year.

Driver Art Arfons in the cockpit of an experimental boat, designed to approach a speed of 300 mph. (UPI PHOTO)

The United States, which during World War II built nearly 5,900 merchant ships, also lost its lead in shipbuilding to Japan, Great Britain, and West Germany.

By 1967 the United States had only one ship among the list of 15 largest and fastest passenger liners in service. This was the 52,000-ton *S.S. United States*, which on its maiden voyage in July, 1952, established record transatlantic crossing times of 3 days 10 hours and 40 minutes eastbound, and 3 days 12 hours and 12 minutes westbound.

THE CHANGING WORLD of SPORT

by HAROLD ROSENTHAL

TV, mobility and money, frolicking down the lane together, have been the handmaidens to sports in the space generation. TV has whisked the living-room snackster into places where only millionaires had previously penetrated; mobility has made the snows of Kilimanjaro as familiar to the skiers as trails of Crawford's Notch. Money, meanwhile, has changed everything.

That smooth green stuff, the best playing surface yet devised by man, has altered virtually every concept of sport as held before World War II. The professional athlete, once directed to use the freight elevator, has now come back and bought the building.

Playing TV's game, sports promoters, with some lower-echelons exceptions, have grown rich beyond their favorite dreams of avarice. Those who did perish along the route could take some small measure of solace from the fact that there were fellows, too, who once ran marginal grocery stores, overwhelmed in the wave of supermarkets and shopping complexes.

Sports cracked or ignored every kind of social and ethnic barrier. Negroes were unknown in baseball and pro football before World War II. There was no rule saying they were unacceptable. They just weren't. Today neither of these games could be played at their current levels of excitement and proficiency without Negro ball players. 1946 was a milestone in sports, with the Dodgers opening the way with Jackie Robinson and the Cleveland Browns doing it in football.

The space generation has made the millionaire athlete no longer some one to be stared at. Ever hear of Billy Haughton? He owns, trains and drives harness horses. Before Billy reached 45 he

Millionaire Bill Houghton, harness driver and trainer of trotters and pacers, winning Messenger Stakes at Roosevelt Raceway, New York. (ROOSEVELT RACEWAY)

had won more than $10 million just by getting trotters and pacers to go "giddy-yap" faster than other trotters and pacers. You don't know the difference between a trotter and a pacer? This, then is ONE field in which you'll never become a millionaire.

Two nasty little wars failed to dim either American participation in, or enthusiasm for, sports for either spectators or contestants. Neither has a nasty little battle between the colleges and the venerable Amateur Athletic Union of the U.S. (AAU) for American control of most of the Olympic sports. Dialog sample: "We provide the talent, maybe 90 percent worth. Look it up." Reply: "Yes, but we give unselfishly of our time and effort running the show so that your post-college athletes will have places to compete and an opportunity to qualify for the Olympics every four years, don't we?" Congress, which should have more important things to do, has tussled with this one without success.

Pleasantly, the affluent society has played an immense role in sports during this period. The automobile has done things other than haul carousing underage youths across state lines in quest of verboten booze; it has also carried sports fans to places the railroads never knew existed. It has provided new and strange places to explore, either with sporting equipment or with that vital bottom-preserving cushion which protects against unyielding concrete in stadiums everywhere.

The automobile has helped man fulfill the age-old desire to be a part of the big scene. It is a desire which goes all the way back to Lief Ericson's succumbing to the pleadings of a couple of underweight Norsemen and signing them on as auxiliary coxswains for the haul to Vineland.

The space generation marked the resumption of Olympic competition, with its customary squabbles and blown-up scandals (Why is it a lady swimmer who is usually the target here of some irate official? Why don't bald gymnasts make trouble on Olympic trips?) The '36 Olympics in Berlin were the last held before darkness settled over Europe. The games were resumed in '48 in London and have since been held in Finland, Australia, Italy, Japan, with the latest set slated for Mexico City.

The era also brought together those super-powers on and off the field, the U.S.A. and the U.S.S.R., for track and field competition. The edge has since been taken from these clashes but when they came head-on for the first time in '58 they simply shoved everything else on the sports pages into the background.

Over the entire scene has brooded the all-seeing, sometimes bloodshot, eye of TV, sometimes making impossible demands, sometimes generating unbelievably heroic drama, and always delivering the cash. It affected everyone from hotdog salesmen ("Get the hell out of the way of the camera!") to architects ("Don't worry about the men's rooms; make sure we have enough camera positions for TV").

In the 60's came that TV producers' dream, intercontinental live sports, bringing with it additional money for promoter and athlete alike. Who would ever have thought a generation earlier that the European rights to a heavyweight championship fight held in Lewiston, Maine would have been worth as much as was taken in at the gate in live money?

TV also served in another capacity—that of keeping the athlete working after his legs were gone and his time cockeyed. From every field, stars of the past moved up to the mike to tell the customers about the prowess of those who had followed them. And most of these made the move rather successfully . . . the Kyle Rotes, the Pee Wee Reeses, the George Kells, the Pat Summeralls, the Sandy Koufaxes and the Bob Cousys.

And everywhere, people were a lot more comfy, too, with indications that this comfort-quality would continue to improve as the space generation took on a little vintage. In Houston, the first major domed arena, fittingly called the Astrodome, came into being in the mid-60's, offering electronic scoreboards, artificial turf and VIP suites way up top.

Athletes got the idea pretty quickly, once it became fairly obvious that this golden flow wasn't going to be turned off suddenly. The baseball players were the first with their player-pensions in the early 50's. The football players wasted no time putting the squeeze on, once pro football emerged as one big highly-saleable TV item.

Pro basketball players, whose predecessors used to dress in the ladies' room (because ladies' rooms are usually just a little more sumptuous in dance halls than men's rooms) rose in stature as though they had been sprinkled with some wonder drug. A half-dozen made it to the $100,-000-a-year class. When these same players were in high school that kind of money would have bought an entire franchise. Even hockey players, to whom a ten-spot was big money back on the farm in Alberta, caught the idea and started to look up lawyers' phone numbers.

Was it all sweetness and light? Well, there was only one blemish, although how much of a blemish can you notice when it's still all plus signs in the ledger? The Associated Press conducted its once-every-ten-years poll in late '67 and came up with news that could be a little unsettling for anyone planning to hand a baseball empire along to his children.

Baseball, said this most impartial of polls (it went to the grass roots—the people who bought newspapers), is no longer the national sport.

What is? Pro football. Well, surely then baseball is No. 2?

Wrong again. College football. The grand old game of rounders, non-invented by Gen. Abner Doubleday in Cooperstown, N. Y. almost 1½ centuries ago, has been relegated to No. 3. After that it's pro golf, whose performers generate a tremendous amount of glamour considering it is a non-contact, no-risks sport.

The big leap upward has been made by automobile racing, with the Indianapolis (big-car) type out in front. A decade ago the sport wasn't even in the top dozen; today it is rated ahead of college basketball, pro basketball, hunting, amateur golf, prize-fighting, track and field, horse racing and hockey.

The proponents of horse racing have marshalled figures to show that the thoroughbreds (flat-racing) and the standardbreds (trotting) attract combined paid admissions of more than 60,000,000 yearly. There is, of course, a certain inducement going for racetracks which no other sports enjoy. You can make a bet on the premises without having to explain your actions later to a plain-clothes policeman.

And now for a closer look at the individual sports:

Auto Racing

Changes in auto racing have been almost as radical as some of the changes in the grillwork and chrome trim on the average car during that same era. From an activity that had only a hard-core of fans, motor sports have burgeoned into a world-enveloping religion. It is carried on live TV from one continent to another, it commands the largest single paid crowd in sports, it makes

An example of changing styles in racing cars, this September 1937 photograph of two racers, seconds after a collision on the track at Hammond, Indiana, is an interesting contrast to the illustrations of the 1948 and 1967 models. (UPI PHOTO)

millionaires of its champions. Once in a while, too, it puts crepe on a doorfront.

The biggest paying sports crowd in the world throngs into the Indianapolis Speedway grounds each Memorial Day to watch the Indy 500, biggest track race for big cars. It fills every one of 208,000 seats, jams into vantage spots on the infield in a pre-dawn rush that reminds movie-goers of the old land-rushes of the West.

No one ever knows how many actually see the Indy race each year. Wait, there are a few; Tony Hulman, who owns the track and some selected members of his ticket department. Hulman's answer to "how many" has always been a smiling "Whatever your guess it'll be a good one."

Hulman, a Hoosier who rescued Indy back in '47 from what seemed destined to be a sub-division cut-up fate, is literally master of all he surveys at the Speedway. The men he and the other auto promoters rub shoulders with are a breed apart. They worry about nothing except perhaps an unusual noise in the engine or about those extra couple of seconds taken during the last pit stop.

The gamble in auto racing is heavy (after particularly bad accidents you can always count on a clamour from some political or religious quarter to call a halt to the "blood-letting"). The stakes are pretty high, too. A half-dozen racing drivers are millionaires, and not from stock tips from friendly leaders in the world of finance, either.

An Indianapolis victory, or one at LeMans, the greatest road race in the world, will do a great deal toward freeing the winner from worry for the rest of his life, barring necessary Sunday evening driving on freeways, of course.

Basically, there are three types of competition, stock cars, sports cars and big cars. Grand Prix racing has been in effect since 1950 as a basis for determining the world championship. Juan Fangio, an Argentine driver, has won it five times. Jack Brabham, an Australian, has won it three times, and Jimmy Clark, a Scot, twice. Stirling

Mauri Rose, winner of the Memorial Day "500" at the Indianapolis Motor Speedway in 1947 and 1948.
(SPEEDWAY OFFICIAL PHOTO)

A. J. Foyt, top championship driver, 1967 winner at Indianapolis "500." (SPEEDWAY OFFICIAL PHOTO)

Moss, a dashing Englishman whose career was ended by a drastic accident, never won world honors although more persons have probably associated his name with speed and dash in driving than any other.

Europe is the main area for long-distance racing, although the U.S. has its own 24-hour race, Daytona, and a 12-hour race at Sebring, Fla. LeMans is the big one. Ferraris have usually dominated this French classic, although other manufacturers have had a look, and in the most recent years it has been Fords out front.

Stock car racing has tremendous appeal because it is, theoretically, a car you could drive out of a show room. With certain modifications, of course. It is this phase of auto racing which accounts for the major portion of the reported 45,000,000 admissions yearly in the U.S.

Like most things, racing cars and ideas about them have changed. Drivers used to sit up like taxi drivers. Now they virtually lie on their backs. For years the Offenhauser front-engine power plants were standard. Ford came to Indy in 1963 with a rear-engine Lotus for the first time, won with one in 1965.

This set up a revolution which moved all power plants to the rear. The newest development has been turbine engines and a 4-wheel drive. U.S.A.C., the governing body in the U.S., has sought to limit turbines by cutting down on the size of the air intakes.

It is men, skilled, heavy-footed and fearless, who must come along to drive these machines, whether they run them on the tracks, roads or goat-paths. Some of the best include A. J. Foyt, who has won more U.S. championships than anyone; Jimmy Hill, America's only world champ; Mario Andretti, youthful sensation out of Nazareth, Pa., in the late 60s; Rodger Ward, who won the 500 twice in a six-year span and was never lower than fourth; Dan Guerney, who first gave other drivers the idea they might switch with profit from one kind of driving competition to another; Bill Vukavich, probably the heaviest-

Juan Manuel Fangio, five-time winner of the Grand Prix of Europe. (MERCEDES-BENZ)

footed of them all, whose final flaming-pyre tribute at Indy horrified even veteran ambulance drivers in the 50's.

The big manufacturers have moved into the act, figuring correctly that the glamour, the increased exposure via TV, would be reflected in increased sales in the younger market. "Fastbacks" bucket seats, console controls, etc., derive directly from auto racing.

There are more than 1,000 tracks in the U.S. The automobile has become a way of life to a majority of the population, both sexes. To a smaller segment of daring men, and their pit crews, the only driving that is really worthwhile is the kind that starts with an aerial bomb and ends with a checkered flag. It's more interesting, they say, than the 9-to-5 rush-hour variety, and the payoff is bound only to improve.

A dramatic action photo of racing cars piling up at the start of 1966 Memorial Day 500-mile race in Indianapolis.

Baseball

Baseball achieved a fantastic height of popularity as World War II came to a close. The superstars—the Bob Fellers, the Hank Greenbergs, the Joe DiMaggios, the Stan Musials, returned from service; the fans flocked to see them.

TV had yet to stick its long electronic snout into the picture (remember, the first national telecast of a baseball game was not to come until 1951 when the Dodgers and Giants clashed in a three-game playoff for the National League crown). Auto factories were roaring around the clock in an effort to meet the ravening demand for cars built during a half-dozen years of war-time restraints.

Money burned in pockets. The floods of goods able to put out the fire had barely started. What better way to spend it than on baseball?

The demand for baseball entertainment was unbelievable. Those outside the big cities read of the exploits of the major-leaguers (the Dodger-Cardinal playoff in 1946 didn't hurt); radio was literally chocked with play by plays, live and reconstructed, or just plain invented.

The fever swept to the promotion-minded as well. Franchises in the majors suddenly took on a multi-million dollars aspect. Phones in major-league front offices rang incessantly with calls from Rio Grande to Walla Walla. Where could one send a down payment for a franchise?

At the height of this madness there were FIFTY-NINE leagues operating. Farm systems were so overloaded that farm directors sometimes were not aware that some youngster had come and gone. The Dodgers at one time had a farm system which included 26 teams.

At the time Fresco Thompson, a former major league player, was farm director for Brooklyn. He was being interviewed when the reporter suddenly found he had run out of note paper. Fresco obliged him with a sheet which looked like some kind of a form. It was. The reporter finished taking his notes on the back of a report on some youth whose dreams ended that afternoon in the wastebasket of some newspaper office along with yesterday's scorecard.

Cleveland, under that master-promoter, Bill Veeck, drew two million. So did the New York Yankees. Other clubs pushed toward that mark.

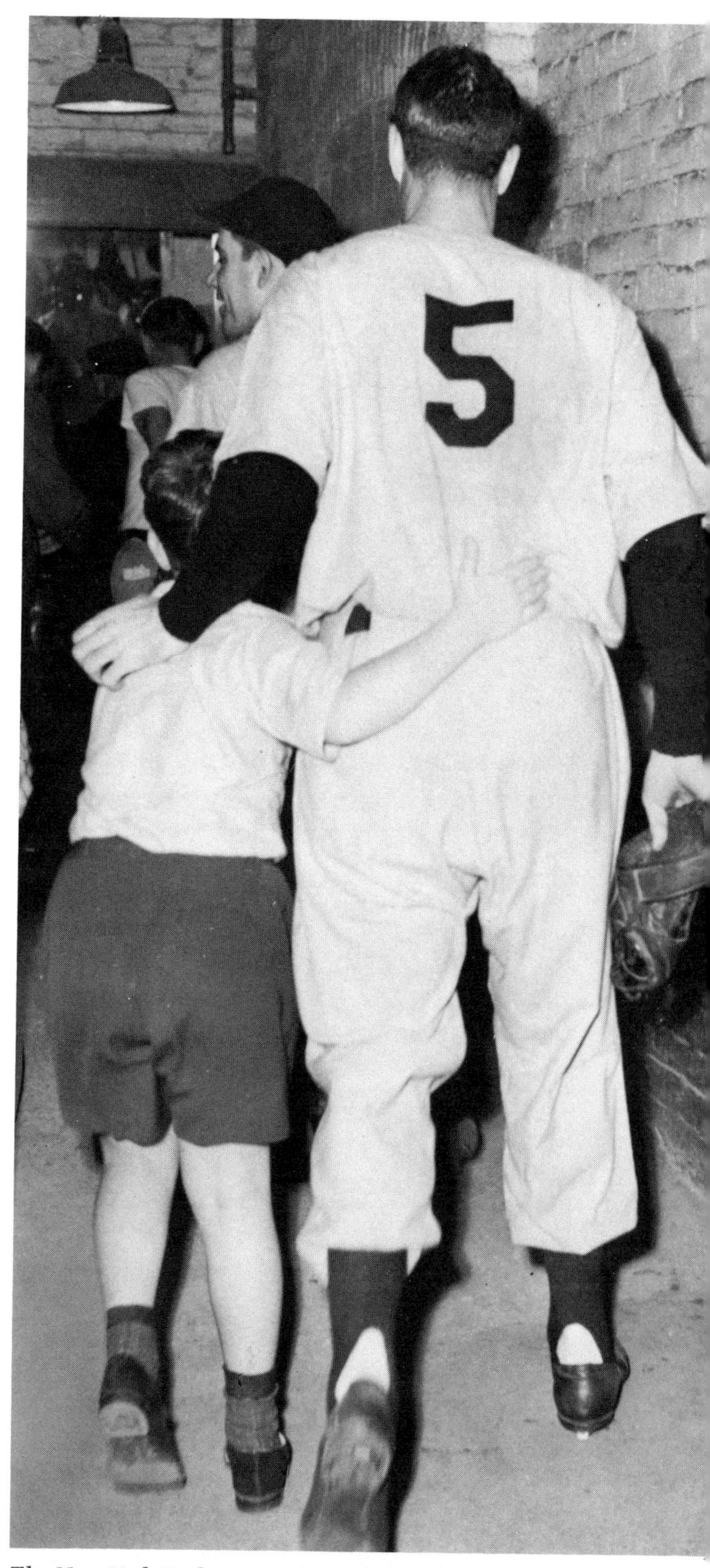

The New York Yankees won the 1949 World Series over the Brooklyn Dodgers in five games despite the injuries that plagued their super star, Joe DiMaggio, shown here after the final game as he trudged back to his dressing room with 8-year-old Joe, Jr. hugging him all the way. (UPI PHOTO)

Ted Williams of the Boston Red Sox, one of the greatest hitters in baseball history, at the time of winning his sixth American League batting championship in 1958 at the age of 40.

Willie Mays, super star center fielder of the San Francisco Giants. (ASSOCIATED PRESS PHOTO)

Everywhere there was undreamed-of prosperity in the sport. The owners, fronted by A. B. (Happy) Chandler, an ex-politico, sat by and amusedly watched the struggle-to-the-death between the established National Football League and the upstart All-America Conference, the latter heavily-financed by race-track money.

The joke was made all the more enjoyable by the fact that most of these embattled football clubs, with their pitiful crowds, were paying baseball clubs nice fat off-season rentals. Obviously, this party would never end.

It did, but it took quite a while. Into the 50's there was a golden flow. Living-room TV sets were still one-to-a-block luxuries. Then, of course, it caught up. Ball games, going more and more to the increased night-time revenues (only the Chicago Cubs in the major leagues were to hold the all-daylight line at Wrigley Field, and still do), started to run into such wierd rivals as Milton Berle, Ed Sullivan, Captain Video and the Friday Night Fites.

Hard times struck in several places. In St. Louis, where Veeck had bought the Browns, you could shoot a moose in the grand stand during a day game. Boston, where the Braves declined in dramatic fashion after winning the National League pennant in 1948, withered. Said general manager John Quinn, "We (the Boston club) have paid for every one of those TV aerials you see on the roofs over in East Boston."

Boston busted out and made it to Milwaukee for a decade in which the club set records at the gate, then set a record for lying about its plans for an eventual move to Atlanta. In Milwaukee in the mid-50s, people paid good weekday afternoon money to see the Pittsburgh Pirates (losers of 103 games in a season) challenge their darlings. They cheered pop fouls, swilled beer, stormed the concession counters as though the Russian paratroopers were already dropping in nearby Waukegan.

TV's blight on baseball was not universal. While the minors died, most of the major league clubs prospered. The majors simply rearranged things. Instead of blowing the bankroll on farm operations they lavished extravagant bonuses on young men who were thought able to make it to the big leagues in a hurry. Every front office today wears fading scars from the mistakes of that era.

Once baseball moved the Boston franchise to Milwaukee and the moribund Browns to Baltimore, the way was open for expansion west. Philadelphia went to Kansas City, and the Coast was next. Football had already preceded it with its switch of the Cleveland Rams to Los Angeles, plus the addition of the San Francisco 49ers to the NFL when the NFL and AAFC merged after '49.

Baseball wasn't quite ready for the West Coast. But it had seen the handwriting about two-team cities (if the hot team was on the road with its TV, the team at home might just as well not bother). St. Louis became a one-team city, as did Philadelphia.

Then in '58 came the biggest of the moves. The Brooklyn Dodgers and the New York Giants, who had been in seven of the previous nine World Series, skipped town for California. Walter O'Malley, Brooklyn Dodger president, executed a series of complicated real estate maneuvers which were to wind up in a Chavez Ravine stadium complex valued at an estimated fifty-million dollars today in downtown Los Angeles. Not quite so ambitious, Giant owner Horace Stoneham settled for an adequate, if windblown, stadium at Candlestick Point outside San Francisco. When these teams left New York they took some of the super-stars of the space generation.

Jackie Robinson, who had smashed the color line with the aid of Dodger front-office boss, Branch Rickey, had retired. An auto accident had put Roy Campanella in a wheel chair for life. But the Dodgers had such stars as Pee Wee Reese, Duke Snider, Gil Hodges and a wild kid lefthander named Sandy Koufax. The Giants had the remnants of a team which had swept the Cleveland Indians four straight in the 1954 World Series, plus Willie Mays, en route to becoming a tremendous star. Out in the Golden West, Walter and Horace were to find pure gold. They also brought California a steady parade of World Series pageants each October.

Back East, meanwhile, the Yankees dominated the sport like no other team in history. Rather than count the times the Yankees were in the World Series, writers would tick off the times the Yankees HADN'T made it since Casey Stengel had taken over as a sort of amusing clown in 1949. There was a break in 1954 when the Indians, with super pitching from such as Early

Mickey Mantle of the New York Yankees, one of the ten leading home run hitters in baseball history.

Stan "The Man" Musial of the St. Louis Cardinals, leading hitter for two decades, won seven National League batting titles.

Sandy Koufax of the Los Angeles Dodgers set several strike-out records in the 1960's, pitching four no-hit games.
(DARRYL NORENBERG)

The Giants' Willie Mays sliding safely to third, Umpire Paul Pryor, and third baseman, Charlie Smith, getting a handful of dirt.
(ASSOCIATED PRESS PHOTO)

Wynn, Bob Lemon, Mike Garcia and Bob Feller, beat them by winning a record 111 games.

In 1959 the White Sox pushed them aside and after the 1960 Series loss to the Pirates, the Yankees pushed Stengel aside as being "too old". His former coach and player, Ralph Houk, took the team and won from 1961 through 1963. Houk then went into the front office and Yogi Berra came off the field to become a winning manager in 1964. Berra lost to the Cardinals and was bounced for his pains.

That was the last time around for the Yankees. Two years later they finished dead last. It was probably one of the greatest flops in sport. For years the Yankees had been synonymous with icy superiority. In fact one of the great lines of the era was "How can you root for the Yankees? It's like rooting for U.S. Steel!"

The list of Yankee greats were household names. Mickey Mantle, playing on gimpy legs, became the super star and the gate attraction so essential in New York after Joe DiMaggio had retired after 1951. There were the tremendous pitchers, Allie Reynolds, Vic Raschi, Eddie Lopat, Whitey Ford. Don Larsen pitched a perfect game in the 1956 World Series. It was no secret that the other clubs counted on the Yankees for at least twenty-five percent of their home attendance.

Not that there weren't stars elsewhere. In Boston the formidable Ted Williams was en route to 521 homers and the distinction of being the oldest (40) ever to win a batting championship. In Los Angeles, Maury Wills was smashing the immortal Ty Cobb's base-stealing record with 104 steals in 1962, the year after Roger Maris had broken Babe Ruth's mark with 61 homers.

In St. Louis, Stan Musial was wrapping up a distinguished career which extended over more than two decades. Stan the Man set a flock of records, including one of having played in 100 or more games for TWENTY-ONE years. Baseball, which has been known to make some monumental blunders was lucky with Stan, probably the greatest playing good-will ambassador the game has ever had. When his playing days were over Gussie Busch, the Cardinal owner, moved him into the front office and then into the general manager's role.

Meanwhile Sandy Koufax, the one-time wild

Carl Yastrzemski holds his leg after falling to the ground when hit by a pitch in the first inning of the third game of the 1967 World Series.

A relaxed moment in the St. Louis Cardinals' dressing room, showing Roger Maris, veteran slugger, exchanging pleasantries with star pitcher, Bob Gibson.

As Bob Gibson pitches in the first inning of the final game of the 1967 World Series, his wife cheers him on.

Umpire Frank Umont halts the third game to warn managers Red Schoendienst of the St. Louis Cardinals and Dick Williams of the Boston Red Sox about "brush back" pitches such as the one that decked Yastrzemski above.

Bob Gibson, pitching star of the 1967 World Series, throws the first pitch of the final game to Joe Foy of the Red Sox.

(UPI PHOTOS)

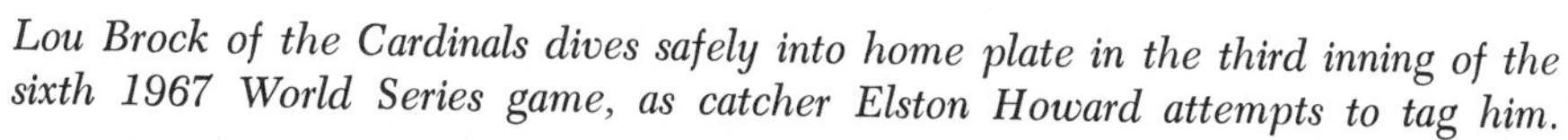

Lou Brock of the Cardinals dives safely into home plate in the third inning of the sixth 1967 World Series game, as catcher Elston Howard attempts to tag him.

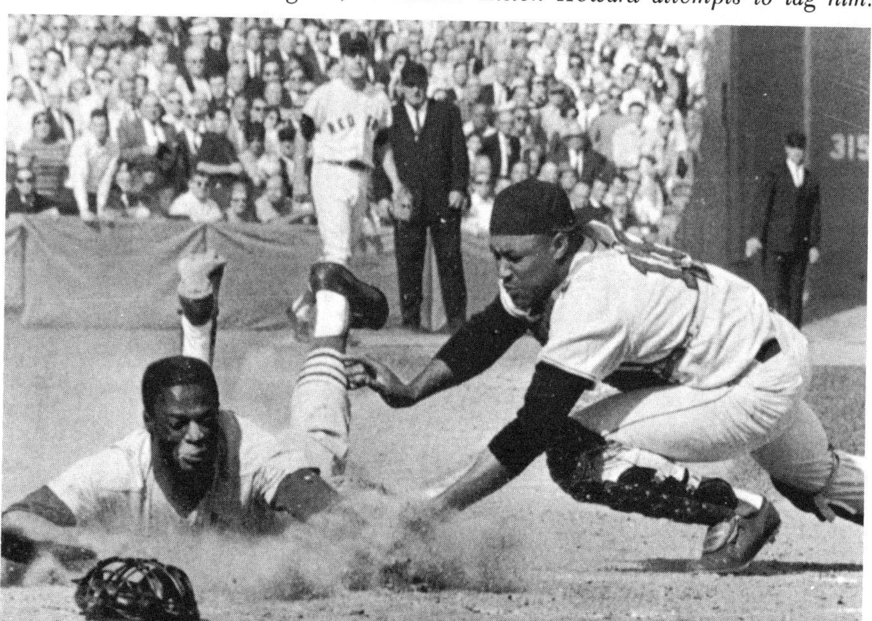

Yankee Roger Maris, in 1961, receiving Brooklyn Prep "Catholic Athlete of the Year" award from Reverend John J. Morrison, S.J., after breaking home run record set by Babe Ruth.

lefty who couldn't find the plate, proceeded to develop into the greatest lefthander the game had seen. Arm trouble forced his retirement after 1966, seemingly at the height of his career. When he departed he left such marks as four no-hit games, 300 or more strikeouts for three years, eighteen strikeouts (twice) and the Cy Young Memorial Award (best pitcher in the majors) three times in four years.

One of the teams Sandy no-hitted was the New York Mets in 1962. That was in the first year of what is unquestionably one of the most unusual teams ever to don uniforms. Koufax's accomplishment was only one of 120 times the Mets were beaten that particular year. At the helm, of course, was Casey Stengel, the most successful manager of his era, who had come back to take the job because . . . "no man is bigger than baseball."

Stengel said he didn't come back to "make a career for himself" (he was already in his 70's) but as it turned out he became one of the most important figures the game has known.

It should be remembered that the pro football explosion was already in progress when Stengel unveiled his rag-tag gathering to the world; culls, misfits, over-the-hillers and an occasional stop-over between psychiatric treatments.

He took this group and built a wildly-excited following for it in an ancient ball park with creaky plumbing. People in New York talked about his tenth-place ball club and ignored the first-place Yankees.

Casey made the Mets synonymous with "we're beat-today-but-watch-us-tomorrow." Millions, young and old, related to that philosophy. They came thronging to the new ball park adjoining the New York World's Fair of '64-65, and when a broken hip sidelined Casey for good in midseason of '65, the Mets had been firmly launched. The story of Stengel's half-century in the game has been the subject for a half-dozen books including one he wrote himself after his discharge by the Yankees was deemed to be the end of a long career. It can best be summed up by the fact that the Hall of Fame circumvented its 5-year rule to move him into his niche there several years ahead of time.

Maury Wills of the Los Angeles Dodgers stole 104 bases during the 1962 season, breaking Ty Cobb's record.

In 1966 baseball's owners got together and did something the National Football League had been smart enough to do a half-dozen years earlier. They packaged their TV, jettisoning the archaic idea of individual deals which made the strong clubs stronger and the weak clubs weaker. It has a long way, however, to go before it catches up to pro football in dollar value.

The game still has plenty of problems but there is a genuine love for it in the U.S. Perhaps the ranks of young men who would play for $150 a month and ride busses in the minors have thinned, but there'll always be the one who will play for nothing, just for the feeling that comes with bending a third strike past some frustrated batter, or for the elation that follows a ball's arc over a distant fence. That's the young man whose name will probably make headlines five, ten or fifteen years hence.

The last game at the Polo Grounds in New York City, September 29, 1957, showing Bill Rigney of the Giants with his arm around Mrs. John McGraw, wife of the former great Giants manager, with other Giants players in the background. (UPI PHOTO)

Casey Stengel, the most successful manager of his era.

Hal Greer (left) and Wilt Chamberlain (right) jam under basket as somebody went tumbling. (PHILADELPHIA BULLETIN)

Basketball

In these days of multi-million dollar TV contracts, players pushing aggressively toward the $100,000 level, owners in pro basketball like to recall how they came to award a franchise to Minneapolis. It was in connection with the fledgling sport's willingness to put on a game wherever a buck could be drummed up. And these weren't exhibitions, either, but regular league games.

At a meeting of the National Basketball Association in Chicago, Max Winter, a soft-spoken promoter from Minneapolis, asked whether he could have a game played in his city? He offered a $25,000 guarantee.

Now in those days, and they weren't too long ago, there were plenty of people sniffing around basketball who talked in thousands but who couldn't ultimately match their quoted figures in cents. Winter looked as though he might be a little different, however. They asked him to leave the room.

"Twenty-five thousand bucks!", said one magnate who remembered the efforts he had made to meet his payroll the previous season. "Let's not give him a GAME. Let's give him a FRANCHISE!"

That's how the Minneapolis Lakers were born, and that's the same franchise that ultimately was sold to Los Angeles for $5,175,000.

TV has been the magic ingredient in pro basketball, as in so many other spectator sports. When the league embarked upon an expansion policy, destined to line up 18 clubs by the early 70's, franchises were pegged at $1,800,000. And there were plenty of takers. Disappointed customers could do their shopping in a rival supermarket set up to take advantage of the various new arenas popping up, and did. The latest challenger to the NBA was the A (for American) BA and the customary flock of injunctions, suits, etc., descended on the bouncing-ball sport.

Action alone was not enough to attract TV. The sport had built-in super stars in such as Wilt Chamberlain, the greatest scorer the game has known, Bill Russell, Bob Pettit, Dolph Schayes, Bob Cousy, Jerry Lucas, Jerry West, Elgin Baylor and Oscar Robertson. Robertson, a great college star at Cincinnati, was undoubtedly the finest all-around performer ever developed. Cousy, now a college coach, was the most magical of the ball handlers.

Chamberlain, a 7-footer able to move like a man a dozen inches shorter, holds the record for 100 points in a game. He has probably taken more money out of the sport than any other performer. Someone once figured that BT (Before TV) Wilt's salary was more than a lot of the league's clubs cleared as a yearly profit.

Pro basketball is a child of the space generation. It was played long before; in fact there were players who got around to playing for a couple of dollars on their day off shortly after Dr. Naismith hung the peachbaskets on either end of that Springfield YMCA gym back in the 90's. It was strictly dance-hall stuff and local-crowd rowdyism, however, until the arena owners in the Eastern half of the U.S. got together right after World War II and set up the BAA.

A half-dozen years later the BAA absorbed the NBL and became the NBL. There was a brief attempt to set up another league by Abe Saperstein, the promotional wizard who had taken the Harlem Globetrotters to every continent except the Arctic and Antarctic. The new loop set up several innovations, including a three-point shot based on distance, but it flopped.

Most agree that the 24-seconds clock was the savior of the game. Prior to that the last minute of each game would stretch drearily as each club took turns fouling and stalling, stalling and fouling.

The clocks were simply a tick-off for everyone to see and hear, set up on opposite ends of the court. You had 24 seconds to shoot after you got possession. It was as simple as that. Colleges, where the customers presumably worry less about getting home, have not installed this electronic prod.

College basketball has not suffered because of the growth of the pro sport. On the contrary, the sport in the field houses, gyms, and arenas has prospered in unprecedented fashion. Every year the NCAA championships draw packed houses wherever held. "Festival" tournaments, and there have been some pretty strange "festivals" dreamed up for basketball tournaments, invariably sell out. In college sports the basketball player is the most traveled performer in the varsity picture.

An occasional scandal in the college ranks has jolted the scene. Most serious one was in the early 50's and it involved City College of New York's NCAA and National Invitation Tourney champion. Ten years later there was another, and this time three or four northeastern colleges were marked. Obviously point-shaving and dumping isn't indigenous to this particular section of the nation. It's more probable that here the District Attorney's men are merely a little sharper, or closer to basketball. Perhaps some of them have played the game.

The premium on height and shooting ability remains pretty much fixed. The six footer has to be a wizard to get a second look from pro scouts. The fellow who can't pop them in from every angle and every distance—consistently—doesn't last too long in the pros. Physical endurance is also a desirable attribute, plus the ability to come back night after night to take a beating under the boards that would ordinarily have the average person yelling for the police.

Pro ball has developed its own folk heroes in two decades. High on the list has to be Arnold (Red) Auerbach, most successful coach of the pros (eight straight playoff championships with the Boston Celtics and now their general manager). Auerbach, himself a college star of modest proportions and talents, merged the abilities of such stars as Cousy, John Kerr, Tom Heinsohn, Frank Ramsey and Bill Russell into unbeatable units. When he moved into the front office he turned over the head-coach's role to Russell, an ex-University of San Francisco player who thus became the first Negro to run a major-league club in any sport.

Arnold (Red) Auerbach, pro basketball's super coach, with eight straight championships for the Boston Celtics.

Robert Cousy of the Boston Celtics, the best ball handler of them all.

Cousy made up for his lack of height (6.1) with a wizardry in ball handling under game conditions never seen before, or since. Spectators and rival players alike were often left limp. He was outstanding as a Holy Cross College player but he became super star in his long career in the pros.

The college spotlight has switched from year to year with the big team being produced in virtually all sections of the nation. Adolph Rupp's Kentucky teams were dominant in the 50's. In the late 60's it was U.C.L.A. under John Wooden, who executed the maneuver of the year when he convinced a 7-foot New York schoolboy, Lew Alcindor, to pursue his further learning 2,400 miles from home.

Colleges have, in the main, provided the amateur talent that has given the U.S. the distinction of never having lost an Olympic contest. Poor judgment and management have caused the U.S. to send so-called national teams to other countries to be drubbed by the likes of Uruguay and Chile, but when it's for the biggest prize of all, the various amateur groups have taken time out from kicking each other in the shins long enough to put its best basketball team on the hardwood—and that one has always been unbeatable.

Boating

The fellows back there in the lab are not only responsible for boating's boom but probably for the fact that there is any kind of recreation boating at all today. When labor costs soared after World War II, boating looked like a dead duck.

The garden-variety, bent-nail carpenter was on his way to the same yearly income as a marine designer. Who was going to be able to have a rotted plank replaced? Do-it-yourself was okay, but not when an amateur's mistake would put a party of five into an unscheduled swimming act five miles offshore.

But technology, in the form of fibre glass hulls, saved the day. Today 90 percent of all hulls are of that virtually indestructible material.

Ditto on the sails. Cotton is a thing of the past. It's Dacron and nylon (the latter for spinnakers). Stronger sail cloth has also meant stronger standing gear, the halyards, stays, etc. Winches are stronger, aluminum masts are lighter and stronger.

And the interest, of course, has skyrocketed in all boating. Among the sailors there are 10,000 Lightning Class 19½-feet sloops registered, a boost of 9,000 since World War II. There are 125 one-design racing classes, there is world competition in the Star Class, there are America's Cup races every few years now instead of every decade.

The boats in which the U.S. defends against all comers are 12-meter jobs, half the size of the original J-Class vessels. The J-Class became obsolete in much the same manner of the dinosaurs; with rising costs their size became ridiculous. And the 12-meters, most claim, give you as good a race, or better.

Young pros, capable and imaginative, have grown up in sailing. Prominent among them have been Harry C. (Bud) Melges Jr., a builder and

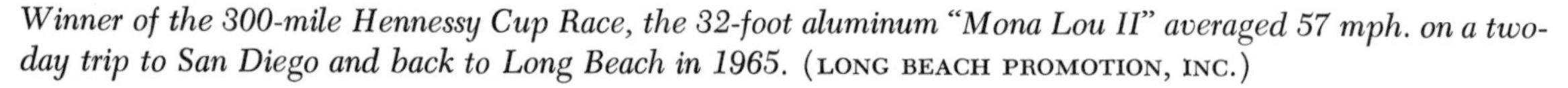

Winner of the 300-mile Hennessy Cup Race, the 32-foot aluminum "Mona Lou II" averaged 57 mph. on a two-day trip to San Diego and back to Long Beach in 1965. (LONG BEACH PROMOTION, INC.)

designer of inland lake scows from Zenda, Wis. Between '59-61, Bud won the North American Yacht Racing Union sailing title three times.

Ocean racing has boomed, in both the Atlantic and Pacific. Man's challenge of the limitless wastes is an eternal one. In 1967 Francis Chichester, a Britisher, was knighted after he had sailed a 45-foot craft singled-handed around the world.

One of every half-dozen persons in the U.S. is interested in some way in power boating. The figure is around 40 million and it is interesting the way it is arrived at by the statisticians of the National Association of Engine and Boat Manufacturers and the Boating Industry Association.

4,138,140 power boats are registered. The rest are boating industry figures. Throw in a little attrition and you have the big figure, multiplied by five, the average per boat you'll find tooling around.

Electronic ignition, eliminating points and breakers and employing high-voltage spark plugs, has cut in half service problems on engines. The lure of the big boats, such as the Gold Cuppers, is still there and with jet engines now the drivers are pressing toward 300 m.p.h. on the water.

The glamour, however, has largely passed to the off-shore powerboat racing, using 36 feet cruiser hulls and twin engines able to generate more than a total of 1,000 horsepower. Sixty miles an hour in waves seven or eight feet high is a lot more thrilling than twice that speed on a lake.

That kind of racing takes plenty of money. There also is still room for the person who watches his pocketbook, thanks to the fiberglass hulls and the development of the inboard-outboard power unit.

Bowling

Bowling's super era traces to the successful introduction of the electronic pin-spotter, that ingenious device which has replaced bored young boys and tired old men in the task of replacing the pins, flattened for the 1,000th time during the evening. What the pin-spotter did, actually, was to make bowling an around-the-clock sport. The machine can't tell time; it operates just as effectively at 3 in the morning as it does at 7 in the evening. Off-hour shortages of pin-boys is just a bit of hardwood folklore, now.

Dick Weber, bowling's three-time winner of National Match Championship (1962, 1963, 1965).

So are some of the $25 and $50 purses of a generation ago. Today's bowlers roll for prizes that would have represented several years of income a couple of decades ago. The Firestone Professional Bowlers tournament in Akron each year carries a top prize of $25,000. Dick Weber, current tops among men in the U.S., has racked up a quarter of a million during the past decade.

Weber was originally a member of the greatest men's team ever put together, the Budweisers of St. Louis. On that same team was Don Carter, who preceded Weber as the leading individual. Others on that fabulous five were Ray Bluth, Tom Hennessy and Pat Paterson. For years they repelled all bidders for the team crown.

So did Marion Ladewig, of Grand Rapids, in the ladies' division. As Marion faded from the picture she was replaced by young aspirants, outstanding among whom has been Millie Ignizio, of Rochester, N.Y.

There are various versions of bowling, duckpins and lawn bowls being among the popular activities. Regulation bowling has made its mark overseas, particularly in Japan. Bowling authorities in the U.S. estimate there are 8,000,000 devotees alone in the organized leagues.

Boxing

Boxing, since its first recorded fervid beginnings (Cain vs. Abel) has managed to turn up strange personalities in stranger situations. The space generation has enjoyed its full measure of these, with perhaps an occasional bonus. To begin, it started with perhaps the best of the heavyweight champions, Joe Louis, and toward the end offered perhaps the most controversial, Muhammad Ali, born Cassius Clay.

Sandwiched in was perhaps the best pound-for-pounder ever to pull on a glove, Sugar Ray Robinson, born Walker Smith. Sugar Ray fought professionally for 25 years, presumably amassed a fortune, winning and losing titles, and established himself as one of the greatest of welterweights (147) and middleweights (160) of all time. He also challenged for the light heavyweight title (175) and missed.

Sugar Ray played the king, in and out of the ring, preferring expensive cars in mauve hues, retinues of in-service personnel, both here and abroad. White promoters frequently accused him of a racist attitude long before the word became fashionable; his frequent pullouts from bouts for the slightest of reasons lent credence to their claims. They could never claim, however, that Sugar Ray short-changed them in the ring.

Sugar Ray Robinson, leading welterweight and middleweight titleholder for twenty-five years. (JOHN CONDON)

Robinson was the big attraction in the era where a flood of free TV killed everything but the big-name fight. The small clubs were extinct by the mid-50's. Sugar Ray would wait patiently for a suitable challenger for one of his titles to be developed somehow (it could be a Hawaiian like Bob Olsen or an Englishman like Randy Turpin or a Mormon like Gene Fullmer), and would then proceed to make everyone rich with his irresistible lure at the ticket wickets.

What Sugar Ray did with his end was his own affair. Eventually age took the spring from his legs and the sting from his punch. Lesser fighters took over his realm.

Joe Louis came out of the Army after World War II one of the biggest men in the country. As an enlisted man he had comported himself with instinctive dignity. His name also was synonymous with legalized destruction within the confines of a ring. He put his title on the line against Billy Conn in June, 1946 and the bout produced the first $100 ringside seat. Louis was involved in

The controversial Muhammad Ali, born Cassius Clay. (JOHN CONDON)

several million-dollar gates but never approached the $2,658,660 of the second Dempsey-Tunney fight in Chicago in 1927.

Louis fought until '49, announced his undefeated retirement, came back to challenge for Ezzard Charles' elimination-series title in 1950 and lost. In his last serious battle he was kayoed by Rocky Marciano during the latter's ascent to the championship. It was the first time Louis had been stopped in the ring since Max Schmeling knocked him out 15 years earlier and he quit for good.

Marciano, like Louis, retired undefeated, and stayed that way. Between him and the controversial Cassius Clay there were Floyd Patterson, Ingemar Johansson of Sweden, and Sonny Liston, as champs.

The heavyweight division produced heavy revenue on big fights, thanks to a specialized form of TV known as "closed circuit." Someone got the idea of pumping the big fight into theatres around the country at high prices and it proved a good one. The payoff from these ancillary activities, as they came to be known, frequently outdid the live gate. It made possible the staging of heavyweight championship fights in such unlikely places as Las Vegas and Lewiston, Maine.

Clay proved easily the most controversial champion to come along in this particular span. Originally an Olympic champion out of Louisville, he was brought along carefully by a group of local sportsmen under professional guidance.

Clay upset Liston in a title fight in Miami Beach, then kayoed him in one round in a fight that was chased out of Boston (and other places) following a sudden hernia operation on Clay. They wound up doing their stuff in Lewiston, Maine in a kind of gymnasium.

Clay became increasingly unpopular in 1966 because of his Black Muslim religious avowals. When he protested his Selective Service re-classification from 4F to 1A he became ostracized in most boxing areas in the country and was forced to find his box offices in Europe and Canada. In early 1967 he was found guilty of refusing induction into the armed forces of his country. Boxing commissions everywhere were quick to vacate his title.

Below Clay and the heavyweights there was precious little to make headlines in the late 60's.

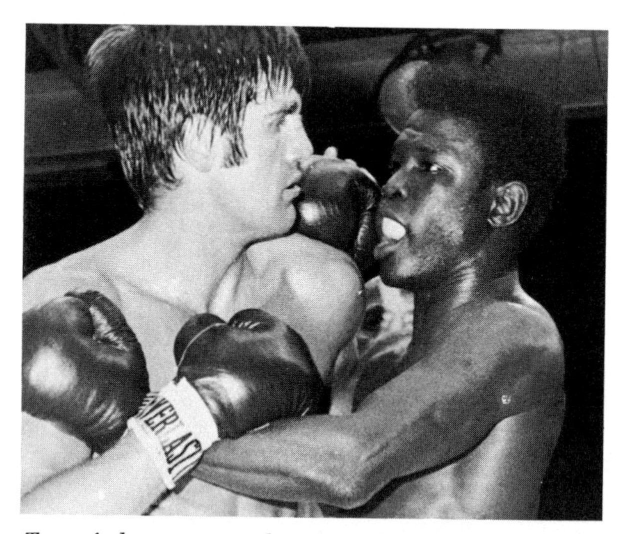

Two of the remaining boxers in the middleweight division, Nino Benvenuti (left) and Emil Griffith, in the first round of their return bout, won by Griffith, at Shea Stadium, September 29, 1967. (UPI PHOTO)

There were more non-Americans than Americans listed in the world championship rosters and American interest in the lighter classes, such as flyweight, bantamweight and featherweight, 112, 118 and 126 pounds, was virtually non-existent. The superior diet of the affluent society, which extended inevitably to the less-privileged classes, had taken care of that. These divisions were taken over by Filipinos, Thais, Japanese and others of the traditionally smaller ethnic groups.

College boxing interest waned during the 50's and 60's. Because of injuries, real or projected, most schools dropped their programs. This area could always be counted upon for a challenger or two in the pro ranks, but this now disappeared. Politicians, self-seeking and otherwise, frequently called for elimination of boxing, especially that for profit.

Amateur boxing has had its difficulties, too, although the U.S. has always managed somehow to come up with a fairly representative team in the Olympics. This, too, traces to the lack of a lure of a professional career. Today, a youth who doesn't know one end of a wrench from another can make more money in some unionized trade just standing and holding that wrench than he would by standing in a dusty ring permitting someone to boff away at his beak. Even the caveman was smart enough not to expose his features to the opposition a second time, unless forced to by a gnawing emptiness in his belly.

The professional football season is long and sometimes snowy, as shown in this view of Len Ford, former star end for the University of Michigan and the Cleveland Browns. (UPI PHOTO)

Football

Pro football's explosive growth in every direction, territorially, financially, and in fan interest, has been by far the biggest story in sports of the past several decades. From a point in the late 40's where the whole apparatus teetered on the brink of bankruptcy, thanks to a bit of unfettered blood-letting between the National League and the short-lived but exciting All-America Conference, the sport has moved to where advertisers gladly pour $100 million yearly into the TV-radio end of the game alone. Well before confirmation by the Associated Press' 1967 poll—the advertisers knew that pro football had become the No. 1 sport in the United States.

Everyone knows how, in 40 years, the price of a pro franchise has soared from $500 (for New York, which the Mara family still holds) to $10 million (for San Diego in the American Football League). Everyone is aware, too, there are middle-aged men around who remember picking up $200 a game, sometimes less, playing in the National Football League.

They could easily be excused for wondering whether they hadn't been born at the wrong time, especially when they read of super stars pushing toward the $100,000-a-year level. They could also be permitted a raised eyebrow or two when a club like Green Bay, engaged in sheriff-ducking only a dozen years earlier, paid a total of more than a million in bonus arrangements to a pair of untried college kids during that final desperate bidding race for talent which directly preceded the merger of the National and American Leagues in June 1966.

Veteran observers are pretty well agreed that there are three clear-cut phases of the pro game. Phase One began when the pros were organized in an auto salesroom in Canton, Ohio, and reached as far as the start of the space generation. It was at this point they made a momentous decision to Platoon (offense and defense) and stuck with it.

The colleges meanwhile vaccilated between unlimited substitution, limited, no-substitution, "wild card" rules, etc., and thereby conceded the pros an appeal edge beyond measurement. They have never been close to catching up; now never will. And rubbing salt into the abrasion is the fact that the collegians are perfectly aware that the pros, in their plush meetings, rate the colleges for precisely what they are in football, regardless of what they are in other fields—a built-in farm system.

Phase Two stretches roughly from the early 50's, when the NFL extinguished the All-America threat, killing all but three of its clubs, Cleveland, Baltimore and San Francisco, and right into the famed over-time game in which the Baltimore Colts and Johnny Unitas beat the Giants for the 1958 playoff crown. Most believe that the playoff was something special in the way of on-the-spot legislation that particular afternoon. Actually the NFL had prepared for just something like this with a rule ten years earlier dictating no playoff could end in a tie.

Phase Three is the current golden one. TV grinds out the money that assures a profitable season no matter what the gate (just as assuredly there could be no profit in pro football today without TV). A benevolent attitude toward the game is demonstrated by the government in its anti-monopoly department. Undreamed of revenue from side-lines and spin-off activities pour in.

Just how lucrative is all this? The championship game between the NFL and AFL from 1968 through 1979 will bring $2.5 million PER GAME. What could you have bought with $2.5

million a generation ago had you gone shopping in football? Probably the ENTIRE NFL, if you had shown yourself to be really in earnest.

That earnest young genius, Pete Rozelle, has played no small part in the incredible pro football explosion. Package-TV was his personal dream, one that he had to struggle to put across. A club getting a quarter of a million for its rights in 1960 had to be subjected to a lot of persuasion to throw it into the same pot as a club getting $50,000. And Pete, after all, had been just a compromise candidate for Commissioner. But Pete persuaded, and pro football rode the electronic waves to overhaul and pass baseball in national interest at a time when baseball was expanding from 16 to 20 major clubs.

The talent, of course, had to be there to capture the imagination. It was. There was Johnny Unitas, a gifted magician, who was to break the record for touchdown passes; his prime target, Ray Berry, who was to catch more passes than anyone who had come before. There was Jimmy Brown, the super-runner and Jim Taylor, who was to pick up a lot more playoff championship money with the Green Bay Packers than Jimmy Brown did with the Browns, but who was destined to be mentioned as a rusher only after Brown. Taylor topped 1,000 yards in five different seasons. Brown did it in seven. In the entire history of the game it has been accomplished a mere 35 times.

There was Bart Starr, and the near-perfect machine Vince Lombardi put together at Green Bay to dominate pro football in much the manner the Yankees did baseball during this era. At Green Bay, Paul Hornung scored 322 points in successive seasons (176 in 1960, 146 in 1961). The 176er came during a 12-game season. Only man who ever came close was Boston's Gino Cappelletti in the AFL. Cappelletti was a pass receiver and kicker, in contrast to Hornung's running and kicking abilities.

There was Y. A. Tittle, whom the Giants picked up almost as an afterthought in a pre-season trade with San Francisco in 1961. Three seasons later Tittle set a major-league pro record of 36 TD passes in one season.

These weren't the only great players in the era which followed World War II. There were the super quarterbacks, like Sid Luckman and Otto Graham, and Bob Waterfield and Bobby Layne and Tobin Rote and Sonny Jurgensen, all fearless, all almost unbelievably skilled. On defense Emlen Tunnell's lifetime interception mark of 79 will probably stand forever.

Football ability came in all sizes and temperaments. There was Eddie LeBaron, who looked like an overweight jockey when he quarterbacked Washington and Dallas, and Big Daddy Lipscomb (his correct name disappeared early in his career) so gargantuan that when he answered "How do I know who to tackle? I just grab a handful and I pick out the one that's got the ball," the opposition was painfully aware that he meant it.

There were speedsters who didn't make it, and speedsters like Bob Hayes, the Olympic champion, who did. In his first two years with Dallas, Hayes set a freshman-soph record for TD receptions, 25.

There were coaches who remembered when they played themselves with one eye on the box office (George Halas) and coaches who marshalled the cold efficiency of business management (Tom Landry, Vince Lombardi and George Allen) to the job. When Lombardi declared

Bart Starr, star quarterback of champion Green Bay Packers.

"There is nothing wrong with controlled violence," or "We either win in this business or we are gone," fan and foe shivered, either with delight or with dread.

Brown and Lombardi easily deserve a few chapters of their own. Brown was outstanding as a college athlete, made it as a star in the pros right from his freshman year. As indicated, he topped 1000 yards in one season seven of nine times. (He got to 996 one year and went 942 in his first campaign.) His top is 1863 yards in '63. As any Phys. Ed. major will tell you, that's well over a mile.

When Brown came out of Syracuse to play for the Browns (surprisingly he was not the first but the FIFTH player to be drafted that year; Hornung, John Brodie, Ron Kramer and Len Dawson were picked ahead of him), Paul Brown was the resident genius in Cleveland. The Cleveland Browns had been one of three AAFC clubs absorbed into the NFL. They showed in a hurry where the talent was with six straight playoff appearances and three victories.

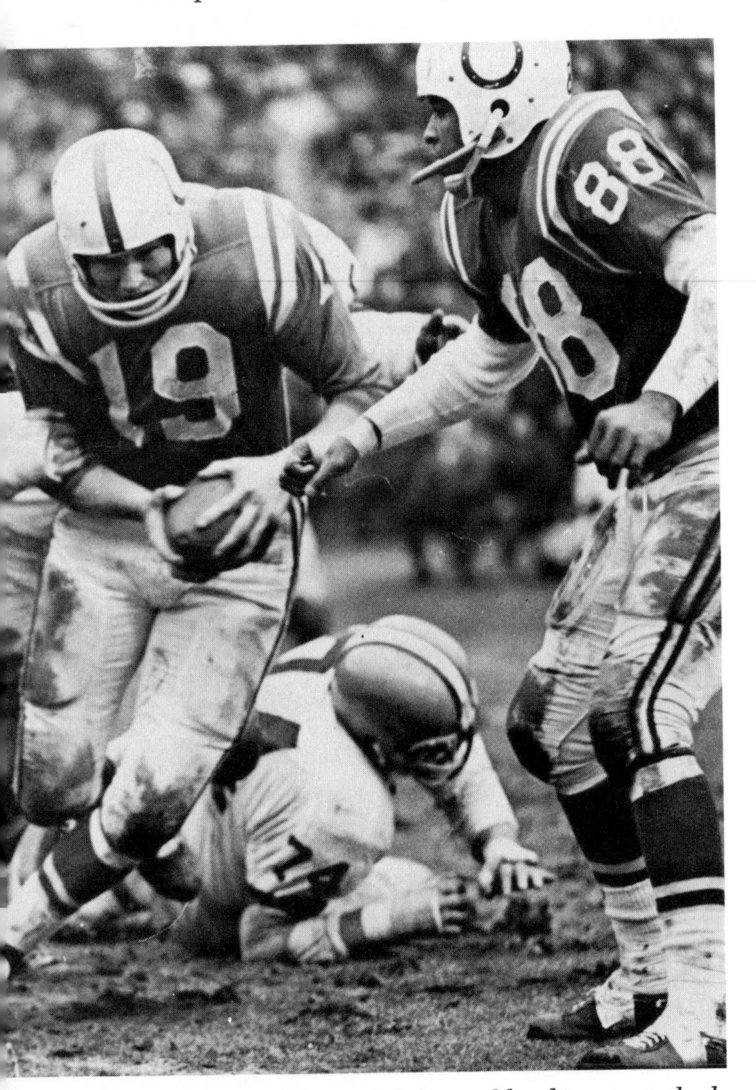

Johnny Unitas, Baltimore Colts' record-breaking quarterback.

An abrasive element ultimately developed between Jimmy Brown and Paul Brown. The player put it up to the new young owner, Art Modell, with a flat, "It's either him or me."

Modell took a deep breath and went for the player. It could have been a couple of deep breaths because this particular shake-off was one of the most expensive in sports, representing a contract of more than a half-million. Jimmy Brown brought the Browns back into the playoff picture in 1964 and 1965 and spearheaded a league championship in 1964. He quit in June 1966 and entered the movie and TV business.

Lombardi decided what he wanted early in life, which is always an edge. He ruled out the clergy and a business career. Vincent wanted to become the best coach of the best football team in the world. He did. Remember those hippy buttons with the strange legends? One read, "God is Alive and Living in Green Bay."

He literally clawed his way up through a series of jobs, including assistantships at West Point under Red Blaik and with the New York Giants under Jim Lee Howell. He thought the Giants could make it as the best team in the world under his drive, but when the Green Bay offer came along he couldn't wait. He accepted in the late 50's and suddenly Green Bay was famous for something other than being the toilet paper capital of the world. He has also provided a steady stream of head coaches for less fortunate places, Norb Hecker in Atlanta, Bill Austin in Pittsburgh, Tom Fears in New Orleans.

Pro football stabilized its rules early and rare is the season when these undergo the smallest of changes, except for some word-clarification. The goalposts stayed on the goal line from 1933 until 1966 when they were offset (the goal line is still the target). The free substitution rule has been in effect since 1949. Protective masks came during the early 50's, as they did in college. Grabbing anyone's mask now means a 15 yards penalty. It used to be only if the runner was involved.

When the AFL started in 1960 it instituted a 2-point rule on conversions (if by rushing or passing) and it has stuck with it. Pro football now works with six officials, automatic timers and enough electronic equipment to operate a nuclear sub. In some cities season tickets are handed down from father to son. In divorce cases there is frequently the burning question, "Who gets the pro football season tickets?"

The pro game survived a sizeable 1963 scandal in which Hornung and Alex Karras, an all-league tackle with Detroit, were suspended for a year for betting. A number of unpleasant headlines followed violent deaths among players, including that of Big Daddy Lipscomb. It all failed however to shake the fans' faith and support. The more fan-faith, the more revenue from all sources, TV, endorsement, gates, etc., a cause-and-effect cycle particularly pleasing to Pete Rozelle, a space generation product himself.

At the start Pete was a publicity man fresh out of the Navy, pushing the University of San Francisco's football team. Seven members of that club made it as regulars in the pros, something which has never happened since. The coach, Joe Kuharich, also went on to a pro career.

A decade and a half later, capitalizing on a combination of brains and opportunities afforded by the dazzling developments in communication, Pete Rozelle had become the most powerful administrator the sports world had ever known.

The colleges have had no such administrator; in fact on the national level there hasn't even been any semblance of competition in publicity and promotion between the colleges and the pros. The pros are highly organized; the colleges, through their conferences, etc., largely resemble a gaggle of semi-feuding fiefdoms. The wonder is that they have been whipped into line sufficiently to make a cohesive enough group to have someone sell their national TV package.

Even so, the college sport, largely because of its inherent tradition, long-time loyalties and excitement, has prospered. It has become the No. 2 sport in the country, and its season is shorter than most. More than 600 colleges play varsity ball. More than 30,000 young men participate. The last count-over gave the sport more than 25 million spectators.

College football has produced its great players, most of whom have gone on to play professionally. The Heisman Trophy is generally rated the top

Jimmy Brown, super runner for Cleveland Browns, topped 1000 yards in rushing, seven out of nine seasons. (TONY TOMSIC)

individual award in college ball. Its winner can usually be discovered high on the pro draft list. Paul Hornung of Notre Dame is generally rated the best of the Heisman Trophy winners.

Colleges have also had their top coaches, men like Red Blaik of Army; Bud Wilkinson, who ran up a record string of Oklahoma victories; Bear Bryant, whose mobile, hard-hitting Alabama teams have dominated football in the South and Southeast; Hugh (Duffy) Daugherty, of Michigan State; H. O. (Fritz) Crisler of Michigan.

In the mid-50's the college people finally put their National Hall of Fame on the drawing board. (The pros have theirs operating at Canton, Ohio.) The college hall will eventually be constructed at New Brunswick, N. J., site of that first intercollegiate game in 1869 between Rutgers and Princeton. Meanwhile a Gold Medal Hall of Fame group, one selectee per year, has already included Presidents Hoover, Eisenhower and Kennedy, Gen. Douglas MacArthur, Byron (Whizzer) White, U.S. Supreme Court Justice, Amos Alonso Stagg and Blaik.

"Arnie's army" watches Arnold Palmer practice iron shots.

Golf

Early in 1967 a sizeable item ran on the business pages which explained better than several volumes the status of golf in the United States. The National Broadcasting Co., it related, had purchased nine of Arnold Palmer's thirteen business interests for "x" millions. Diversifying was how the radio fellows put it.

Arnie, of course, would join them as a consultant, etc. They, in turn, would get special credentials in "Arnie's Army," that vast vocal following which Palmer has built in one of the most dramatic examples of relating to the sporting masses by any pro athlete anywhere.

Palmer is one of the most popular athletes who ever said "thank you" for a paycheck. He is also the first golfer who has been associated with the faceless millions instead of the comparative handful which follows the actual play, or the larger number which have made newspaper accounts of golf required reading. Whether this is all impact on the part of TV, the times, or just an ectoplasmic reaching out is something that will be debated a long time after the Latrobe swinger has racked up his clubs. Any evaluation of the sport during this era which doesn't put him right on top —not only in golf but up there in ALL sports— misses the mark.

There are a half-dozen men around who have won more titles than Palmer and there have been others who have picked up more prize money than he has along the money circuit. The Palmer name, however, is magic. If there is any question, check with him on his assigned wave-length as he flies his near-million dollars worth of private airplane around the country.

Palmer, Jack Nicklaus, Sam Snead, Ben Hogan, Gary Player, have been some of the names which have stirred the imagination during the past two decades. In the women's play it was Mildred (Babe) Zaharias, a super performer into the mid-50's until cancer ended her life. Such women as Patty Berg, Louise Suggs, Betsy Rawls, Mickey Wright, have also occupied the spotlight. Mickey could have been the best, with four women's open titles in a seven-year span.

Nicklaus, an Ohio Stater, won the open in the 1962 playoff, at 27. Since then he has compiled a young-player's record unmatched since the days of Bobby Jones. He is the first golfer to top one-quarter million dollars in a single year.

Ben Hogan, who dominated the game in the early 50's, won the open four times. He got to the final in 1956, shooting for No. 5, and missed. Only Jones and Willie Anderson, a turn-of-the-century performer, had also won it four times.

No amateur has won the U.S. open since Johnny Goodman in 1933, although Marty Fleckman, a Texan from Port Arthur, came close in 1967. Fleckman led after three rounds, blew it the last time around.

TV has changed golf. It has added its all-seeing eye to the enormous pressures already weighing

Louise Suggs, one of the great golfers.

Patty Berg, winner of the U.S. Women's Amateur title in 1938, the U.S. Women's Open in 1946, and many other tournaments.

Looks as though the girls play rough, but actually it is only a sign of Judy Kimball's disgust after missing a putt in her final round of the Titleholders' tournament in Augusta, Georgia, in 1964, while playing with Marilynn Smith (right). (UPI PHOTO)

on the contestants. It has caused committees to accede to special pairings, fool with starting times, etc., so that the prime contenders can get to the camera holes at the prime time. The U.S. Open used to be played on three days with thirty-six holes on the last day. It's now four days of eighteen holes each. It programs better that way.

There has been virtually no change in the ball and club, or in the basic idea of knocking it in with a minimum of strokes and a maximum of 14 clubs. According to the National Golf Foundation, 8½ million play at least 15 rounds a year.

Just how lucrative has this game become? Would you steer YOUR son into the racket, or would you treat him the same way if you caught him with a putter as you would if he bounced a pair of dice on the living room table?

Remember Jimmy Demaret, he of the fancy-colored shirts and slacks back in the late 40's? Jimmy was top money winner along the pro circuit in 1947 with a total take of $27,000. Twenty years later, Billy Casper banked $121,000 for a similar effort. The fellow who finished THIRTY-TWO places behind Billy in the final financial standings made a thousand dollars more than Demaret had twenty years earlier.

The late Tony Lema tossed his putter in glee as he birdied the first hole of a sudden death play-off to win the Cleveland Open over Arnold Palmer in June 1964. (UPI PHOTO)

Selected as one of the top ten photographs of 1966 by UPI Newspictures, this shows Jack Nicklaus (left) and his caddie (right) in their mutual delight as Jack birdied the fifteenth hole during the 1966 Masters Tournament at Augusta, Georgia. (UPI PHOTO)

Hockey

Scratch a hockey player, major-league variety, and you will find (a), a Canadian and (b), one of the toughest athletes playing for pay. There has been a sports axiom which says just about everything concerning hockey players. It is in the form of a semiserious question concerning the length of recovery from a tonsils operation by various kinds of pro athletes.

Baseball players? Six months. Football players? Six weeks. Hockey players? Between periods.

Further probing will reveal hockey players to be infinitely more affluent than their counterparts twenty years ago. The average salary in the National Hockey League is reported as $16,000. Few of the stars made this figure at the start of the past two decades.

Detroit Red Wings' Gordie Howe – 624 career goals through 1966-67.

Chicago Black Hawks' Bobby Hull–"The Golden Jet."

Hockey was one of the last pro sports to accept expansion. For two decades it was a tight little six-team loop, concentrated in Canada's two leading cities and the remainder in the U.S., all on the Eastern side of the Mississippi. The sport's vogue was reflected in its annual draw of 95 percent of capacity.

Then for the 1967-68 season, the league doubled in size and went Coast to Coast. Added to the original Montreal Canadiens, Toronto Maple Leafs, Chicago Blackhawks, Boston Bruins, New York Rangers and Detroit Red Wings were the California Seals (San Francisco), Los Angeles Kings, Minnesota North Stars, Philadelphia Fliers, Pittsburgh Penguins, and the St. Louis Blues.

The move involved 120 of a possible 360 major league hockey players. In return, each of the six existing clubs received two million dollars. This figure, plus the expected revenue from a three-year TV contract, should down-pedal any uneasy conversation about possible dilution of talent.

Hockey has never lacked talent. It is the dream of every boy who laced a skate in Canada to play in the big leagues. Rare indeed have been the hockey bonuses to match the big ones in pro football, baseball or basketball. Probably the best have gone to Jean Beliveau, a Montreal center a few years ago, and Bobby Orr, the latest of the big bonus players who signed with Toronto.

The sport has never lacked for eye-catching stars, and there have been plenty since World War II. After the '60-61 season, Maurice (the Rocket) Richard, of Montreal, retired, with the most career goals, 544. That number has since been surpassed by the Red Wings' Gordie Howe, who entered his 22nd season in '67-68 with 624. Behind him and coming fast is Chicago's Bobby Hull, with 360 goals in 10 seasons. Hull's 54 goals in '64-65 is a record.

Prior to 1947 hockey clubs played 50 games a season. In '49-50 it was upped to 70, and now it's 74. In the past two generations, with rare exception, the top has been shared by Montreal, Detroit and Toronto. The Stanley Cup, emblematic of the playoff championship of the league, is the oldest trophy in professional sports competition in North America.

Harness Racing

Harness racing was one of the few space generation sports which zoomed without benefit of TV. The sport shook the hayseed from its hair in the early 40's, installed plenty of betting windows, made a few vital adjustments, then watched the money come in.

Adjustments included moving from day to night racing, switching from complicated heats to single-dash competition, and installing an automobile-mounted starting gate which eliminated exasperating recalls of previous eras. The last was a lot tougher than it sounds; it had to be invented first.

Not even the wildest of dreamers of the early 40's could foresee crowds of 50,000, such as have been drawn to Roosevelt Raceway, in Westbury, L. I., the pioneer in big-time trotting. Horses hauling wagons a little faster than others earning close to a million. Aw, come on!

Nor could anyone imagine trotting promoters scouring far corners of the globe for talent to spice up the big stake races. It used to be that farmers raced on their free afternoons at state fairs. Now trotting in the U.S. has gained more of an international aspect than thoroughbred racing.

A visiting French mare, Roquepine, is rated one of the greatest of trotters. She has pushed over the $600,000 mark in earnings, has won the Prix d'Amerique in France and the Roosevelt International in the U.S.

Among the pacers, Bret Hanover, horse of the year as a 2, 3 and 4-year old, is generally rated greatest. A son of Adios, regarded as the greatest of the progenitors, Bret Hanover earned a record $922,616.

Harness racing also has made millionaires of a number of trainer-drivers, men like Billy Haughton and Stanley Dancer. Virtually every state in the nation has harness racing, since the sport is a pretty basic one, but only fifteen states offer mutual betting.

Horse Racing

His name, Kelso, sounded like some new detergent being pushed on TV, but Bohemia Stables' super star won 39 of 63 starts from 1959 through 1966. When they put him out to pasture he had racked an all-time money mark of $1,977,896.

His name was Johnny Longden and he looked like a smallish grandfather. Lots of people wondered what he was doing up there on a big horse. When he finally hung up his tack after the 1966

Kelso—"Horse of the Year" five straight years. (N.Y.R.A.)

season, Longden had an all-time mark of having finished in front in 6,026 races.

No one but a wife-beating, child-intimidating degenerate goes to a race track, to gamble away the rent and grocery money. Obviously. In the space generation the national total year attendance at flat races, (as distinguished from trotters) rose from 17,914,908 to 47,020,456. And the money handled moved from $1.2 billion to $3.5 billion. That's an awesome amount of degeneracy, and the painful part is that it is encouraged by state governments which take their share right off the top. It's axiomatic that however poorly other roads are marked, a motorist can never get lost on his way to a race track.

During the twenty years following World War II, a host of super steeds have clattered down to the wire first, but Kelso is generally rated the best. Five straight years he was voted Horse of the Year honors. He was invariably sent away at post time the odds-on favorite. And he seldom let his backers down.

In this particular era only two horses have made it to the Triple-Crown, that much coveted sweep by a three-year old of Kentucky Derby, Preakness and Belmont Stakes. They were King Ranch's Assault in 1946 and Calumet Farm's Citation two years later.

International competition also blossomed in the U.S. in this interlude. The Washington (D.C.) International, an autumnal test at Laurel, has attracted some of the world's best, including Russian horses. American horses have won about half of these races, with French, English, Venezuelan and Australian mounts sharing the rest.

Willie Shoemaker aboard Damascus (N.Y.R.A.)

An international flavor also became apparent among the jockeys riding in the U.S. with the appearance of such top flight South and Central Americans as Braulio Baeza, Manuel Ycaza, Avelino Gomez, Angel Cordero and Eddie Belmonte. The biggest winner working, however, was still Willie Shoemaker, who had a shot at Longden's record.

The record amounts paid out for horses continued to zoom along with everything else. Syndication ownership for breeding purposes became big business. Biggest ever was the $150,000 per share, 32 shares, on Buckpasser. This made his syndication value just a shade under $5 million. He was slated for stud after the 1967 campaign.

Shooting

All forms of shooting—trap and skeet, pistol and rifle, boomed in the space generation. An estimated 20,000,000 hunting licenses alone were in effect in 1967. This figure had doubled within a decade.

There were a number of unusual developments in the shooting sports. Trap and skeet enjoyed an upbeat because construction of homes, roads and shopping sites cut drastically into the hunting lands. Shooters took advantage of shot-gun facilities close to home, facilities which could be accommodated within a 200-yards complex.

As in most sports, quality in shooting improved. The United States was able to boast the world's best in pistol (Joe Benner and Bill Blankenship) and the top rifleman, Gary L. Anderson, a divinity student at the San Francisco Theological Seminary. Anderson, like the others, is a U.S. Army man. He is left-handed and has held a half-dozen world titles.

Other developments in shooting included an increase in hand loading (the assembly of the bullets by the shooters themselves instead of using store-bought ammunition) and the reduction in weight in the over-all bullet. Gun people have experimented with rocket-projectile bullets and propellants which are little more than bits of activated cotton.

American shooting heritage goes back to Dan'l Boone and the squirrel rifles and nothing has happened recently to dim the image.

Skiing

The American skier may not be the fastest down the slope, nor the furthest coming off the jump, but he has the jump, by far, on the rest of the world fraternity in the matter of getting fastest to where the snow is whitest. The American skier could be the most traveled in the history of sport —any sport, both in numbers and distance.

He (and his date) turn up today in a wide variety of tempting sites—Europe, South America, and even a bit of Africa. He comes armed with the finest equipment, ranging from cold-defying clothing to epoxy and fiberglass runners. Sticking out of a pocket can be discerned the corner of the return trip portion of his excursion or special-rate airplane ticket which he'll be using to get back home in a week or two.

Winter in New England, with skiers dotting the slopes of Spruce Peak as they enjoy their holiday vacations at Stowe, Vermont, in December 1965. (UPI PHOTO)

United States Olympic Skier—Billy Kidd.

With figures like a mere $200 for a round-trip ride to assured skiing in some foreign clime, it is hardly good economics to stay home and brood over the lack of snow. The ulcers which could develop could prove far costlier.

Skiing has never been a nickels-and-dimes affairs but its devotees (now numbered at 4 million in the U.S., or approximately four times as great as the figures of pre-World War II) have always felt that the skiing dollar was one well invested. Today, good roads and jet travel take the skier virtually anywhere so he can indulge in everything the sport has to offer, ranging from the thrill of speed to the thrill of recognition (opposite-sex department) around the fireplace.

Groomed trails, snow-making machinery, better lifts and base facilities provide the skier today with a sport superior to that which the earlier kings of the runners enjoyed. The runners, incidentally, are no longer of wood, the material favored by all, going back to the Vikings.

Wood has been phased out in favor of aluminum-steel combinations, plastic-metal and epoxy-fiberglass. And that thin undergarment will keep today's week-end skier warmer than an Arctic explorer clad in a walrus suit.

Except for the teaching pros, skiing remains an amateur sport. In international competition the U.S. has come up with gold-medal Olympic winners in Andrea Mead Lawrence and Gretchen Frazer. Among the men, Buddy Werner, the alpine ace, was the best until he met an untimely end in a Swiss avalanche in 1964. The current world star is France's Jean Claude Killy, whose handsome gallic looks do him no harm on TV.

Similarly, TV does the sport no harm, but enhances the interest. No one goes out just to watch skiing, so the medium can't hurt the gate, as it does in some sports.

Up to the 60's the Austrians were dominant in the men's events on the world level. They were gradually supplanted by the French. Killy's predecessor was Tony Sailer (pronounced Sighler), an Austrian. America's best is Billy Kidd, a transplanted Vermonter who was a silver medalist in the 1964 Olympics. Billy was still a collegian moving up to the '68 games. Suzy Chaffe, another Vermonter, is tops among the current ladies.

Good coaching has brought American skiers along at an accelerated pace. Outstanding in this group has been Bob Beattie, head coach of the U.S. Olympic team. Like Kidd, Beattie is a transplanted New Englander who has found the lure of the Colorado mountains irresistible.

Jean-Claude Killy of France speeding down the course to win the Men's Giant Slalom at the World Series of Skiing in Vail, Colorado, in March 1967. (UPI PHOTO)

Soccer—America's newest spectator sport.

Soccer

Soccer is the No. 1 sport in the world but its efforts to achieve an even remotely similar position in the U.S. have, to date, been largely unsuccessful. In its latest attempt it has TV, a hitherto-unavailable factor, going for it on a regular contractual basis. It also has for the first time big-league promotion, plus backers who won't abscond with the gate receipts leaving the dusty players and officials to get cleaned up as best they can via the wash basins in the men's room.

Whether soccer rises to the level of other money sports in the United States, there is no question about its status around the globe. Its World Cup arouses a fever unmatched in any sport. People simply don't bother to go to bed the last couple of days of the World Tournament. When England beat West Germany in the 1966 final (Telestar put it on live in the U.S., causing TV executives to put aside their blocks long enough to bark, "Get that for us!") the entire United Kingdom went on a binge. Similarly, air accidents, such as that which wiped out the Torino team of Italy in 1949, have plunged countries into national mourning.

Although it is widely played at all levels in the U.S., soccer generally is not understood by the sports-going public. To it, there isn't the surgical skill of top baseball or the brute, elemental force of pro football at its crunching best.

Yet, elsewhere people have been known to stop wars (insurrections, anyway) to see a big match. The biggest star, Pele, a Brazilian, is a millionaire several times over. Prices on international soccer stars sold from one country to another make some baseball and football transactions appear like deals in second-day old fish.

As indicated, the jury is still out on soccer in the U.S. TV money, plus backing by football and baseball people, anxious to have their dollars and stadia working additional months of the year, might result eventually in one big successful pro loop. It would have to be sprinkled liberally with foreign stars until American kickers come of age.

This will take time, obviously. The U.S. has won only one match in all its World Cup efforts, upsetting England in an early round almost twenty years ago. There has been no indication of any noticeable improvement in local talent.

The verdict on Pele is imprinted indelibly, however. The slum son of a soccer player who never quite made it in Sao Paulo, he moved from a 75-dollars-a-month performer status with Santos to a quarter of a million a year with the same Brazilian club. He was a World Cup performer at 15; twice he has led the Brazilians to soccer's global honors. He was injured in the '66 tournament, a fact which most observers say prevented the Brazilians from scoring an unprecedented three straight.

Brazil has rewarded its national hero in a manner unknown in the U.S. Money? As much as he wants, via real estate, tithes by the coffee industry, etc. That's only half the piece.

The other is that he is the first living Brazilian to be declared a "national treasure." This means that he can't be sold, just as though he was some priceless piece of art or sculpture. That's how Edison Arantes do Nascimento (5.9—145 lbs) is listed on the books of the Ministry of Culture.

Back to the U.S. where soccer struggles for a portion of the spotlight. The sport has always had a following although it is generally agreed ethnic rooting has hurt its aspirations, rather than helped.

Back in the 20's, Hakoah, of Vienna, enjoyed an American tour which matched any. Big matchups (Santos-Milan), etc., have filled ball parks in the U.S. and Canada. As a steady diet it has languished, however, drifting uncertainly between the football and baseball which Americans rate 1-2.

The soccer-TV relationship is an unusual one. Usually the Big Eye moves in on something already firmly established, for the purposes of skimming the cream. Frequently TV has caused more long-range injury than help through its support. This is one instance, however, where, if soccer makes it in the U.S. to the level of a major sport, it will be only because someone big in TV had thought it would be a good idea.

Basically the sport hasn't changed much in the past couple of generations. It's still played eleven to a side, only the goalie can touch the ball with his hands and there is a premium on durability. Substitutions are held to a bare minimum.

Around the world it's called "football" or its phonetic equivalent. We call it soccer, a corruption of the word "association." The big gamble in the soccer world today is that it's sudden association with TV will result eventually in a flood of gold that will make all other sport-art forms in this country look like schoolyard exercises.

Swimming

One April afternoon in 1927, Johnny Weissmuller, still a few years from becoming Tarzan of the Apes, plunged into the waters at Ann Arbor, Mich., in a big A.A.U. meet and emerged with a 100-yard free style world mark of 51 seconds. It was one of those well-before-his-time performances. It was to stand for almost a generation, until Alan Ford, a Yale varsity swimmer, shaved a few fractions in 1947.

Swimming records today stand no chance of such longevity. In fact records have been broken while the new champ is still toweling himself. It's a little cruel but it is largely true that in swimming, this year's record-breaker is usually next year's has-been. Very few Olympians have repeated, which means winning performances stretching over four years are rarities.

Some of the Australians like Murray Rose, David Thiele and Dawn Fraser (Miss Fraser won the 100 in 1956, 1960 and 1964 before she was set down for ten years for a Tokyo Olympiad escapade) are some of these rare ones. Particularly in the ladies' department the time schedule runs something like champion at twelve, record-holder at fourteen, retired TV personality at seventeen. Miss Fraser's epic feat, maintaining world superiority in one event for a decade, has to be tantamount to an average person's living to the age of 175.

Gold medal winner of the Women's Springboard Diving at Tokyo in 1964, Ingrid Kramer of Germany, shows her championship form. (UPI PHOTO)

The Americans are the best swimmers. More records have been broken in the Yale University pool (site, off and on, of both the collegiate and national AAU championship meets) than any other splash-site in the world. Don Schollander, an Olympic champion and record-breaker before becoming a Yale freshman, has to be the most attractive swimmer of his generation. In a national poll in '65 he was acclaimed the top athlete of the country, beating such super-stars as Mickey Mantle, Willie Mays, Oscar Robertson, Willie Shoemaker and Jimmy Brown. And the balloting was done by hard-eyed sportswriters and broadcasters, who presumably had set aside all factors except excellence under pressure.

Swimming hasn't changed much in the past couple of decades. The crawl is still the fastest of strokes; there isn't a faster way of getting off than the flat-out flop, legs already kicking. The butterfly was introduced (a sort of reverse breast stroke) in this era.

For a while there was an interesting vogue of hair-shaving to cut down on resistance in the water, but it was probably largely psychological, even though a number of swimmers reported improvements of several seconds. The Japanese, tremendous before World War II, never quite caught up to the Americans and Australians when the Olympic competition was resumed.

Synchronized swimming became an organized sport in the postwar period, and there have always been enough strange men available, willing to maim, and be maimed underwater, to stage the national water polo championships each year. Once in a while an Esther Williams comes along

America's Jeanne Collier (left), silver medal winner, and Patsy Willard (right), bronze medal winner, with Ingrid Kramer of Germany, gold medal winner at the Tokyo Olympics. (UPI PHOTO)

The Women's Olympic 100-meter Backstroke final at Tokyo in 1964, a close race won by Cathy Ferguson of the United States, with Christine Caron of France second, and Virginia Duenkel of the United States third. (UPI PHOTO)

as a champion and makes it big in the movies but for the most part swimmers eventually make model husbands and wives in middle-class communities where they sit at poolside and keep a wary eye on the children.

No one has ever kept a log on the number of persons who swim. The registered athletes in college, school and AAU competition is only modest, but how about the number of bathing caps, sunburn lotions, ear plugs and nose clamps, not to mention sand pails and shovels, sold yearly? Besides you have to be able to swim to get into some of the more esoteric sports like surfing, skin diving, water skiing, aquaplaning, etc.

Swimmers are a good deal smarter today, too. Anyone who announces that he or she will swim the English Channel is looked upon as some kind of a nut rather than a hero-to-be. In 1967 some young lady made a fuss and went off pouting because they wouldn't let her try to swim the English Channel in topless fashion. All right, what would she have done after she got there?

The winning American 400-meter relay team at the Tokyo Olympics, (left to right) Mike Austin, Steve Clark, Gary Ilman, and Don Schollander. (UPI PHOTO)

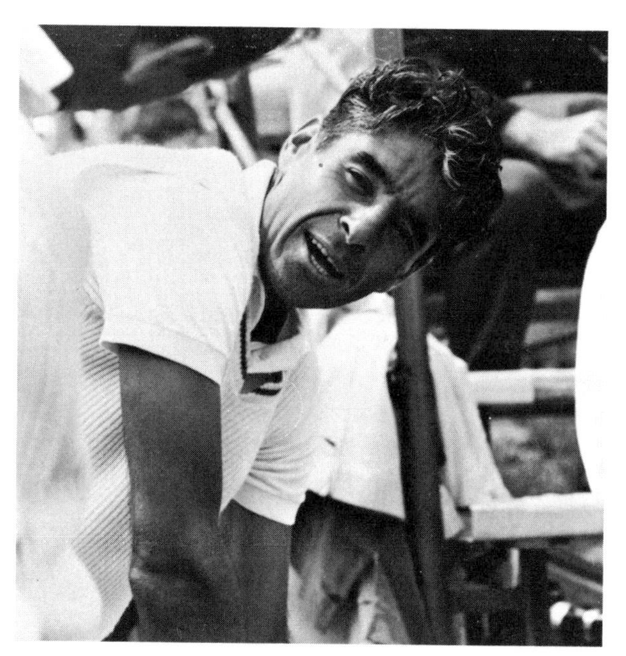

Pancho Gonzales, one of tennis' top stars of the 1950's.

Australian Rod Laver, first lefty to win Grand Slam of Tennis.

Tennis

Tennis enjoyed a normal growth during the space generation but the sport failed to maintain its previous position as a glamorous one for a variety of reasons. These ranged from a skid in American talent to a refusal of world tennis to sanction "open" competition between the top amateurs and the pros.

Although Richard (Pancho) Gonzales of California was rated one of the finest net artists ever to grace the game in the mid-50's, or any other period, he didn't approach the crowd appeal of a Don Budge, an Ellsworth Vines, or other pre-World War II stars. Jack Kramer, who was the first of the big stars after the war, had considerable appeal but Big Jake, too, was caught between tennis' archaic management and the on-rushing promotional efforts of the money sports.

It was the same in the women's department. Helen Wills, Helen Jacobs and the super stars were gone. In their stead appeared such top performers as Maureen Connolly, Althea Gibson, Margaret Smith and Mario Bueno, but there wasn't much box office magic here, either. Miss Connolly might have been a big draw except that her career was cut short by a horse-riding accident.

Miss Gibson, first Negro player to win a major tennis title, turned pro, found pickings slim, eventually gravitated to golf. In the late 60's Billy Jean King, a talented Californian, emerged as the top U.S. player with the potential to top the rest of the lady players in the world for a considerable period.

Tennis' grand slam—the Australian, French, English and American titles all within a single season of competition, is one of the really rare efforts in sport. Don Budge accomplished this just before the outbreak of World War II. It wasn't to happen again until Rod Laver, a red-headed Australian of modest physical proportions, turned the trick. He also was the first left-hander to do it.

Australia sent an unbroken stream of top-flight performers to dominate world courts—in Melbourne, Paris, London and Forest Hills. Although they made the transition quickly to the pro ranks

Althea Gibson of New York (left) and Darlene Hard of Montebello, California (right), at Wimbledon in 1957, when Miss Gibson became the first Negro to win a singles title in the Wimbledon events. (UPI TELEPHOTO)

Lew Hoad, Australian tennis star, with his second trophy as winner of the Wimbledon Men's Singles Championship, in 1957. (UPI PHOTO)

to capitalize on their headlines they were still in sufficient supply to make the Davis Cup, emblematic of world amateur supremacy, virtually an Aussie fixture. The U.S. had started with a bang, winning it the first four years after World War II, but through the 50's they were able to win it only twice. Only U.S. victory in the 60's came in '63.

Nothing transpired to change the basic format of the game. Major world tournaments continued to be held on grass, and the majority of players in the world continued to play on non-grass surfaces, ranging from concrete to clay.

Rosemary Casals of San Francisco, one of the younger American women tennis stars. (UPI PHOTO)

Despite the efforts of scoring innovators, "40-love" and "deuce" continued to ring out from the umpires' chairs. James Van Alen made strenuous efforts to introduce his simplified scoring system in the U.S.—basically where every point counts and winning an extended set means winning a match. In the forseeable future, however, it will still be best two out of three sets for the ladies and best three out of five for the men in big championship play.

Tennis tradition in the U.S. is tremendous, going back to the eras of Maurice McLaughlin, Big Bill Tilden, Little Bill Johnson, Vines and Budge. More people play tennis than ever. The ruling body in the sport in this country has made sporadic efforts to promote in the manner of other successful sports. Stymieing it, however, has been the bull-headed refusal of World Tennis Federation members to open things up to the amateurs and pros.

Principal bloc opposition stems from the Iron Curtain countries, apparently quite satisfied with the status quo.

Tennis' forseeable fate seems that a greater number of people will play, follow the sport, and lavish enthusiasm on it, but not nearly in the proper relation to the population growth.

Track and Field

Track and field rates with the oldest of sports. It goes back to the time our original ancestors discovered that a flung rock, smacking squarely on target, somehow didn't kill a sabre-toothed tiger. It just made him a little madder. The first track records, set on that particular Neanderthalic afternoon, have improved steadily.

Most dramatic moment of the space generation for the spiked-shoe set came in 1954 when Roger Bannister, an Englishman, pierced the four-minute mile barrier. Its drama came from statements only ten years earlier, from scientists in physiology to physics, that this would forever be impossible. There were charts to prove it, plus graphs to show the same impossibility for the 16-foot pole vault and the 60-foot shot put, all marks since eclipsed not once but many times.

Scientists have since become a little cagey on track predictions. Today the stuff is fed into a computer and if it doesn't work out you can

Jackie Robinson, great second baseman of the Brooklyn Dodgers, during spring training, 1953. (UPI PHOTO)

Ted Williams, Boston Red Sox super star, at l during game against Philadelphia Athletics Shibe Park, Philadelphia. Buddy Rosar, of t A's, is behind the plate. (UPI PHOTO)

LEFT: *Mickey Mantle and Roger Maris, of the New York Yankees, and a bat boy in a spring training game against the Cincinnati Reds at Tampa, Florida. The "M" boys were one of baseball's major attractions.* (UPI PHOTO)

RIGHT: *Joe DiMaggio of the New York Yankees on the occasion of his retirement as an active player. Governor Thomas Dewey is in the background.* (UPI PHOTO)

LEFT: *Stan Musial of the St. Louis Cardinals in his familiar batting stance at Busch Stadium, St. Louis, September 28, 1963.* (UPI PHOTO)

Craig Breedlove walks away from his specially designed racing car, the "Spirit of America" in which he established a new ground speed world's record of 600,601 miles per hour at Bonneville Salt Flats, Utah, November 11, 1965. (UPI PHOTO)

Cornelius Warmerdam, great pole vaulter of the early post-World War II period, and the first of the 15-foot pole vaulters. (UPI PHOTO)

One of the most popular events in the winter Olympics is figure skating. Here Emmerich Danzer, men's World Figure Skating Champion performs in Vienna, Austria March 3, 1967. (UPI PHOTO)

Joe Louis, world Heavyweight Boxing Champion during and after World War II. (UPI PHOTO)

Pancho Gonzales, great amateur and professional tennis champion of the post-World War II period. (UPI PHOTO)

Professional basketball became a major attraction in the post-World War II years. George Mikan, with the ball in this photograph, was the first super star. (UPI PHOTO)

Sam Snead at the National Open Golf Tournament, Medinah Country Club near Chicago June 16–18, 1949. (UPI PHOTO)

Ben Hogan putts as Jimmy Demaret watches. (UPI PHOTO)

Competitors in the first World Series of Golf, Firestone Country Club, Akron, Ohio, September 7, 1963, included, from left to right, Arnold Palmer, Julius Boros, Jack Nicklaus and Bob Charles. (UPI PHOTO)

Water skiing came into its own as an internationally popular sport in the years following World War II. (UPI PHOTO)

The last leg of the 400-meter relay in the swimming meet of the 1964 Olympics, held in Tokyo, Japan. (UPI PHOTO)

Part of the vast crowd in Wembley Stadium, London, July 29, 1948, during the Olympic track meet. Shown here is the Olympic flame which traditionally is carried from Elis, Greece, site of the first games more than 2500 years ago, to the host stadium. (UPI PHOTO)

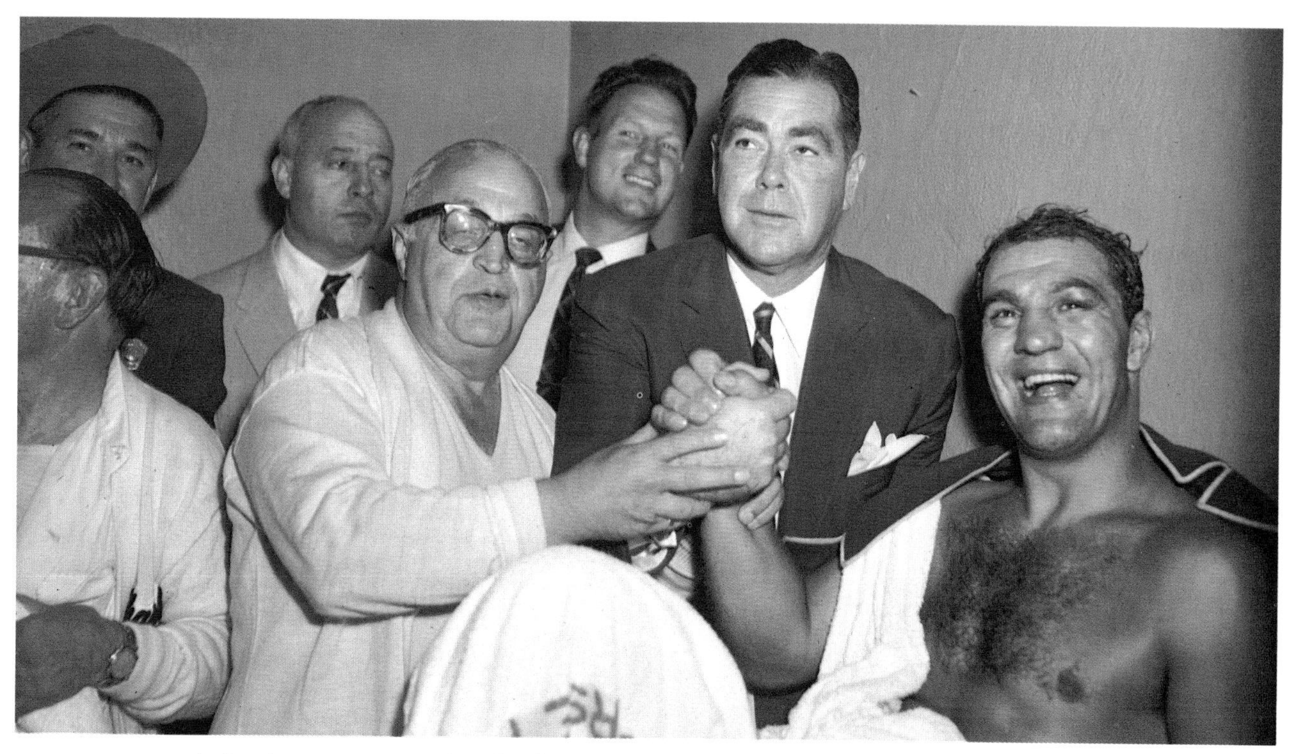

A dressing room scene after the fight, showing the champion, Marciano, with his trainer, Al Weill, and manager, Jim Norris. (UPI PHOTO)

The world's heavyweight boxing championship fight between Archie Moore and Rocky Marciano, September 21, 1955, won by Marciano. (UPI PHOTO)

John Thomas (left) of the United States receives the silver medal for second place in the high jump at Tokyo in 1964, with Valery Brumel of the U.S.S.R. to his immediate left, and John Rambo (right) of the United States, third place medal winner. (UPI PHOTO)

Valery Brumel of the U.S.S.R., world and Olympic record holder in the high jump, at the Tokyo Olympic games. (UPI PHOTO)

One of the most successful amusement enterprises of the century is Disneyland, Anaheim, California, which opened in 1955. Although designed as an amusement park for children, millions of people of all ages have been thrilled by its many varieties of entertainment, as shown in these six views. (UPI PHOTOS)

ABOVE: *Opening day at the New York World's Fair, April 22, 1964.* (UPI PHOTO)

LEFT: *The Space Needle and general view of the 1962 World's Fair in Seattle, Washington.* (UPI PHOTO)

BELOW LEFT: *Ferris wheel and general view of the "La Ronde" amusement area at Expo 67, Montreal, Canada, 1967.* (UPI PHOTO)

BELOW: *The Atomium, the striking symbol of the Brussels World's Fair of 1958.* (UPI PHOTO)

Roger Bannister, English medical student and first man to run the Mile in less than four minutes, crashed his way into athletic history by completing the Mile in 3 minutes 59.4 seconds, at Oxford, England, in 1954. (UPI PHOTO)

Jim Ryun of Lawrence, Kansas, leading Kenya's Kipohoge Keino in the "Emsley Carr" mile in London, August 12, 1967, won by Ryun in 3 minutes 56 seconds. (UPI PHOTO)

always blame it on a defective transistor. The Russians have fed Olympic track data into one of their pet machines and have come up with some interesting figures: The Olympic winner in the year 2000 will have to hustle the 100-meters in 9.7 (the record is 10 flat), and he is going to have to high jump 7 feet 10½ inches.

Once Bannister broke through in the mile, the rest followed. Since that memorable occasion the four-minute standard has been battered more than 300 times. Breaking four minutes today isn't even a 100 percent guarantee of a finish among the top five in a national or international meet.

The mile, perhaps because it has every ingredient—endurance, speed, judgment of pace and a fan's panoramic view of the struggle, has been a favorite with American track and field audiences for several generations. Oddly, it was more than a generation between American world record holders.

Glenn Cunningham, the tireless Kansan, established a world mark in 1934, held it until 1937, when it was lowered by Sydney Wooderson, an Englishman. Until 1966, all record breakers proved non-Americans. Then Jim Ryun, another Kansan, came along and wrested it back with an amazing 3.51.3. It was doubly amazing because Ryun was a teenager, just a college freshman, when he accomplished this feat. Mile superiority usually is associated with athletic maturity.

Ryun's vistas were unlimited. No one that young had ever achieved a similar pinnacle so early. His lean good looks also made him a tremendous favorite among the younger set, live and on TV. Indoor promoters chased him like mad because a banked track offering Ryun was assured box office.

Indoor track has enjoyed a boom, breaking out of a small established Eastern-Midwest circuit (New York, Boston, Philadelphia, Baltimore, Cleveland and Chicago) to reach the West Coast and arenas all over the country. Traditionally held in New York, the National A.A.U.'s were moved to Albuquerque. TV revenue permitted the moguls to gamble on an unusual site and the fans backed their move. Indoor tracks, conforming to the basketball-hockey layouts for which arenas are generally built, measure 11 laps to a mile.

A number of other barriers were broken during the past decade, barriers which were the focal points of fan dialogue for years. The 16-feet pole vault, once regard an impossibility, is now well beyond 17 feet, and the customers are wondering who the first 18-footer will be. The fiberglass pole, with its coiled-spring effect, has been the means for smashing all the records. The shot put has moved from 60 to 70 feet.

The high jumpers got to 7 feet and kept going. Valerie Brumel, the Amazing Russian, established the world high jump mark of 7.5¾ before a motorcycle accident cut short his career.

The one imagination-stopping barrier which still stood into the late 60's was the 9-seconds 100 yard dash. They had worked it down to 9.1 and the record-holder, Bob Hayes, was unusual on a number of counts. He not only looked like a football player but he was one, and a very good one. In fact Hayes turned pro to play with the Dallas Cowboys in the National Football League.

There was a wide assortment of spiked-shoe heroes and heroines, in the two decades following World War II. Harrison Dillard, the U.S.'s best hurdler, failed to qualify for the 1948 Olympics. Undaunted, Dillard managed to qualify in the

100-meter dash. He surprised the world by winning the final. In 1952 he made certain he wasn't eliminated in his hurdling specialty, and won that final.

Peter Snell, a world-beating distance runner from New Zealand (three Olympic titles spread over the 1960-'64 games) set a world indoor 1,000-yard mark. The time, 2:06, is especially significant because this was the first time Snell had ever seen an indoor track.

Abebe Bikila, an Ethiopean soldier, thrilled the world when he won the Olympic marathon title without shoes, not once but twice. Emil Zatopek, a Czech soldier, was an amazing performer in the early 50's. In '48 he won the 10,000-meter Olympic title; in '52 he won the 5,000 and 10,000 AND the marathon.

Women stars came and went but some of the names that stuck with the fans were Fanny Blankers-Koen, a Netherlander who won the 100, 200 and 80-meter hurdles in the 1948 games; and Wilma Rudolph, a lanky American Negro girl who won the 100 and 200 a dozen years later.

The U.S. and Russia got together in a massive dual meet in Moscow for the first time in 1958 and met on several occasions subsequently, both in the U.S and in Russia. The Olympic games were moved back to the North American continent for 1968, set for Mexico City (the last time had been Los Angeles in 1932), and were also awarded to Munich, Germany for 1972.

A bitter squabble of lengthy duration blemished the picture in the 60's, with the National Collegiate A.A. seeking to wrest control of amateur sports from the A.A.U., the solo governing body representing the International Sports Federation (and thus the only one able to certify American athletes for international competition).

The bickering reached the Halls of Congress with neither side inclined to concede much. It was prestige rather than money because the colleges control 100 percent their one big-money sport, football.

The A.A.U.'s No. 1 display in this argument has been its almost 100 percent voluntary work in the advancement of amateur athletics in the U.S. They offer that without the A.A.U. there wouldn't have been any further athletic careers to pursue once college men were through with varsity sports.

Parry O'Brien, great shot-putter and discus thrower, who broke the 60-foot barrier in the shot-put event in June 1959. (UPI PHOTO)

And Some Conclusions

There is an inevitable element of danger in sport. An ankle-tackle will bring a 230-pound fullback crashing to the ground like a riven oak. A jolting forearm shiver by a lineman can addle a rival's brains; a 90-mile an hour fastball, zeroing on a batter's head, obviously carries the germ of destruction.

There is danger in the mad dash of a hockey forward blasting through a solidly-packed defensive line as skate blades flash and sticks swing. Certainly the devasting right hand landing on a fighter's exposed jaw has to be rated one of the more serious hazards to life and limb.

But have these been the most dangerous pastimes of all in the past couple of decades? Not by a long string of tables, as compiled by the insurance companies who have an intensive interest in such matters, an interest heightened by a little item known as "benefits to survivors."

The most dangerous sports, say these, are auto racing, sky-diving and scuba diving. All three of these activities are among the "new" sports, and have soared to increased heights. There are now 30,000 drivers in the U.S. in all forms of motor racing. There are 25,000 sky divers who make 10 jumps or more a year, according to the Parachute Club of America. The divers, skin and scuba, total is being checked pending their all surfacing simultaneously.

The death rate in sky-diving, until that dreadful accident in mid-1967 when a miscalculation wiped out 16 jumpers who landed in Lake Erie, has been pegged mostly around the first jump. Fully 15 percent of all fatalities had come on the first try. Ironically, in that watery disaster, most of the jumpers were credited with at least 100 leaps.

Auto racing has claimed about as many in recent years as it did a decade ago, which means a definite improvement because so many more racing drivers are now behind the wheel in sports car, stock car, big car and drag racing.

Keeping track of fatalities in scuba (that's with oxygen equipment) and skin (that's without) diving, is a comparatively new activity. Most of the victims were inexperienced. They drowned in comparatively shallow water.

The space generation has known its sports tragedies, certainly. They have ranged from top players succumbing to mysterious diseases to an entire team, like the U.S. figure skaters, being wiped out in an airplane crash. Dozens of spectators have been killed in a single accident at Le Mans as cars hurtle out of control. Youngsters vibrant and confident, have ridden the high combers in surfing, brilliantly alive one moment, dead and broken the next. Hunters continue to mistake each other, motorcyclists plummet off narrow mountain trails.

These deaths is a price exacted for participation in the most active, exciting era sports has known.

Category	Associated Press Poll 1950, First Half-Century	1950-'67
Male Athlete	Jim Thorpe	Arnold Palmer
Female Athlete	Babe Didrickson Zaharias	Dawn Fraser
Baseball	Babe Ruth	Stan Musial
Football	Jim Thorpe	Jimmy Brown
Prize-fighting	Jack Dempsey	Sugar Ray Robinson
Basketball	George Mikan	Wilt Chamberlain
Track	Jesse Owens	Jim Ryun
Golf	Bobby Jones	Arnold Palmer
Tennis	William T. Tilden	Rod Laver
Swimming	Johnny Weissmuller	Don Schollander
Horse Racing	Man o' War	Kelso
Biggest upset	1914 Braves	N.Y. Giants' 1954 Series victory over Cleveland.
Most Dramatic	Dempsey-Firpo Fight	Baltimore Colts' 1958 NFL playoff victory.

Washington: Pray Silence for Yastrzemski

By James Reston

Perhaps the best example of the interrelationship between the world of sports and everyday life in the United States of America in the years of the late 1960's is brought out in this article, which so succinctly sets forth the contradictions, confusions and contrasts of our daily life as compared with the certainties of sports.

A jubilant locker room scene near the end of the 1967 season, after the Boston Red Sox downed the White Sox 6 to 2. From left to right are outfielder Reggie Smith; outfielder Carl Yastrzemski; infielder George Scott; and catcher Mike Ryan. (UPI PHOTO)

These are hard days to write about politics in the United States. The country is in another of those lovely hypnotic trances over sports, and every time you try to write the word "Johnson," it comes out Yastrzemski.

This is something more than the annual madness over the baseball World Series. When President Johnson made a major address on the war in Vietnam the other night, N.B.C. estimated his television audience at between nine and ten million. The next day, when Carl Yastrzemski and his implausible Red Sox gored Minnesota in the last game of the regular season, the TV audience was between twenty and 25 million.

The frenzy in the capital of the Commonwealth of Massachusetts, of course, has even surpassed the excitement at the election of John F. Kennedy. Even that old chestnut about Beantown has been rewritten:

"And this is good old Boston/ The home of the bean and the cod/ Where the Lowells talk only of baseball/ And Yastrzemski gets signals from God."

Getting into the Senate gallery for the current debate on Vietnam is easy, but getting a ticket for a Washington Redskins pro football game is now an impossibility. The total TV audience for all the pro games on a Sunday averages over 25 million. College football attendance last year for all games was 25,275,899, and it promises to go even higher in the next three months.

This is more than a fad or a habit. It could be the natural reaction of the people to an incomprehensible age where games are about the only things in the news that come to a clear and definite end. The Red Sox, of course, are straight melodrama. They have gone from spectacular futility to triumphant success in one short season, but even this does not explain the psychological reaction of the fans.

Who's Ahead?

The hunger in the country is for something precise and understandable. This is what is back of the "win or get out" fever on the war. A foreign policy is a process without beginning or end and nobody ever quite knows who's ahead, including the big coach in the White House. But sports are different, because, paradoxically, they are almost the only things in the news that remain the same.

The rules and specifications are rigid, and the officials are omnipotent. On the umpire's say-so, a strike is a strike, even if it's a ball. The tests are simple for all alike: four downs to make ten yards, three strikes and you're out, and the rewards and punishments are sudden and often dramatic.

If a pitcher gives up three straight unambiguous home runs, nobody says he is really a nice fellow who didn't mean to get into trouble: they take the bum out. Sports are not like politics: they pay off on results and not on intentions, and everybody understands, except of course, the poor pitcher.

The Vanishing Hero

Another reason for the rising popularity of sports in these confusing days is that they still produce recognizable heroes in an unheroic age. Heroism we have had in this war as usual, but in world politics today there are few heroes. Johnson in Washington, Wilson in Britain, Brezhnev and Kosygin in the Soviet Union, and what's-his-name in Germany are all symbols of a mechanical rather than a heroic age, and even de Gaulle seems determined to prove the truth in Emerson's bitter conclusion that "Every hero becomes a bore at last."

But Yastrzemski is a hero to millions who cannot even pronounce his name, and so he will remain until one day, as happens to all men, he strikes out with the bases loaded in the ninth. Meanwhile, even the Cabots and the Lodges are talking to him in Boston, and Tom Yawkey is mentioning $100,000 for next year's pay, which is heroic in any league.

Pageantry and All That

Finally, there is some pageantry in American life, thanks mainly to sports. Pageantry was something the Founding Fathers set out to abolish in America as a reaction to the pageantry of the British Crown, and they did a fairly good job of it. The result is that we have few majestic occasions in our national life, even at the installation of a college president or the coronation of a bishop or a beauty queen.

But a football stadium on an American autumn Saturday afternoon, crowded to the rafters and blazing with color, with the flags flapping and the bands playing the hymns of the great state universities—this is something more than a game. It may be an escape, but it is a pleasant escape, even on TV with all those singing commercials for beer.

There is nothing like the crisp autumn air and the bands, crowds, and antics of a football game to make one forget the problems of the world. (UPI PHOTO)

SHOW BUSINESS in the SPACE AGE

by ***ROBERT J. LANDRY***

Entertainment in the space age has been marked, as so much else in our economy, by extended or revolutionary new technology. But invention and broad reorganization of production processes cannot account for the emotional, rebellious and controversial aspects, the angry young playwrights, the morbid young humorists, the frantic gyrations of go-go girls, the breakdown of censorship, the teenage dictatorship over pop musical taste, the fantasy response to innumerable movies offering wildly improbable sexy sleuths like Agent 007. Such details reflect the general cultural climate, a standard-breaking and standard-making period.

Entertainment itself has been derided; campus drama critics mounting a campaign to submerge the Broadway theatre in contempt. Entertainment has also been perverted; a smut-obsessed cafe comic, the late Lenny Bruce, bcoming a sort of folk hero of sick comedy with a clientele that doted upon his abuse of authority, success and piety. Finally, an off-Broadway play openly reviled in scabrous terms the President of the United States.

A wide stream of pessimistic protest against life and society has coursed through much of the "intellectual" drama and movies of these latter years. Disgust with a world shadowed by dread of the H-bomb and fallout, disillusionment with human nature and the administration of justice are reflected, also intense fascination with the dregs of humanity. These and the use of anti-heroes in theatrical (as book) plotting all figure in the various new schools of drama. Followers speak of "The Theatre of The Absurd" or "The Theatre of Cruelty." The German Communist playwright, Bertold Brecht, has had an enormous influence since the war in both Europe and America. Samuel Beckett's *Endgame* drama presented two characters on stage, both living in and speaking from garbage cans.

"Way-out" plays of this sort are chiefly presented off-Broadway, or in campus repertory theatres, or in the various urban clusters of the so-called "avant-garde." Though such drama is little known to, or seen by, average American citizens, it does not mean that the example of pessimism does not spread outward from the limited exposure of such works and viewpoints. There has been, to be sure, a strong critical reaction against such plays which many see as sick, destructive, anarchistic.

Continuous dispute revolves about extreme brutality, the sadistic love or exploitation of violence as a form of thrill. Objection has repeatedly been voiced to the violence depicted on stage, screen, in paperback novels, cartoon

Eric Burdon and the Animals—novel names and novel costumes feature in modern musical groups.

Narrow escapes and wildly implausible "showdowns" build suspense in James Bond movies.

comics for children. Defenders answer that any daily newspaper proves that fiction does not invent, but only mirrors brutality. Psychologists and social workers tend to reject the idea that children imitate fiction. Delinquency, they say, is more plausibly traced to poverty, broken families, poor educational opportunities.

Brutality rather than sex license is a prime motive of censorship in various countries, including Great Britain, which cuts out violence, while being liberal regarding sex scenes. Many Asiatic countries, led by India, are profoundly shocked by gangster and western film violence.

Fans tend to identify theatrical history with the personal fate of various glamorous personalities. Hence the Freudian profiles in the wake of Marilyn Monroe's pathetically premature demise. Or the cult to the memory of James Dean, a young actor whose mania for speed hurled him into legend. Then there was the madcap romance in Italy of Elizabeth Taylor and Richard Burton while hotly pursued by reporters and photographers. More recently there has been the unusual situation of the actor (George Murphy) as U.S. Senator or Governor of California (Ronald Reagan) and the actor (Peter Lawford) as brother-in-law of a President. Entertainers, of late, rate status in "Society," and very definitely in the financial community, because of the fact that many stars earn $250,000 to $750,000 a year. Cary Grant a few years ago commanded $1,000,000 per film, plus a percentage of its profits. Nor was he alone.

Show folk began moving into political activity and agitation in the depression, and some of them acquired the reputation of being actual Communists or "fellow travelers." This put them, and others who were innocent, under attack. In its extreme form, such attacks on talent became an organized "blacklist." One newsletter regularly "informed on" performers, often with scant proof. Finally a theatrical attorney, Louis Nizer, pressed litigation successfully on behalf of an entertainer, John Henry Faulk, against the newsletter.

Thus, change and challenge in show business has not been limited to new tinted tubes, curved screens, optical and sound devices designed to bombard the senses, transistorized trumpets and rock organs. Usually this dilemma arises when mankind is confronted by new gadgets. To what uses will the tools be put? Remember that radio, which was supposed to advance brotherhood, was employed by Hitler to spew hatred. The British art critic of long ago, John Ruskin, when invited to comment on the original cable to India asked, "But what have you to say to India?"

Reminder of a Simpler Time

Since we here deal with so vast a canvas, it will place the show business of the space age (1946 to the present moment) in perspective to briefly recite a few essentials about the immediately preceding war period. At that time, commercial amusements in the United States attained a fine, final, almost careless rapture of prosperity despite rationing, price freeze, travel difficulties, curfew and the rest. Show business in 1941, the year of Pearl Harbor, was dominated by motion pictures (perhaps 18,000 theatres, though data is unreliable) and radio-broadcasting (950 local stations, four networks, around 30,000,000 home sets). Both these media operated under codes of good taste and had a strong family tone. By then,

Famous billboard soliciting funds for USO, the entertainment "arm" for GI's.

vaudeville was quite, if not long, dead, though cabarets, cafés, hotel dining rooms with orchestras and singers were fairly numerous. What was left of so-called burlesque as a form of organized entertainment had evolved—many would say degenerated—into mere strip-tease, a peculiar American kind of peep-show fated to become, in export, the fad of Paris after liberation.

What else comprised American show business on the brink of our involvement in global warfare? The usual clutch of traveling circuses and carnivals, the usual flurry of county and state fairs, roadside pageants, amusement parks, and a few surviving tent shows, summer stock companies. Include forty-odd deficit-financed symphony orchestras and a few score of wandering piano and violin virtuosi. But these latter, like Broadway stage hits, grand opera performances and ballet, were more rumor than experience so far as most Americans were concerned. The general public turned for its "produced" diversion to the movie screen, the home receiver, the parlor phonograph. The latter was already a conspicuous influence in the spread of classical music appreciation. Concerts conducted by Arturo Toscanini had sold some 20,000,000 records.

Up to Pearl Harbor, great masses of Americans still felt the penury of the long depression, so that, after 1941, the war put money into people's pockets in amounts beyond their then averages. Hook this sudden flush of income to the psychological truism that any nation at war is haunted by boredom and loneliness and is desperate for diversion. Millions of families were uprooted and scattered with resultant widespread anxiety which generated a mood, or market, for entertainment. This opened unprecedented opportunities for performers. Thousands of old-time vaudevillians came temporarily back to show business to help fill the draft-created talent void and cater to the draft-created hunger for amusement.

Quite frankly, American showmen and performers "enjoyed" the war (1942-3-4-5) because they then had things very close to their fancy. This was partially true in much more austere Great Britain. The significant theatrical point is that the quality of entertainment in wartime is subordinate to the indiscriminate yearning for relief from tension or boredom. Young men on leave, especially if about to be shipped out, and their families and sweethearts, were almost compulsively "on the town" and tended to be heedless of costs for farewell good times. While much free show was provided soldiers and sailors via Stage Door Canteens, USO Clubs, churches and temples, many in service craved big nights that were expensive. Young officers paid scalpers $50 a pair for tickets to a smash musical like *Oklahoma* and even $30 for a straight comedy like *Harvey* (which ran 1,775 performances).

Evidences of Sophistication

Americans approached World War II with a sophistication lacking in 1917. The long radio debate over "isolationism" versus "interventionism" may have helped. Certainly there was much skepticism about synthetic sentiment, old-style patriotic boasts. Soldiers dancing with their sweeties would hoot down any civilian in a dinner jacket who broke in on the dance to vocalize *He's 1-A In The Army and 1-A In My Heart.* Titters too, for foolishness like *Good-Bye, Mama, I'm On My Way To Yokohama.*

Not that there was no hysteria around, but it seemed essentially erotic, with teenage girls unbearably excited by the tenor voice of a then-boyish Frank Sinatra, already known as "Swoonatra."

American radio programs attained a very special high-mindedness and devotion to morale and cooperation with the Office of War Information, under Elmer Davis. Many advertisers contented themselves with mere trademark mention, dropped hard-sell for the duration. It was the heyday of prose poets like Norman Corwin and Archibald MacLeish. Never before, or since, perhaps, have broadcasts been so consistently intellectual and public-spirited.

The opposite extreme probably was represented by noisy cabarets. The musicians and comedians in such places had to be old men (i.e. over 38) immune to conscription. In some "liberty towns" the fun stations occupied entire blocks, as was true of the West 52nd Street area in Manhattan, which operated a veritable carnival midway complete with a shill before every portal. The jazz flavor conferred the nickname of "Cat's Alley."

As for the film industry, it luxuriated in crowds, crowds, crowds. Every week during the war years the theatres of the United States and

Film star Marlene Dietrich, one of hundreds of "soldiers in greasepaint" during World War II.

Canada sold about 75,000,000 admissions, a sales estimate singularly independent of whether the films unreeling were magnificent or mediocre. People were prisoners of gasoline rationing, compelled to accept diversion according to walking distance or bus-line access and schedule. Hundreds of film houses in proximity to three-shift war factories operated 24 hours a day, often well filled in the middle of the night. It was crazy but profitable, the norm of abnormal times.

Soldiers in Greasepaint

The Federal government acknowledged the importance of bringing entertainment to the troops, no matter how remotely stationed. Show tours, under Special Services' auspices, reached the farthest outposts of global warfare. Militarily picked, cleared, vaccinated, dressed and transported, these paid performers became known as "soldiers in greasepaint."

Some 38 of these performers are known to have lost their lives while with the troops, one a famous dancer, Tamara, another a superb juggler, Bob Ripa. Non-fatal injuries to entertainers were far more common, the best-known case being that of the famous stage and radio singer, Jane Froman, who was so badly injured in an airplane accident off Lisbon that she required repeated surgery for many years, to the detriment of her career. Carole Lombard, wife of Clark Gable, was killed while on a War Bond-selling tour.

The late, great "Mammy" singer, Al Jolson, entertaining troops overseas.

GI's, the world's largest "captive" audience—and the most appreciative one.

Cutbacks and Adjustments

Peace broke out in 1945, though there was the Korean War in store a few years later. Entertainment-wise, the first fast victims of restored routine were the instant cabarets and other cash separation centers of the bored soldiers on pass and the off-shift war workers. These places had been of the mood momentary. Radio programs resumed hard-sell and film theatres, their crowds falling off, went back to dish nights.

The film industry had one strong anchor to windward in the form of foreign sales. American producer-distributors in the early 1950's were earning perhaps 45% of their gross rentals overseas, a take-out of around $225,000,000 annually. This was, to say the least, a very comforting economic factor against the stay-at-home habit of television.

Television proved earth-shakingly competitive to all other forms of amusement and advertising. It would be literally a decade before the radio, film, magazine and newspaper industries learned to live, with poise, in an economy complicated and agitated by TV.

It was immediately apparent that television programs were going to be enormously costly, thereby grabbing more of the advertising dollars. Against this risk, advertisers were hypnotized by the idea of product-in-use demonstrations in the parlors of America. Such visibility justified the costs. Consumers, in their own way, were entranced by a medium that added sight to sound and set up a sort of movie theatre in the home, though old movies were not originally available to television.

At the outset, network leaders asserted with absolute, if misguided, conviction that all television entertainment would originate "live." But events cancelled this promise and today practically all TV programs are on film, which means prerecorded.

Outwardly, television programming followed the example, and ran on the same tracks laid down by radio. But in subsequent adaptation to inflation, the whole pattern of deal-making changed. In radio the big advertising agencies had literally produced the entertainment, but in television all the ad agencies did was produce the inserted commercials.

Television advertising is sold much more by bargaining and less by rigid price cards than was radio. A poorly-rated program, in its last months or weeks on the air, may sell its commercial

Songs, Playbills, Programs spanning a half-century of the theatre.

minutes at knockdown prices. By the mid-1960's, a TV "commercial minute" in a network program had a cost range of from $25,000 to $60,000, depending upon prime time and popularity (that is to say, presumed audience size) ratings.

Radio studio payroll conditions had been modest indeed compared to television studio payrolls. A contrast of the early 1950's found that a daytime soap opera episode on radio could be managed with no more than 11 employees, including the actors, whereas a similar daily episode on television demanded a minimum of 35 employees in the studio.

Television has woven itself inextricably into American family life. After, or with, theatrical feature films, there is little doubt that TV is the over-riding mass appeal medium. Despite this success, there has continued unremittently a drumfire of criticism from professional viewers, teachers, the public generally, members of Congress and the Federal Communications Commission. One chairman of the FCC, Newton Minow, branded the television program schedules a "cultural wasteland," thereby delighting the fault-finding elements in the country while angering the networks and stations. It is now part of American folklore that the so-called "Golden Age of Television" came at the beginning of the medium, roughly 1948 to 1958. Young directors and writers were then comparatively free to deal with challenging ideas and fictional materials. Later they would complain that committees of advertisers had intervened, insisting upon "safe" plots, stereotyped westerns and murder stories. At the present time, television-trained men are almost the only new directors recruited for theatrical features.

"Crazy Guggenheim"—Frank Fontaine's beloved comedy character.

In their defense, television officials have argued that they are not in the business of offending anybody or of inviting counter-attack upon themselves. Nor are they pleased when confronted by demands to grant "equal" time, at no charge, in the name of fairness. The most celebrated case of a network granting free opportunity for a political answer came after Edward R. Murrow on CBS excoriated Senator Joseph McCarthy. The latter presented his reply some time later.

The Electronic Acceleration

Electronics has been the great accelerator of amusements, as well as much besides in late years. The electron tube infused the old vacuum tube, on which radio-broadcasting was based, with enormously increased power. Television, and later color television, stereophonic sound in film theatres, community antenna television, tollvision, closed-circuit transmissions and other innovations since the war derive from the science of electronics.

A factor of television delay in this country, other than war curbs, was a business feud between the Radio Corporation of America, spokesman for electronics, and the Columbia Broadcasting System, originally an advocate of its own "mechanical disc" method of telecasting. The Federal Communications Commission gave the decision to RCA.

The post-war expansion of film theatre technology put various new trade names into circulation. There was a Three-Dimension (3-D) system of exhibition, requiring the spectator to wear spectacles. Then came the three-panel Cinerama process, which created a renaissance in travelogues. CinemaScope, Panavision, Todd-AO (American Optical), Technirama 70 and Dimension 150 are other "widescreen" processes. Meanwhile, at the various scientific displays in connection with Montreal's World's Fair of 1967, there was explicit promise of even more communications wonders ahead, with due impact presumably upon entertainment media.

The Revolution in Music

Popular music has been a radical change area in space age amusements. Recording and reproducing technology has undergone not one or two, but a dazzling array of improvements. Often these changes have had the practical commercial bonanza effect of rendering much of the existing recordings and mechanisms useless. A first big breakthrough was in 1950 when the Long-Playing (LP) record came as a sensation. Theretofore, a platter ran three to five minutes, but would now spin for forty minutes.

With new hard-surface materials, improved know-how, and the "microgroove" track, the high fidelity phase opened. An enlarged and prosperous middle class helped, as it helped all branches of entertainment. The audience for records became enormous, with a solid phalanx of disk-crazy teenagers a considerable escalation in itself.

With two-channel stereo, cartridge tapes, albums of all sorts, a separate boom in speech and documentary records, the annual value of recordings kept rising, reaching $600,000,000 a year by the mid-1960's. There were literally hundreds of small, independent "labels" on the market and an unending outpouring of new musical ideas and talent.

The sale of musical instruments increased, much of it due to the electronic influence in juicing up various instruments. An electrical guitar, powered for big beat and ear-assaulting pandemonium, almost has become an essential toy for every growing, red-blooded American boy. Elvis Presley has been a big influence and so, too, the British foursome, The Beatles.

Discothèques and Jukeboxes

Powered turntables have become the basis of a new kind of dance hall, the Discothèque. It has been estimated that there are perhaps 5,000 of them in the country. There is no official count. But add discothèques to teenagers to radio disk jockeys to jukeboxes, and the by-products of the phonograph industry are suggested.

Jukeboxes constitute an enormous music-related network. Nobody knows precisely how many there are in cafés, bars, clubs, lodges, pizza and ice cream parlors for the high school trade. There may be 500,000 jukes operating by coin.

At the peak of the Rock 'n' Roll Era—few "production" houses remain in existence. (ARSENE STUDIO)

The New York Rock 'n' Roll Ensemble, one of many groups of which an important ingredient is visual publicity.

For the owners of copyrights, the galling fact about them, whatever their numbers, is that they use copyright music for profit, but pay no performance fees to the creators and publishers of the music they play. The situation is a legal fluke because such a thing as a jukebox was never imagined in 1909 when the copyright law was enacted; hence, the loophole which music men hope eventually to plug.

During about half the years of the space age, the U.S. Congress has been trying to write a new copyright law that the various elements of the economy would accept. Meanwhile, music copyright owners depend for collection of performance fees upon two licensing organizations, the American Society of Composers, Authors and Publishers (founded in 1914) and Broadcast Music, Inc. (founded in 1940). The two air media, theatres, cafés, dance halls, etc., all pay for the music they play on an involved point-rating system.

Counting in phonograph sales, instruments, performance fees and everything else which comprises the U.S. music industry, this is now a giant big business with an annual volume of at least one billion dollars.

Rewards of Genius

Irving Berlin is the standout example of a fabulously popular and wealthy composer of pop tunes. From his *Alexander's Ragtime Band* in 1913, Berlin's outpouring of hits was constant for 55 years. Right after World War II, he set up a fund, for the benefit of Boy and Girl Scouts of America, assigning to it his royalties and performance fees from various of his compositions. It tells much of the economics of song hits to cite the payments to this Fund, through December 31, 1966, of a total of $446,974.32 from four Berlin songs:

God Bless America	$354,957.64
This Is The Army	47,092.85
Give Me Your Tired	33,942.23
This Is A Great Country	10,981.60

Although pop music has been expanding its multiple markets for the last two generations, there has been a simultaneous decline in the employment of musicians. It set in with the demise of movie house stage bands and vaudeville pit orchestras, circa 1930. At one point, the frustrated American Federation of Musicians decided its members would make no further records ever, and stuck with this attempted boycott some 18 months. Union tooters are convinced that recordings kill live employment. When the union tried in 1941 to force radio stations to hire staff orchestras, which the broadcasters said they did not need, Congress came to the rescue of the stations by passing a law that stopped the musicians. A further disappointment for musicians, as regards employment on regular salary, developed when television program producers tended to use library tapes for background and bridge music.

Riding Gain

A master technician in modern amusement media is the sound, or volume control, engineer. He was present of yore in the radio studios "riding gain" on the needle, which duty was simple-seeming, but worthy of respect. Since then, microphones and amplification have grown in importance and use. Perhaps only grand opera makes a point of feeling "disgraced" by microphones. Everybody else uses a hand-mike, or has a hidden mike sewn into his garments. All this means that the sound engineer is the indispensable collaborator in broadcasting and recording studios, behind scenes at stage musical comedies and night club floor shows, and for outdoor events in summertime. The control panel is the very heart of big capacity "arena show business," making it possible.

Through the "mixing" panel, little voices are made to seem big, notes and words emitting from almost invisible lips half a block and more away are rendered intelligible, even "intimate." Mikes and amplifying permit the illusion that long-haired youths with a range of three chords on a juiced-up guitar are versatile musicians. Take away electronic support and many modern entertainers would be helpless. Sound control opens ball parks to talent like The Beatles, Joan Baez, Pete Seeger. In another context altogether, it permits 100,000 New Yorkers to come within the range of His Holiness Pope Paul VI celebrating Mass.

It is not being suggested here that large assemblages are a contemporary invention. In ancient Greece, 4,000 years ago, there were amphitheatres accommodating 40,000 and more. The difference is that the Greeks of antiquity relied upon favorable hillside terrain for ideal acoustics, whereas this generation turns to the sound engineer and his electronic gadgetry.

Another tribe of microphone-made folk are the "western and country" entertainers. They found their first breaks in radio hillbilly days, but have

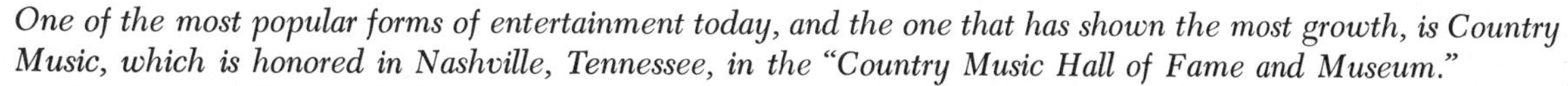

One of the most popular forms of entertainment today, and the one that has shown the most growth, is Country Music, which is honored in Nashville, Tennessee, in the "Country Music Hall of Fame and Museum."

Show Business in an Arena.

since standardized and organized their special kind of musical entertainment. Nashville, Tennessee is the western and country music headquarter city.

Out-Size Arenas

Of course, arenas and auditoria serve many contemporary purposes other than entertainment—sports, notably, political rallies, business conventions, community celebrations. They constitute an essential civic facility, drawing business traffic. Nor are arenas confined to large cities. In Louisiana, the 64,000-population city of Monroe erected a 2,245-seat theatre and an 8,000-capacity arena as part of a $6,500,000 project, meaning a per capita investment of about $100.

In such out-size halls or open-air places all over the land rendezvous screaming teenagers to hail their favorite combos dispensing the big beat with electronic gadgetry. Many of these young talent groups give themselves intentionally arresting names, as The Moby Grape, The Grateful Dead, The Loving Spoonful, The Ultimate Spinach, The Mothers of Invention, which go beyond the imaginative theatrical billing adopted by certain strip-tease ladies, namely, Candy Barr, Paddy Wagon, Norma Vincent Peel, Blaze Fury. The pun in theatrical billing goes way back, often associated with vaudeville acts of long ago, only their choices now seem "square" indeed, names like Salt & Pepper, Harvard & Yale, Hill & Dale.

Many, perhaps most, of the youthful combinations reach fame exclusively through the phonograph record. They are ever intent upon creating big-selling disks earning a heavy play in the jukes or on the radio disk jockey programs. If a hit record can put unknown youths into boxoffice orbit, it is necessary to point out the sad reverse of the fact: namely, should the knack be lost, or luck run out, popularity can shrivel to zero, sending the lads back to the barbers.

Radio City Music Hall

It may seem contradictory, but it is a fact of present entertainment economics that only "flash popularity" attractions want enormous seating capacity. Film houses have retreated almost entirely from the gingerbread movie palaces built in the 1920's before radio and talking pictures developed. The one remaining situation of this kind is the Radio City Music Hall in Manhattan. It has 6,200 seats, scaled up to $3 top. With the movie, there is presented a 55-man orchestra, separately an organist, also the famous "Rockettes" line of girls, plus a ballet corps and a vocal choir. These are the regular payroll talent. For each change of show several special turns are added.

Loew's Capitol on Broadway cut its capacity practically in half to create a new setting more suitable for modern widescreen or road show performances. Scores of yesteryear film temples, with ornate decor and militarily-drilled ushers, are no more. In some instances, their balconies were converted into an upstairs theatre with a separate show and boxoffice.

A solitary vaudeville operation continues, the Apollo on 125th Street in Harlem. This is an important showcase for Negro rock, folk, spiritual, jazz and comedy talent.

As to jazz, it has persevered, but been somewhat sidetracked by the teenagers' preference for

World-famous Radio City Music Hall, home of the spectacular Rockettes.

Gingerbread Movie Palace of the 1920's—a reminder of the past.

Sean Connery (James Bond) attacks a "female" enemy—in reality, a man.

the less original, but louder forms of big beat. Jazz has usually been considered among the most truly creative contributions of American, and especially Negro American, talent.

Road Show Films

Smaller audiences paying higher prices sum up the road show, or reserved seat, film policy. Behind this procedure are the hopes of building a long preliminary run, for prestige's sake, before the film goes into "grind" release. Road-showing is not new, but until recently was infrequently adopted. It is still pretty much a big city practice, although it has spread to some film theatres located in shopping plazas. The original road show film was the D. W. Griffith epic of 1915, *The Birth Of A Nation.*

It says something about the upgrading of theatrical films in the past 20 years, that road-showing has greatly increased, that film festivals have multiplied, that hundreds of colleges now teach film appreciation or film production skills, and that the film "buff" is so numerous. The "buff" is not to be confused with the gushy and romantic film "fan." A buff tends to be a serious adult student of the cinema, a reader of intellectual criticism. He has little, if any, interest in the love affairs of stars.

Film festivals had a beginning prior to World War II when Benito Mussolini's regime established the one at Venice. Italy then had a very fine film school. The Communistic dictatorships were also quick to recognize film as an art, by which they usually meant a propaganda means, and they train technicians well.

American Film Institute

The United States was slow to teach the arts of film production, and shockingly negligent about physically preserving its own film classics. The old (and inflammable) nitrate prints disintegrated into dust when not properly stored. The new acetate film stock of our times is more durable, as well as fireproof, so that helps. Only in 1967 were Federal funds made available to establish an American Film Institute, of which much is expected. Curiously, French film archives have often been far more respectful to old American movies than were the Americans.

In the space age, there has been an emphatic

International Market for Theatrical and Television Films, Milan, Italy.

shift in the artistic standing accorded the motion picture by intelligent people. As films have moved up in prestige, its former position as low man on the arts totem pole has been assigned television, which, with the exception of news and documentary programs, does not often draw esthetic praise.

Enhanced respect given theatrical films reflects the liberation of product from the "mass production" system of yesteryear Hollywood, also the impact of new directors working in the film industries of Great Britain, France, Italy, Russia, Sweden, Japan and other nations.

Films being made and exhibited in the late 1960's differ sharply from those of 20 years before. Many factors have brought this about, of which the previously mentioned censorship retreat is one. Only a few years ago, the word "virgin," used humorously in Otto Preminger's *The Moon Is Blue,* was the occasion of a public dispute. Since then, word taboos have been broken in all directions, though it is hardly true, as extremists claim, that "anything goes." There is little reason to suppose that the vulgar speech of gutter and barracks is ever going to become generally acceptable on screen or television, the two major mass media. Perhaps it is significant that a victory over the New York State censorship at the time meant little to the boxoffice of Shirley Clarke's film *The Connection.* Its use, some eleven times, of a four-letter word usually not acceptable in formal entertainment, although common in novels, became a cause célèbre. Albany, for a time, held up the then-necessary license.

No account of amusements in the space age could withhold mention of the New York "film underground," a group of free-lance producer-writer-directors who finance their films privately and typically shoot with non-union crews. The

An elaborate setting near Madrid, Spain, for the film, "The Fall of the Roman Empire."

finished movies are often unreeled in clandestine circumstances. They tend to an overwhelming preoccupation with homosexuality and narcotics as subject matter.

Hollywood Condescends

At the outset, the major Hollywood studios tended to scorn television as a child's plaything. The film industry was slow to modify its own plans, or to seek partnerships with the new medium. The long, fat years may have slowed the reflexes of the then reigning "czar" of the film colony, Louis B. Mayer, who had for years collected the largest salary, $800,000 a year, paid to any American. What more immediately distressed and frightened the Hollywood power structure was the threat of another consent decree. The Anti-Trust Division of the U.S. Department of Justice had exacted reforms of trade practices as early as 1940, but it looked like far

Europe's first drive-in theatre shows this double feature—Audrey Hepburn and Gary Cooper on the screen in competition with members of the audience who are imitating the performance of the professionals. (UPI PHOTO)

"Oscar"—coveted award of the Academy of Motion Picture Arts and Sciences.

more drastic compulsory reform would be imposed. It came early in 1950. The second consent decree which the film industry was forced to sign stipulated that the studio divest themselves of all theatre holdings, cease "block booking" and refrain from other practice held to be in restraint of trade.

It will suffice to make the historic point: "Divorcement" of studios from theatres, in the wake of television competition, truly ended the old order in Hollywood. It would have the side result of slowing production by the studios themselves, while encouraging aggressive new "independent" producers.

Nothing was simple. Nothing happened except after much trial and error. But the film industry moved gradually, with many wailings for the good old days, toward new ideas and themes, fresh talents. The object was to get people back into the theatres and that necessitated building many new theatres, following population to outlying areas, and offering attractions that could counter the home tube popularity of, say, Milton Berle.

The inside clique which had long ruled in Hollywood had accepted and worked with the American system of state, city and church censorships. But Johnny-come-lately producers opposed arbitrary limits on subject matter. They were intolerant of any official intolerance of their pictures. In a series of appeals to the United States Supreme Court by independents and importers, the censorships were nearly all put out of business in one of the great basic changes of the space age.

Today, of course, the film industry and the television industry are extensively collaborating. In a real switch, two of the networks, ABC and CBS, now produce feature films intended, in the first instance, for theatres, with television playoff later. Hollywood is now as much a television as a theatrical film-producing center.

Subsidy and Subscriptions

Separately, there has been impressive progress in the cultural performing arts. The $146,000,000 complex of buildings which comprise Lincoln Center in New York is only the largest gesture of this nature. New community centers of the same sort exist in Los Angeles, Houston, Seattle, Indianapolis, Saratoga Springs, Montreal, Toronto, Miami.

Ingenious financing has been developed to bring such performing arts complexes into being. First off, there is often condemnation of land. Lincoln Center stands where slums once stood. Lincoln Center drew upon Federal, State, City, private corporations, foundations, and individual contributions. Even foreign governments, notably West Germany and Austria, made donations. It is to be noted that one of the edifices, the New York State Theatre, was an outright $19,000,000 gift voted by the legislature in Albany.

Inflation and an economy clouded by high taxation have made this many-sided financing necessary. The wealthy individual donor is still around, and still counted upon, but in no way able to absorb a whole season's deficit as was long true of, for example, the Boston Symphony.

A leap forward by the New York City Opera, which specializes in modern, folk and American works, has been made possible largely through numerous grants from the Ford Foundation.

The two key terms of opera, symphony, ballet, dramatic repertory are "subsidy" and "subscription." Otherwise these arts would succumb to deficits and could not continue in existence. Another designation for subscription is "preorganized audience." Tickets are sold in blocks and ahead of time so that the attraction avoids catch-as-catch-can, and is insured against bad

Metropolitan Opera House at New York's new modern Lincoln Center. (LOUIS MELANCON)

The New York State Theatre at the Lincoln Center for the Performing Arts, valued at $19,300,000, on the occasion of its opening night, April 23, 1964, with performances by the New York City Ballet and a scene from "Carousel" by the Music Theatre of Lincoln Center. (UPI PHOTO)

Tom Ewell in one of the perennial revivals of "Life With Father" –longest running play of the century.

weather, breakdown of transport, or other adverse conditions.

"Subscription" was widely adopted well before the war for the various community concert series and for the touring stage plays of the Theatre Guild. Since then it has spread, indeed become general. A full 97% of the Metropolitan Opera tickets for an entire season are pre-sold to subscribers, all the money being in hand before the season's first curtain rises.

There is, of course, the disadvantage to the last-minute patron that he often is unable to secure admission to a cultural event. Everything is already sold. Hunter College in New York recognized this situation in the fall of 1967, when it adopted a policy of holding a stated percentage of tickets for window sale. It spoke of restoring "spontaneity" to concert-going.

Legitimate Theatre

As for the legitimate, or Broadway, theatre of stage plays and stage musicals, here there is justified use of the old half-mocking, half-affectionate term, "the fabulous invalid." Forever dying, never dead, or so it often has seemed. The first squeeze came when the legitimate, and especially the touring company was caught between talking pictures, radio and unemployment. Later the complaint was ever-rising costs, a famine of playwrights. Broadway's own former tally of 72 playhouses slipped to the present 32. Once the block on 42nd Street between Seventh and Eighth Avenues in Manhattan was solid with legit stands. They are still there but long since on grind movie policy.

Efforts to reverse the downward trend of theatrical real estate in midtown Manhattan have included building code modifications to permit office space to be built over auditoriums, and liquor control regulations to permit theatres to operate bars, as in London. But these inducements have not amounted to much. There have also been periodic campaigns in recent times against theatre ticket scalping but the main result has been to drive the practice underground, not to halt it. The fact remains that when a play is a hit, everybody proceeds to milk it, well knowing that 75% of all stage productions fail in any year.

Against the flops and the losses there are, from time to time, the fabulous successes. *My Fair Lady*, a musical based on an earlier straight comedy of George Bernard Shaw, earned perhaps $9,000,0000 on an original investment of $300,-000. The film rights were sold for $5,000,000 and the Warner movie will end up one of the great money-makers of screen history.

Off-Broadway is sometimes represented as an answer to the decline of Broadway. But little shows presented to small audiences at reduced admission rates are only a token offset. This sort of cellar theatre has developed in many big cities all over the country. In some instances quite vital productions and very promising talent have attracted notice, as with "The Second City" troupe of Chicago. The former restaurant, the dark film house, the abandoned church have their usefulness to side-street legit but hardly restore "the fabulous invalid".

Broadway, proper, with a recent average of 60 productions annually against some 200 a year in the mid-1920's, is a high-risk business whose successes continue to be glamorous, though comparatively few in number. The season of 1948-49 on Broadway represented 1,325 playing weeks for all shows and a boxoffice income of $28,640,700. The tally for the season of 1964-65 was fewer playing weeks, 1,250, but a substantially higher money yield, $50,462,765, which reflected the higher prices charged to get in. For the same contrasted seasons there was not too much change in road dates for touring stage attractions. It was $23,657,900 the season of 1948-49 and $25,929,115 for the season of 1964-65.

New York City regards the legitimate theatre as its greatest appeal to tourists, convention delegates and lovers of the drama who regularly throng the city in season "to see the plays." No other city has over six or seven playhouses against Broadway's 32, from which it is apparent that, despite all risks and shrinkages, the kind of entertainment to which Shakespeare devoted himself, and before him, by thousands of years, a number of wonderfully gifted Greek dramatists, is still with us.

Will television, when it becomes another home relay system of the electronic phenomenon, help the legitimate theatre by broadening its public? We do not know, yet, but many optimists ardently describe golden years ahead.

"Get Me To The Church On Time" is the theme of this scene from "My Fair Lady," one of the memorable musicals of the late 1950's. (UPI PHOTO)

Felicia Weathers as Elisabetta in opera, "Don Carlos." Negro singers became grand opera stars in post-war era. (B. F. BAKONYI)

Faster Travel

The jet airplane plays a role in theatrical life. As the spread of railroads in the 19th Century opened up vaudeville and touring legitimate shows, so has the jet quickened international bookings. In the old days, an Enrico Caruso would leisurely cross the Atlantic by ship and spend the entire season singing at a single opera house. Not so with the great singers today. They are literally here today and on another continent tomorrow. It is not exceptional for a tenor to jet from, say, La Scala in Milano (Italy) to Covent Garden (in London) to the Colon (in Buenos Aires), then back to, say, Paris, Barcelona, Belgrade, then over-Atlantic again to the Lyric Opera (Chicago) and out over the Pacific to Japanese and Australian engagements. Jets have made "all the world a stage" in a sense Shakespeare never implied. They also are the necessary means of "cultural exchange." When the Bolshoi Opera of Moscow arrived for three weeks at Montreal's Expo 67, some 429 persons stepped out of giant jets, while 105 tons of costumes and scenery came ahead by ship.

Nearly all talent today moves either in the skies or by prearranged bus and truck. Circus performers drive their own cars or trailers, seldom sleep or eat on the lot as in the old times. Circus paraphernalia is now lightweight, emphasis upon aluminum, and travels from town to town in their own fast-haul motor vehicles.

Fast aircraft has also stimulated the unique desert centers of gambling in Nevada, where big-name singers and comedians are part of the come-on of Las Vegas, Reno and nearby oases.

Cultural Exchange

"Cultural Exchange" has been conspicuous between the U.S. and U.S.S.R., but has been much more widespread than that. Our State Department has consciously used American talent to win friends for us in countries all over the world. The government subsidy of tours has introduced the people of faraway lands to live American talent, often for the first time, the natives knowing Americans only through Hollywood movies. In more recent years, the State Department has favored shipping out college choirs, orchestras and other "amateur" talent, often for budget limitation reasons. The success of these essentially youthful aggregations among their foreign audiences has apparently been genuine, and they have the side advantage for diplomacy of being good mixers with the natives. However, other observers contend that the United States ought to be represented only by its finest professionals and not by amateurs.

The American concert platform circuits have meanwhile presented entertainment companies and musical aggregations from many countries, usually with the originating nation picking up the jet fares tab. We have welcomed folk dancers, singers and musicians from Spain, Portugal, Greece, Bulgaria, Poland, Israel, France, Africa, Korea, Japan, the Philippines, Mexico and so on.

Richard Rodgers (center) and Oscar Hammerstein (right), with musical director Harry Sosnick, contributed immortal musical plays and songs to the theatre.

New York City Ballet production of "Midsummer Night's Dream," the first ballet filmed in the United States.

About World's Fairs

Another form of "international" entertainment draws attention, namely World's Fairs. Suspended during the period of hostilities, these resumed in 1957 with the Brussels World's Fair, in which a kingdom of 9,000,000 population organized itself to play host to 40,000,000 visitors, a dozen years after it was an occupied country. There was a small World's Fair (less than 100 acres) in Seattle in 1962. Then came the, in many ways, ill-fated New York World's Fair of 1964 and 1965, which had been privately promoted by politicians, public relations counsels and bankers, but without the sanction of the International Bureau of Expositions in Paris. Following this New York fair's conclusion, there was a good deal of crepe hanging as to the whole situation and future of World's Fairs. It was asserted that these were obsolete, that people were now too knowledgeable, too traveled, too sophisticated to really care. It was further said that a World's Fair could no longer provide scientific or artistic leadership, as in the past, because the pace of innovation outran the years of necessary make-ready. We may now presume to doubt these gloomy ideas, since the stunning success of the Montreal World's Fair of 1967 adequately answered the charge that the vitality and popularity of such events were exhausted.

Montreal's Expo 67 differed from New York in putting its stress on entertainment of all kinds, whereas amusements had been notoriously neglected at Flushing Meadows in favor of industrial showmanship. Montreal also organized an elaborate program of performances in local theatres by great musical, operatic, dramatic and dancing companies from all over the world. The business arrangements which made these visits possible suggest the ingenuity of the Canadians, and the alternatives to excessive investment risk. Under the World Festival of Entertainment, directed by Gordon Hilker, Expo 67 provided theatre, staff, advertising, ticket handling, food, lodging, local transport, laundry, and so on, and paid every member of a visiting company $12 daily pocket money in Canadian currency. Against this, the government of origin picked up the company's jet fares tab and paid the regular salaries.

Government-to-government "cultural exchange," or any variation thereof, is not, however, the whole thing. It should be remembered that the rock 'n' roll "British Invasion" of America in the 1960's was without assistance of any kind.

Negative Factors

Many American stage actors actively oppose the bringing over of British actors, on the grounds that Americans could as well play the roles. They contend that managements often import British players to save money, but American managements deny any saving, since they must defray travel costs and other expenses for Britons. Moreover, it is questioned that, for the particular roles, Americans are artistically as satisfactory as the Britons, all of which offers us a glimpse of "job anxiety" within theatrical union ranks. Similar antagonism to "newcomers" of any nationality, including American, characterizes

Theatre in the Round—audience surrounds small stage, actors are costumed and carry props, but lights take over scene changes. (CHARLES J. RICH)

several of the Hollywood studio craft unions. The more candid members put it plainly: they have a stake in their jobs and will protect their seniority from erosion at all costs. The "closed doors" of Hollywood unions impose a depressing barrier for young would-be directors and cameramen.

Negro actors also complain that they are excluded from opportunities on the screen. They have exacted promises, at several times, of improvement in casting practice, but continue dissatisfied with their "calls." One Negro actor put his complaint wittily: "If they can't get Sidney Poitier, they rewrite the part for a white actor!" So there is no lack of internal dissension, and of many kinds, in show business.

A sustained campaign to stop comedians and entertainers resorting to "racial stereotypes" began during the war years as part of the counter-propaganda against Hitler's race hatred. This has changed the nature of humor in our times. There is now limited use of jokes at the expense of Negroes, Jews, Irish, Italians or other ethnic segments of the population. "Dialect" has become controversial. Blackface minstrels (white men satirizing Negroes) have disappeared from sophisticated centers, though preserved by village amateurs in some sections.

Meanwhile, amusements mirror the tone of the American culture generally. Very definitely, entertainment is now mobile. The old river showboats are extinct, but performers now go to sea to do their acts for the passengers on pleasure cruise ships. They receive a salary plus first-class passage. These cruise ships have kinship to the Catskill Mountain hotels of the depression years, where talent went with the beet, or borscht, soup. Just recently the Holiday Inns, a chain of motels, has launched separate "Dinner Theatres" adjoining their plants, presenting a simplified stage comedy with food for a fixed charge of $6 a head.

So we see modern merchandising influencing entertainment in many ways, and political tensions finding an echo on stage, screen, home receiver and floor show. The good and the bad, the happy and the disturbed aspects of our environment come through to us in entertainment.

The Rolling Stones, one of the favorite English pop singing groups, in some areas rivaling the popularity of the Beatles. (UPI PHOTO)

CIVIL RIGHTS and INTEGRATION

The greatest domestic issue of the United States during the two postwar decades was the effort to attain greater civil rights for the Negro people who make up 10 to 12 percent of the population. A century after being freed from slavery by the Civil War, Negroes still had not achieved full equality as citizens.

Racial prejudice and economic discrimination in both the North and the South forced the majority of Negroes into a second class status. Negroes did not receive equal education, handicapping them in seeking employment. Labor unions and employers discriminated against Negroes, forcing them to take unskilled and low-paying jobs. Proportionately more Negroes than whites were unemployed and on public welfare. Most Negroes were forced by racial prejudice to live in slum areas that became all-Negro ghettoes. Even Negroes who could afford better housing were prevented by racial prejudice from moving into middle-class white suburbs.

Throughout the two decades there was a movement of Southern Negroes to the Northern cities. And at the same time there was a movement of whites from the cities to the suburbs. As a result, by the mid-1960's many American cities, including the nation's capital, Washington, D.C., had populations that were more than 50 percent Negro.

During the twenty-year period Negroes made greater gains in civil rights than in any similar time span since the Reconstruction Era. A handful of Negroes rose to higher positions than ever before attained by members of their race—appointed to the President's cabinet, to the United States Supreme Court, and to influential jobs in most industries and professions. But many Negroes felt that the majority of their race still were oppressed. Protests and riots occurred frequently, particularly in the Negro slum areas of the cities.

Infantrymen in Korea in June 1951, in pursuit of retreating Communist forces after capturing anchor points in the Iron Triangle. The armed forces were desegregated years before schools and various other public establishments. (UPI PHOTO)

The Supreme Court in June 1952, showing, from left to right in front row, Felix Frankfurter, Hugo L. Black, Chief Justice Fred M. Vinson, Stanley F. Reed and William O. Douglas. In back row, from left to right, are Tom C. Clark, Robert H. Jackson, Harold H. Burton and Sherman Minton. (UPI PHOTO)

Beginnings of the Postwar Civil Rights Movement

In 1946 the United States Supreme Court, led by Chief Justice Fred Vinson, ended the "Jim Crow" discrimination against Negroes in interstate transportation. The ruling in the case of *Morgan* v. *Virginia* struck down a state law that required Negroes to sit only in seats reserved for members of their race on interstate buses.

But also in 1946 the United States experienced more Negro lynchings than in any year since the Depression of the 1930's. The nation was horror-stricken when a mob of about 25 persons killed four Negroes, two men and their wives, near Monroe, Georgia, on July 25. Earlier that day one of the Negro men had been released on bond from jail where he had been held on charges of wounding a white man with a knife. The other victims were the man's wife, her sister, and her sister's husband. Late in the year a federal grand jury failed to indict anyone for the crime. In two other lynch-slayings of Negroes during the year in Mississippi and Louisiana, eleven men were indicted but were acquitted when brought to trial.

Responding to a public outcry against the lynchings, President Truman appointed a Committee on Civil Rights on December 5, 1946, to investigate the entire status of civil rights in the United States and to recommend new legislation. Addressing the committee, Truman said:

"I want our Bill of Rights implemented in fact . . . we are not making progress fast enough."

Six months later, in June, 1946, the President spoke to the annual conventions of the National Association for the Advancement of Colored People (NAACP) and said:

"As Americans, we believe that every man should be free to live his life as he wishes. He should be limited only by his responsibility to his fellow countrymen. If this freedom is to be more than a dream, each man must be guaranteed equality of opportunity. The only limit to an American's achievement should be his ability, his industry, and his character."

In October, 1947, the President's Committee on Civil Rights issued a lengthy report that detailed needed new laws and called for "the elimination of segregation, based on race, color, creed, or national origin, from American life." The committee particularly denounced the "separate but equal doctrine" that had been established by the Supreme Court in 1896 upholding the legality of state laws segregating Negroes. Similarly, two months later, a Commission on Higher Education appointed by President Truman reported its recommendation that all educational segregation should be eliminated and that federal funds should be withheld from any institutions practicing discrimination. The report said:

> "The first condition toward equality of opportunity for a college education can only be satisfied when every qualified young person, irrespective of race, creed, color, sex, national origin, or economic status is assured of the opportunity for a good high school education in an accredited institution."

President Truman who had forced the armed services to integrate Negroes rather than continue to have all-Negro units, called on Congress to adopt the civil rights legislation recommended by his special committee, and later encouraged the Democratic party to adopt a strong civil rights plank in its platform for the 1948 presidential election. Southern Democrats headed by Governor J. Strom Thurmond of South Carolina bolted from the Democratic convention to set up their own States' Rights, or "Dixiecrat," party in an effort to defeat Truman and his civil rights program, which called for federal anti-lynching laws, antipoll-tax laws, and a federal fair employment practices law. Although Truman lost the electoral votes of Alabama, Louisiana, Mississippi, and South Carolina to the "Dixiecrats," he won the election.

Although the presidential election provided wider consideration of the problems of civil rights, the most concrete action in 1948 came from the United States Supreme Court. With three justices abstaining, the Supreme Court by a 6 to 0 opinion refused to uphold real estate contracts that contained a so-called "genleman's agreement" preventing the sale or use of property by Negroes or Jews. President Truman continued to press for civil rights legislation, but a coalition of Southern Democrats and conservative Republicans prevented such action.

Increasing Tempo of the Civil Rights Movement

The United States Supreme Court continued to lead the nation toward more equal civil rights in the 1950's. In *Sweatt* v. *Painter* in 1950 the Court held that a segregated law school for Negroes in Texas did not provide equal opportunity for education. In following years the Court upheld this decision in other cases that slowly opened up most Southern universities and colleges to Negro enrollment, although as late as 1963 the federal government had to take over the Alabama National Guard to force the University of Alabama to admit Negro students.

Encouraged by their success in gaining admission to previously all-white institutions of higher learning, Negroes began to bring suits to attempt to overthrow the laws in 21 states that provided for segregation in the public schools. Five of these cases were argued before the Supreme Court in its 1952-1953 and 1953-1954 terms. The chief counsel for the NAACP was Thurgood Marshall, who more than a dozen years later became the first Negro appointed as an associate justice of the Supreme Court. Finally, on May 17, 1954, Chief Justice Earl Warren handed down the unanimous ruling of the justices overturning the "separate but equal doctrine" and ordering the public schools to end segregation.

Earl Warren, Chief Justice of the Supreme Court, which ruled unanimously in favor of desegregation in the case of Brown v. Board of Education of Topeka, 1954. (UPI PHOTO)

U.S. Supreme Court Decision in Brown v. Board of Education of Topeka

—decision prepared by Chief Justice Earl Warren and approved unanimously by all eight associate justices, May 17, 1954

These cases come to us from the States of Kansas, South Carolina, Virginia, and Delaware. They are premised on different facts and different local conditions, but a common legal question justifies their consideration together in this consolidation opinion.

In each of the cases, minors of the Negro race, through their legal representatives, seek the aid of the courts in obtaining admission to the public schools of their community on a nonsegregated basis. In each instance, they had been denied admission to schools attended by white children under laws requiring or permitting segregation according to race. This segregation was alleged to deprive the plaintiffs of the equal protection of the laws under the Fourteenth Amendment. In each of the cases other than the Delaware case, a three-judge federal district court denied relief to the plaintiffs on the so-called "separate but equal" doctrine announced by this Court in *Plessy v. Ferguson*, 163 U.S. 537. Under that doctrine, equality of treatment is accorded when the races are provided substantially equal facilities, even though these facilities be separate. In the Delaware case, the Supreme Court of Delaware adhered to that doctrine, but ordered that the plaintiffs be admitted to the white schools because of their superiority to the Negro schools.

The plaintiffs contend that segregated public schools are not "equal" and cannot be made "equal," and that hence they are deprived of the equal protection of the laws. Because of the obvious importance of the question presented, the court took jurisdiction. Argument was heard in the 1952 Term, and reargument was heard this Term on certain questions propounded by the Court.

Reargument was largely devoted to the circumstances surrounding the adoption of the Fourteenth Amendment in 1868. It covered exhaustively consideration of the Amendment in Congress, ratification by the states, then existing practices in racial segregation, and the views of proponents and opponents of the Amendment. This discussion and our investigation convince us that, although these sources cast some light, it is not enough to resolve the problem with which we are faced. At best, they are inconclusive. The most avid proponents of the post-War Amendments undoubtedly intended them to remove all legal distinctions among "all persons born or naturalized in the United States." Their opponents, just as certainly, were antagonistic to both the letter and the spirit of the Amendments and wished them to have the most limited effect. What others in Congress and the state legislatures had in mind cannot be determined with any degree of certainty.

An additional reason for the inconclusive nature of the Amendment's history, with respect to segregated schools, is the status of public education at that time. In the South, the movement toward free common schools, supported by general taxation, had not yet taken hold. Education of white children was largely in the hands of private groups. Education of Negroes was almost nonexistent, and practically all of the race were illiterate. In fact, any education of Negroes was forbidden by law in some states. Today, in contrast, many Negroes have achieved outstanding success in the arts and sciences as well as in the business and professional world. It is true that public school education at the time of the Amendment had advanced further in the North, but the effect of the Amendment on Northern States was generally ignored in the congressional debates. Even in the North, the conditions of public education did not approximate those existing today. The curriculum was usually rudimentary; ungraded schools were common in rural areas; the school term was but three months a year in many states; and compulsory school attendance was virtually unknown. As a consequence, it is not surprising that there should be so little in the history of the Fourteenth Amendment relating to its intended effect on public education.

In the first cases in this Court construing the Fourteenth Amendment, decided shortly after its adoption, the Court interpreted it as pro-

Thurgood Marshall, first Negro member of the U.S. Supreme Court, took the oath to "do equal right to the poor and the rich" at the opening session of the Court, October 2, 1967. (UPI PHOTO)

scribing all state-imposed discriminations against the Negro race. The doctrine of "separate but equal" did not make its appearance in this Court until 1896 in the case of *Plessy v. Ferguson, supra*, involving not education but transportation. American courts have since labored with the doctrine over half a century. In this Court, there have been six cases involving the "separate but equal" doctrine in the field of public education. In *Cumming v. Board of Education of Richmond County*, 175 U.S. 528, and *Gong Lum v. Rice*, 275 U.S. 78, the validity of the doctrine itself was not challenged. In more recent cases, all on the graduate school level, inequality was found in that specific benefits enjoyed by white students were denied to Negro students of the same educational qualifications. *Missouri ex rel. Gaines v. Canada*, 305 U.S. 337; *Sipuel v. Board of Regents of University of Oklahoma*, 332 U.S. 631; *Sweatt v. Painter*, 339 U.S. 629; *McLaurin v. Oklahoma State Regents*, 339 U.S. 637. In none of these cases was it necessary to re-examine the doctrine to grant relief to the Negro plaintiff. And in *Sweatt v. Painter, supra*, the Court expressly reserved decision on the question whether *Plessy v. Ferguson* should be held inapplicable to public education.

In the instant cases, that question is directly presented. Here, unlike *Sweatt v. Painter*, there are findings below that the Negro and white schools involved have been equalized, or are being equalized, with respect to buildings, curricula, qualifications and salaries of teachers, and other "tangible" factors. Our decision, therefore, cannot turn on merely a comparison of these tangible factors in the Negro and white schools involved in each of the cases. We must look instead to the effect of segregation itself on public education.

In approaching this problem, we cannot turn the clock back to 1868 when the Amendment was adopted, or even to 1896 when *Plessy v. Ferguson* was written. We must consider public education in the light of its full development and its present place in American life throughout the Nation. Only in this way can it be determined if segregation in public schools deprives these plaintiffs of the equal protection of the laws.

Today, education is perhaps the most important function of state and local governments. Compulsory school attendance laws and great expenditures for education both demonstrate our recognition of the importance of education to our democratic society. It is required in the performance of our most basic public responsibilities, even service in the armed forces. It is the very foundation of good citizenship. Today it is a principal instrument in awakening the child to cultural values, in preparing him for later professional training, and in helping him to adjust normally to his environment. In these days, it is doubtful that any child may reasonably be expected to succeed in life if he is denied the opportunity of an education. Such an opportunity, where the state has undertaken to provide it, is a right which must be made available to all on equal terms.

We come then to the question presented: Does segregation of children in public schools solely on the basis of race, even though the physical facilities and other "tangible" factors may be equal, deprive the children of the minority group of equal educational opportunities? We believe that it does.

In *Sweatt v. Painter, supra,* in finding that a segregated law school for Negroes could not provide them equal educational opportunities, this Court relied in large part on "those qualities which are incapable of objective measurement but which make for greatness in a law school." In *McLaurin v. Oklahoma State Regents, supra,* the Court, in requiring that a Negro admitted to a white graduate school be treated like all other students, again resorted to intangible considerations: ". . . his ability to study, to engage in discussions and exchange views with other students, and, in general, to

The first day of desegregation in Greensboro, North Carolina schools, September 3, 1957. (UPI PHOTO)

learn his profession." Such considerations apply with added force to children in grade and high schools. To separate them from others of similar age and qualifications solely because of their race generates a feeling of inferiority as to their status in the community that may affect their hearts and minds in a way unlikely ever to be undone. The effect of this separation on their educational opportunities was well stated by a finding in the Kansas case by a court which nevertheless felt compelled to rule against the Negro plaintiffs:

"Segregation of white and colored children in public schools has a determined effect upon the colored children. The impact is greater when it has the sanction of the law; for the policy of separating the races is usually interpreted as denoting the inferiority of the Negro group. A sense of inferiority affects the motivation of a child to learn. Segregation with the sanction of law, therefore, has a tendency to (retard) the educational and mental development of Negro children and to deprive them of some of the benefits they would receive in a racial (ly) integrated school system." Whatever may have been the extent of psychological knowledge at the time of *Plessy v. Ferguson,* this finding is amply supported by modern authority. Any language in *Plessy v. Ferguson* contrary to this finding is rejected.

We conclude that in the field of public education the doctrine of "separate but equal" has no place. Separate educational facilities are inherently unequal. Therefore, we hold that the plaintiffs and others similarly situated for whom the actions have been brought are, by reason of the segregation complained of, deprived of the equal protection of the laws guaranteed by the Fourteenth Amendment. This disposition makes unnecessary any discussion whether such segregation also violates the Due Process Clause of the Fourteenth Amendment.

Because these are class actions, because of the wide applicability of this decision, and because of the great variety of local conditions, the formulation of decrees in these cases presents problems of considerable complexity. On reargument, the consideration of appropriate relief was necessarily subordinated to the

Reverend Martin Luther King, Jr., the first of ninety defendants to go on trial, charged with conspiring illegally in a city bus boycott, escorting his wife across the street as they left the Montgomery County Courthouse for the lunch recess, in March 1956.
(UPI PHOTO)

primary question—the constitutionality of segregation in public education. We have now announced that such segregation is a denial of the equal protection of the laws. In order that we may have the full assistance of the parties in formulating decrees, the cases will be restored to the docket, and the parties are requested to present further argument on Questions 4 and 5 previously propounded by the Court for the reargument this Term. The Attorney General of the United States is again invited to participate. The Attorneys General of the states requiring or permitting segregation in public education will also be permitted to appear as *amici curiae* upon request to do so by September 15, 1954, and submission of briefs by October 1, 1954.

But the Supreme Court's decision was resisted by many states and local communities. Sometimes violence flared. For example, in 1957 President Eisenhower called out federal troops to force the integration of public schools in Little Rock, Arkansas, after Governor Orval Faubus ordered the National Guard to bar Negroes from entering previously all-white schools. Many states and communities did move to integrate their public schools, but by the late 1960's many all-Negro schools continued to exist both in the North and in the South.

Although the Supreme Court had outlawed segregation on interstate transportation in 1946, Negroes continued to be forced to sit in special sections on local buses in many Southern communities. In 1956 Martin Luther King, a Negro Baptist minister, rose to national prominence by leading a boycott by 50,000 Negroes in Montgomery, Alabama, against segregation on the local buses. In the years that followed King led many protests against segregation as president of the Southern Christian Leadership Conference, which urged Negroes to use non-violent methods in obtaining their rights. In 1964 the 35-year-old King was awarded the Nobel Peace Prize for his work—the youngest person ever to win the award.

Under President Eisenhower in 1957 and 1960 the first civil rights laws since Reconstruction were passed by Congress. But, because the Congress was controlled by the Democratic party, much of the credit for the passage of these laws went to Lyndon Johnson, at that time majority leader of the Senate. These measures were designed to help Negroes obtain equal voting rights. The 1957 act established a federal Civil Rights Commission and gave the federal government the authority to ask for injunctions against local governments in cases where Negro voting rights were being violated. The 1960 act strengthened these measures.

In the early 1960's many Negro and white "Freedom Riders" began traveling through the South and staging sit-ins at restaurants to force these eating places to desegregate. Many of these demonstrators were jailed, but many restaurants that previously had been segregated began accepting Negro customers.

Martin Luther King and other Negro leaders organized a huge "Freedom March" on Washington, D. C., on August 28, 1963, in which about 200,000 persons took part. The demonstrators called upon the government to end all segregation and bring equality to Negroes. President Kennedy called on Congress to meet the Negro demands, and in an address to the nation said:

> "One hundred years of delay have passed since President Lincoln freed the slaves, yet their heirs, their grandsons, are not fully free. They are not yet freed from the bonds of injustice. . . ."

In his first State of the Union address to Congress in 1964, after assuming the presidency upon the death of President Kennedy, President Johnson urged:

> "Let this session of Congress be known as the session which did more for civil rights than the last hundred sessions combined . . ."

Congress responded with the passage on July 2, 1964, of a sweeping new Civil Rights Act. It forbade discrimination in hotels, motels, and restaurants in any way connected with interstate commerce. It banned racial discrimination by unions and employers engaged in interstate commerce. And it empowered the Justice Department to bring school desegregation suits. The Voting Rights Act, passed by Congress on August 4, 1965, gave the Justice Department the authority to force local communities to register Negroes and allow them to vote. But in 1966 Congress failed to pass new civil rights legislation that President Johnson had requested which would have ended discrimination in the sale and rental of housing to Negroes.

During the late 1960's, some Negro leaders became more militant in their demands for better treatment. Stokeley Carmichael, chairman of the Student Nonviolent Coordinating Committee (SNCC), coined the slogan "Black Power," which came to be a symbol for more violent action on the part of Negroes.

Almost every city in the United States experienced Negro riots. In August, 1965, Negro mobs in the Watts district of Los Angeles burned and looted property estimated at $50 million before 14,000 National Guardsmen brought the riot under control. A total of 34 persons were killed and more than 4,000 were arrested in the Watts disorder. Similar riots hit New York City, Chicago, Cleveland, Boston, Newark, Detroit, and dozens of other cities.

THE REVOLUTION in EDUCATION

Because they were in the midst of it, the members of the Space Age generation were not always aware that a revolution was underway in the schools that they attended. Major factors were at work bringing many changes to education.

The population explosion and the mushrooming of suburban areas caused dramatic increases in school enrollments. It necessitated the building of thousands of new schools and the training of hundreds of thousands of new teachers.

More changes in curriculums and ways of teaching took place in the two decades than in any other period of American history. Teaching machines, computers, and many other innovations were introduced as educators sought ways to improve student learning.

Private foundations, and state, local, and federal government agencies poured billions of dollars into the educational systems, turning the "knowledge industry" into big business.

And the explosion of scientific and technical knowledge brought new burdens to both teachers and students who were forced to learn more than previous generations because there was more to learn.

The GI Bill of Rights and Teacher Shortages

To encourage veterans of World War II to go to college and resume their education that had been interrupted by the war, the federal government provided financial assistance under the GI Bill of Rights. Veterans were paid a subsistence allowance of $75 or more a month as well as their tuition, fees, books, and other expenses. As a result, in 1946 about half of the 2 million students enrolled in colleges and universities were veterans.

The flood of veterans on the college campuses doubled the enrollment of many schools. At many institutions military barracks were moved from abandoned army training centers to provide temporary housing for the new students. And the colleges launched huge new building programs to provide more permanent classrooms and dormitories.

The United States also came out of World War II with a shortage of teachers in the public schools. It was estimated that 350,000 teachers had left the profession during the war. The average salary of teachers in 1946 was $1,700 a year and educational groups began demanding that this be increased to a minimum of $2,400 a year to attract more persons into the profession. That year President Truman called for substantial federal aid to education, but his plea was ignored by Congress.

The Student Population Explosion

By the early 1950's the first children of the Space Age generation began to go to public schools in rapidly increasing numbers. The number of students in public schools had remained fairly stable at about 25 million from 1930 to 1950. But in the early 1950's more than 5 million additional children—mostly the children of war veterans—entered the public schools. To accommodate this growing student population

The old one-room school, or "little red schoolhouse," was one of the casualties of the consolidations that had begun before World War II and were completed in the school building programs of the space age. (UPI PHOTO)

Thousands of new schools have been built during the space-age years using many innovations in architecture—for example, this school-in-the-round in Daly City, California. (UPI PHOTO)

from 60,000 to 75,000 new classrooms had to be built each year, and the number of teachers had to be increased in like amounts.

The student population explosion continued and by the mid-1960's more than 42 million children were attending public school—an increase of nearly 70 percent since the end of World War II. More than 800,000 additional teachers were employed in the period from 1950 to 1965, increasing the number of public school teachers to more than 1.7 million. To encourage more and more teachers to enter the profession, teachers' salaries were quadrupled, rising to an average yearly salary of nearly $7,000 by the late 1960's.

As the children of the Space Age generation grew older the colleges and universities began to feel the impact of the population explosion by the late 1950's and 1960's. By 1965 more than 5.5 million students were attending universities, colleges, and junior colleges. Many new colleges were built and existing institutions of higher education doubled and tripled their enrollments.

"Why Can't Johnny Read?"

When Russia launched Sputnik, the first artificial earth satellite, into space in 1957, an outcry arose from the American public wondering what was wrong with the schools if the United States was not able to maintain its lead over the rest of the world in scientific know-how. Critics released survey reports showing that many children were not able to read materials designed for their grade levels. And attacks were leveled at school administrators and teachers for not emphasizing science and mathematics in the curriculum.

As a result Congress in 1958 passed the National Defense Education Act. This measure made federal aid available to schools to improve their programs in mathematics, science, and foreign-language instruction. It resulted in the schools introducing such innovations as the language laboratory, which made it possible for students using microphones and headsets to listen to themselves speak foreign languages while receiving individual instruction from a teacher. Federal funds also were used to improve science laboratories in many schools. With federal encouragement a "New Math" curriculum was designed and introduced to schools in an effort to give students a better understanding of the subject, and other new curriculums were designed for such science subjects as biology, chemistry, and physics.

At the same time the schools were under increasing pressure to eliminate racially segregated classrooms, as already discussed in the chapter "Civil Rights and Integration."

Increased Federal Aid to Education

Throughout the two decades broadly based federal aid to education had been blocked in Congress because of fears that federal control of education would result from federal aid. But in 1965, largely because of the persuasive powers of President Johnson, Congress passed the Elementary and Secondary Education Act, which provided more than $1 billion in federal funds for schools serving low-income families as well as additional hundreds of millions of dollars for the improvement of libraries, instructional materials, and supplementary educational services. And in 1966 Congress increased the amount of federal money allocated to elementary and secondary education to more than $6 billion.

The increasing flow of money to the schools enabled educators to buy much-needed books and equipment and to begin experimenting with new ways to improve the quality of instruction.

BIG GOVERNMENT GETS BIGGER

While the Space Age generation was growing up, the federal government was growing larger. As well as playing a more important role on the international stage as one of the world's two super powers, the American government also took an increasingly active part in almost every aspect of domestic affairs.

One gauge of the increasing size of the government was the amount of money it spent. From 1947 to 1967 the annual expenses of the government almost quadrupled—from $40 billion in 1947 to about $145 billion in 1967. This meant that, while in 1947 the government spent an average of $280 per year for every man, woman, and child in the United States, in 1967 the government was spending about $725 per year—or over twice as much—for every person in the population.

Another gauge of the growth of the government was the number of people it employed. In 1947 there were about 2 million civilian government workers, but by 1967 this had grown to about 2.6 million—an increase of about 30 per cent.

New Cabinet-Level Departments

Although countless bureaus, commissions, and agencies have been created since the end of World War II, perhaps the growth of the federal government is best illustrated by the addition of four cabinet-level departments to the executive branch.

The Department of Defense, created by the National Security Act of 1947, replaced two previous cabinet-level departments that had existed from the beginning of the American government—the War Department and the Navy Department. The new Secretary of Defense became a member of the President's cabinet and under him were placed the Secretaries of the Army, the Navy, and the Air Force. Headquartered in the Pentagon Building in Arlington, Virginia, across the Potomac River from Washington, D.C., the Department of Defense became the single "biggest business" in the world with annual expenditures of more than $50 billion a year in the late 1960's. The first Secretary of Defense, was James V. Forrestal, appointed by President Truman in 1947. His successors were

The United States Army's "Sprint" anti-missile missile as it flashed away from a launcher during a test at White Sands, New Mexico, March 26, 1965. (U.S. ARMY—UPI)

Louis A. Johnson (1949), George C. Marshall (1950), Robert A. Lovett (1951), Charles E. Wilson (1953), Neil H. McElroy (1957), Thomas S. Gates Jr. (1959), and Robert S. McNamara (1961).

The Department of Health, Education and Welfare was created in 1953 as the result of recommendations by the Hoover Commission on Organization of the Executive Branch of the Government. It took over administration of the following agencies: the Social Security Administration, which administers benefits for old age, medicare, disability, and survivors; the Public Health Service, which works to control disease and other health problems; the Office of Education, which supervises the various programs of federal aid to education; the Food and Drug Administration, which enforces federal laws concerned with food and drugs; the Vocational Rehabilitation Administration, which aids the states in rehabilitating civilians who have job handicaps; and the Welfare Administration, which is largely concerned with child welfare. The first Secretary of Health, Education and Welfare was Oveta Culp Hobby, appointed by President Eisenhower in 1953. Her successors were Marion B. Folsom (1955), Arthur S. Flemming (1958), Abraham A. Ribicoff (1961), Anthony J. Celebrezze (1962), and John W. Gardner (1965).

The Department of Housing and Urban Development was created by Congress in 1965 to take over programs previously administered by the Housing and Home Finance Agency aimed at improving housing and helping cities beautify and improve themselves. The first Secretary of Housing and Urban Development was Robert C. Weaver, appointed by President Johnson in 1966. Weaver, who had been administrator of the Housing and Home Finance Agency since 1961, was the first Negro ever appointed to a position of cabinet-rank.

The Department of Transportation was established by Congress in 1966. It took over administration of the Federal Aviation Agency, the Bureau of Public Roads, the Coast Guard, and the safety functions of the Civil Aeronautics Board, the Interstate Commerce Commission, and the National Transportation Safety Board. The first Secretary of Transportation was Alan S. Boyd, a former member of the Civil Aeronautics Board, who was appointed by President Johnson in 1966.

Other large agencies that were not of cabinet-rank created during the period included:

The Atomic Energy Commission, which was established by the Atomic Energy Act of 1946, and which in 1947 took over the Administration of the atomic energy program that had been developed by the War Department's Manhattan Project. The annual budget of the AEC in the late 1960's was about $2.5 billion a year—six times that of the Department of State.

The National Aeronautics and Space Administration was established by the National Aeronautics and Space Act of 1958. It took over the personnel and facilities of the former National Advisory Committee for Aeronautics, and administered the nation's space program. The agency's budget in the late 1960's provided for expenditures of more than $5 billion a year.

The Office of Economic Opportunity was set up by the 1964 Economic Opportunity Act to administer the federal government's war on poverty. In the late 1960's its annual budget was more than $1 billion.

This is the entrance to one of the Qumran Caves along the shore of the Dead Sea, where Bedouin tribesmen found the first of the Dead Sea Scrolls in the summer of 1947. In 68 A.D. Roman troops from Jericho conquered this early Jewish settlement, causing the inhabitants to conceal their sacred writings in clay jars and hide them in the caves above their village. (UPI PHOTO)

THE EXPLOSION of SCIENTIFIC KNOWLEDGE

Underlying many of the most important changes during the growing-up decades of the Space Age generation was the explosion of scientific knowledge. With many more scientists than ever before, and with more money and effort being put into scientific research than in any period of the past, every field of science blossomed with discoveries and insights.

New Discoveries About the Past

In the fields of archaeology, anthropology, and geology, scientists made many new discoveries about the past of man and the earth. One of the most important discoveries was that of a tool for more accurately dating the age of prehistoric objects. This tool—called radiocarbon dating—stemmed from the discovery in 1947 of an isotope in nature called carbon 14. The finding was made by a University of Chicago scientist, W. F. Libby. Because carbon 14 decays at a steady rate, half of any given amount disintegrating every 5,600 years, it is possible for scientists to measure the age of something by determining the amount of radiocarbon it contains. This tool enabled scientists to determine that man and the earth itself were both much older than had been previously believed.

In 1947 an Arab shepherd boy discovered a group of ancient scrolls in a cave by the Dead Sea near Jericho. These scrolls and additional ones found in the area in the early 1950's turned out to be the earliest known manuscripts of the Bible, having been written in the first century A.D. The manuscripts included all or parts of all the books of the Old Testament. The scrolls are believed to have belonged to a Jewish religious sect called the Essenes. Some of the writings were in Aramaic, the language spoken by Jesus. The find was particularly significant to Biblical scholars, because the scrolls were about a thousand years older than any other known text of the Bible.

In 1953 the British scholar Michael Ventris

Jesuit scholar, Father Roberto Busa, and IBM engineer, Paul Tasman, check by computer the compilation of the index of a major portion of the 2000-year-old Dead Sea Scrolls. (UPI PHOTO)

The "big eye" of the Hale Telescope, dedicated June 3, 1948, weighs 530 tons but has the balance of a fine watch. The light enters the center shaft, is reflected into a lens, and photographed for study. (UPI PHOTO)

succeeded in deciphering the ancient writings of the people of Crete. The language, called linear B, had baffled scientists for many years. Ventris found that the writing was a form of Greek instead of an independent language, as scholars had believed. The discovery resulted in a reassessment of the place in history of the ancient Minoan civilization of Crete as a predecessor of the Greek civilization. A decade later Russian mathematicians deciphered the hieroglyphics of the ancient Maya Indians of Central America by using a computer that tried all possible letter combinations against the language.

Until 1957 most scientists believed that the earth was about 3,350 million years old. But in that year American scientists, using radiocarbon dating, found that meteorites are about 4.5 billion years old. They added almost a billion years to the earth's age by a new hypothesis that the earth, too, must be 4.5 billion years old, because it must have been formed at the same time as the meteorites.

The age of man also was extended back into time. Dr. Louis S. B. Leakey of Kenya discovered the remains of an ancient tool-making man in Tanganyika in 1959, naming him Zinjanthropus, or East African man. Two years later University of California scientists J. F. Evernden and Garniss H. Curtis, using radiocarbon dating, placed Zinjanthropus' age at 1,750,000 years—about three times as many years as anthropologists previously believed man had existed on earth.

The Universe Becomes Larger

The development of new instruments and the sending of robot cameras into space brought many startling developments in astronomy during the two decades. Spacecraft, sent to the moon, Mars, and Venus, relayed back information and photographs that forced astronomers to discard or change many theories about earth's neighbors.

On June 3, 1948, the 200-inch Hale telescope was dedicated at the Mount Palomar Observatory of the California Institute of Technology. It was the largest optical telescope in the world. Fourteen years later, in 1962, the world's largest radio telescope, with a 300-foot saucer-like antenna, was completed at Green Bank, West Virginia.

In the years after World War II more and more astronomers became interested in mapping the source of radio waves coming from distant parts of the universe. The identification of radio waves from space had first been made as early as 1931, but it was not until the 1940's and 1950's that astronomers had devoted much effort to trying to map their origin.

Then, in June, 1960, Rudolph Minkowski of the Mount Palomar Observatory finally discovered one of these distant sources of radio waves with the Hale telescope and actually photographed it. The object, named 3C 295, appeared on the photograph to be nothing more than a small star, but close examination of its spectrum revealed that it was billions of light years away from the earth and speeding away at the unheard-of speed of about 67 thousand miles a second. By 1966 about 100 of these objects, named quasars or quasi-stellar objects, had been photographed, some of which seemed to be traveling away from earth at speeds equal to 80 percent of the speed of

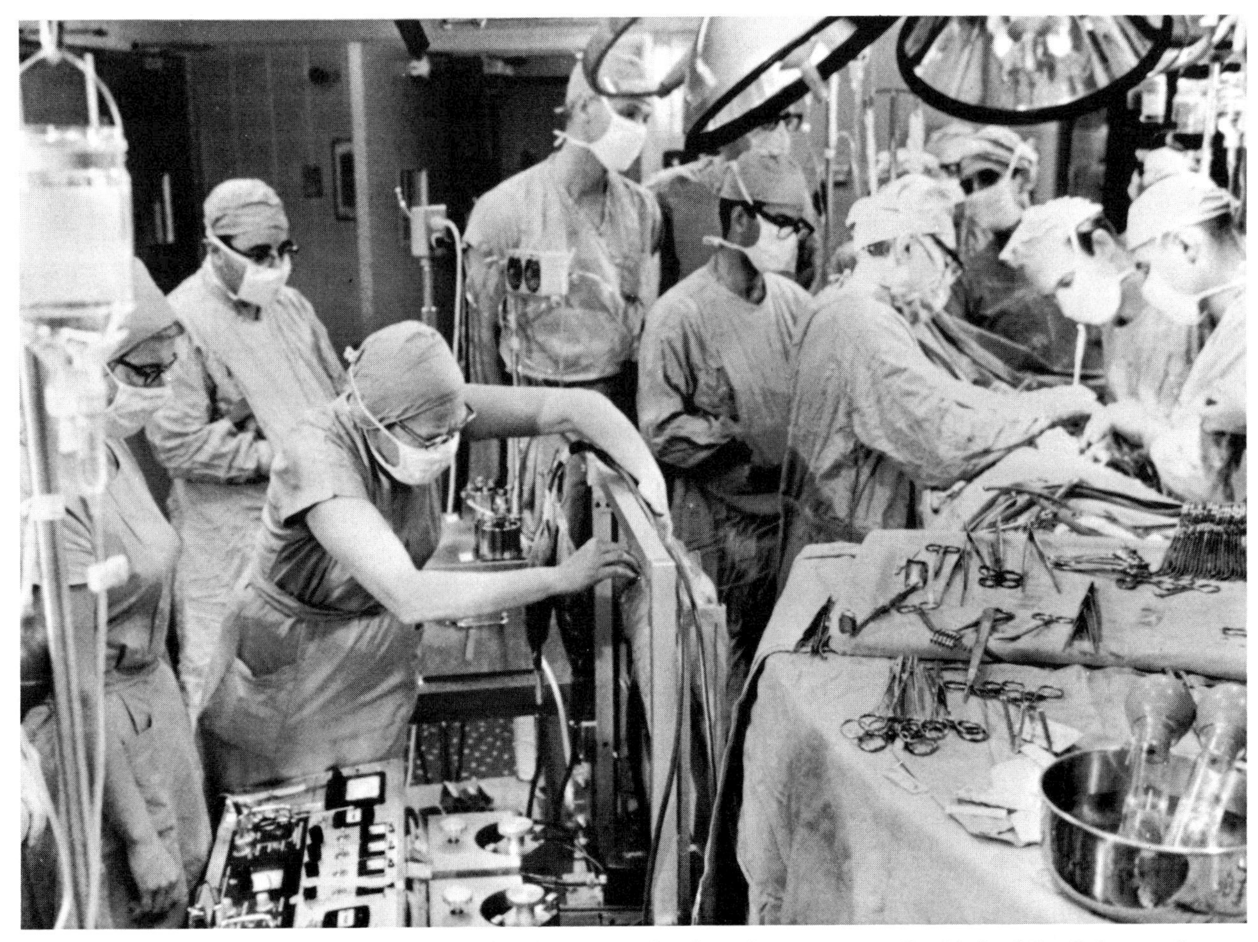

The heart surgery room at Houston's Methodist Hospital, where heart surgeon, Dr. Michael De Bakey, and a team of heart specialists implanted an artificial heart in the chest of 65-year-old Marcel De Rudder during five hours of surgery in April 1966. (UPI PHOTO)

light. One of these quasars, 3C 9, was calculated to be 8.7 billion light years away—the most distant object known to man when it was discovered in 1965 by astronomer Maarten Schmidt of the Palomar Observatory.

Another new type of object in space was discovered in 1965 by astronomer Allan Sandage of the Palomar Observatory. These new objects, called quasi-stellar blue galaxies by Sandage, did not seem to give off radio waves like quasars, but produced about 100 times more radiation than an ordinary galaxy. Like quasars, these blue galaxies seemed to be traveling away from earth at tremendous speeds; one was calculated to be moving away at 125,000 miles a second.

New Discoveries About Matter and Energy

While astronomers were finding out about the expanding universe, chemists and physicists were looking inside matter and energy. A whole new area of study called high-energy or elementary particle physics evolved. About a hundred elementary particles were observed, identified, and classified, as were anti-particles. This research, most of which was beyond the comprehension of the layman, led in the 1960's to theories that there might exist an anti-earth or even an anti-universe that would be negative counterparts.

Somewhat more understandable to the layman was the use by physicists and chemists of particle accelerators, such as cyclotrons, to bombard various elements with atomic particles to produce isotopes of existing elements as well as sometimes to produce new elements. From 1944 to 1961 ten new elements were discovered in this way—Americium, Berkelium, Californium, Curium, Einsteinium, Fermium, Lawrencium, Mendelevium, Nobelium, and Promethium. Six of these elements were discovered by Dr. Glenn T. Seaborg and his associates at the University of

After the administering of the Sabin vaccine became possible, through the oral method in a series of sugar lumps, there was no problem for anyone. (UPI PHOTO)

California. In 1961 Seaborg became chairman of the United States Atomic Energy Commission.

In the new branch of solid-state physics, scientists developed the transistor and the diode, which led to more compact circuits and the elimination of vacuum tubes in electronic devices. In the 1960's the development of the laser, a device that could greatly amplify light, brought about unique new uses of light, for example as a cutting tool in delicate surgical operations.

Developments in Medicine and Health

The most outstanding development in medicine during the two decades was the elimination of poliomyelitis, more commonly called polio or infantile paralysis. The first break-through came in 1949 when three Harvard University bacteriologists, John F. Enders, Frederick C. Robbins, and Thomas H. Weller, discovered how to grow polio viruses. This enabled Dr. Jonas E. Salk of the University of Pittsburgh to produce a vaccine which in April, 1955, was declared successful after it had been tested on nearly 2 million students. Six years later, in 1961, a new polio vaccine that could be taken as a pill was approved for use. It had been developed by Albert Sabin of the University of Cincinnati. As the use of the polio vaccines spread, the number of cases of the crippling disease fell from more than 50,000 a year in the 1950's to almost zero in the 1960's.

Thousands of new drugs were developed to treat diseases. Some of the more outstanding were ACTH, which began to be used in 1949 to aid sufferers from arthritis, and isoniazid, a drug discovered in the 1950's, which radically changed and improved the treatment of victims of tuberculosis, eliminating the need for complete bed rest in most cases.

Huge sums of money and many hours of scientific research were spent during the two decades in pursuit of ways to prevent cancer and heart disease. Although some progress was made, no preventive was found for either disease and this search was part of the unfinished business left to the Space Age generation.